TOLERANCE AMONG THE VIRTUES

For Rich Miller

All best,
JRB

TOLERANCE AMONG THE VIRTUES

John R. Bowlin

PRINCETON UNIVERSITY PRESS
Princeton and Oxford

Published by Princeton University Press,
41 William Street,
Princeton, New Jersey 08540

In the United Kingdom: Princeton University Press,
6 Oxford Street, Woodstock, Oxfordshire OX20 1TR

press.princeton.edu

ISBN 978-0-691-16997-2
Library of Congress Control Number: 2016935713
British Library Cataloging-in-Publication Data is available

This book has been composed in Sabon Next LT Pro

Printed on acid-free paper ∞

Printed in the United States of America

1 3 5 7 9 10 8 6 4 2

For Nicholas and Isaac

CONTENTS

TOLERANCE AMONG THE VIRTUES

INTRODUCTION

During the spring of 2000 I attended a cockfight in Collinsville, Oklahoma. I tell the tale of that visit and reflect on its significance in the epilogue, but here the point regards the confusion and puzzlement it precipitated. I went to Collinsville as a citizen seeking information about an activity that many in the state wanted to ban. A referendum was scheduled for later that year, and I had never seen a fight. My hunch was that I would find it objectionable and yet tolerable. I assumed that I would vote against the ban in solidarity with the rural and Native peoples who opposed it. But I was mistaken. In fact, I found the fights horrific in their seductive violence and vile in their visible effects. I left Collinsville thinking that the proponents of the referendum were right. Cockfighting was intolerable; a ban would be best.

This judgment was unexpected and disorienting. It caught me off guard, and after a week I came to doubt it. Or rather, I came to doubt that I understood it well enough to maintain it. Did my conclusion that cockfighting was unbearable bear witness to my own intolerance? Intolerance is a vice. Its act wrongs other another person. It denies them a good they are due. (But what was that good and under what conditions was it due? I didn't know.) Did this mean that my refusal to honor this request for toleration was somehow unjust? More troubling still was another thought: was the solidarity I felt for my fellow citizens who led rural lives and claimed Native identities in fact false? Did my refusal to tolerate this violent and (to my mind) objectionable portion of their local traditions signal my own smooth hypocrisy? Was my claim to solidarity more apparent than real? And then the worst thought of all: was I being played? In the stories of tolerance that we tell, hardscrabble towns in the American Bible Belt are not its natural home, and yet toleration was precisely what the members of cockfight clubs across the state were asking from people like me, urban and suburban inhabitants of Tulsa and Oklahoma City. Was their request as much a semblance as my solidarity? Was it a mask that they would remove once they secured the tolerance they wanted but would never offer in return?

After a while I tried to revise my judgment, muster some tolerance, and so escape these discomforts, but this didn't work. The act was too difficult, its odd combination of objection and endurance, and besides it felt wrong. To my mind, cockfighting wasn't just objectionable, but intolerable. So I tried indifference. I tried not caring about cockfighting, about the tasks of citizenship, and about the solidarity I felt, whether real or imagined. But this didn't work either. Like Augustine so many centuries before, I had *seen* a cockfight. I had chosen to attend, and I had been captivated by its spectacle, its strange combination of violence and beauty.[1]

INITIAL DISCOVERIES

The truth is, I didn't know how to tell the tale of that trip to Collinsville, to say what I had seen and give an account of its significance. So I did what I have been trained to do. I read around in the relevant literature, some of it scholarly, some of it not. My reading led to a course, the course to a handful of articles, and the articles to this book. It also led to three initial discoveries. First, I discovered that my discontent was widespread. Whatever I read, wherever I turned, there it was. Journalists, theologians, moral philosophers, hipster youth pastors, political theorists, popes, radical critics, college evangelists, political operatives, and scholars of religion—all could be found deploring the resort to toleration in response to the differences that divide us, resenting the praise this act so often receives, and resisting the thought that a virtue might be its cause.[2] The sources of their discontent turn out to be multiple, and yet as we shall see in chapter 1, criticism of tolerance and its act, whatever its source, typically functions as a medium of discontent with modernity. By these lights, toleration is a distinctively modern response to disagreement and difference, and its ills are variations on modernity's own. When it is endorsed nevertheless, the act must be unmasked as a swindle, as a cover for either domination or moral collapse. It must be replaced with some other response. A just political society will leave it behind. A community of hospitality and welcome will proceed without it.

---

1 *Libuit attendere*, says Augustine, when he saw two cocks fighting in a courtyard. He attended to them. He chose to do so, and it pleased him. *Ord.* I.8.25. For Burkean reflections on suffering that captures our attention, reflections designed to diminish our habit of moralizing our captivity see Bromwich, "How Moral Is Taste?"

2 Here's a representative list of the discontented, one of each. Niebuhr, *Beyond Tolerance*; Bretherton, *Hospitality as Holiness*, 121–126; Herman, "Pluralism and the Community of Moral Judgment"; Dobson, *Be Intolerant*; Brown, *Regulating Aversion*; Ratzinger, *Truth and Tolerance*; Žižek, *Violence*, 105–139 and "Tolerance as an Ideological Category"; McDowell and Hostetler, *New Tolerance*; GOP chairman Reince Preibus (Elbow, "Reince Preibus Doesn't Like the Word 'Tolerance'"); and William O'Meara, "Beyond Toleration."

Of course, I also discovered friends of toleration, those who endorse the act, praise its performance, and admire its prominence in modern lives and politics. Still, whatever I read, wherever I turned, there was very little talk of the virtue that perfects resort to this act, even among its friends. This was my second key discovery. Tolerance is infrequently theorized as a virtue, as a habitual perfection of action and attitude. Few make the effort; some even deny that tolerance is a virtue.[3] Instead, most scholars and critics, friends and foes alike, have subjected the *act* of toleration to scrutiny, the act of patiently enduring a person, action, or attitude that is thought to be objectionable in some way, and this has put the debate on precisely the wrong footing. As we shall see, an act of toleration can be good or bad, right or wrong, depending on the ends and circumstances of the act. Some objectionable differences should be patiently endured; others should not. But this means that those who care deeply about certain resorts to the act, who defend those resorts as right and required, and who, as a result, are inclined to declare the act itself essentially good will be accused of moral blindness by those who concentrate on examples of the act that fall short of the right. So too, those who feel nagged or coerced to endure what they consider intolerable and who, as a result, are inclined to declare the act itself essentially bad, will be counted among the intolerant by those who consider the act essentially just and good. So goes the contemporary debate, or at least a good portion of it: misguided judgments about the moral status of the act in general are used as proxies, as smokescreens, in debates over specific instances of the tolerable and the intolerable, over what should and should not be patiently endured, while the virtue that attends to this distinction is hardly considered.

Given the sources and motivations that have shaped the revival of virtue theory in recent years, this might seem understandable. That revival has, for the most part, looked to premodern accounts for inspiration, to the ancients and medievals. If toleration is, as most assume, a modern response to the moral and political challenges posed by diversity and difference, then we should not expect the revivalists to care about the virtue that causes right

---

3   The logic of these explicit denials will be considered in chapter 1. For examples, see Gray, *Two Faces of Liberalism*, chap. 1; Hauerwas, "Hauerwas on 'Hauerwas and the Law'"; Heyd, "Is Toleration a Political Virtue?"; and MacIntyre, "Toleration and the Goods of Conflict," 153–154. To his credit, MacIntyre admits that *acts* of toleration can be just, but he does not consider whether these just acts require a distinct virtue that belongs to justice. He also insists the acts of *intolerance* can be *just*, and this odd sounding remark should have prompted him to ask about virtue and vice. In the current generation of moral philosophers, theologians, and political theorists, only a handful have: Compte-Sponville, *Small Treatise on the Great Virtues*, 157–172; Fiala, *Tolerance and the Ethical Life*; Forst, "Tolerance as a Virtue of Justice" and *Toleration in Conflict*, 502–517; Horton, "Toleration as a Virtue"; Newey, "Tolerance as a Virtue"; Oberdiek, *Tolerance*; Sabl, "Virtuous to Himself"; Tinder, *Tolerance and Community*; and Vainio, "Virtues and Vices of Tolerance."

resort to this act. They don't find it in the premodern sources they borrow and adapt; they don't even look. And why should they? After all, for many, the point of the revival is to locate alternatives to the moral discourses and practices of modernity, discourses and practices that toleration is thought to exemplify, that elicit our discontent, and that provoke the search for moral resources in a time before tolerance, before the eclipse of virtue.

Not surprisingly, most friends of toleration are willing to accept this story that pits act against virtue across the threshold of the modern. For them, a perfectionist account would only entangle toleration in the metaphysical complications and moral compromises of premodern virtue. Such an account would have to refer to ends given by nature and thus to a myth that naturalizes what is in fact contingent, presumably to the benefit of some and the detriment of others. It would have to speak of communal norms and tradition-bound lives and thus endorse an implicit patriarchy. It would accent the imitation of moral exemplars and thus threaten the individuality and special dignity of persons. And its account of desire, intention, and happiness would betray a disregard for duty and allow self-interest to infect even the most praiseworthy actions. Better then, to theorize the act not the virtue, toleration not tolerance, and thus avoid perfectionism's difficulties, or so these friends of toleration conclude.

With friends and foes of toleration largely united in their disregard for the virtue that perfects resort to the act, it's hard to presume otherwise. And the difficulty is compounded by the fact that most historians believe that toleration emerged in the modern period, not as a virtue was cultivated and praised, but only as self-interest took hold and swords were sheathed at the conclusion of the wars that followed the Protestant Reformation. But then there's this. In some circumstances, in response to some persons and objectionable differences, an act of toleration is clearly right and good. In some instances, its patient endurance is clearly required and failure to respond with this act is plainly unjust. Moreover, the conflicts of judgment and love, attitude and action, that afflict our various social and political relationships would seem to make right and regular resort to this act indispensable for their persistence and flourishing. No doubt, participation in this activity, this regular resort, can be difficult and devotion to its ends unstable, but once its special goodness is conceded, it's hard to avoid speaking of degrees of excellence, of better and worse, with respect to participation and devotion. And of course, once there is an aspiration to do better, perhaps even habitually so, then talk of the virtues that perfect participation in this activity, in its judgments and loves, will be hard to resist.

Third, and finally, I discovered that the confusion and discontent that surround toleration, the assumption that it appears only as modernity does, and the refusal to find its source and perfection in a moral virtue have made it nearly impossible to see its relationship to love's endurance or consider the virtue that perfects this work of love, the virtue that the Apostle Paul calls forbearance.[4] Both the tolerant and the forbearing respond with patient endurance to at least some of the differences, disagreements, and moral imperfections that afflict their relationships and communities. For the tolerant, this act comes as right and due, for the forbearing as love's endurance. Given the identities and differences that unite and divide these virtues and acts, we might expect to find them treated together, as the siblings that they are, and yet this happens rarely and almost always to ill effect. Scholars who see their relationship and treat them together tend to be Christian theologians, and they tend to pit forbearance *against* tolerance. They draw a distinction between the two in order to mark the boundary between good and evil, sacred and secular, grace and nature, ancient wisdom and modern hypocrisy, real virtue and clever vice— vice that parades in virtue's garb. No one, as far as I can tell, has tried to regard them together, as sibling virtues, while simultaneously resisting the temptation to scapegoat tolerance in order to secure advantage for a certain interpretation of sin and grace, a certain account of secular modernity, or a certain position in contemporary debates about the tolerable and the intolerable. I discovered, in other words, that the confusions and resentments that confound contemporary attitudes toward tolerance have not only distorted Christian appropriation of this Pauline inheritance, but also prevented scholars and critics of all kinds, whether Christian or not, from reflecting on love's response to disagreement and difference.

TASKS

My efforts in this book follow from these discoveries. First and most basically, I explicate and defend a perfectionist account of tolerance, the virtue that belongs to justice as one of its parts. There are many studies of toleration understood as an act or a set of practices or policies. Some accent historical emergence; others attend to theoretical justification. But we have very few historically informed, conceptually nuanced studies of tolerance, the associated virtue. My efforts supply just that, and in this respect they open up

---

4   Paul assigns the perfection to God and uses the word ἀνοχή (*anoché*) (Rom 2:4) to describe its act. He also locates an equivalent norm and activity in the community created by God's forbearance. Here he uses the words βαστάζειν (*bastazein*) (Rom 15:1) and ὑπομονή (*hupomone*) (Rom 15:4–5). The members of this community are to endure each other's differences, retain each other's company, and so bear each other's burdens. He implies that this activity recapitulates and so bears witness to divine perfection. It helps sustain the community that God's forbearance and Christ's sacrifice have created (Rom 15:1–6).

a fresh topic. For the most part, tolerance, the virtue, isn't what is discussed when toleration is, except occasionally by implication or as a result of imprecise speech. And, as we shall see in chapter 1, on those few occasions when tolerance is discussed directly, it is often to discount the ideals it embodies and the sources of action it provides. Acts of toleration are needed, so the argument goes, but not by virtuous means, not by the perfection of habit. This book offers a reply to precisely this disregard of tolerance. For the friends of liberal societies and their regimes of toleration, interest in the effort should go without saying. Those societies will flourish, their regimes of toleration sustained, only as their inhabitants are equipped with the virtue (at least in some measure) and capable of cultivating it in others. As for the resentful foes of those regimes, they should be interested too, if only because an account of the virtue and its semblances clarifies what should and should not be resented in this area of our common life. And both should be interested in holding together coalitions of reformers and revolutionaries in the struggle to achieve justice, and this, even when their differences threaten to break them apart and undermine the struggle.[5]

In the pages that follow, I take up a number of tasks. I show how failure to count tolerance among the moral virtues goes a long way toward explaining the anxieties and discontents that swirl around resort to its act (chapter 1). I consider how tolerance, like justice, appears in all times and places as a concept employed (at least implicitly), as an act performed (at least sporadically), and as a seedbed of acquired virtue (chapter 2). I specify what an instance of acquired tolerance looks like: what matter it regards, what ends it intends, what hopes it can have, what passions accompany it, and what other virtues assist its act (chapter 3). And I identify the terms we will need, the vocabulary we must deploy, in order to speak of this virtue with clarity and precision (chapter 4). Since toleration's patient endurance is but one possible response to the problems of association posed by difference and disagreement, I consider the attitudes the tolerant will have toward these other possible responses—acceptance, indifference, exit, coercion, contest, and correction (also chapter 4). And I offer a novel account of the tolerance that distinguishes societies like our own—liberal, democratic, and pluralist (chapter 5). Finally, I consider the sibling relations that obtain between tolerance and forbearance, two habitual perfections of the will and its acts (chapter 6). Forbearance perfects our response to differences that are in some

---

5 In the chapters that follow, we will see how tolerance has limits, how its patient endurance comes to an end. In the struggle for justice, one such limit will regard partners. We may find ourselves among Leninists, anarchists, democratic republicans, pacifists, just warriors, black nationalists, deep ecologists, radical Protestants, traditionalist Catholics, and so on. However we identify ourselves, decisions will have to be made about which of these to tolerate as fellow travelers and which are too much trouble given the aims we share with the others.

way objectionable, but it abides within friendships and its patient endurance comes as friendship's love. It comes as love's endurance. It was the Apostle Paul who spoke most vividly and famously of a love that endures all things (1 Cor 13:7), and Christians will refer to a species of this act and its attendant virtue that come by God's grace and that abides within friendships animated by God's love. Others will not. They will refer to a love that endures within ordinary friendships and a virtue acquired by ordinary means. In this final chapter, I give an account of both kinds of forbearance, both the customarily acquired and the graciously given. I identify their similarities and differences, and I develop a vocabulary for speaking about their various sibling relations with tolerance.

I create this conceptual framework on appeal to assumptions we already make and commitments we already have. Most of us assume that differences can divide persons and communities—differences in moral and political commitment, in religious belief and practice, in activities loved and habits formed. So too, most of us make judgments about the significance of these differences and about the complications that some might pose to our social and political arrangements. And most of us have ideas about which differences are in fact objectionable, in what way and to whom, and about the various responses that might be offered in reply. Most of us are committed to offering responses that are just and due, and most of us hope to offer right responses with greater ease and consistency across a growing variety cases. I begin with these commitments and assumptions. Along the way, I make a number of specific judgments about the tolerable and the intolerable, and I offer reasons in defense of what I say. Still, for the most part, my purpose is not to distinguish the commitments, lives, and actions that deserve to be tolerated from those do not. Crucially, I do not assume that judgments about the tolerable and intolerable follow from a single principle. As far as I can tell, they don't. There appears to be no one substantive way to mark the distinction, no general rule that can be handed down by the theorist and applied by the people. As we shall see, the circumstances that must be considered before toleration's act of patient endurance can be offered as right and due are simply too many and the judgments that must be rendered too various for any one principle to capture them all. What's needed instead are persons who are attentive to those circumstances, who have identified the differences and disagreements that disrupt their political communities and social relationships, and who are disposed by habit to offer right responses in reply. What's needed, in other words, are tolerant persons, persons who have acquired the virtue in some measure, who understand that its principal act can be justly required not merely expedient, and who are committed to sustaining their social and political relationships despite the differences that divide them and in accord with virtue's norm. My task is to describe the contours of this virtue, its act, ends and circumstances, to spell out its sibling relations with forbearance, and to consider how these virtues function in our households, friendships, citizens organizations, and political communities.

A number of benefits accrue from this shift in attention from toleration as act and policy to tolerance as virtue and sibling to forbearance. Four stand out. First, we will acquire a clearer, more precise sense of what these virtue concepts amount to and how they ought to be applied. This is urgently needed. Both have fallen into disrepair; tolerance in our public discourse, forbearance in our friendships, and both in those social and political relationships that require acts of both justice and love. The counsels of resentment would have us abandon both or replace one with the other. This book counts those counsels false. We would be foolish to relinquish these virtues, regard them as competitors, or resist referring to them when we speak of excellence in response to the differences that divide us. Better, I think, to concede the perfection they bring to persons and acts and the good they offer our communities. Better to learn how to use these virtue terms, adjust their criteria of application, and so speak more precisely about right response to disagreement and difference. This is the conceptual work that I take up in the chapters that follow.

Second, once we acquire a better understanding of how to apply these concepts, and once we dismiss the counsels of resentment that proceed without this wisdom, we should face one less obstacle on the way to a more honest and transparent debate about the disagreements and differences that unsettle our political lives and social relationships. That is, it should be harder to scapegoat tolerance as a means of opposing the patient endurance of some specific difference or as a way of shutting down debate over what can and cannot be tolerated. At the very least, those who know how to apply these concepts can oppose these tactics and encourage more ordinary means of debate. If my political society or religious community tolerates what I consider intolerable, and if I hope to convince my friends and fellow citizens to recast their judgments, then I will have to offer reasons that regard the concrete differences in dispute, reasons that offer new ways of distinguishing what is tolerable from what is not. And my success or failure in this effort will turn on the character of those reasons, on their power and authority in this particular setting, not on the outcome of a phantom debate about the moral status of tolerance.

Third, this effort should help us develop a chastened, more self-conscious account of modernity. If, as I shall argue, tolerance appears as concept, act, and seedbed of virtue in all times and places and in all kinds of social and political relationships, then we can no longer point to tolerance in order to mark the difference that modernity makes. The tolerance found in modernity's liberal societies might be distinct from other varieties found in other times and places, but the point is that there are other varieties. Historians have already begun to describe them and so encourage us to rethink the relationship between tolerance and modernity, but theory has lagged behind history.[6] Locating tolerance among the virtues should help theory catch up.

Finally, by theorizing tolerance and forbearance together we will see how virtues that regard the same material object and generate the same material act can themselves be regarded as siblings, as similar yet distinct. Both tolerance and forbearance regard human actions in response to objectionable difference, both generate acts of patient endurance in reply, and it's this shared object and act that enables us to see their family resemblances and pair them across the divide between love and justice. So too, by theorizing them together we can see how a right response to the differences that threaten the peace and persistence of a social relationship will depend in large measure on the character of the relationship itself. Different social relationships require different responses, generate distinct demands, and elicit diverse hopes. Thus, the need for two distinct virtues. Moreover, by regarding tolerance and forbearance together and noting the biblical and theological terms that Christians have used for speaking about love's endurance we will acquire an example of how the actions and perfections of a particular religious community might stand in relation to those found in liberal democracies. Differences will come into focus, but only against the backdrop of a shared desire to cope with persistent disagreement, a shared interest in sustaining social and political relationships, and a shared concern to specify and coordinate the demands of love with those of justice. The hope is to complicate the distinction between secular and religious moral discourses and so identify resources for each on either side of the divide.

SOURCES

Four sources inform this effort and contribute to its content. The thought that tolerance could be explicated in perfectionist terms comes from Stanley Cavell, who assumes that talk of virtue's perfection is required whenever we identify a special goodness in human action and whenever there is opportunity to do better or worse with respect to desire and performance.[7] It also comes from Steven Macedo, William Galston, and others who have

---

6   See, for example, Nederman, *Worlds of Difference*.

7   For Cavell, moral progress requires reflection on the activities a virtue is said to perfect and on the "unthoughtful philosophy" of those who claim to understand what perfection entails. Quite often the claim is one's own, and thus a certain kind of self-criticism may be required, a self-repudiation that might be revelatory. It might reveal genuine bewilderment about those same virtues and activities, and this might compel further reflection on them. It might elicit "exploratory responses," and this might yield conversion of self, claim, and practice. "Such ideas are implicit in Emerson's picture of finding ourselves on a series of stairs. Philosophy is here transfiguring, one could hastily say internalizing, the ancient idea of the

encouraged us to think that liberal democracies require a virtuous citizenry.[8] My effort differs from theirs in that it aims at a much more determinate conception of virtue, one that attends not only to matter, act, ends, and circumstances, but also to the tight connection between social location and normative demand and to the sibling relations that can obtain among virtues. Tolerance is important because of the quite specific virtue it is; because of the special goodness its patient endurance embodies and because of the crucial role this act plays in the various communities we love and activities we take up. But it is also important because it stands among a number of moral virtues that matter for those of us concerned with educating students, building teams, exercising citizenship, forming coalitions, and maintaining friendships. Here I'm thinking not only of cardinal virtues such as justice and courage, but also of faith, hope, perseverance, and honesty. Like tolerance, these latter virtues play a crucial role in sustaining these activities and perfecting our participation in them. Like tolerance, they are misunderstood and undertheorized. Our speech about them tends to be imprecise and so prone to distortion and misuse. My hope is that the determinate account of tolerance I provide and the vocabulary of virtue that I develop can be used as models for those who might work up these other virtues.

The thought that tolerance and forbearance should be regarded together comes from Ernst Kantorowicz, from his reading of the twelfth-century Norman Anonymous in his famous study, *The King's Two Bodies*.[9] In the political theology of the Norman Anonymous, a king, an ordinary human being, acquires authority to occupy his office only as the Holy Spirit makes him a *gemina persona*—one thing by nature, another by grace. His *persona mixta* "mirrors the duplication of natures in Christ," and this duplication enables him to participate in Christ's temporal rule.[10] The image helps us see how different virtues can nevertheless be siblings. It draws our attention to the fact that two formally distinct natures can be united by a common matter that each regards, and this fact can be used to reflect on the relations that obtain between virtues united in material object and yet specifically distinct, some as distinct as nature is from grace or as love is from justice.

The thought that tolerance and forbearance might be regarded as sibling virtues and that a vocabulary could be developed to bring clarity and precision to that regard comes from Thomas Aquinas. I solicit assistance from him in every chapter, and the assistance is largely conceptual. That is, I do not

---

self as on a path, concentrating rather on the implicit features of taking steps, learning to walk away." Cavell, *Little Did I Know*, 461, 499.

8   Macedo, *Liberal Virtues*; Galston, *Liberal Purposes*.

9   Kantorowicz, *King's Two Bodies*.

10   Ibid., 58.

explicate and defend an interpretation of Thomas's account of these virtues, and the reason is simple. He doesn't have an account to interpret. He does mention *acts* of toleration in his discussion of a proper response to Jewish rites and beliefs, and he does refer to *acts* of forbearance in his discussion of fraternal correction. But in neither case does he move beyond mere mentioning. He doesn't provide detailed reflection on these acts, on their matter, objects, and ends, and he says very little about their social settings, circumstances, and limits. He never considers their possible relations, and he does not theorize either of them as a virtue. So it's not *his* account of these matters that I develop. Rather, it's Aquinas's treatment of various topics—action and habit, natural law and acquired virtue, justice and charity—that I borrow and adapt in my perfectionist account of tolerance and its sibling, forbearance. At times, I do my best to get Thomas right in his own terms. At times, I extend his inquiries in ways that he does not but could have, perhaps even should have. And at times, I draw inferences from what he does say while assuming commitments he does not have. As I said, my goal is to rectify two virtue concepts that have fallen into disrepair, whose criteria of application are uncertain and confused. For this task, perhaps surprisingly, there is no better conversation partner than Aquinas.

The ironies here should not go unnoticed. Many of Thomas's modern champions are allied against toleration; they consider the act essentially bad.[11] While most of those who consider toleration essentially good would never dream that a medieval Christian theologian could best provide the conceptual resources we need in order to describe the act and identify the virtue that generates right resort to it. And yet it is precisely these conceptual resources that Aquinas provides. Along with Plato, Aristotle, and the Stoics, he is one of the great theorists of the virtues. In fact, he surpasses all others because he comes late enough in the history of virtue theory to have identified most of the relevant topics and problems, assess what others have proposed, and respond with gratitude, correction, and innovation. And, crucially for our purposes, the concrete concerns that motivated Thomas's theorizing about the virtues should prove helpful from the vantage point of modern efforts to theorize difference and endurance, correction and coercion, loyalty and exit. He was writing in order to instruct people who were charged with the spiritual care of parishioners and parishes, monks and monasteries—that is, with particular communities in which important differences in judgment and love were likely to cause problems of association and where members had to respond in accord with the norms of justice and love.

---

11 Not all. John Knasas finds an account of tolerance in Thomas's treatment of the natural law, in its defense of human dignity. On his rendering, tolerance is principle and act but not exactly virtue. See his *Thomism and Tolerance*. For a quite different coordination of natural law and tolerance, see chapter 2.

Those communities turn out to have quite a lot in common with our own universities, political coalitions, and social movements, as well as with contemporary parishes, congregations, and religious communities. And those problems of association turn out to be roughly our own. As I said, Thomas does not theorize tolerance or forbearance, but he does share our interest in responding well to disagreement and difference, he does think that patient endurance is quite often the right response, and he does provide the conceptual resources we need to identify the habitual sources of this act.

And finally, the thought that we need these conceptual resources if we hope to sustain the social and political relationships we care about and to work with others to rectify their imperfections comes from Albert Hirschman and his justly famous *Exit, Voice, and Loyalty*.[12] In many ways, his book and mine are siblings. Both of us sort through the options that are available to participants in a relationship or organization that is in some way imperfect or dysfunctional. Both of us develop a vocabulary that accounts for those options and that identifies their reasons and circumstances. Both of us are interested in the reasons that warrant staying put in a deficient relationship or deteriorating organization and in the contestation and correction that can nevertheless come from those who do. But there are also formal differences. Most significantly, Hirschman does not provide a perfectionist account of these matters. He does not speak of virtue, tolerance or any other. Rather, it's the complications of judgment and desire that occupy his interest, judgment and desire in response to conflict and decay within an organization or relationship, not the possibility that perfection might come to these responses. Indeed he doubts that it can. The psychological and institutional mechanisms that conspire against "any stable and optimally effective mix" of right responses are simply too powerful, or so he thinks.[13] The complications of judgment and desire are simply too many and "the forces of decay" too persistent.[14] Fair enough. But it is one thing to doubt that an optimal mix of responses can be fixed in advance and applied like a rule. It is another to doubt that some particular mix is better than others in response to the deficiencies of some particular organization or relationship. And it is another thing still to doubt that this better mix can be known, desired, and rendered in act. As we shall see, it is precisely the complicated character of these responses that should encourage us to imagine degrees of perfection with respect to them and to consider the possibility that some of us will do better than others across a range of circumstances, some even habitually so.

12   Hirschman, *Exit, Voice, and Loyalty*.

13   Ibid., 125.

14   Ibid., 124.

SIBLING INQUIRIES

Tolerance is my principal concern, but, as I have said, I will also consider its sibling relations with forbearance. For this latter task, I make use of both secular and religious discourses and I assume that sibling relations obtain here as well, among these discourses. These different tasks and discourses hang together in one book, one *mixta libro*, for the same reason that tolerance and forbearance, acquired by ordinary means, belong to the same family as the forbearance that, by Christian confession, comes by grace alone. Despite their different aims and formal principles, they share a common material object: action in response to the objectionable differences that divide persons within a social or political relationship. These inquiries, like these virtues, share this object. It is the most basic matter about which each regards.

Christians have a long history of borrowing and adapting secular philosophical discourses for the purposes of explicating the faith they confess and the hopes and loves they have. One might say that Christian theology is nothing but this combination of secular wisdom and prophetic piety. So it will come as no surprise when the concepts explored and distinctions drawn in chapters 1 through 5 find their way into the discussion of gracious forbearance in chapter 6. Readers who are interested in this combination will want to work their way through all six chapters. But what about those readers who care about the material object of my inquiries but have no interest in the theological efforts of chapter 6? Should they pull up short and close the book before the end?

They may, of course, but then there's this. Christians are not the only people who need light shed on the relationships that obtain between the virtues that belong to justice and those that perfect our loves. If both virtues generate actions in response to the difficulties posed by difference and disagreement, then we need some way of hammering out a vocabulary for speaking of such matters. It so happens that Christians, because of their preoccupation with both love and justice and because of their attention to unity and difference within relationships, have already taken up the hard work of hammering out such a vocabulary. Secular readers might wish to learn from these efforts, to borrow successes and avoid missteps. Some will want to do this very selectively. In Aquinas's case, they will resist his account of virtue offered by grace, by divine action, but even here there may be something to learn. It might be, for all I know, that a thoroughly secular conception of grace and its virtues could be developed, and it may be that Aquinas's efforts could be naturalized to this effect. This is something I leave for others to explore.

The point is that secular readers may want to follow the inquiry to the end, and not out of ethnographic curiosity, or at least not only, but also to understand for themselves something about forbearance. This makes perfect sense, and not simply because tolerance comes into focus against the backdrop that forbearance provides, but also because forbearance and its act have a natural life. Indeed, as we shall see, the account of divine love and gracious forbearance developed in chapter 6 proceeds by analogy with these natural realities. But suppose we reverse the vectors. As I said, Christian theologians have a long history of borrowing and adapting secular philosophical sources, an appropriation made possible by the common material objects that so often unite these inquiries. But here the possibility that I am imagining cuts the other way: these shared material objects make theological resources candidates for borrowing and adapting by secular theorists. What purposes might motivate the borrowing and adapting, I cannot say in advance. Rather, I simply note that when moral philosophers and political theorists find something useful in the discourses of charity, for example, they should not overlook the theoretical resources that the theologians have already developed. Those resources may well leaven their efforts. An example makes the point.[15]

In the third and final section of *The Reasons of Love*, Harry Frankfurt considers the self's love for itself. In any kind of love, "the lover cares about the good of his beloved for its own sake." He wants to "protect and pursue the true interests of the person whom he loves," and in this case the beloved is himself and the interests are his own.[16] To love oneself, one must be devoted to the interests and projects one happens to have, and not for their instrumental pay off but for their own sake. The trouble of course is that this assumes wholehearted devotion to those interests and projects, and for most of us this assumption cannot be made. Most of us have hearts that are divided. Some of our projects and interests elicit ambivalence and self-doubt, not undivided devotion. Some of our loves generate second thoughts and hesitations, not reflective endorsement.[17] Frankfurt's response to this antinomy of self-love is to admit that wholeheartedness is an ideal, to concede that most of us fall short, and to encourage a certain lightheartedness when we do. "At least be sure to hang on to your sense of humor."[18]

---

15   Other examples include Nussbaum, *Political Emotions* and Rose, *Love's Work*. In the modern period, it was the Romantics who recognized the benefits of naturalizing the supernatural, of secularizing "inherited theological ideas and ways of thinking." I am suggesting that moral philosophers and political theorists would benefit from following their lead. See Abrams, *Natural Supernaturalism*, 2.

16   Frankfurt, *Reasons of Love*, 85.

17   Ibid., 91–95.

18   Ibid., 100.

It's a compelling account, less its concluding advice. Ambivalence and self-doubt are not the only attitudes of a divided heart. Others are more serious. Projects and interests that cannot be endorsed by the better self we long to become may elicit contempt for the self that remains captive to them. The better self's critique signals a transformation hoped for but not yet achieved. In cases like these, despair and self-hatred can come, and it's unlikely that a sense of humor can stave off their arrival, not in every instance. What might? Well, again, there are theological resources that could be secularized, adapted, and endorsed. There is a long and rich history of theological reflection on self-love for an imperfect self, a love that originates in the gracious regard of another. Correction and forbearance are aspects of that love, offered by the self we hope to become to the self that remains committed to cares we despise. Both acts are geared to the divided and broken souls most of us have, and when offered and received, they bear witness to the first beginnings of self-transformation, of progress toward wholeness.

In this particular instance, secular theory could benefit from acquainting itself with theological resources precisely because it is already attentive to the place of love in our lives. For the most part, however, moral philosophers, political theorists, and historians have ignored love's response to the conflicts and differences that divide us. They have mostly attended to the act of toleration, and they have struggled to bring its moral substance into focus. The solution, I suggest, is to shift attention to the virtue that perfects resort to this act, to bring this virtue into focus along with its sibling, forbearance, and to learn from the theological discourses that describe love's endurance. This, in any event, is the solution I explore in the pages that follow.

ABBREVIATIONS
AND TRANSLATIONS

THOMAS AQUINAS

DC	*Quaestio disputata de caritate*
De vert.	*Quaestiones disputatae de veritate*
DFC	*Quaestio disputata de correctione fraterna*
DV	*Quaestio disputata de virtutibus in communi*
SCG	*Summa contra Gentiles*
ST	*Summa theologiae*

ARISTOTLE

Metaph.	*Metaphysics*
NE	*Nicomachean Ethics*

AUGUSTINE

c. Acad.	*Contra Academicos* (CCSL 29)
civ. Dei	*De civitate Dei contra Paganos* (CCSL 47, 48)
conf.	*Confessiones* (CCSL 27)
e.	*Epistolae* CI-CXXXIX (CCSL 31B)
lib. arb.	*De libero arbitrio* (CCSL 29)
ord.	*De Ordine* (CCSL 29)
pat.	*De patientia* (CSEL 41)
Trin.	*De Trinitate* (CCSL 50, 50A)

CAESAR

BGall.	*Bellum Gallicum*

CICERO

Inv.	*De Inventione*
Leg.	*De Legibus*
Off.	*De Officiis*
Par.	*Paradoxa Stoicorum*

LACTANTIUS

Div. inst.   *Divinae institutiones*

For the most part, I have relied on the English translations listed in the bibliography. I have checked the translations of Thomas's works against the best available Latin editions, also listed in the bibliography. I have frequently modified these translations in order improve their clarity and sharpen their connection to the literal sense. In a few instances, I have made my own translations, noted in the footnotes.

CHAPTER 1

TOLERANCE AND RESENTMENT

Begin with the ordinary facts of pluralism, present in some measure in every time and place, but perhaps more apparent in our own, where differences of various kinds—moral, religious, ethnic, and other—press hard upon us and where disagreement about the relative merit of various goods, commitments, and activities confound our life together. Some of these differences and disagreements threaten the basic union of wills that every society assumes. These require rough magics—coercion, constraint, expulsion, or withdrawal. Others are less threatening to that union, and to these the tolerant respond well, most often with patient endurance, an act designed to maintain the society shared with those they endure and autonomy with respect to the differences in dispute.[1]

It is because of these facts and threats, and because this desire for social union remains in spite of them, that tolerance has, from time to time, been counted among the virtues, one of the parts or aspects of justice that nearly every society cultivates in some way and praises in some measure.[2] Of course, as virtue and act, tolerance is not the only solution to the problems

---

1   By "tolerance" I refer to a virtue that perfects our capacity to act in certain ways in accord with certain norms and reasons and to a collection of actions and attitudes associated with that perfection. Leaving to one side an important caveat, a "tolerant act" is one that conforms to those norms and reasons. It is an act of toleration that is right and good. By "toleration" I mean either the license given to the one who is endured to speak and act in certain ways across certain lines of disagreement and difference, or the activity of enduring some objectionable difference. These distinctions will become more precise and others will be added as the argument unfolds. They are summarized at the start of chapter 4.

2   So for example, in the fourth century, Lactantius locates tolerance within justice and considers it an unavoidable feature of its principal parts, piety and equity (*Div. inst.* v.15, 20).

of association posed by the diversity of goods and loves. Nor should it be. At the same time, not every difference or dispute can be regulated by law, suppressed with coercion, or avoided by exit. And so in most times and places peaceful coexistence is secured, at least in part, by cultivating the habits, attitudes, and practices of the tolerant. In this, at least, ancients and moderns agree. Cicero notes that the just and pious will shun coercion and endure dissent in religious affairs, for the gods love purity of mind above all,[3] while J. B. Schneewind insists that John Rawls's theory of justice, in both its metaphysical and its political variants, is best regarded as a "modern liberal democratic view of toleration."[4] No matter how they are situated in time or place, the tolerant act justly and the just act tolerantly. They give what justice demands to those from whom they are divided by disagreement and dissent, and, in their paradigmatic act, what they give is a willingness to bear the burdens of these disagreements and endure the company of these dissenters for the sake of the common life they share.

This much is plain. Problems of association, of peaceful coexistence among individuals and groups, are constant and unavoidable, and the appeal to toleration is common. So is the defense of certain instances of the act as right and good, as truly tolerant. Still, those problems and that appeal do acquire an urgency from time to time, and we appear to live in one of those times. Two reasons stand out. The first regards "the immediacy of difference, the everyday encounter with otherness, [that] has never been so widely experienced," not only in societies like ours—liberal, mobile, ethnically diverse, technologically advanced, stubbornly religious—but also in societies quite different from our own.[5] Almost everywhere globalization has made difference that was once distant now proximate. At the same time, the liberal variety of tolerance offered in response to these circumstances comes packaged with certain deficits, difficulties, and threats that challenge its friends and provoke its foes. It's no wonder, then, that ours is a heyday of discourse and dispute about tolerance.[6]

---

3 This is Lactantius's interpretation of *Leg.* II.8 found in *Div. inst.* v.19.13, 26; 20.3, 7. For commentary see Digeser, *Making of a Christian Empire*, 109. Forst (*Toleration in Conflict*, 37) assigns the first modern use of *tolerantia* to Cicero, who notes that the wise person will exhibit "tolerance in human affairs, [and] contempt for fortune" (*tolerantia rerum humanarum, contemptione fortuanae*; *Par.* vi.27). My own treatment of tolerance is decidedly less Stoic.

4 Schneewind, "Bayle, Locke, and the Concept of Toleration," 12.

5 Walzer, *On Toleration*, 6–7.

6 At times, the differences that generate problems of association, problems that tolerance might address, are real and substantial. At other times the differences apprehended are merely apparent, or, at the very least, less substantial than the parties in conflict imagine. And it may be that globalization has a hand in this if only because new proximity tends to make minor differences seem major. For a discussion of this dynamic, see Ignatieff, "Nationalism and Toleration."

It has happened before. There have been other such heydays, other periods when peaceful coexistence was difficult to muster and when appeal to acts of toleration and to the perfection of this act was both considered and challenged: in the earliest Christian churches, in the late Roman Empire, in early modern Europe, and no doubt in other times and places. In each instance, debate abounds, and not simply about the variety of tolerance that might address this or that particular problem of association, but also about the essential goodness of its basic act and its status as a virtue. For every Lactantius defending the act and praising its consequences, there is usually a Porphyry decrying its vice.[7] For every Locke there is an Assheton to confront and a Proast to debate.[8] Our time and place reproduce the pattern. Liberal tolerance is proposed as one solution to the problems of association we confront, and straightaway critics emerge, highbrow and low, left and right, all denouncing the false promise and counterfeit character of the virtue and the dangerous and domineering spirit of its act.

A COMMON LOGIC OF COMPLAINT

Some argue that tolerance offers an inconsistent, and thus unstable, response to the problems that pluralism poses. It comes overburdened with paradoxes. It demands what we cannot deliver. The tolerant dislike, and at times despise, what they are obliged to endure, a feat that few can manage. Most of us resolve this conflict between duty and desire by putting aside our objection to the differences in dispute. This in turn enables us to forgo the disapproval that makes pluralism a problem and tolerance a possible solution. Indifference is the fallout, which in turn confirms the suspicions of those who worry that tolerance requires impossible moral compromise and comes packaged with a contemptible metaphysical minimalism. For these critics, even a morally robust tolerance, one that shuns indifference and holds fast to disapproval, carries the taint of moral danger, decadence, and betrayal. For of course, why should we tolerate beliefs that we consider false, actions we consider vicious, social practices we consider dangerous or scandalous, institutional arrangements we consider cruel or corrupt? Why should we cut deals with the wicked and keep company with the confused when we could just as well coerce their conduct or forsake their company?

Consider, for example, Bruce Bawer's remarks in his somewhat awkwardly titled essay, "Tolerance or Death!", from the December 2005 issue of

---

7   See Digeser, *Making of a Christian Empire*, 91–114.

8   See Assheton, *Toleration disapprove'd and condemn'd* and the first of Jonas Proast's three responses to Locke: *Argument of the Letter.*

Reason.com.[9] Bawer argues that the variety of tolerance that distinguishes liberal democracies is ill suited to our times. It's the virtue that enables the mullahs to preach hate and the terrorists to kill the innocent. In a similar vein, Mark Steyn writes that liberal democracies are incapable of acting with force and confidence when their way of life is challenged by moral decay from within and by unjust violence from without. Schooled in patient endurance, in easygoing open-mindedness, the inhabitants of liberal democracies tend to respond to these challenges by mustering ever more tolerance. Craven and foolish, they can't resist concluding that intolerance of other people's intolerance, other people's wickedness, is, well, simply intolerable.[10] Pope Benedict XVI offered remarks of the same kind, although considerably less heated. While still Joseph Cardinal Ratzinger, he argued that "the fundamental problem of our time [is] the question of truth and toleration." The problem, as Ratzinger sees it, is that the modern "commandment of tolerance and respect for others" comes packaged with "the notion that all religions are ultimately equivalent," which in turn denies the exclusive character of the truth that Christians confess about Christ and humanity, sin and salvation. He asks, "If tolerance is one of the foundations of the modern age, then is not the claim to have recognized the essential truth an obsolete piece of presumption that has to be rejected if the spiral of violence that runs through the history of religions is to be broken?" The Christian, he insists, must "resist this ideology of equality," this false account of truth and freedom, this "all-inclusive tolerance."[11]

Others offer criticisms from the perspective of the tolerated. By their lights, the problem with tolerance is not that it is unstable, that it dissolves into relativistic indifference. Rather, the problem is that it begins with judgment and ends in condescension. For these critics, tolerance is a morally inadequate response to the problems posed by the plurality of lives and commitments precisely because it assumes unjustifiable inequalities of moral authority and political power. Some disapprove and endure, others are judged

---

9   Bawer, "Tolerance or Death!"

10   Steyn, "It's the Demography, Stupid."

11   Ratzinger, *Truth and Tolerance*, 102, 105, 210, 214. Ratzinger returned to these themes in the homily he delivered as dean of the College of Cardinals at the votive mass of April 18, 2005 that immediately preceded his election to the papacy (Ratzinger, "Homily *Pro Eligendo Romano Pontifice*"). He writes, "Today, having a clear faith based on the Creed of the Church is often labeled as fundamentalism. Whereas relativism, that is, letting oneself be 'tossed here and there, carried about by every wind of doctrine,' seems the only attitude that can cope with modern times. We are building a dictatorship of relativism that does not recognize anything as definitive and whose ultimate goal consists solely of one's own ego and desires." For a powerful response, see Stout, "House Founded on the Sea."

and tolerated. According to these critics, societies like ours must move beyond judgment and tolerance to recognition and acceptance.[12]

Even the friends of tolerance provide weak praise. As act and attitude, tolerance is useful, they say, perhaps even indispensable, for coping with disagreements and differences both large and small, and yet praise rarely proceeds beyond instrumental accounting. Tolerance is good because it helps us get along in spite of our differences, which is to say, in effect, that if we could get along without it, we would. A tepid endorsement indeed.

Notice the common logic of these quite different criticisms. Tolerance is too difficult to muster, too condescending. Tolerance is complicit in the worst vices of liberal societies. Tolerance encourages a passive-aggressive politics, a gentle and self-deceived paternalism that in fact betrays our commitment to the equal dignity of all. Tolerance must be overcome; the conditions that demand its exercise must be escaped. Pick a complaint, any one will do. Each begins with a certain disregard for the world we inhabit, a world where the diversity of human goods and the relative indeterminacy of human loves generate conflict among lives and commitments that are entrenched and inescapable and where societies large and small secure right relations among members only as toleration's act is offer in response to at least some of these differences and only as some variety of the virtue is cultivated and praised. In order to free us from the obligation to endure certain differences and remain in certain dysfunctional relationships, these critics reject this world. They deny its unavoidable reality; they disregard the goodness embedded in its difficulties. They yearn for a world where pluralism was less perplexing and where tolerance was unnecessary. Some long for a world to come, some starry future where difference will not threaten nor disagreement divide, and where equal standing and shared first principles will generate mutual respect, acceptance, and appreciation. In this future, there will be no problems of association that might require toleration as a solution. Others yearn for a fanciful past, where pluralism was not so pressing and where the challenges of peaceful coexistence were not met with a remedy so unheroic and unambitious, so overburdened with ambivalence and moral compromise, so content with disagreement's sorrow. And note, these latter, wistful yearnings are encouraged by the standard history. On this account, as act and potential virtue, tolerance is a modern affair, a moral innovation that emerged in the wake of the wars of religion that followed the Protestant Reformation. It acquired merit only as religion became relatively private, the public square

---

12   The complaints of the tolerant will be considered in this chapter, those of the tolerated in chapter 2. For evidence that fear of judgment, of its implicit intolerance, has led many Americans to recast tolerance as indifference or acceptance, see the survey data in Wolfe, *One Nation, After All*, 275–322.

relatively secular, and associations of all kinds relatively voluntary.[13] For those who accept this account, and most do, tolerance is so closely bound to the norms and ideals of liberal society and to a certain image of secular modernity that our attitude toward one portion of the package typically bears on the others. This tight packaging has enabled liberals to consider tolerance their own, a moral advance that distinguishes their time and place from all others. But it has also offered the foes of liberal society and secular modernity another reason for discontent with tolerance, and, no surprise, the resentment that so many feel for tolerance confirms their complaints with liberal modernity.

The reasons that provoke these criticisms are not immediately apparent. One is tempted to offer an easy explanation. Tolerance *deserves* our complaints; it ought to be resented. Why? Because it asks us to do or endure what we would rather not. Few of us want to tolerate what we find objectionable or to be tolerated by others. The tolerant do not want to restrain their outrage and the tolerated would prefer to be accepted. The first act with regret and the second receive what is given with little gratitude. Both would prefer to live in a world where tolerant attitudes and practices were unnecessary. Given this response, it's no surprise that tolerance is resented and its place among the virtues doubted.

But this can't be right. If it were, we would expect other virtues to be resented for roughly the same reasons, but for the most part they're not. At times, we don't want to be treated justly or to act among the just, and yet this aversion rarely yields global complaint against justice. Specific judgments about the just and the unjust are often resented, as is the authority those judgments sometimes have over other considerations, but rarely do these resentments touch justice *in se*.

Or, rather, discontent with this or that collection of authoritative judgments about the just and the unjust is rarely expressed in across-the-board complaint against justice, but not so with tolerance.[14] Of course, one

---

13   For recent examples of the standard history, see Creppell, *Toleration and Identity* and Zagorin, *How the Idea of Religious Toleration Came to the West*. Both offer excellent accounts of the emergence of modern varieties of tolerance. At the same time, both assume that these varieties exhaust what tolerance might be and thus both support the Enlightenment's image of premodern Europe: repressive and coercive, it could not regard tolerance as a virtue. Both assume that before the modern period tolerance was always considered a vice. For doubts about this history and this image, see Bejczy, "Tolerantia" and the essays in two recent collections: Nederman and Laursen, eds., *Difference and Dissent* and Laursen and Nederman, eds., *Beyond the Persecuting Society*.

14   *Qualified* complaint with justice remains quite common. Consider Marx's critique. What Marx resents is not the concept per se, but rather its deployment as an ideology in social conflicts and our failure to see that its material content derives from the function it plays in a given mode of production. His treatment of the "so-called rights of man" in "On the Jewish Question" follows this pattern. (See Tucker, ed., *Marx-Engels Reader*. For commentary, see Wood,

suspects that the critics exaggerate, that their complaints in fact regard specific judgments about the tolerable and the intolerable, not tolerance *in se*, and yet something about the virtue enables them to couch their complaints in comprehensive terms.

In the next section I will consider what this something might be that encourages this odd resentment of the virtue itself. For now I want to pursue another explanation, one that involves attention to how philosophers and theologians talk about tolerance. At first, this might seem odd. If complaint and resentment are relatively widespread, then why not cast a wide net and look at first order expressions of opinion: polling data, editorials, newsletters, reading lists, weblogs, and so on? Why not describe the actual lives and practices that embody these opinions, complaints, and resentments? Well, for starters, I assume that philosophers and theologians give ordered, condensed, and reflective expression of these same widely held opinions, and I assume that their reflections begin with lives and practices. They do not create what they say out of nothing. The concepts they employ and the arguments they advance are not artifacts of their own making. Rather, philosophers and theologians begin with the lives, commitments, and judgments of actual communities of discourse. They spell out the norms implicit in those lives and put those commitments and judgments in order—gathering them together, tracing their inferential relations, making imbedded commitments explicit, offering reasons in defense of some, and suggesting revisions of others. And it is this reflective and expressive character of their efforts that I am after. When it goes well, reflection brings concept, commitment, and judgment into focus. It helps us see what they amount to, what revisions of belief and practice they encourage, and what reasons are needed to maintain them. And even when it goes poorly, it encourages reflection on our own reasons for maintaining this belief or making that inference, our own understanding of how norm and commitment made explicit ought to affect judgment, conduct, and linguistic usage.[15]

This is how I intend to make use of the philosophers and theologians discussed in this chapter and beyond. More often than not, their efforts go well, but not entirely so. Concept, commitment, and judgment are brought into focus, but distortion remains, either in what is said about tolerance, or

---

"Marxian Critique of Justice.") Or consider those who champion self-esteem as a primary goal of upbringing and education. They don't *say* that they resent justice, but they do describe countless acts of warranted criticism and just grading as cruel or harsh. They want us to replace the question of what criticism is just and due with the question of what remarks are likely to build up self-worth. And finally there is Stanley Hauerwas's infamous, hyperbolic, and often misunderstood insistence that justice is a bad idea. See *After Christendom?* For clarifications, see Hauerwas, *Performing the Faith*, 215–241. I owe this qualification to Melissa Lane.

15   For an explication and defense of this rationalist and expressivist account of philosophy, see Brandom, *Articulating Reasons*, 1–77.

in the practical proposals made. My hunch is that at least some of the sources of resentment reside in these distortions and that a good number of these distortions follow from our failure to grasp what it might mean for tolerance to be a virtue annexed to justice.

But there's more. Philosophical and theological efforts are not simply expressive, they also provide warrants. They give ordered, reflective expression of judgments and commitments implicit in certain lives and practices, and in turn, those expressions justify certain judgments and commitments, certain practices and lives. There is, as John Rawls put it, a kind of reflective equilibrium and a kind of trade in authority between abstract expression and the concrete realities that are the objects and sources of reflection.[16] That said, there is also trouble hidden in this trade, trouble in the divide between the concrete and the abstract, the reflective and the practical. When philosophers and theologians make explicit the specific commitments embedded in actual lives and practices they typically resort to abstractions that mask the expressive character of their efforts, even from themselves. Abstraction is, of course, a trademark of these disciplines, and yet the abstract character of certain concepts tends to encourage forgetfulness of their concrete origins, of the lives and practices that are the primary objects of reflection. It tends to mystify and so mislead.

Our contemporary debates about tolerance display the mischief that philosophical and theological abstractions can do and the resentments they can encourage. This resentment comes from many quarters and for many reasons, and yet more often than not it is an abstract idea, tolerance itself, that receives complaint. But this can't be quite right. If tolerance is, as I shall argue chapter 2, a natural virtue embedded in the form of life human beings happen to lead, if it is geared to ends we all desire and activities we cannot avoid taking up, then it is unlikely that the virtue itself can be resented. As Nietzsche points out, resentment of human life, and of the virtues that come packaged with it, is hard to maintain. When it is said to exist, we should doubt that it does and instead look for self-deception at work, for a hidden desire to transform some feature of that life or some understanding of those virtues.[17] When the abstract ideas of philosophers and theologians encourage and mediate these resentments, we should try to uncover the concrete commitments embedded in the abstractions they employ. More often than not, these concrete commitments will be the real objects of complaint, not the abstraction, not the virtue itself. Once this reality is exposed, these resentments tend to lose both their critical power and their claim to universality.

---

16 Rawls, *Theory of Justice*, 578–580.
17 Nietzsche, *On the Genealogy of Morals*, 97–163.

Suppose we take this advice to heart. Suppose we regard the resentments directed toward tolerance itself as in fact directed toward specific judgments about the tolerable and the intolerable.[18] In that event, we could also assume that complaint with this or that specific collection of judgments will be embedded in the abstract terms used by the resentful. And we could assume that at least some critics will want to keep their complaints with a specific regime of tolerance hidden, embedded in the philosophical or theological abstractions they employ. Why? Because disagreements about the tolerable and the intolerable, about the specific activities and things that are or are not objectionable and that may or may not deserve our patient endurance, are often painful and frequently difficult to resolve. What better way to circumvent this difficulty and avoid this pain than to convince us that this debate isn't worth having? If tolerance itself deserves our complaints and resentments, then why bother with debate about specifics? Or, perhaps more to the point, what better way to *win* such a debate by stealth, to displace one account of the tolerable and the intolerable and replace it with another. Convince us that tolerance itself deserves our complaints and resentments, that it is always an unworkable, morally dubious solution to the problem of peaceful coexistence among differences, and you will most likely weaken commitment to the dominant account, the one you resent, and in turn create opportunity for an alternative regime of tolerance to emerge.

My hunch is that this is how things often work. The critics of this or that specific regime of tolerance make use of the mystifying potential in philosophy and theology to exaggerate their grievances. At the same time they borrow the authority of these discourses to convince us that their grievances are sound, that tolerance itself ought to be refused. Combine this dynamic with the fact that tolerance appears to have certain features that, as we shall see, encourage these complaints and real trouble emerges for societies that wish to determine their affairs democratically. If we become convinced that the real issue is tolerance *in se*—with the essential goodness of its patient endurance and its status as a virtue—not the merit of this or that particular account of the tolerable and the intolerable, then debate about the tolerable limits of difference will be distorted and preempted. The mystifications that philosophers at times work upon themselves will be inflicted upon the rest of us.

Although some philosophers and theologians exploit this mechanism of resentment willingly and desire these outcomes self-consciously, most do not. Most are appalled to find their arguments and distinctions used by others to generate global resentment toward tolerance. Most will insist that

18 That certain ideologies of tolerance need critique, no one doubts. The confusion comes in mistaking the ideology for the reality, the particular account of tolerance for its perfect instantiation. For a vivid example, see Wolff, Moore, and Marcuse, *Critique of Pure Tolerance*.

they don't want their efforts used in this way. Fair enough. But if the concrete sources of their abstract discourses are easy to forget, and if, as a result, their efforts are easy to misuse and their authority easy to borrow, then attention must be paid. If there is something about tolerance itself that encourages mystification and global complaint, then surely we must redouble our efforts.

UNSTABLE TOLERANCE

Consider the following opportunities to exercise tolerance. An adult bookstore appears on your street, across from the public library and two blocks down from the post office and the middle school. Or perhaps you live in South Florida and a Santerian priest moves in next door. He and his wife raise chickens, pigeons, and goats, not for consumption or companionship, but for ritual sacrifice in rites of initiation and healing. It appears that the couple serves a small community and that these rites take place in their home, most likely in a basement room set apart for worship. Or suppose you live in rural Oklahoma, down the street from a Native American Church, where some of your fellow citizens routinely ingest peyote in sacred ceremony. Or, finally, imagine you are the pastor of a church that has been invited to join a citizen's organization whose members include congregations that confess beliefs you consider heretical and support policies you consider unjust. The organization is working to reform unfair lending, housing, and voter registration practices in your community. You share these aims, this commitment to justice, but you wonder whether it would be right for your congregation to work in this company.

Each instance, it seems, calls for the actions and attitudes of the tolerant. The activities in question—selling pornography, sacrificing animals, using hallucinogens, confessing certain beliefs, and endorsing certain policies— are considered objectionable by some, and as such they may generate problems of peaceful coexistence among neighbors and fellow citizens. They may create obstacles to shared action among potential coalition partners. And let's assume for the moment that these activities are not matters of "Civil Interest," as John Locke put it. They do not appear to regard those outward things—life, liberty, health, and property—that fall under the authority of the "Civil Magistrate," of those charged with care for the political community. At the very least, they do not seem to threaten those civil interests in any direct or obvious way, and thus they do not appear to be candidates for regulation by "the Laws of Publick Justice and Equity, established for the Preservation of those [interests]."[19] Rather, these activities

19 Locke, *Letter*, 26.

appear to fall between the unbearably harmful and the harmlessly unobjectionable, the two extremes that frame the domain where tolerance operates
and where problems of association are addressed by its act.

Those who commend a tolerant response will insist that these activities
belong in this domain even as they concede that some are not only objectionable but also injurious. The porn industry does generate harms of various kinds. Santerians do kill animals. The easy availability of hallucinogens
can cause all sorts of trouble and woe. And those who judge certain beliefs
importantly false or regard certain policies as dangerously unjust will very
likely consider them potential sources of scandal, of moral and spiritual
harm, when they are endured, not resisted.

None of this can be denied. At the same time, legal remedies would likely
make things worse. Criminalized activities tend to generate criminals, and
this is best avoided, particularly when there are less coercive means of changing objectionable behaviors: correction, shaming, public protest, and so on.
Still, George Fletcher speaks for many when he wonders whether these activities can be both regarded in this way and tolerated nevertheless. By his
lights, the psychological dynamics of tolerance and the infrequent resort
to its act should lead us to doubt this possibility. Those who at first exercise some measure of tolerance in attitude and act will most likely surren-
der to this dynamic and follow this history. Some will exit the relationship
that requires toleration's act. They will move out the neighborhood; they
will refuse membership in the citizen's organization. They will forsake the
common good of a shared life, and they will abandon the power and mutual
support that might come from working with others for the sake of shared
ends. Others will remain in the relationship for the sake of these benefits,
but only as they abandon their resistance to what they at first found objectionable and endorse some other attitude, perhaps indifference, perhaps
acceptance. Still others will remain in the relationship but magnify their
complaints. They will no longer consider the difference in question objectionable yet tolerable, but intolerably harmful and thus subject to the coercive force of law.[20]

Why is this the likely progression of one's initial response to objectionable difference? Because tolerance is, according to Fletcher, inherently unstable—both the virtue and its act. At its core lies a psychological conflict
that the initially tolerant soon find intolerable, insufferable. They must endure what they dislike and, all things being equal, would prefer to abolish.
Their objections quite naturally generate "an impulse to intervene and reg-
ulate the lives of others." At the same time, countervailing reasons of some
sort convince them "to restrain that impulse . . . [and] suffer what they would

---

20   Fletcher, "Instability of Tolerance."

rather not confront."[21] And, since all those who suffer quite "understandably prefer an easier way," the tolerant typically reconsider the objectionable activity or thing that requires their patient endurance and relocate it among the unbearably harmful or the harmlessly unobjectionable.

Recent history seems to confirm Fletcher's diagnosis. Consider how responses to pornography tack between these two extremes while artfully steering clear of the middle realm that tolerance regards. Some have argued that pornography harms women precisely because it eroticizes inequalities of power. Access to all kinds should be regulated by law, they say, not tolerated by informal agreement.[22] For a time in the mid-1980s, many found these arguments convincing. City councils in Minneapolis and Indianapolis passed ordinances that would allow citizens who believe they have been harmed by pornography to take civil action against anyone involved in its production or sale. But these ordinances did not survive First Amendment challenge, and even if they had, attitudes were changing. By the turn of the millennium, pornography and its milder cousins were ubiquitous, in most American homes just a mouse click or channel change away. Considered objectionable by most just one generation past, pornography is now widely accepted, or, if not accepted, then regarded with indifference.

Fletcher's hunch—that debates about objectionable difference tend to tack back and forth between acceptance, indifference, and legal coercion, while ignoring the rigors of patient endurance—can also be seen in the Supreme Court's response to peyote use in the Native American Church. What might be considered merely objectionable and thus potentially tolerable has been transformed by legal judgment into the unbearably harmful and potentially suppressible.[23] But in other instances, this transformation has not been so easily made. Consider the objections that Santerian animal sacrifice has elicited in South Florida. Harms have been catalogued and ordinances passed, but in each instance the courts have ruled against those who wish to restrict this activity, largely because the harms offered in justification have been both insubstantial and ordinary. In certain settings, the animals used in Santerian sacrifice may well pose real threats to public health, but these threats so closely resemble those that accompany ordinary farming and ranching that one suspects the ordinances were passed to suppress the merely objectionable,

---

21   Ibid., 158–159. For similar worries about the instability of tolerant attitudes and the difficulty of acting tolerantly, see Raphael, "Intolerable."

22   For an argument to this effect, see MacKinnon, *Toward a Feminist Theory of the State*.

23   See *Employment Division, Department of Human Resources of Oregon v. Smith*, 494 U.S. 872 (1990). In response to *Smith*, congress passed the Religious Freedom Restoration Act of 1993, which the Supreme Court restricted to federal matters in *City of Boerne, Texas v. Flores*, 521 U.S. 507 (1997). In response to *Flores*, twenty-one states have passed their own RFRAs that apply in their own jurisdictions.

not the intolerably harmful.[24] When the dynamic that Fletcher describes fails in this way, some other response to objectionable difference will no doubt emerge, and, if his hunch is right, it will not be tolerance. Indifference will grow, perhaps acceptance, and if neither of these emerges, then no doubt some other response will circumvent the suffering endured by the tolerant as they endeavor to do what, in the end, he insists they cannot do—restrain their desire to act intolerantly toward the activities they find objectionable.

Surely there is some truth in what Fletcher says. Acts of toleration can be difficult to produce. Objecting to this or that, wishing to intervene, and, at the same time, restraining that desire and enduring what one despises—this can be a painful and unstable state of mind. Still, if Fletcher's account is taken to be authoritative and exhaustive, then the critics of tolerance will likely feel vindicated, their complaints confirmed. They will reason like this. When differences in commitment and activity elicit objections and generate divisions, toleration is often recommended as a solution to the problems of association that follow. At the same time, we are told that the judgments and desires that generate this act are unstable. They are not easily had or sustained. Those of us who give them a try frequently lapse into indifference or acceptance. These attitudes will, of course, generate actions that resemble toleration's patient endurance of objectionable difference.[25] We will live and let live, but not because we have managed to combine objection and restraint, but rather because we believe nothing with conviction, or failing that, because we accept uncritically what our recent ancestors, courageous and upright, would have found abominable, intolerable. Either way, the tolerance we are encouraged to exercise in practice conspires with our meager virtue and lands us in a contemptible nihilism, a traitorous moral flabbiness. On this account, tolerance is a kind of vice in disguise. Its ideal can be achieved only in semblances of its act, semblances that give the appearance of virtue, appearances that enable the weak and vicious to pose among the virtuous and strong, to be counted among the tolerant. Given the praise it receives nevertheless, why not resent this swindle, this virtue that invariably arrives as well-dressed vice? Combine these commitments and inferences with the common belief that tolerance is found exclusively in modern, liberal societies, societies that some say encourage this kind of moral collapse in all im-

---

24   For the U.S. Supreme Court ruling on the effort in Hialeah, Florida to ban animal sacrifice, see *Church of Lukumi Babalu Aye Inc. v. Hialeah*, 508 U.S. 520 (1993). For Fletcher's discussion, see "Instability of Tolerance," 163–164.

25   Indeed, the resemblance is quite often so close that only the truly tolerant can mark off indifference from acceptance and distinguish each of these from acts of true tolerance. As we shall see in chapter 3, it is precisely this ability that, in part, distinguishes their virtue. The tolerant display their moral excellence as they draw these distinctions among actions so similar in appearance that they easily confound the rest of us.

portant matters, and this resentment is confirmed in a broader landscape of assumption and criticism.

These are not Fletcher's inferences and conclusions. His aim is not to discount tolerance, but simply to call attention to its instability and display our tendency to replace it with some other response to differences that generate social struggle. Still, its most common critics assume that those who encourage tolerance in fact recommend moral collapse, and Fletcher's account confirms this assumption.[26]

Now consider the other dynamic of impossible tolerance and objectionable difference that Fletcher describes, the one that leads to the other boundary of its act.[27] Here, the objectionable and potentially tolerable is recast as the unbearably harmful, and one might conclude, as Fletcher seems to, that this is simply the end of tolerance. In a way it is. The difficulty of sustaining tolerant attitudes toward the objectionable can lead to this recasting, and, when successful, this recasting does indeed terminate the need for tolerance in both attitude and act. Some consider this self-consuming dynamic unavoidable, and they find it displayed in Locke's famous treatment of the act.[28] On Locke's rendering, the objects of toleration's patient endurance are all those activities and things that do not fall under the jurisdiction of the civil magistrate precisely because they have no bearing on those civil interests that he (or she) is obliged to preserve.[29] Locke calls these activities and things indifferent, which is somewhat misleading. Certain individuals and communities might not respond with indifference to the activities and things that the magistrate counts among the indifferent, but no matter. Indifference is determined by civil interests, and this determination sets toleration's scope. One might object to this or that, but so long as it shows up on the magistrate's list of indifferent actions and things it will not be subject to legal constraint. In these circumstances, toleration is best. Of course, circumstances might change and what was once judged indifferent might be considered in a new light, and it's the magistrate's consideration that matters here. Recall Locke's example: "the washing of an Infant with water." In itself, such washing is an indifferent thing, and thus one may not appeal to the magistrate for relief if one happens to object to the manner in which infants are washed in the church down the street. Normally, washing

---

26   For a sampling of popular complaints that equate tolerance with acceptance or indifference and thus with moral betrayal and collapse, see McDowell and Hostetler, *New Tolerance*. For a similar collection, but this time pitched to evangelical youth, see Dobson, *Be Intolerant*.

27   Fletcher, "Instability of Tolerance," 163–164.

28   Some will contest this interpretation, but no matter. The point here is not to get Locke right. Rather the point is to indicate how a plausible interpretation of Locke's account of toleration can contribute to the current climate of resentment toward tolerance.

29   Locke, *Letter*, 39.

does not fall under the magistrate's jurisdiction. But not all times are normal. "If the Magistrate understand such washing to be profitable to the curing or preventing of any Disease that Children are subject unto, and esteem the matter weighty enough to be taken care of by a Law, in that case he may order it to be done."[30] In times like these, failure to wash, once an indifferent matter, is now potentially harmful and thus a civic concern.

Notice the fallout. Acts of toleration require a domain of indifference, and on Locke's rendering the civil magistrate determines its scope. As almost anything indifferent can become an object of civil interest, toleration becomes a solution to problems of peaceful coexistence only as the magistrate's rule becomes potentially limitless. Given the right circumstances, communities and individuals can be denied their authority over any one of the indifferent activities and things that, given their other commitments, they hardly consider indifferent. For some, this conclusion quite obviously makes toleration's act a dubious, perhaps a dangerous, solution to the problems posed by objectionable difference. When this political dynamic is combined with the psychological one the Fletcher describes, toleration becomes, for these critics, literally intolerable. As they see it, every defense of the act includes a subtle apology for potentially limitless state authority over human affairs. Toleration's advocates may not *intend* to extend the reach of state power in this way, but surely the tolerance they recommend generates this consequence by accident and in disguise. Add this unwelcome outcome to the impossible psychological demands that Fletcher contends the tolerant must meet as they endeavor to generate this act and real trouble emerges. Since these demands can be escaped as the magistrate expands state authority over indifferent things, casts some among the unbearably harmful, and thus diminishes toleration's domain, those who try to produce its painful act may be disposed to appeal for this kind of relief, which, for obvious reasons, the civil magistrate will be eager to supply.

No one should accuse Locke of wanting to expand the reach of state power over the indifferent activities and things that most individuals and communities hardly consider indifferent; indeed, his aims were just the opposite. He wanted to safeguard local control and individual autonomy. Nevertheless, according to these critics, a political culture that embodies Locke's account of toleration is too often despotic in consequence precisely because it grants wide authority to the civil magistrate over affairs that traditionally fall under the jurisdiction of local associations—families, churches, guilds, and so on.[31] Because toleration is conceived on the divide between the un-

---

30 Ibid., 40.

31 For a forceful statement of these views, see Conyers, *Long Truce*. In a concluding chapter ("High Tolerance") Conyers tries to imagine what an uncorrupted tolerance might look like. In this, his efforts resemble Budziszewski's in *True Tolerance*. Both combine complaint and

bearably harmful and the harmlessly unobjectionable, and because it is the civil magistrate who specifies the character of this divide, presumably in accord with state interests, every defense of the act is in fact a defense of state power over these associations. It includes tacit approval of state intervention whenever their affairs become matters of civil interest. Equally troubling is the fact that toleration's domain will be as contested as political authority is. It too will be subject to the capricious, irrational, and often violent vicissitudes of power. Either way—either as pawn or as participant in power politics—it is not at all clear that toleration can deliver what it promises. Its friends insist that it can bring civil peace as it secures freedom from state intrusion, but its foes have reason to doubt that it can.

Here, as before, Fletcher's aims are descriptive not critical, and yet if his account of unstable tolerance is accepted, then, once again, his philosophical efforts provide cover for these complaints. And notice, once this cover and these complaints are combined with the praise that tolerance receives in societies like ours, resentment comes, it follows in turn. If tolerance amounts to *this*, this semblance of virtue, and if its act generates this threat to our rightful authority over our ordinary associations, and if, as virtue and act, it is commended, practiced, and praised nevertheless, then we should not only oppose its practice and resent its praise, but also resist the conditions—the diversity of life and commitment—that encourage our fellow citizens to commend it.[32]

Fortunately, it is not at all clear that Fletcher's remarks exhaust all there is to say about tolerance or that the inferences its critics might make from those remarks are in fact justified. Consider, first, the psychological dynamic that Fletcher describes. Surely he is right. Quite often it *is* difficult to object and endure at the same time, and many of us will seek to avoid this difficulty by casting about for some other attitude toward objectionable

---

revision. Unfortunately, both justify their complaints and revisions only as they mistake a semblance of virtue for the real thing. As we shall see below, it's a common mistake, often made on Augustine's authority.

32   Lee Yearley would have us distinguish "counterfeit virtue," which involves actions that appear virtuous but in fact are not precisely because they mask an intention to deceive, and "semblances," which generate appearances of virtue but without that intention. My concern is with the latter but I use the phrases interchangeably, largely because as I doubt the distinction can be drawn as neatly as Yearley assumes. Those who act from a semblance of virtue are often convinced that they *are* virtuous and would have us believe that they are. They act as the virtuous do but without due regard for the good that virtuous acts instantiate in themselves. They don't see the mistake that they have made, and thus they present themselves as fully virtuous. Do they intend to deceive? No, but they deceive nonetheless, and we are likely to hold them accountable for this failure to portray themselves truthfully. See Yearley, *Mencius and Aquinas*, 17–23.

activities and things.[33] At the same time, it is not at all clear that this ordinary moral weakness warrants Fletcher's conclusion that tolerance is too unstable to recommend as one possible solution to the problems posed by disagreement and difference. If we assume that tolerance is an ordinary human excellence, and if we place it among the other moral virtues, we soon discover that this psychological dynamic distinguishes virtue in general, not tolerance in particular. And if this is right, then Fletcher's doubts about tolerance are hardly warranted. If this is right, then the inferences from difficulty to complaint and from instability to resentment are hardly justified. Or, put another way, if his doubts about tolerance are warranted because of the psychological dynamics it shares with the other virtues, then we would expect him to express doubts about justice, courage, and the rest, which of course he doesn't. We would also expect the critics of tolerance to extend their complaints and resentments to these other virtues, which of course they don't. Place tolerance among the virtues and we soon discover that its instabilities are hardly unique, just as the moral traps it lays for those weak in virtue are hardly exceptional. At the same time, we will discover that tolerance does have an unusual relation to its semblances. Combine this unusual relation with the psychological dynamics it shares with the virtues in general, and we find that tolerance does indeed generate special opportunities for confusion and thus for resentment.[34]

SEMBLANCES OF VIRTUE

Consider, then, the virtues in general and begin with Aristotle's account in book II of the *Nicomachean Ethics* and with Aquinas's interpretation of that account embedded in his treatment of courage.[35] In general, all of the moral virtues fulfill roughly the same function. All perfect our ability to know, desire, and act for the sake of those ends that are both choiceworthy and difficult to know, desire, and achieve. Were these ends not choiceworthy, we would have no reason to love them or pursue them in action. Were they not difficult to know and love aright, we would not need to be perfected by habit in order to respond to them well and pursue them with right action. Since we do many things, many habits are needed to perfect our agency, and each habit is distinguished from every other by the good it regards and

---

33 Just how often this difficulty arises and thus how frequently this instability emerges will be considered in chapter 2.

34 Do these opportunities for dispute, confusion, and resentment attach to tolerance alone? No, but they are unusual, shared only with those virtues that we tend to confuse with their semblances—pride, docility, self-reliance, piety, humility, and the like.

35 Aristotle, *Nicomachean Ethics*, 1104b5–1105a16. Hereafter *NE*.

the difficulties it addresses. So for example, there is the good that can be achieved in human affairs when we give to others those actions and things that they are rightfully due.[36] At the same time, most of us know what Thomas points out: that it is often quite "difficult to find and establish the rational means" that would give to others what they are in fact due in this or that circumstance.[37] And it is for precisely this reason that we need those intellectual virtues, prudence in particular, to guide our inquiries and perfect our judgments. By the same token, there are, as everyone knows, certain "obstacles to the establishment of this rectitude in human affairs," above all passions that too often confound our ability to judge well about the right and the good and that too often suspend our willingness to follow better judgment to right intention, sound choice, and praiseworthy action. For this reason we need temperance, courage, and the other virtues that perfect our relations to the various objects that elicit our various passions.[38] And finally, most of us find it difficult to desire right relations in each of our many affairs and to do so with the constancy of habit, and it is for this reason that we need a will informed by justice.

Notice what follows once we grant that the moral virtues regard the difficult and the good. The virtuous are those who pursue the good—habitually, promptly, and with a certain pleasure—despite the fact that difficulties of various kinds threaten to interrupt their various pursuits.[39] This absence of instability is, in part, what their perfection in virtue involves, and this constancy of character is what it means to say that they are strong, that they act at the limits of their powers. The courageous, for example, respond well, not simply to ordinary difficulties and commonplace dangers, but also to the gravest threats and most pressing challenges. Confronted with demands of this magnitude, they respond with fear and daring in right order, which in turn enables them to judge well and to act for the sake of the good that they know to be best, the good that justice requires. For them, the greatest obstacles to right action, are, quite literally, transcended by their habitual disposition to respond in each instance with passions of the right kind and intensity. Indeed, we might say that, in their case, the exercise of virtue floats free of its origin in the difficulties and dangers of this world. The ordinary obstacles to right action are, for them, hardly obstacles at all.

By contrast, those of us with little or no virtue will confront real obstacles to the good we hope to achieve and the happiness we hope to have in the difficulties and dangers of this world. When we are told that we must be

36 Here I follow Aquinas. See *ST* I-II.60.2–3; II-II.58.3.

37 *ST* II-II.129.2.

38 *ST* II-II.123.1.

39 Thus, if a person "stands firm against terrifying situations and enjoys it, or at least does not find it painful, he is brave; if he finds it painful he is cowardly" (*NE* 1104b7–8).

courageous, that we should give virtue a try, we are put off by its rigors. More often than not, our meager, unstable virtue collapses under the challenge and we recast our account of the circumstances of choice and thus diminish our need for a virtuous response. We might conclude that the end we had hoped to achieve, the end that demands resort to a courageous act, is in fact a matter of indifference, not desire. Or, if that proves impossible, we might pursue this end, but then insist that the unacceptable threats posed in its pursuit are in fact acceptable. The good threatened is in fact less worthy of our care than we had first thought. Or, we might argue that the means proposed to achieve this end, means that present difficulties and dangers, are far from best. Some other, less arduous course of action would be a better choice. All of these tactics are well known, all are designed to excuse us from acting as the virtuous do, all circumvent virtue's demands by deception, and all produce moral postures that are subject to unmasking.[40]

If this account is right, then it appears that instability afflicts every virtue that falls short of perfection, not simply tolerance, and this shared affliction appears to be an ordinary consequence of the difficulties that every virtue regards. Given this ordinary feature of the virtues in general, the tendency of tolerance to dissolve into some other moral posture hardly justifies Fletcher's doubts about the virtue as a source of civil peace. Courage, justice, and the rest display similar tendencies, and yet no one appeals to this fact in order to suggest that we can (or should) proceed without them. Rather, most of us acknowledge the difficulty of thinking, feeling, and acting as the virtuous do in precisely those circumstances of extremity that most urgently require virtue's act. We admit that we fall short of moral perfection most of the time and that we squirm out of virtue's demands more often than we care to admit. Even so, in a cool hour we recognize the virtues for what they are, for the goods they instantiate in themselves and for the benefits they secure when their acts succeed. In fits of justice and charity, we take note of those who lay hold of these goods and obtain these benefits, and we grant them the honors they deserve.

But of course, a cool hour slips away, fits pass, difficulties mount, and most of us return to dodging the demands of this or that virtue and, at times, resenting the fact that we fall short of its measure. *This* species of resentment is an ordinary consequence of the difficulties that *every* virtue regards, and it does not deny the perfection it assumes. Rather, it bears witness to the au-

---

40   The religious establishment in the American South employed these tactics and postures during the heyday of the civil rights movement, only to be exposed as cowardice in Martin Luther King, Jr.'s forceful replies. King's criticisms were effective precisely because most of us have little difficulty imaging the decay of virtue or seeing the difference between courage and its semblances once they have been carefully described and distinguished. See his April 16, 1963, "Letter from Birmingham Jail," published in a revised form in *Why We Can't Wait*.

thority of that perfection, to the demands it makes and our struggle to measure up. It is not the resentment that we find directed toward tolerance itself, where the virtue is despised, not as arduous excellence, but as vice in disguise. *Both* kinds of resentment follow from the difficulty and instability of virtue in general, but the instability that afflicts tolerance generates actions that encourage us to confuse the virtue and its semblances, the real thing and its opposing vices dressed in virtue's garb. It's this unusual consequence of virtue's ordinary instability that distinguishes tolerance from most other virtues, and it is precisely this confusion that causes a good portion of the resentment that attaches to the virtue itself. No doubt, semblances of virtue are often mistaken for the real coin, but as far as I can tell this common confusion rarely follows from the difficulties and instabilities that afflict the virtues in general, and once it does emerge by other means with respect to other virtues it does not, as far as I can tell, diminish our regard for them. Consider again courage. As Aristotle points out, it has a number of semblances that we often mistake for true perfection, and yet rarely do these mistakes come packaged with contempt for the virtue itself.[41] In fact, if anything, just the opposite is true. In our confusion we extend the admiration we have for courage to its semblances. But not so with tolerance, where confusion of true and apparent virtue typically generates suspicion of the virtue itself and resentment of the praise it so often receives. Moreover, these extraordinary inferences from an ordinary confusion seem easy to make, easy to imitate. And, as I have said, some of our best moral philosophers and theologians have made them and, on their authority, others have been encouraged to follow suit.

The argument goes like this. As a virtue, tolerance regards those activities and things that fall between two extremes, between the unbearably harmful and the harmlessly unobjectionable. The tolerant know which activities and things fall within this domain and they respond to each as each deserves, quite often with an act of toleration, of patient endurance. Like all virtuous persons, they act with the constancy of habit, with ease and pleasure, with one eye on the good they hope to achieve and another on the good they find in the act of virtue itself. But of course, most of us have little virtue and what little we have falls short of perfection. We act tolerantly in response to objectionable differences of modest consequence but struggle with those that matter. When we succeed, it's only as we restrain ourselves—only as we choke down our outrage and stifle our desire to oppose the differences we despise—and most of us find this act of self-restraint too difficult to produce much of the time. How can one despise and endure patiently at the same time anyway? So, more often than not, our imperfect tolerance, like our deficient courage, collapses into moral postures that are incapable of

41 See Aristotle's discussion at *NE* 1116a17–1117a29.

producing right action.[42] Confronted by the important difficulties that the tolerant address well—by judgments that are difficult to make and differences that are painful to endure—those of us with little virtue abandon our objection to what we at first, and quite rightly, found odious and instead generate some other attitude, perhaps indifference, perhaps acceptance. And, as we have seen, the attitude that emerges produces a semblance of virtue's act. In most instances, the external actions of the indifferent and the accepting will be difficult to distinguish from those of the tolerant. They will live and let live, but not from tolerant habits and motives. They dodge the virtue but not its outward appearance, not its external act.[43]

What follows is the now common confusion of tolerance with a couple of its semblances, of the real thing with some of its opposing vices dressed in virtue's clothing. Other virtues have semblances that enable the morally mediocre to pose among the virtuous from time to time, but few deteriorate under the demands of virtue's difficulty into a moral posture that can produce a semblance of virtue's external act. Courage, again, has semblances such as fearlessness that give the appearance of virtue in habit and act, and yet on the whole imperfect courage tends to collapse into fearful moral postures that are incapable of producing actions that resemble those caused by genuine courage.[44] By contrast, imperfect tolerance tends to collapse under the difficulties it must address into moral postures that enable those without the virtue to act as the tolerant do, at least in external appearance. As perfect tolerance is rare and painful differences many, most assume that tolerance is nothing but these postures, nothing but blithe indifference that quickly melts into easy acceptance. Indeed, most of its critics are quick to assume that tolerance simply *is* this moral collapse. And, fearing moral collapse, some will not only decry tolerance but also flee to the *other* boundary of its domain. Looking for a solution to the problems of association that disagreement and difference invariably generate, unable to combine objection and endurance as the virtuous do, and appalled by the smooth indifference and contemptible acceptance that is so often mistaken for tolerance, they reassign the objectionable and yet potentially tolerable to the unbearably harmful and possibly dangerous. They become reactionary advocates of law and order, of coercion and constraint.

42   It might be the vice we call intolerance, the habit that tends toward an unjust response to the differences that can divide us. This vice has various actions: false indifference, undue acceptance, misplaced objection, and so on. Or it might be the absence of real virtue: some combination of moral weakness and self-deception.

43   Note, indifference and acceptance are not always vicious responses to difference. In some circumstances they are quite obviously virtuous. Here they are vicious precisely because they discount the truly objectionable character of the difference in question.

44   See Aristotle, *NE* 1116b25–1117a4.

Such is our lot, or so many believe. Moral collapse or heavy-handed paternalism; these are the options that tolerance offers those of us who are morally mediocre and who cannot, as a result, resist the instability that comes packaged with virtue's difficulty. And yet many are convinced that these options are essential to tolerance itself, not consequences of ordinary instability and commonplace moral weakness. They are, after all, its common yield. Tolerance must then be a vice, just as the praise it receives nevertheless must be resented and its friends resisted.

The trouble with this conclusion should now be apparent. Resentment that rests on confusion, on the inability to distinguish true tolerance from its semblances, is hardly justified. What's needed, then, is a better account of the virtue, one that helps us escape this confusion and avoid the potentially unhappy political consequences of its instability. Fletcher is surely right, this instability does exist; the evidence is overwhelming. But the point is that this fact does nothing to discredit tolerance, especially if we locate it among the virtues and assume the following. First, every account of tolerance needs to include a discussion of its limits, of the indifferent and the acceptable on the one hand, and of the intolerable and potentially coercible, on the other. And note, this discussion scarcely amounts to criticism. It is, rather, a portion of the work that must be done in order to specify the domain of virtue's act. Second, because every account of tolerance comes loaded with concrete judgments about the tolerable and the intolerable, every account is open to contest and dispute, not about tolerance itself, but about its substance, scope, and limits. This is inevitable. And third, because tolerance is a virtue, the best way to resolve these disputes is to cultivate and acquire the habit of acting tolerantly.[45] Why? Because, as I will argue in chapter 3, we say that a person is tolerant when she exhibits endurance, acceptance, indifference, and constraint with respect to the right actions and things, in the right circumstances, and to the right degree. Right judgment about concrete matters such as these is the very soul of this, and every other, moral virtue. But this means that tolerance itself cannot be justly resented simply because it includes these judgments, or because they are difficult to make, or because the conflicts and disagreements that tolerance is expected

---

45 Tolerance is an acquired moral virtue. It is acquired, as other moral virtues are, by imitation and habituation—by being initiated into certain activities or social practices, by coming to regard their ends as worthy of pursuit, by recognizing certain persons as exemplary practitioners, by imitating their words and deeds, by reproducing their intentions, judgments, and choices, eventually by habit, and by innovation on this inheritance. Most of these activities have institutional supports (legal codes, educational curricula, religious rites, civic rituals, and so on) and reproduce various relations of power. The same can be said of intolerance the vice. It can be acquired by custom, and certain institutional arrangements and regimes of power can help cultivate its malicious will with respect to difference and distorted judgments about the tolerable and the intolerable. For Thomas's discussion, see *ST* I-II.51.2–3; 63.2; 78.2–3.

to address are frequently reproduced in our debates and contests over its substance, scope, and limits.

There will be winners and losers here, but the losers should lament their loss and the regime of tolerance that emerges, not that the matter was decided by debate and certainly not the virtue in dispute, not the goodness of its act.[46] Nor should tolerance be resented simply because those with little virtue tend to avoid its difficult judgments and painful endurance by casting the merely objectionable and potentially tolerable among the intolerably harmful or the harmlessly indifferent. What *can* be lamented is that societies like ours encourage this kind of vice, this corruption of tolerance. We tend to be relatively skittish about explicit moral contest and we tend to diffuse its sources by reducing matters that provoke disagreement to those that do not. There is nothing wrong with this strategy, not per se, but it does create the impression that moral judgments can be avoided (even when they can't be) and it does encourage us to resort to this strategy whenever judgment becomes difficult and disagreement likely. At times we should make this resort, at times we shouldn't. The tolerant will know how to distinguish these times, and yet because most of us fall short of perfect virtue, those of us who live in societies like ours will be tempted to make this resort whenever difficulties and disagreements arise.

Such is the way we live now. At the same time, we should keep in mind that this dynamic reaches beyond tolerance to justice, its home and principle, and while we might, in some instances, lament the dynamic, few of us resent *this* virtue. Those of us with ordinary measures of justice built into our souls surely dodge its difficulties more often than we should. We reduce judgments about the just and the unjust to calculations of utility. We sidestep rights and downplay wrongs, and yet few regard justice with contempt simply because of its instability among the morally imperfect. Why then regard tolerance differently? If lament we must, then we should consider how few of us respond as the tolerant do to the objectionable differences that give us the most difficulty, that cause us the most pain when endured. At the same time, we can't take this lament to a fever pitch without resenting the virtue and discounting its excellence. What we can decry is philosophers who encourage complaints and critics who provoke resentment simply because they overlook how tolerance stands among the other moral virtues and how the virtues in general stand among various difficulties.

---

46 The variety of tolerance that we find in democratic societies is specifically geared to enduring losses in public debate and affairs. The tolerant bear these losses well and endure the company of the victors, hoping that, when their day comes, they will receive the same tolerance in return. See Bowlin, "Democracy, Tolerance, Aquinas."

VIRTUE AND RESTRAINT

The collapse of virtue into a semblance is one consequence of the difficulties and instabilities that confound the moral virtues, tolerance among the rest, but there are others. Bernard Williams, for example, agrees that tolerant states of mind and affection are difficult to maintain. Endurance is not easily combined with dislike, to say nothing of hatred or repugnance, and he admits as much. At the same time, he recognizes that in certain circumstances dislike can be tempered, its impulse to action restrained.[47] Fear of one's own intolerance, its postures and consequences, can encourage self-control. So can hatred of the cruelty that intolerance can inflict on others. In either case, acts of toleration can result, but not from a tolerant state of mind, not from a tolerant collection of loves and desires. An impulse to act intolerantly is, after all, being restrained. In this way, Williams can acknowledge the self-consuming instabilities of tolerance the virtue, while endorsing *acts* of toleration produced by other than virtuous means. And of course, to say that acts of toleration are largely products of self-restraint is equivalent to saying that tolerance the virtue is irrelevant. As Aquinas reminds us, the virtuous exhibit what the self-restraining do not—a unity of internal state and external action. By habit they acquire both "an aptness to a good act" and "the right use of that aptness." The just, for instance, are not only capable of giving to others the good they are due by right, but they are inclined to do so with a prompt will. They desire what is right with a settled habit, and their actions accord with their desires. Thus Aquinas can say that, in general, "a virtue is that which makes its possessor good" insofar as it generates the right kinds of rational loves and desires, and in turn these loves and desires make "his work good likewise."[48]

Some will be perfectly content with this concession to imperfection, this reduction of virtue to self-restraint. They will consider it a sign of our moral maturity, of our recognition that acts of toleration, of patient endurance, are not impossible even as the virtue might be. Relations between persons divided by difference can be set right, they will say, but not on appeal to virtue. In fact, some will contend that this is how things ought to stand. Judith Shklar, whose views Williams borrows and adapts, insists that a society like ours cannot endorse tolerance the virtue without undermining the conditions that generate toleration's act. Divided by disagreements about the best kind of life and threatened with factional violence, liberal societies proceed without "a *summum bonum* toward which all political agents should

---

47 Williams, "Toleration."

48 *ST* I-II.56.3, cf. *NE* 1106a16–17.

strive."[49] They do not have any "particular positive doctrines about how people are to conduct their lives or what personal choices they are to make."[50] They shun grand schemes of moral and spiritual perfection and instead have but one mundane aim: "to secure the political conditions that are necessary for the exercise of personal freedom."[51] So too the citizens of liberal societies tend to be more appalled by the cruelties and terrors of political life than impressed by the positive liberties that politics at its best is designed to secure. Though divided in love, they are united in fear of a *summum malum*, physical cruelty, and it is this combination of common love in absence and shared fear in abundance that generates both their suspicion of moral perfection and their high regard for acts of toleration.[52]

Why suspicion? Because each moral virtue regards some good, some end that its actions seek, and because different specifications of that good will generate competing, often incompatible, examples of that virtue, of candidates for moral perfection. Notice the fallout. A society that disagrees about the goods that ought to be known, loved, and pursued in the best kind of life and that proceeds with its affairs nevertheless will not assume substantial agreement about the determinate character of specific virtues, or rather it ought not. So too it must resist every "tendency to offer ethical instruction," every desire to cultivate a collection of virtues that might enable its citizens to choose and live well.[53] Failing this, violence will erupt as competing accounts of the ends worth pursing and the virtues worth cultivating generate competing regimes of ethical instruction. It's this violence and this cruel, coercive tutelage that the citizens of liberal societies fear most and "would avoid if only [they] could." Happily, tolerance reduced to self-restraint provides the means.[54] Citizens are offered the freedom they need to pursue their own loves and craft their own lives. In return for this measure of autonomy they must endure loves and lives quite different from their own. On this rendering, tolerance is not a virtue, not a "mode of human perfection," not a portion of the happiness that all human beings desire according to their kind. It can't be. Liberal societies have no shared account of such things and much fear of the cruelties and terrors that so often accompany didactic, perfectionist politics. As such, they cannot assume a determinate conception of tolerance or cultivate the virtue among citizens without undermining the conditions of their common life. Acts of toleration produced by self-restraint will have to suffice. All we can say in their

49   Shklar, "Liberalism of Fear," 27.
50   Ibid., 21.
51   Ibid., 21.
52   Shklar, *Ordinary Vices*, 1–44.
53   Shklar, "Liberalism of Fear," 33.
54   Ibid., 27.

defense "is that if we want to promote political freedom, then this is appropriate behavior."[55]

So goes Shklar's antiperfectionist account of liberal toleration and autonomy.[56] The question, of course, is whether it makes sense, and it's not clear that it does. There is no reason to deny that individual autonomy is a substantive human good or that the inhabitants of liberal societies agree that it is.[57] In fact their agreement here, about this, is one of the things that distinguishes their political life. Since habits that regard actions are specified, in part, by the good ends their acts are designed to achieve, there is no reason to doubt that certain habits are specified by the goodness of autonomy. Nor is there reason to doubt that autonomy's intrinsic goodness extends to these habits. If, by liberal lights, an autonomous life is best, then we should not be surprised when liberals count autonomy's habits among the virtues, tolerance among others. Nor should we be surprised to discover that liberal societies have an interest in cultivating these virtues. Families, schools, community organizations, playing fields, and the like—these will be the seminaries of liberal virtue.

Williams amends Shklar's account of tolerance in roughly this way. At the same time, he concedes that her efforts capture most of the facts on the ground.[58] Those with high regard for individual autonomy might consider tolerance a virtue, but in practice acts of toleration are largely a product of fear and self-restraint. Williams offers two reasons for this concession. First, as a virtue, tolerance simply demands too much. Its exercise is just too difficult. One must retain one's conviction that certain actions and things are objectionable while at the same time transcending one's desire to put a stop to those actions and things, presumably out of love for individual autonomy. And, if that were not difficult enough, one must see as much merit in the intrinsic goodness of transcending this desire and acting tolerantly as one does in the civil peace that tolerance is designed to secure.[59] Williams suspects that most of us will fail to meet these demands. Most of us will manage to restrain ourselves, produce acts of toleration, and secure the benefits of civil peace only as we are moved, not by virtuous states of mind, but by the commonplace motives Shklar recounts: fear of violence, hatred of cruelty, and moral compromise for the sake of survival.[60]

---

55 Ibid., 34.

56 An alternative account of liberal tolerance will be considered in chapter 5.

57 What this agreement amounts to and whether "autonomy" best describes its substance are matters of dispute and will be considered in chapter 2.

58 Williams, "Toleration," 25.

59 Ibid., 26.

60 Of course, some of us will be incapable of producing acts of either kind with any consistency. When confronted with the most divisive difference, we tend to act neither as the

For others, the difficulty of acting tolerantly out of virtuous motives is irrelevant, if only because they doubt that tolerance is a virtue in the first place. Their reasons are *not* Shklar's. They do not find talk of virtue incompatible with love for individual autonomy. Rather, their complaint cuts the other way. While they inhabit liberal societies, they do not regard individual autonomy as liberals do, as an intrinsic good, as an indispensable aspect of human flourishing. This in turn leads them to doubt that the habits geared to autonomy stand among the virtues, tolerance among others. And, as they find no intrinsic goodness in tolerant attitudes and deeds, they will need some other reason to restrain themselves and act as the liberal and tolerant do. Williams thinks that "appeals to the misery and cruelty and the manifest stupidity involved in intolerance" may do the trick, as might attention to self-interest and survival.[61]

Such are the ordinary realities of the way we live now. Persons and opinions are no longer confined by national or regional boundaries. Friends and foes of individual autonomy and its virtues find themselves living together, rubbing elbows and butting heads. In this context, civil peace requires mutual toleration, and if Williams is right, humdrum motives do most of the work. Friends of liberal autonomy may find tolerant states of mind and affection impossibly difficult to maintain. Its foes might refuse to locate tolerance among the moral virtues. And yet both can act with patient endurance in response to the differences they despise, but only as they are compelled by their hatreds and fears to restrain themselves in spite of themselves.

All of these matters deserve further scrutiny, above all the thought that the world can be neatly divided into those who consider autonomy good and tolerance among the virtues and those who do not. We also need to consider the assumption, shared by both friends and foes of tolerance, that it is a moral innovation of the modern period and that the liberal variety exhausts what it might be. This will be the work of subsequent chapters. For now it is enough to see that, despite their differences, the views shared by Williams and Shklar create multiple opportunities for resentment. Both think that toleration requires deliberate self-mastery. Both think its act is ordered to the ends of individual autonomy. And both think that toleration's self-restraint can be found only in societies that count individual autonomy among the best things and threats to it among the worst, physical cruelty above all. For Shklar this means that toleration abides in liberal societies alone and that only liberals have sufficient reason to respond to objectionable differences with acts of patient endurance. For Williams it means that

---

virtuous do, nor with self-restraint. If we hope to keep the peace, we may have to avoid the objectionable person or thing altogether. For treatments of this strategy, its timing and rationality, see Elster, *Ulysses and the Sirens*, 36–111 and Hirschman, *Exit, Voice, and Loyalty*, 21–54.

61   Williams, "Toleration," 25.

the illiberal inhabitants of liberal societies will endure what they despise only as they are compelled or encouraged by some other collection of loves and fears.

Suppose we bracket their differences, at least for now, and consider the opportunities for resentment provided by the views they share. Suppose their efforts confirm one's own assumptions and experience: tolerance is nothing but self-restraint, either *in se* or in fact. And suppose one is certain that a combination of civil peace and autonomy cannot be had without regular resort to acts of toleration. Well, in that event, one will have to assume an inherently resentful moral posture. Why? Because one will have to do what one would rather not, and because one cannot act against desire without resenting the restraint that generates the act.

Consider continence. On Aquinas's rendering, *continentia* is a variety of self-restraint. It is also an imperfect antecedent of temperance, the virtue that regards our relations to objects and pleasures of taste and touch. By imperfect antecedent I mean a disposition to produce right external actions for less than virtuous reasons, actions that, when repeated, might contribute to the formation of a virtuous habit. The point here is that continence is not virtue, and it bears the marks of this deficit. The continent have an inordinate appetite for one or more of these objects and pleasures, inordinate because they know that injustice will be done, that other goods will be lost, if they allow love to generate desire and if desire is followed and fulfilled. So, they restrain themselves deliberately, willfully.[62] They secure or protect these other goods, but not with the ease and pleasure that accompanies the pursuit of an end that they know to be best and love with an undivided heart. Rather, they act regretfully, perhaps with sorrow, with their eyes on incompatible goods, each of which they desire in this instance. They know full well that they cannot have them both and that they must forsake one for the other. And of course, in these circumstances, resentment comes easily. Why? Because the continent cannot have all that they desire, because they suffer as a result, and because they assume, as most without virtue do, that they cannot diminish their suffering by reforming their desires. In their minds, it is the world that conspires against them, or rather, its contingent arrangement of things that precipitates their incompatible loves. In this instance, the world is so arranged that they cannot have the good that brings pleasure without forsaking the good they prefer. As they can imagine a different arrangement of things, one more compatible with their passions and desires, they cannot help but despise the way things are now and yearn for an arrangement that did not require self-control and suffering. This sour combination of hatred and yearning, this is resentment.

62 *ST* I-II.58.3.2; II-II.143.ad 1.

Tolerance reduced to self-restraint works in much the same way. Through acts of self-control the tolerantly self-restraining endure what they despise and what they would rather intervene against. They would prefer to take action, but they resist this urge for the sake of some other good, one that intervention would forsake. Like the continent, the tolerantly self-restraining act with sorrow over the loss of a good forsaken, in this instance, the good of taking action against the objectionable action or thing and rearranging the world in the image of their desire. And, like the continent, they suffer this loss for the sake of something else, although the passions involved have different vectors. The continent suffer the absence of a good that they love but refuse to pursue. By contrast, those who act tolerantly through self-restraint suffer the presence of something objectionable, something that they despise and would oppose but cannot without the loss of some other good that they prefer. Regardless of the cause, suffering entails a kind of passivity, and we are tempted to say that those who endure difference through self-restraint act unwillingly, that they are compelled by the circumstances they find themselves in. But this isn't quite right. They want peaceful relations in the society they share with those they endure. This is the good that they love, the end that they intend. At the same time, they find themselves in circumstances that compel resort to means that, all things being equal, they would not otherwise choose. All things being equal, they would not restrain themselves and endure what they despise. If circumstances were different, they would shun this resort. Still, the point is that things are not equal, not in this circumstance. So they choose to endure objectionable activities and things, and surely their choice is deliberate, willful, even if it would not be made "outside of the actual circumstances of the case."[63]

The caveat matters. It affects how the tolerantly self-restraining regard their plight and how we assess their sacrifice. They know that their self-restraint is voluntary and their losses deliberately sacrificial, and yet at the same time they are convinced that their desires cannot be altered and that they are, as a result, victims of circumstance, not hostages of their own character. This is, as I have said, an ordinary attitude of those without virtue, but it is also a consequence of the confidence that their self-restraint assumes. Restraint would be unnecessary if they were not convinced that their objections were sound and, all things being equal, their interventions justified. Of course, in this instance all things are not equal and self-restraint is necessary, but it would be unthinkable without prior confidence in the objection made against the hateful thing and in the justification offered in defense of intervention. Resentment and self-pity result from this collection

---

63   The phrase is Aquinas's and comes from his discussion of mixed minds, divided loves, and puzzling voluntariness (*ST* I-II.6.6).

of attitudes, judgments, and passions. As the tolerantly self-restraining can imagine a world in which the objectionable activity or thing did not exist, or, failing that, one in which objection could be relieved by active opposition, they yearn for a different world. At the same time, they despise the conditions of this one, where restraint is necessary and invariably comes with suffering and sorrow. They know that acting with tolerant self-restraint gets them the social peace they want in the circumstances they find themselves in, but for them, the act is just a tool for achieving this end, and they would prefer some other means, or, failing that, some other world, one that makes resort to these means unnecessary.

What matters here is the assumption that tolerance is nothing but self-restraint. It is not a virtue, not a human perfection, not a habitual source of desires and actions that are just and good in themselves quite apart from the social peace that they may or may not achieve. If this is true, then tolerance is indeed an inherently resentful response to disagreement and difference. But if it isn't, if tolerance cannot be reduced to self-restraint without abandoning certain moral ideals or discounting our capacity achieve them, then we cannot say that tolerance comes loaded with resentment everywhere and always or that resentment is a justified response to the sacrifices it requires. In the next two chapters, I will argue that tolerance is indeed a virtue, that we cannot easily ignore or set aside its ideals. For now, however, it is enough to see that this is how things stand with the other moral virtues. When philosophical description reduces a virtue to its imperfect antecedent, the resentment that distinguishes the imperfection becomes virtue's norm. It becomes as justified as virtue is. When this reduction is refused, this same resentment loses its warrant. It becomes a mark of imperfection, not of virtue.

Consider again courage. All things considered, the conditions that call for its act are unwelcome. Difficulties and dangers are hardly objects of levelheaded desire, even by the courageous. The subjunctive state of their wills, their velleity in Aquinas's useful idiom, is negative toward those very conditions (*ST* I-II.13.5). They wish they could avoid them even as they know they cannot. By contrast, it is the rash, Aristotle tells us, not the courageous, who yearn for wars and storms at sea in the hope they might exhibit their prowess.[64] But they are impetuous boasters and foolhardy pretenders. Their courage is but a semblance of the real thing, and it is their yearning that betrays them. More often than not, they cower and flee when the dangers they desire suddenly appear. "Brave people, on the contrary, are eager when

---

64 The courageous might seek out difficulties and dangers of a lesser sort. Some projects are worth doing precisely because they pose the right kind of challenges. Some activities are desirable precisely because they include dangers and terrors that attract because they can be escaped. Burke locates our taste for the sublime in this latter desire. See Burke, *Philosophical Enquiry*, I.6–7, 18. Thanks to Jeff Stout for this qualification.

in action, but keep quiet until then."[65] They neither yearn for difficulties and dangers nor resent them when they arrive. They know that acting well and doing well among the threats and struggles of this life require the virtues, courage among others. They know that courage generates the right kind and measure of fear and confidence, not through the difficult restraint of excess but through the ease of habit. And they know that acting courageously is painful precisely because it involves responding well in the midst of the gravest dangers and standing firm among the most pressing difficulties.[66]

At the same time, "the end that bravery aims at seems to be pleasant, though obscured by its surroundings."[67] When the courageous succeed, when their acts achieve their ends, delight follows. When the battle is won and right relations are restored, when the ship survives despite the storm, the courageous take delight. This much is obvious, but it's not all that Aristotle has in mind. The remark also regards the activity itself, not just the consequences of success. For the courageous, responding well to difficulties and dangers is fine, a worthy pursuit regardless of its success or failure in achieving other ends. It is good in itself and thus an independent source of delight. As Aquinas puts it, "the brave man intends as his proximate end to reproduce in action a likeness of this habit" and he is afforded delight as he simultaneously acts courageously and achieves that end.[68] This delight may well be "obscured by its surroundings," by the hard work that must be done and the pains that must be suffered, but the courageous bear this unwelcome suffering well and consider this act fine. It is good in itself, and the courageous act as they do, at least in part, because they know that it is.

By these lights, the virtuous are distinguished from the merely self-restraining by their ability to see the good in acts of courage themselves and by their willingness to regard this good as a proximate end of their actions. They are also distinguished by the habitual ease with which they act, and these are related matters. If I know and love the good that comes with an act of courage, then the end that act is ordered to achieve does not exhaust my reasons for acting. The good in the act itself provides another and it is a reason that comes with its own guarantees. The external end may or may not be achieved by my act of courage, but the good that is the activity itself is had and enjoyed whenever I act. With this additional motive, with its guaranteed benefits and satisfactions, it's no wonder the courageous act with ease. By contrast, the self-restraining can regard those acts only as a means to some other end. Since these means often include pain and suffering, and since they are thought to instantiate no goodness in themselves,

---

65   *NE* 1116a9.
66   *ST* II-II.123.4–6.
67   *NE* 1117b3.
68   *ST* II-II.123.7–8.

they are best avoided, presumably by pursuing an end that does not require resort to them. Combine this presumption against these particular means with the threat of failure that haunts nearly every imaginable progression from chosen means to external ends and the hesitations that confound the merely self-restraining come into view. And, as we have seen, resentment will accompany their hesitations. If one cannot see the intrinsic goodness in acting courageously, and if seeing this goodness is a portion of what it means to have courage, then the hard work of restraining one's fears and forcing oneself to act as the courageous do will surely generate resentment. At the same time, if courage is no mere tool, if it is a real virtue, then this resentment will be unjustified. It will be a sign of virtue in absence, not of the unavoidably resentful character of courage.

Tolerance, I want to suggest, works in same way. Like courage, it comes with our humanity, with the life we lead according to our kind. Like the courageous, the truly tolerant act with negative velleity toward the circumstances they find themselves in, toward the goods they must sacrifice and the losses they must suffer as they endure the objectionable differences of another. And like the courageous (but unlike the tolerantly self-restraining), their negative velleity is not a source of resentment. They know that differences in life, judgment, and love create regular opportunities to make use of their virtue, and they recognize the intrinsic goodness of its act. When they offer acts of patient endurance that are right and due, they not only intend to secure the ends external to their act—social peace in the society they share with the tolerated and autonomy across their differences—but they also hope to reproduce their virtue's goodness, to make it actual.

The self-restraining, by contrast, have an imperfect grasp of this goodness and manage to act as the tolerant do only as they have assessed the tactical merits of doing what they would rather not. When they conclude that they must restrain their desire to intervene, compel themselves to endure what they dislike, and retain the company of the objectionable, they do so, not with ease and delight, but with regret and resentment over the losses they must bear, the moral compromises they must make, and the circumstances they confront. And of course, it is one thing to restrain oneself and act as the virtuous do, quite another to be justified in acting with resentment. As with courage, so long as tolerance is counted among the virtues, this justification will be denied the merely self-restraining even as this resentment will be difficult to avoid.

My point should now be plain. By reducing tolerance to self-restraint, at least in practice, Williams and Shklar encourage the assumptions and resentments that the self-restraining are already likely to have. As most of us can be counted in their company, most of us will be encouraged to assume what many already suspect: that tolerance necessarily involves violent self-policing, never the ease and delight of virtue. With this assumption confirmed, most of us will come to resent tolerance, to despise its sometimes painful act and loath the conditions that require its labors. And we will now have these attitudes confirmed by philosophy's authority. One might reply that Williams at least escapes this charge precisely because he reduces tolerance to self-restraint in practice alone. It remains a virtue in concept and a real option in fact, even if that option is, as he insists, rarely exercised. Fair enough, but for Williams, the option applies to liberals alone, to those who count liberal versions of autonomy among the best things. *They* can count tolerance among the virtues and by Williams's lights even the self-restraining among them will be encouraged to do so by their love for liberal autonomy. All others—and this includes not only the illiberal inhabitants of liberal societies, but most human beings in most times and places—will find it impossible to regard tolerance as a virtue precisely because they do not think that autonomy is good, or so he concludes.

Imagine Williams is right and then imagine what the illiberal inhabitants of liberal societies will be told on his authority. "We do not expect you to act virtuously from tolerant states of mind and affection. Indeed, we doubt that you can. At the same time we expect you to act as the tolerant do, to find some other motive to restrain your impulse to intervene against the objectionable. This you must do because you happen to reside in a society that considers this (for you) impossible virtue one of the principal solutions to the problems of peaceful coexistence posed by disagreement and difference. While you are incapable of imagining or exhibiting an important moral excellence, you must nevertheless do what you can to muster its resentful substitute."

Here, resentments are compounded by resentments. Suppose you believe, as most do, that Williams is right: tolerance is a contingent idiosyncrasy of liberal societies, a consequence of their high regard for a certain kind of individual autonomy. As I mentioned above, the standard histories of toleration would give you reason to believe that it is. In addition, suppose by upbringing or recent conviction you doubt that this kind of autonomy is one of the best things. And finally, suppose that you nevertheless live in a liberal democracy. In that event, you will not only be encouraged to make contemptible moral compromises and to take on a resentful, self-restraining moral posture, and you will not only be told that you are incapable of exhibiting one of the principal virtues of the society in which your reside, but it is likely that your complaints with that society will be mediated through your resentments and that your resentments will be exaggerated by your complaints. If tolerance is, as Williams contends, simply liberalism in action, then your double resentment for tolerance will be an expression of your discontent with liberal society. So too, your discontent with liberal society will confirm and amplify your resentment. It is a toxic mix, encouraged and justified by the historical tale that has helped shape liberalism's self-image and by a philosophical account of tolerance that expresses that image and confirms that tale.[69]

In our day, discontent with liberal, democratic varieties of tolerance and autonomy comes from many quarters. Quite often it comes from communities within those political societies—immigrant communities with non-Western origins, religious communities with traditional commitments and lives. These communities hope to reproduce themselves—their traditions, norms, and virtues—and quite naturally they feel threatened when commitment to the liberal variety of individual autonomy and its attendant virtues diminishes the authority they need to fulfill their hopes. In many instances these are sensible threats to feel and reasonable complaints to have. How they are resolved—creeping assimilation, sectarian withdrawal, compelled restraint, or violent resistance—is one of the principal and ongoing dramas of contemporary liberal democracies. As my task is neither prophesy nor prescription, I will not predict how these dramas will play themselves out in individual cases or suggest how they should. Rather, my aim is to clarify the languages and practices of tolerance so that they might be put to good use in these dramas, and, as we have seen, removing tolerance from the list of virtues that all human beings might exercise and yoking its act to the pursuit of one good alone, liberal autonomy, prevents this good use. It distorts debate and fuels resentment. What's needed, then, is a better account of tolerance as concept, act, and habitual perfection, one that shows how it is in some way natural to us, how its act can be regarded as right and due in nearly every time and place and in all kinds of social and political relationships, and how it brings some measure of tranquility and autonomy wherever it is found.

As I said, these tasks will be pursued in the chapters that follow. My hope is that my efforts will make it harder to resent tolerance *in se*, which in turn should make it difficult to use suspicion of tolerance and confusion about its act as a medium of wholesale discontent with liberal democracy. If this effort succeeds, specific judgments about the tolerable and the intolerable will remain divisive, but it will be obvious that those judgments should be the objects of discontent and dispute, not tolerance itself. More positively, once tolerance is recast in this way there should be no doubt that it can function as one source of social peace in societies divided by disagreement and difference. On its own, the insistence that tolerance is in some way

69 Williams and Shklar are not the only philosophers who express this image and confirm this tale. Joseph Raz is another. He contends that "toleration is a distinctive moral virtue only if it curbs desires, inclinations, and convictions which are thought by the tolerant person to be in themselves desirable. Typically, a person is tolerant if and only if he suppresses a desire to cause harm or hurt which he thinks the other deserves. The clearest case of toleration . . . is where a person restrains his indignation at the sight of injustice or some other moral evil." Raz, "Autonomy, Toleration, and the Harm Principle," 162.

natural to us, that it emerges from our human form of life, does nothing to resolve these disputes or secure this peace, but it should prevent us from supposing that the virtue and its act are irrelevant to these aims or harmful to these societies.

RESENTING TOLERANCE, IMAGING FORBEARANCE

The account of tolerance and resentment that I have considered thus far turns on the distinction between a virtue, its semblances, and its imperfect antecedents. I have assumed that tolerance is a virtue, even as many do not. Many suspect that it is something else—either a vice dressed in virtue's clothing, or self-restraint that replaces an impossible virtue. Resentment follows. It's easy to despise a vice that passes as a virtue, and far easier once you are confident that the virtue in question is in fact an imposter. So too, it's easy to resent the demand for virtue's act when its source has been reduced to painful self-restraint. When some of the most influential treatments of tolerance authorize these conclusions and encourage these resentments, it's easy to conclude that the virtue is nothing but these frauds.

All of this should sound familiar to those acquainted with any account of the moral life that accents the virtues, where the hard work of distinguishing the just, courageous, and wise from those who merely seem so is one of the principal tasks of responsible social criticism. When Aristotle discusses courage, he also considers those dispositions and actions that resemble true virtue but fall short in various ways.[70] When Cicero considers Marcus Cato and Gaius Laelius, he insists that while "they bore a certain semblance and likeness to wise men" and were counted as such by those ordinary people who "enjoy and praise things that do not deserve praise," in fact their virtue fell short of real perfection.[71] The pattern is ancient and ordinary, and it is repeated in those traditions of social criticism that have emerged in the Christian churches, especially those that bear the marks of Augustine's effort to specify Christian difference across the divide between virtue and semblance. It was Augustine who insisted that he could see through Roman virtue to vice lurking below and who pursued his criticism in order to encourage both contempt for (or at least ambivalence about) pagan virtues and admiration for Christian alternatives.[72] With that Augustinian inheritance in mind, consider how Glenn Tinder's criticism of tolerance repro-

---

70   *NE* 1116a17–1117a29.

71   *Off.* III.13–16.

72   Sometimes it's contempt: when he counts pagan virtue, not as holy, only less vile (*civ. Dei* V.13). Sometimes it's ambivalence: when he calls Regulus, the bravest and most distinguished of the Romans (*civ. Dei* I.24), and then discounts this virtue on account of the

duces this pattern. Like Augustine, he claims to see through apparent virtue to real vice lurking beneath, and his confidence follows from the difficulties and instabilities that secular critics of tolerance are eager to point out. As an alternative, he proposes forbearance, a Christian virtue that corrects the deficiencies of tolerance.

Tinder begins as one might expect, by acknowledging the hard facts of disagreement and difference and by pointing out the challenges that accompany them. Maintaining civil peace is one such challenge. Maintaining the confidence of one's convictions while keeping company with various differences is another. As Tinder assumes roughly Fletcher's account of unstable tolerance, it hardly surprises when he insists that the virtue solves the first challenge only as it exacerbates the second. "The idea that there are numerous and conflicting truths, or, to put the same idea in other words, that there are numerous and conflicting illusions—all shaped mainly by the historical situations of those clinging to them—is, for many people, nearly irresistible."[73] The assumption that tolerance is essentially unstable only confirms this mood of temptation and threat. Tolerance "easily becomes acquiescence in the submergence of truth into a shifting variety of opinions and impressions."[74] For Tinder, the committed Christian, the conclusion is plain. Tolerance "cannot be acceptable to the followers of the God of Israel," to Jews and Christians alike. Rather, the faithful must "develop a new attitude toward the religious and cultural confusions surrounding them that is tolerant, yet, in refusing any dalliance with relativism, is distinct from traditional tolerance." To mark the distinction, Tinder borrows from the Apostle Paul and calls this attitude "forbearance," which he describes in interesting detail.[75] For now, consider a couple of things about Tinder's criticism and conclusion.[76]

---

impiety that accompanies it (*civ. Dei* XIX.25). For an account of this rhetorical strategy that accents the ambivalence, see Lamb, "Commonwealth of Hope," especially chaps. 4 and 6.

73 Tinder, "What Can We Reasonably Hope For?," 33.

74 Ibid., 33.

75 Ibid., 33.

76 This was not always Tinder's view. See his *Tolerance: Toward a New Civility* and *Tolerance and Community*. The latter is a rewritten version of the former. In each he describes, not a virtue, not a moral perfection, but a disposition and an attitude that enables one to "tolerate beliefs, practices, or habits differing from one's own" (Tinder, *Tolerance and Community*, 1). He explores the warrants for this attitude, the suffering it requires, the social context that is favorable to it, and the limits that bring it to an end. In neither version does he pit secular tolerance against a theologically charged alternative. In fact, in the preface to the latter version he insists that a secular account of tolerance can be spiritually meaningful (ibid., ix), and when he concludes, he infuses spiritual content into his own account. True tolerance keeps faith with "humanity and truth in times that tempt us to despair of everything but immediate pleasure. . . . [I]t is a readiness (borrowing a phrase from an unknown follower of Saint Paul) for speaking and hearing 'the truth in love' (Eph. 4:15)" (ibid., 240). Five years later, this

First, as with Augustine's criticism of pagan virtue, Tinder's complaint with tolerance turns on a moral sleight of hand. The trick works like this: locate a semblance of secular virtue, assume that it is regarded as *true* virtue by wide consensus, expose the wickedness hidden within the semblance, insist that the secular consensus cannot see the sham precisely because it participates in that wickedness, and then, finally, contrast what the consensus considers virtuous (but in fact is not) with true perfection, with Christian justice, piety, and wisdom. As the consensus cannot imagine real virtue, either faintly or in full, without the assistance of the Holy Spirit and the witness of the church, it is not the hypocrisy of one's opponents that is unmasked, not their failure to distinguish real and apparent virtue, but their inability to make the distinction. It is their sinful, moral blindness that the trick puts on display.

By these lights, the courage and self-restraint that enabled Rome's citizens to live in freedom and Rome's legions to conquer and rule were in fact mere semblances. They amounted to nothing more than the ability "to bridle ... baser desires" for power, pleasure, and luxury by unleashing lust for human praise and glory (*civ. Dei* V.13). One vicious desire checked a few others. And when this ruse failed and love for glory was overcome by these baser desires, counterfeit virtue was maintained and Rome's descent into transparent wickedness was curtailed, at least for a time, by encouraging fear of external domination (*civ. Dei* I.31; II.18). Thus Augustine concludes famously: these "virtues" and desires were not yet holy, they were only less vile (*civ. Dei* V.13). He also points out that "the holy apostles did not do this." They did not seek glory for glory's sake. In fact, they preached the name of Christ where it was hated, in places that brought curses and reviling, not honor and welcome. And yet, like those ancient Romans, they prevailed nevertheless. They "conquered hard hearts and filled them with the peace of righteousness" and in turn received glory in the church. "They did not rest in that glory as if it were the virtue which they sought as their end. Rather, they referred that glory itself to the glory of God, by Whose grace they were what they were": good men in essence, not simply in appearance, men who received the glory that is due true virtue and who offered it to God in humble gratitude for his grace and for their goodness (*civ. Dei* V.14).

By this same logic, the justice and modesty that Lucretia exhibited as she took her own life was, in fact, nothing of the sort. Why? Because she was either an unwilling and thus innocent victim of Tarquinius's lust, or a willing and thus adulterous coconspirator. If she was unwilling, then her self-slaughter was murderous and base, an unjust attack upon her innocent self. If willing, she was neither chaste nor pious to begin with (*civ. Dei* I.18–19).

---

generous attitude toward tolerance has vanished, so too the possibility that secular and theological discourses might be mutually leavening.

As the Romans prefer to count her innocent, Augustine thinks we must conclude that she took her life, "not from love of purity, but because of a weakness arising from shame," because of her vanity, and because of her inability "to bear patiently the infamy that another had inflicted upon her." By contrast, those Christian women who suffered in the same way during Alarac's assault on Rome are still alive precisely because they refused to regard themselves as guarantors of male honor and Roman propriety, a regard that, in Lucretia's case, elicited both murderous shame and love for human glory. "Within themselves, indeed, by the testimony of their own conscience, they have the glory of chastity. Moreover, they have it in the sight of God, and they require nothing more" (*civ. Dei* I.19). So too, Cato's suicide was not a virtuous consequence of his just love of honor, of his unwillingness to live diminished and disgraced under victorious Caesar. It was, rather, arrogant self-assertion, a natural result of his colossal pride, of his unwillingness "to give Caesar the glory of pardoning him." By comparison, Job's steady endurance in difficult times exposes Cato's cowardice (*civ. Dei* I.24). It shows his suicide to be "an act demonstrating not honor forestalling villainy, but weakness unable to sustain adversity" (*civ. Dei* I.23).[77]

In each case, Augustine's criticism is designed to show how praise of pagan virtue, of courage, modesty, justice, and so on, in fact expresses moral collapse. But it's a transparent trick, cheap and easy. We've seen it before. Reduce a virtue to its semblance and then decry this counterfeit perfection and resent its unmerited praise. Cast its friends among the morally lost, its critics among the elect, and then propose an authentic alternative, not a vice clothed in virtue's garb, but a real perfection. Augustine resorts to this trick against his own ambivalence about all human virtue, even the best of which he considers morally ambiguous, and it is his critical ambitions that get the best of him.[78] He hopes to make the difference between Christian and pagan virtue as stark and obvious as the difference between good and evil. To achieve this aim he must recast every pagan virtue in the mold of

---

77 Augustine's treatment of the rape of Lucretia has complexities with respect to genre, aim, and context—both historical and theological—that my remarks skate past. For an important interpretation, see Webb, "Rape and Its Aftermath".

78 Augustine's better instincts are on display in his eschatological account of temporal virtue in *civ. Dei* XIX.27, where the distinction between pagan and Christian virtue, so prominent throughout book xix, largely fades from view. Combine these instincts with the incarnational treatment of virtuous love that we find in *conf.* IV.vi.11–xii.19 and the fallout is an account of temporal and eternal virtue that, in many ways, tracks my own in chapter 6. For an account of the incarnational and eschatological aspects of Augustinian virtue, see Bowlin, "Augustine Counting Virtues." For an account of hyper-Augustinian anxieties about virtue's semblance, an inheritance that bears directly on the emergence of modern moral philosophy, see Herdt, *Putting on Virtue*. Tinder's critique of tolerance exhibits this inheritance, as do the philosophical accounts of the virtue he assumes.

sin and then explain how his pagan opponents could so easily confuse virtue and vice. So he identifies pagan virtue with virtue's semblance, with sin
that's hard to recognize. This makes the trouble with pagan virtue obvious
and the comparison with a Christian alternative easy. In this way, criticizing
pagan virtue and resenting the praise it receives become a means of specifying Christian difference.[79]

If we allow "pagan virtue" to refer loosely to any praiseworthy habit that
the Christian critic cannot locate in the moral and theological inheritance
of the churches, then, on Tinder's rendering, tolerance is a pagan virtue. In
aim and substance, his critical efforts reproduce the Augustinian pattern. He
wants to distinguish a Christian response to disagreement and division from
what he finds on offer in liberal democracies, and he wants to commend
this Christian alternative. He knows that tolerance (as virtue and source of
action) is offered and praised, and, on the borrowed authority of secular
philosophers like Fletcher, he assumes that its semblance—nihilistic indifference—is what it actually amounts to. He assumes, in other words, that
societies like ours encourage a vice and call it a virtue, that most of us cannot see the mistake, and that Christian forbearance emerges as a compelling
alternative once our confusion has been exposed. When we recommend
tolerance we in fact encourage moral collapse. Christians can see through
this ruse to the vice hidden below precisely because they can offer forbearance as substitute and savior. As a friend once put it to me, "Christians don't
tolerate; we love."

But Tinder's criticism succeeds only as we fail to think of tolerance as a
virtue with semblances and imperfect antecedents that we can distinguish
from its genuine article. Or, more precisely, it succeeds only as we concede
the authority of those misleading philosophical treatments of tolerance that
either ignore or discount the importance of these distinctions and reduce

---

79 Wetzel argues that Augustine collapses secular virtue into human sinfulness, and against
the bishop's better instincts. See his "Splendid Vices and Secular Virtues." My debt is substantial.
Wetzel's efforts clarify Augustine's own, and they indicate how Augustine's failure to distinguish secularity from sin has been put to use by contemporary theologians eager to locate the
difference that Christians lives and virtues might make. The desire to mark these differences,
whatever they might be, and to make them as sharp and substantial as possible, has occupied
some of our best theologians in recent years. In part, the motive has been to restore integrity
to Christian lives and commitments after centuries of Constantinian captivity. In part the motive has been to resist the new Constantinian settlement that has emerged in recent years between the Republican Party and certain strains of American Protestantism. All of this is to say
that Tinder's critique of tolerance and his resort to this prominent strand of Augustinian social
criticism occur in a broader landscape of anxiety about Christian difference in politics and
morals, a landscape dominated by John Milbank's efforts and Stanley Hauerwas's encouragement. For Milbank's resort to Augustine's slight of hand against secular virtue, see *Theology and
Social Theory*, 326–438. For Hauerwas's praise of Milbank's Augustinian resorts, see Hauerwas,
After Christendom?, 21–22 and Hauerwas and Pinches, *Christians among the Virtues*, 55–69.

virtue's act to hapless indifference or misplaced acceptance. This failure and this concession are, in this Augustinian context, motivated by a desire to mark Christian difference and secure Christian commitment, but these gains are ill gotten. If the difference between true tolerance and its semblances comes into focus after just a little reflection, and if most of us, "pagan" and Christian alike, can grasp the difference on the slightest provocation, then Tinder's complaint, his resentment, and his specification of Christian difference all fall flat. And note, his efforts turn on our ability to see how he draws this distinction *and* on his assumption that we can't ordinarily draw it, or at the very least that we typically don't. Either way, he assumes that most of us have unwittingly reduced tolerance to a species of moral nihilism and that most will dismiss the virtue once sound criticism brings us to our senses.[80] It's an unconvincing collection of assumptions, and it casts doubt on his effort to show that "pagan" virtues are as different from their Christian cousins as evil is from good. Certainly, the virtues that Christians praise and that help perfect their lives and relationships will be distinct in *some way*. They will be situated in social relationships that include the God of Israel as a middle term, and their acts will be ordained to love's union with God and neighbor. This much, at least, Christians will confess. And yet the various relations that obtain between these virtues and their "pagan" counterparts are likely to be more complicated, and more interesting, than Tinder imagines.

Whether Augustine eventually imagines genuine moral virtue that does not have love for God and neighbor as its explicit final end remains a matter of scholarly dispute.[81] This is not the place to resolve it. Beyond dispute is the fact that Augustine refers to patient endurance in response to some objectionable of differences. To Marcellinus's doubts about the possibility and merit of Christian citizenship, he notes the political benefits of Christ's injunction to forgive and forbear. Justice and piety will come to the city and peace to its affairs only as Christ's "outstanding example of forbearance" (*exemplum singulare patientiae*) is reproduced among its citizens.[82] To Donatist refusal to endure difference within the church, he praises the "examples of the Prophets and the Apostles, namely, that we are to bear with the wicked,

---

80 Augustine's criticism turns on the same assumption. He says that pagan Rome considered Cato's suicide courageous even as he insists that his readers, some of them Roman pagans, can follow his arguments and count it a vice. He even admits that Cato's friends made arguments of the same kind. Like Augustine, they saw *infirmitas* in this act, not virtue's strength, and they drew the same conclusion (*civ. Dei* I.23). His suicide followed from vice posing as virtue. Robert Dodaro's interpretation of *civ. Dei* book I confirms this reading, although it's unlikely that he would accept my complaint with this variety of Augustinian social criticism. See *Christ and the Just Society*, 27–43.

81 For doubts that he does, see Wetzel, "Tangle of Two Cities." For a defense of that possibility, see Lamb, "Commonwealth of Hope."

82 *E.* 138.13.

so as not to desert the good, rather than to desert the good so as to cut off the wicked" (*malos esse potius tolerandos, ne deserantur boni, quam bonos deserendos, ut separentur mali*).[83] In each instance, it is love's patient endurance that he commends, a disposition of our hearts and a work of charity designed to bring peace to the city and unity to the church. It is not an act of just endurance, one that emerges from extraecclesial roles and relationships and that is ordained to their ends. It is, rather, a requirement of the person's status as a member of the city of God on its temporal sojourn. And the benefit it brings to those extraecclesial roles and relationships will be entirely a consequence of this love's work upon them. In this respect as well, Tinder is simply following Augustine's lead.[84]

A WAY FORWARD

At this point, three tasks are needed to sort out our attitudes toward tolerance, our strange combination of admiration and ambivalence. First, we need an account of tolerance as an acquired virtue that is in some way natural to us, one that identifies its internal and external sources, its psychological dynamics, its acts, ends, and circumstances, and its dependence upon a handful of other moral virtues. Second, we need to identify the distinguishing marks of the tolerance that we find in modern, liberal societies. If tolerance is natural to us, then its modern self-image will have to be recast. If it is not a moral innovation that can be assigned to modernity, then we need a better, more precise account of the variety that in fact emerges in the modern period. And finally, we need to consider love's endurance, the virtue the perfects resort to this act, and the relations that obtain between this virtue, forbearance, and its sibling, tolerance. Tinder would have us believe that they are as different as vice is from virtue. One is chosen only as the other is rejected. One is a deliverance of grace, the other a consequence of fallen nature. One belongs to those who share something like Tinder's theological commitments, the other to those who do not. As I have said, this can't be right, but then, what is? If both virtues generate acts of patient endurance, tolerance as an instance of justice, forbearance as an expression of love, and if both acts have a special goodness that cannot be denied, neither tolerance by those

83   *E.* 108.vi.16. Here he scolds Macrobius, Donatist Bishop of Hippo, for Donatist failure to forbear differences within the church.

84   For another example of this hyper-Augustinian inheritance in Christian social criticism, see Karl Barth's treatment of tolerance as semblance of virtue and the forbearance of Christ as alternative. *Church Dogmatics*, I/2, 299–303. For resistance to this inheritance, see Fergusson's theological case for toleration, *Church, State, and Civil Society*, 72–93. For Barth's account of a tolerance informed by the forbearance of Christ and offered as love to those who lead corrupt, perverted, or otherwise unjust lives, see *Church Dogmatics*, IV/3, 493–496.

who share Tinder's theological commitments, nor love's endurance by those who do not, then we need an account of their similarities and differences. Crucially, we need to see how they might be found, how they might function, within both secular and religious lives.

Locate tolerance among the virtues, reconsider its modern features, and spell out its various relations to forbearance. Do all this, and the heat of recent debates might be replaced with a more reflective light, and this light might illumine some of the relations that obtain between secular and theological moral discourses. This, at least, is the hope.

CHAPTER 2

A NATURAL VIRTUE

But is tolerance in fact a virtue? In the previous chapter we noted that some critics doubt that it is. Some contend that the demands the tolerant must meet and the moral compromises they must accept give us reason enough to strike the virtue from our list. When its cultivation is encouraged, we should object, or so they insist. When it is praised nevertheless, we should resent its false merit and decry the moral dangers posed by its undeserved repute. We also noted that these complaints and resentments are difficult to sustain once we locate tolerance among the other moral virtues. In that company, tolerance behaves roughly as those virtues do. Like the others, it is difficult to cultivate and exercise, its antecedents and semblances are easily mistaken for the real thing, and it is connected to a whole cast of others virtues by way of dependence and resemblance. When these ordinary features of virtue in general are assigned to tolerance in particular, complaints and resentments can be sustained only as we ignore our better judgments about what the virtues entail and how they function. When complaints and resentments persist nevertheless, the fault can be charged to moral inattention, some of it culpable, some of it not, some of it motivated by passions and interests that corrupt judgment, some of it caused by nothing more than the ordinary difficulties that every moral virtue regards.

But this reasoning is largely circular and self-justifying. It addresses some of the most common complaints and resentments only as it asserts what they deny: that tolerance is a natural virtue, that like courage and justice it is an indispensable source of human flourishing, and that it instantiates genuine human goodness in its own habit and acts. But how do we know that this assertion is sound?

The claim has two parts: that tolerance is a virtue, and that it is somehow natural to us. Warrants are needed for both parts, and for the first, they come without much trouble. Thomas points the way. When he considers whether hope (*spes*) can be a virtue, he appeals to Aristotle's authority (*NE* 1106a16–17) and replies that "the virtue of a thing is that which makes its subject good, and its work good likewise. Consequently wherever we find a good human act, it must correspond to some human virtue" (*ST* II-II.17.1). When he asks whether friendliness (*affabilitas*) is a virtue, he sharpens the point: "since virtue is directed to good, wherever there is a special kind of good, there must needs be a special kind of virtue" (*ubi occurrit specialis ratio boni, ibi oportet esse specialem rationem virtutis*) (*ST* II-II.114.1). When he asks whether *veritas, sive veracitas*—truth, or truthfulness—is a special virtue, he sharpens the point even further: a "special kind of goodness (*specialem rationem boni*) will be found where there is a special order (*determinato ordine*) . . . whereby our externals, either words or deeds, are duly ordered in relation to some thing (*debite ordinantur ad aliquid*)" (*ST* II-II.109.2).

With these remarks as a starting point, let's assume that responding well to differences in judgment, love, and form of life, above all to differences that are objectionable in some way, is a human action that embodies a special *ratio* or form of goodness, one distinct from others. It is, after all, an action that mediates human relations and sets them in due order, not in general, but across various divides of objectionable difference, and it's this special aspect of its act that generates its distinct formality and specific goodness. Given this special aspect, given these divides of objectionable difference, given the right order between persons that we all desire, it behooves us to secure the special goodness of this act. Let's also assume that the offer of patient endurance in response to objectionable difference of the right kind, in the right circumstances, and for the sake of the right ends is the paradigmatic example of this good act. And finally, let's assume that there can be moral development with respect to this response, that one can grow in tolerance and thus act in ways that are right and due with ever more ease and consistency and across an ever greater number of cases and differences.

If we assume all this, and if we follow Thomas's lead, then there must be a virtue that corresponds to this act, in this instance a virtue that regards operations as its matter, one that is connected to justice and that the tolerant use when they act. But why *must* this be so? In general, why is it that every human action that instantiates a special *ratio* of goodness has a corresponding virtue? Thomas doesn't tell us, at least not directly, but a reply can be inferred from what he does say. He tells us that human actions are, by definition, voluntary, which is to say that they have their origin in us, in our own reason and will (*ST* I-II.6.1–2). But this means that when we identify a good human action, we locate its goodness not simply (or even principally) in the external operation done, but also (and more significantly) in its internal sources, in the intending and commanding that actually generate the act (*ST* I-II.6.4). We recognize that a right external operation has its origin in these good internal acts, that it can be thwarted by violence, and that when it is (when misfortune of this sort *does* occur) goodness nevertheless remains in the internal principles of the external action that failed (ibid.). It follows that we count a human action good in the fullest sense when its internal sources are good, and when the powers that produce them are disposed by habit to do so with consistency and ease. It is precisely this habitual perfection that the moral virtues provide.

Perfection comes in two varieties. There is, first, the habitual ability to perform a good act (*facultas ad bonum actum*). In the case we are imagining, this aptness to act entails judging which differences are in fact objectionable and in what way, determining what response to them would in fact be right given the circumstances that matter, and having a prompt will to act in accord with this determination (*ST* I-II.56.3). And, second, there is the right use of this ability (*recte facultate utatur*), in this instance the habitual will to translate the good intention elicited by the aptness to perform a tolerant act into an action that is in fact tolerant. Insofar as tolerance is a moral virtue it confers both of these perfections on the tolerant. It not only gives them a prompt will to do tolerant actions, but it also makes them act tolerantly. Tolerance confers precisely this twofold perfection, and we know that it does precisely because we know that good intentions are not good enough. The ability to generate them promptly but without the additional desire to execute what is intended provides an aptness to do well but no inclination to do well actually. If this were all that moral virtue entailed, it would, in effect, reduce by half the perfection that tolerance and the others exhibit. They would be virtues only in a relative sense (*secundum quid*) precisely because the aptness to act that they confer would come without a settled desire to exercise that aptness (ibid.).[1]

Less obvious is the fact that it is a reflective judgment about the goodness of virtuous action itself that inclines the virtuous to act on their right intentions. If the tolerant begin with a prompt will to do tolerant acts, then they will in fact act tolerantly, in accord with that prompt will, only as they come to regard tolerant acts in a certain way, as goods of a certain sort. More precisely, they will act upon their habitually tolerant intentions only as they regard *rightful* acts of patient endurance as both good in themselves, and thus choiceworthy, and as best, and thus surpassing all other options in the circumstance of choice. Indeed, we can speak of virtue *simpliciter* only as an

---

1   In this respect, they would be more akin to sciences and crafts, virtues that reside in the intellect (*ST* I-II.56.3; 57.2–4).

aptness to act tolerantly is combined with desire informed by this judgment about the relative goodness of tolerant acts (ibid.). Forgo this judgment, and once again we have virtue, but only by half. And since this judgment, this right reason about things to be done, arrives consistently only as virtue perfects the practical intellect, we can say that tolerance, like the other moral virtues, is perfect and complete only as it comes packaged with prudence. Its response to objectionable difference is habitually just and good only as its desire is informed by reason that is habitually right (*ST* I-II.58.4; 65.1).

So tolerance is a virtue precisely because tolerant acts embody a special aspect of goodness. But is it a virtue like courage and justice? Like them, is it a natural virtue? Does it somehow come packaged with our humanity? Well, suppose that we could show that as concept, act, and potential perfection tolerance in fact turns up in substantially different times and places. In the standard history, it emerges in the modern period and distinguishes the moral lives and political practices found in liberal democracies. But the standard history misleads. The special goodness in a rightful act of toleration has been identified and commended outside of the modern West—in Lactantius's plea for pagan endurance of Christian dissent from public worship, in Augustine's response to Donatist dissenters who have been compelled in and pagans opponents who share the public square, and in Aquinas's response to Judaism, to name just three.[2]

By itself, however, I doubt this evidence warrants the conclusion that tolerance is, as concept, act, and potential perfection, in some way natural to us and that its varieties tend to turn up everywhere and always. Still, if, on other grounds, we suspect that it comes packaged with our humanity, then finding it elsewhere would indeed confirm our suspicion.

Begin, then, with a traditional account of the virtues in general. Everything is what it is and not some other thing because of the ends it pursues and the actions it performs, all in accord with the kind of thing that it is. This applies to oak trees and aardvarks, hound dogs and human beings.[3] When *we* act for the sake of the ends characteristic of our kind, when we do so rationally and well across a variety of circumstances and with the ease of habit, we become, we might say, a perfect instance of the kind of thing that we are. We are virtuous according to our kind and happy as a consequence of our virtue. And note, happiness comes for more than one reason. It comes,

---

2   Recent treatments of premodern tolerance include Boguslawski, *Thomas Aquinas on the Jews*; Bowlin, "Tolerance among the Fathers"; Digeser, *Making of a Christian Empire*; Drake, *Constantine and the Bishops*; Garnsey, "Religious Toleration in Classical Antiquity"; Kahlos, *Forbearance and Compulsion*; Laursen and Nederman, eds., *Beyond the Persecuting Society*; and Sutherland, "Persecution and Toleration in Reformation Europe."

3   The same applies to heavy bodies that fall and fires that burn (*ST* I-II.26.2, 109.1; II-II.26.3). For commentary, see Brock, *Philosophy of Saint Thomas Aquinas*, chap. 2.

in part, because virtue conspires with good fortune to generate success in action. That is, more often than not, the virtuous among us achieve the ends they intend and enjoy the happiness that success in action brings. But happiness also comes in some measure regardless of success or failure. It comes because the virtuous perform the activities characteristic of our kind with excellence and because happiness, by these lights, is nothing but this excellent performance, nothing but this perfection in being. Since we perform activities of different kinds and pursue ends of various sorts, perfection comes to our agency and happiness to our lives only as we acquire and exercise many virtues. And a virtue can be considered natural to us whenever we locate an activity characteristic of our kind that cannot be performed well and a pursuit that cannot succeed without the habitual perfection it provides. By these lights, tolerance can be counted among the natural human virtues precisely because there are activities and pursuits that distinguish our humanity that cannot be perfected without it, without a habit that disposes us to right performance of these particular acts and success in these pursuits.

So goes a formal case for finding tolerance among the virtues natural to us. In the remainder of this chapter I will unpack its assumptions, spell out its warrants, and address some of its critics. Three complaints stand out. Some resist the picture of our humanity that this formal case assumes. For these critics, human beings and human agency cannot be perfected by this particular habit. By their lights, tolerance distorts our nature, corrupts our agency, and diminishes our humanity. Perfection arrives only as we forgo tolerance and locate some other solution to the problems posed by disagreement and difference to peaceful coexistence. For others, it is not the relation between human nature and virtue that deserves scrutiny but rather the metaphysics of substance assumed by that relation. For these critics, we cannot speak of human beings as a natural kind without committing ourselves to that dubious metaphysics. For others still, it is the moral consequences of those assumptions that generate doubt. To claim that tolerance is a deliverance of our humanity, that it shows up in some guise everywhere and always, ignores the undeniable and stubborn facts of moral diversity. It binds our lives in a moral straightjacket that is said to be natural, but in fact is not. By these lights, nature talk is always a swindle and a hoodwink, always a slight of hand in a game of power, where one local moral regime with utterly contingent sources and prospects confronts its rivals by asserting a natural, and thus, necessary basis for its virtues, commitments, and practices. Combine this doubt with the standard history of tolerance, where the virtue emerges only as Reformation Europe convulses, and every reference to changeless humanity and necessary virtue becomes difficult to sustain.

With the last two complaints, the proof is, so to speak, in the philosophical pudding. That is, it remains to be seen whether the account of natural virtue that I develop below with the help of Aquinas and Wittgenstein in fact commits us to dubious metaphysical assumptions and self-congratulatory assertions of moral universality. We shall see. In that account, justice is treated first, only then tolerance, so patience will be required. In the meantime, the first complaint needs to be addressed. It is, in some respects, similar to those we considered in chapter 1. Like them, it expresses certain attitudes and resentments toward tolerance, and like them it does so with philosophy's authority. But there are differences. The complaints we considered in chapter 1 begin with misunderstanding and end in scorn. They begin with insufficient attention to the dynamics of virtue in general and to tolerance in particular, and they end with contempt for the moral compromises and self-restraint that tolerance is thought to demand. They presuppose no grand claims about virtue and nature, just confusion about the true character of tolerance, its antecedents, semblances, and corruptions. These complaints can be put aside and this contempt abandoned as this confusion is cleared up and these dynamics spelled out, or so I argued. This new complaint is slightly different. It begins with the indignities the tolerated are thought to endure, with the condescension that tolerance appears to require, and concludes with a theory about human nature that, in effect, removes tolerance from the list of virtues that perfect our humanity. In place of tolerance it offers an altogether different solution to the problem of peaceful coexistence across lines of objectionable difference.

POWER, THEORY, AND VIRTUE

Barbara Herman follows complaint to theory along this track.[4] Tolerance, she contends, is an inadequate, dangerous, and ultimately self-defeating response to moral diversity and disagreement. The tolerant endure what they dislike, not because they find intrinsic worth in toleration's act, in the right relations it creates when it succeeds, or in the company it allows them to keep. Rather, they act as they do because they have no other options. Given the circumstances they find themselves in, given the aims they happen to have, they can do no other. With false smiles and hidden frowns, they tolerate in public and disdain in private.[5] They regard the tolerated, not as equals, not as members of a common moral community, but as competitors with whom they "negotiate agreements from within their separate spheres of value" and as strangers whom they live among but never with.[6] More often than not, their disapproval and disdain creates "a moral culture of oppression," one

---

4   Herman, "Pluralism and the Community of Moral Judgment." For another example of this track, but with a theological twist, see O'Meara, "Beyond Toleration."

5   Herman, "Pluralism and the Community of Moral Judgment," 61.

6   Ibid., 67, 61.

that disregards the "legitimate political claims" of the tolerated "for equality and civil rights."[7] It is, after all, the powerful who tolerate, who could coerce but endure instead, and the weak who plea for endurance. At the same time, these same attitudes and inequalities make it difficult for the tolerant to sympathize with other lives and commitments, and this in turn makes it unlikely that they will recognize the harms that mark toleration's proper limits. Everyone agrees that substantial harms must not be endured, that the tolerant must distinguish the harmlessly objectionable from the intolerably harmful, and that this distinction is often geared to local commitments and attitudes, to specific cultures and contexts. A joke in one social setting might degrade and insult in another. An act considered benevolent by some might be received as a humiliating slight by others. But this means that tolerance cannot be exercised in a context of pluralism without sympathetic attention to cultures and contexts quite different from one's own, and it is precisely this sympathy that the tolerant typically lack. Their "laissez-faire" attitude toward disagreement and difference, their cultivated moral indifference, discourages this kind of cross-context attention.[8] More troubling still, these attitudes and postures of the tolerant tend to make ordinary acts of justice difficult to perform. In most instances we cannot treat others justly without first knowing quite a number of details about them, and yet the tolerant, smug and self-satisfied, resist this knowledge and rest easy in the ignorance their virtue seems to encourage.[9]

For Herman, the conclusion is obvious. Tolerance is no virtue. It cannot be our "first moral response to pluralism."[10] The conclusion surely follows from the account of tolerance she assumes, but then why assume as she does? Why concede authority to her account? What prevents us from proceeding as we did in the previous chapter, from asserting that tolerance is indeed a virtue and insisting that whatever this virtue amounts to it cannot function as Herman assumes? Well, of course, nothing does, and I will develop arguments of precisely this kind in the pages that follow. That said, Herman's failure to distinguish true virtue from mere semblance is hardly the sole source of her complaint. Her principal concern regards the relation between human nature and moral colloquy, and her complaint follows from her account of that relation.

On Herman's rendering, tolerance undermines the conditions that make moral discourse, debate, and judgment possible. Since our nature is expressed as we engage in moral colloquy of precisely this sort, tolerance, in effect, prevents the full expression of our humanity. So goes the argument. It

7 Ibid., 61.
8 Ibid., 61–62, 67–68.
9 Ibid., 64.
10 Ibid., 76.

turns on Herman's understanding of moral colloquy, her sketch of the conditions that govern moral discourse, and on her account of the obligations that bind all who participate. Moral colloquy, she contends, assumes membership in a community of moral judgment, a community constituted and regulated by a collection of shared principles that create a common deliberative field.[11] These principles are designed to mediate and resolve conflicts among "local value claims" and thus preserve the community of moral judgment and the common deliberative field that constitute the "conditions for moral development and colloquy: the conditions necessary to secure what Kant calls the 'public use of reason.'"[12] Anything that strikes against this shared moral community, this common deliberative field, is "an impermissible hindrance to the effective expression of human rational agency."[13] Anything that makes this community more inclusive, that expands its boundaries through "mutual adjustment" of local values, should be encouraged. Indeed, we are obliged by the rational agency we share "to extend the community of moral judgment" and thus give practical expression to "the kingdom of ends as a cosmopolitan ideal."[14]

If this is right, then tolerance can be cultivated, practiced, and praised only as we ignore this obligation and, in turn, forsake our humanity. Why? Because tolerance begins in the absence of Herman's variety of moral colloquy, in disagreement, disapproval, and division, and in some instances the tolerant are content to let these conditions stand. At the very least, they make no transcendent appeal that might enable us to resolve our disagreements, overcome our divisions, and put aside our need for mutual endurance and burden bearing. Some refuse this appeal because they doubt the existence of moral principles that, in origin and warrant, transcend the local values they are thought to govern. Others doubt that we have easy access to whatever transcendent principles there happen to be. But regardless of their metaethical commitments, the tolerant assume that moral disagreements and divisions are common, that at least some are unavoidable, and that we need to carry on as well as we can in spite of them. Human beings love many different goods, rank them in competing, often contrary, ways, and lead, as a result, many distinct, and at times, incompatible lives. Disagreement and dissent follow, and the tolerant assume that these ordinary consequences of our shared humanity can be managed, but never overcome. Some disagreements can be put aside, some conflicts resolved, but many remain and these require other resorts—coercion, tolerance, expulsion, or exit. For Herman it

11 Ibid., 68–69.
12 Ibid., 68, 75.
13 Ibid., 75.
14 Ibid., 76.

is precisely these assumptions and resorts that prove "the inappropriateness of tolerance."[15] If disagreements are not mediated by objective moral principles that express the value of rational human agency, then invariably they will be decided by fortune's arbitrary rule, by inequalities of "power and trading advantage."[16] Some lives and commitments will trump others. Some will flourish, others will fade; some will be tolerated as they are, others will be transformed by intolerant coercion. In the end, conflicts among different lives and commitments will not be resolved by mutual adjustment to objective principle, but kept in check by violence, fear, and moral compromise. In this context, our nature will find neither expression nor perfection precisely because our conduct will not be ruled and measured by principles that establish a community of objective moral judgment, a community that makes possible the fullest exercise of our rational agency.[17]

Against the backdrop of these criticisms, Herman argues that Kant's moral theory offers a solution to the problems of peaceful coexistence that avoids these troubles with tolerance. As I mentioned above, some of these troubles emerge only as Herman confuses virtue and semblance, and one wonders whether she could justify her resort to moral theory once this confusion is cleared up. No doubt, we are disposed by our nature to engage in moral colloquy, and surely moral colloquy is unimaginable apart from some agreement in moral principle and judgment. That said, it is far from obvious that true tolerance emerges only in the absence of colloquy and community, or that this absence is encouraged once it emerges. Nor is it certain that we should assume, as Herman does, that tolerance both presupposes and perpetuates inequalities of power. Certainly, an act of patient endurance can be ordered to unjust ends, to oppress, control, or humiliate, and it can be used to sustain arbitrary lines of inclusion and exclusion. That said, these facts hardly distinguish this act from others that mediate our social and political relationships and that we are inclined to endorse. Acceptance, indifference, recognition, love, and countless other actions: these can also be used as instruments of injustice across differentials of power. As we shall see, both assumptions are difficult to sustain once a place is cleared for tolerance among the virtues.

Still, Herman's most important complaint with tolerance does not depend on these confusions. She is right to insist that the tolerant are content to let some moral disagreements and divisions stand, and that some versions of the virtue do not demand the pursuit of cosmopolitan ideals. Most do not require us to extend the bounds of the tolerant community to in-

15   Ibid.
16   Ibid., 72, 67.
17   Ibid., 72–73.

clude human beings as such.[18] At the same time, it is not at all clear that these aspects of tolerance clash with our shared humanity or suppress the expression of our rational agency. They might in fact enable the tolerant to concede their authority, their undeniable reality. And of course, if the latter is the case, then it is not tolerance that distorts our humanity and prevents its perfection. Rather, it may be Kantian moral theory that in fact tilts against nature.

With this possibility in mind, consider Herman's complaint against consequentialist moral theories. When confronted with conflicts among lives and commitments, consequentialists propose "rules of value translation, so that disputes can be resolved through single scale balancing or weighing." With this scale in hand, they hope to gather together the many goods that human beings can know and love, compare their values, and reveal the merely apparent character of their various conflicts. But it's a false hope, says Herman, precisely because of the "difficulty of establishing commensurability among goods."[19] The many things that we love are distinct in kind and so too in value. Their goodness cannot be captured in single measure. The theorist who tries to locate such a measure will invariably ignore these differences and discount this complexity. They will disregard the facts on the ground and flatten out love's response to them, and this conclusion remains even if the fears and hopes that motivate the resort to theory are, as Herman insists, perfectly sensible.

This is what surprises. Like the consequentialist, the Kantian moral theorist fears the predictable conflicts that follow from the diversity of human goods and loves, and she hopes to avoid the violence and condescension that so often accompany our response to them. Like the consequentialist, she thinks that a successful moral theory will address this fear as it identifies a common deliberative field that will, in turn, secure this hope. Herman's theory identifies a deliberative field that unifies judgment, not a common measure that unifies objective value, but the fallout is much the same: disagreements are resolved, conflicts are avoided, and, ultimately, our need for tolerance is overcome.[20]

Given these common hopes and fears, and given this shared desire to replace virtue with theory, one wonders whether the criticism that Herman addresses to the consequentialist recoils on her own efforts. One wonders whether we couldn't lament Kantian principle as she does consequentialist calculations and for roughly the same reason. Herman contends that

---

18 For one such version, see Lessing, "Nathan the Wise."

19 Herman, "Pluralism and the Community of Moral Judgment," 68. The most elegant and forceful argument to this effect remains Taylor, "Diversity of Goods."

20 Herman, "Pluralism and the Community of Moral Judgment," 68.

disagreements among lives and commitments can be resolved on appeal to moral principles that are available to all and that can, when put into effect, give full expression to our rational humanity. But this implies that those lives and commitments that fall victim to the transcendent principles of Kantian theory are unjustified and irrational. It implies that we are somehow less than fully human when we live those lives, retain those commitments, and carry on among their various conflicts. Of course, most of us have at least some commitments and pursuits that should be revised or abandoned given the other things we happen to believe and desire, the authorities we have good reason to trust, and the evidence that has become available. And of course, few of us consistently revise or abandon as we should. Disordered passions and unshakable interests too often get in the way, tripping up our efforts to amend belief and adjust desire. Motivated irrationalities of this sort are common and none of us are immune. At the same time, it is difficult to believe that these ordinary moral and intellectual imperfections can be cleared up and our rational humanity offered its fullest expression only as our parochial commitments are vetted by transcendent moral principle.

To see the difficulty, consider the fact that Herman gets the relationship between principle, on the one hand, and action and commitment, on the other, exactly backward. She contends that actions and commitments can be considered rational only as they measure up to moral principle, and yet more often than not we are less certain about the principle that measures than we are of the rationality of those same doings and believings. For the most part, we assume that our actions and commitments are rational by default, that they are innocent until proven guilty. We do not grant them this license because we have, in every instance, good reasons at hand that justify what we think, say, and do. In fact, more often than not we proceed without reasons of this sort, without providing explicit justification for our actions and utterances. In most instances there's simply no need; there are no doubts about what was said or done that must be addressed. And it is precisely because reasonable doubts appear sporadically in our daily affairs that we have good reason to proceed as we typically do, acting and believing in accord with the commitments we happen to have but without resort to the explicit warrants that might provide justification. Of course, doubts do emerge; challenges do come. When they are reasonable, warrants must be provided and inferential relations among concepts and commitments must be made explicit. More often than not these efforts succeed, usually as we spell out the relations that obtain between certain actions and commitments and certain authorities in matters of conduct and belief that are themselves immune to doubt, at least for now—our senses, our parents, our best friends, a sacred text, a moral exemplar, the National Academy of Sciences, and so on. But even when these efforts fail and belief needs to be revised and conduct recast, we need not discount the rationality of what was said or done before these efforts were made. As long as inattention to doubt cannot be charged to negligence, disordered passion, or failure of nerve, our rationality is preserved. By the same token, this effort to justify what was said and done should not lead us to conclude that we must subject all that we say and do in the future to this same kind of scrutiny. The need to justify comes by way of the reasonable doubts there happen to be and the authorities whose challenges require an answer. When those doubts and authorities are absent, we can proceed with the commitments we happen to have and with the activities we are prone to pursue but without explicit resort to reason giving and without reservation about the rationality of our thinking and doing.[21]

Now consider the principles of the moral philosophers. *They* tend to be guilty until proven innocent. Sensible doubts about them seem to emerge at every turn, and philosophers struggle to find reasons that might justify commitment to their favorite principle. Success is typically fleeting. Soon enough, others will develop arguments that discount those reasons and support some other principle. This is why moral philosophy's terrain tends to be so contested and its principles so various and uncertain.[22] And this is why it makes little sense to suggest, as Herman does, that our actions and commitments can be counted rational only as they accord with philosophical principle. A principle with dubious warrants can hardly assess the rationality of actions and commitments that we quite sensibly suspect are innocent until proven guilty, and, in most instances, this is precisely how things stand. We tend to have far less confidence in the reasons that might justify commitment to this or that philosophical principle than we have in the presumptive rationality of the actions and commitments the principle is asked to assess. In fact, more often than not we assume that the lines of assessment and authority ought to be reversed and that ordinary commitments ought to judge the principles proposed by the moral theorist. And, strangely enough, Herman inadvertently offers evidence in favor of this reversal when she puts her own principles to work.

Consider, for example, her remarks about autonomy and moral authority. As we might expect, Herman insists that Kantian notions of autonomy are incompatible with nearly every effort to vest "any person or group with ultimate deliberative authority, whether fathers, councils of elders, or experts."[23] And of course she's right. Authority of this sort rarely accords with the

21 I am indebted to Robert Brandom's treatment of action, commitment, and entitlement. See *Making It Explicit*, 157–180, 204–206.

22 And not only in our day. In the early fifth century, Augustine could note how "philosophers have devised a great multitude (*multa et multipliciter*) of different arguments concerning the supreme ends of good and evil" (*civ. Dei* XIX.1).

23 Herman, "Pluralism and the Community of Moral Judgment," 74.

principles that govern a Kantian deliberative field, and surely many of us who inhabit liberal democracies share her commitment to some version of those principles. But not all will. Some of our fellow citizens and some inhabitants of other times and places will consider the matter quite differently. The authority relations that some of us might reject on appeal to Kantian principle, they might accept, and with good reason. Their epistemic context might offer no other sensible option, or, at the very least, no reasonable objection to certain kinds of paternalism. At the same time, our own attitudes about moral authority are more complicated than Kantian principle allows. We are more ambivalent than Herman imagines. Our democratic instincts cut one way; our hunch that freedom needs authority cuts in another. Herman hopes that resort to moral principle can resolve this ambivalence, but it's not that easy, and her passing remarks about modern medicine puts the difficulty on display.

The moral authority of physicians is suspect, she thinks, precisely because it depends upon an exclusive expertise cloaked in the "obscurity of unnecessary Latin," which in turn threatens the autonomy of patients. But this isn't quite right. The trouble is not so much that this complaint casts doubt on the deliberative authority of all sorts of practices that we might admire—legal, scientific, religious, and so on—but rather that our minds are mixed. We don't want paternalistic medical care, where physicians determine the ends they seek on our behalf. We don't want them to decide what a healthy life amounts to or what activities a healthy body ought to be able to perform, not without input from us. At the same time, most of us want our physicians to participate in the discussions that determine those ends and that specify the moral content of a healthy life. Their special expertise hardly diminishes their authority in these discussions. In fact, just the opposite is true. Most of us grant them some authority precisely because of their special mastery of medicine's practices and judgments. We want our physicians to exercise the authority that comes with this mastery, and most of us cannot revise or abandon this desire simply on the merits of moral theory's principle. Rather, most of us would temper the demands of principle in light of this desire.

The fallout should be obvious. If the principles that moral theorists propose can be assessed and revised by ordinary commitments and desires, then it makes little sense to say that moral colloquy presupposes a deliberative field that is plotted and mapped by principle. Better to say that the moral principles we happen to endorse are embedded in the various communities of moral colloquy there happen to be. They emerge and become explicit in the exchanges we happen to have, in the give-and-take of reasons. By the same token, if epistemic confidence in our ordinary commitments and desires tends to be greater than the confidence we ordinarily have in the principles that moral theorists propose, then it makes little sense to say that our rational nature is perfected, that it is given full expression, only as those commitments and desires have been tested by principle. Better to say that perfection comes as virtue does and that assessment and revision of commitment and desire will proceed as they should when the moral and intellectual virtues are firmly in place. Better to admit that moral theory cannot resolve our disputes about the right application of virtue terms or inoculate us against the possibility that virtue had will sometime fail. So too, if our rational humanity cannot be perfected by a moral principle that vets our various commitments, governs our many desires, and confines us to a single deliberative field, then perfection must come in spite of the diversity of human goods and loves and regardless of the conflicts that result. This diversity and these conflicts must be unavoidable features of the life we lead, or, at the very least, unavoidable features of the way we live now. It follows that we will flourish according to our kind, not as theory overcomes these features, but only as our judgments and desires are perfected by those virtues that attend to them.[24]

No doubt, some will find everything I have said so far unconvincing. Some will remain sympathetic with Herman's Kantian cosmopolitanism and her account of public reason, moral principle, and human nature. And, of course, this is hardly surprising. Disagreement about metaethical matters abounds. Friends and foes of this or that collection of first principles are constantly butting heads, and in societies like ours we have kept these disagreements from becoming sources of discord and violence by casting metaethical differences among the actions and things we are willing to tolerate. Herman is unhappy with this settlement because it allows most of these disagreements to remain in place and because its generous account of rationality tends to bless all sides that do. As she takes pains to point out, these aspects of toleration's settlement conflict with her own account of public reason, but her discontent ignores the ordinary facts of metaethical disagreement.[25] Isn't it

---

24 Christians will add a caveat. The conflicts and sorrows that accompany the diversity of human goods and loves are neither necessary nor unavoidable. They are, rather, consequences of sin. No doubt, the potential for conflict and sorrow was there before Adam fell, lurking in the various incompatibilities among the diverse goods that human beings love. But that potential creates no necessity. Had Adam not sinned and humanity remained in paradise that danger would have been diffused by wise judgment, or so Christians confess. It is for this reason that Aquinas assumes that law would have governed sinless Eden. Law is not essentially coercive; it need not restrain. It is, rather, "an ordinance of reason for the common good, made by him who has care of the community" (*ST* I-II.90.4), and presumably the diversity of goods in Eden would have generated need for ordinances that coordinate their various incompatibilities (*ST* I.96.4). (Presumably that "him" could just as well have been "her.")

25 The fact that some contemporary theorists of public reason consider toleration a constitutive condition of rational colloquy only confirms the point. See O'Neill, "Public Use of Reason." Some even pair a theory of toleration with an account of tolerance the virtue. Of these, Rainer Forst's account is the most theoretically sophisticated, and it offers a stark

wishful thinking to suppose that one's favorite moral theory could win the day, convince us all, and suspend our need for tolerance of metaethical difference? Isn't philosophical harmony of this sort unimaginable, and if so, doesn't Herman's unhappiness with tolerance depend in part on her inattention to these philosophical facts on the ground? Isn't it a consequence of the false hope that accompanies this kind of moral theorizing?

answer the question [handwritten margin note]

NATURAL LAW AS NATURE'S GRACE

Suppose the argument so far is largely correct. Metaethical principle cannot suspend our need for tolerance precisely because its appeal to nature goes largely unanswered. Principle cannot unify judgment in its image or recast conduct by its rule, if only because doing so disregards the presumptive rationality of too many of those same beliefs and actions. Suppose this much is right. In that event, we cannot look to metaethical principle in order to resolve the various disagreements, disputes, and conflicts that come packaged with the diversity of human goods and loves and that seem to make tolerance a natural virtue, as indispensable as courage or justice for perfecting agency and securing happiness in the life that human beings actually

---

alternative to my own (*Toleration in Conflict*, 449–517). In basic matters of ethical theory, we stake out fundamentally different positions: on whether moral reasons, norms, and actions are distinct from other kinds; on whether the just and the right can be disentangled from the good and the best; on whether the normative requirements of practical reason are uniform and universally binding; on whether these requirements transcend the social and political relationships they set right; on the relation between religious belief and moral judgment; on the character of moral personhood; and on how to interpret Wilfred Sellars on the myth of the given. Forst looks to Kant and Habermas for inspiration and support, I look to Aquinas and Wittgenstein. These differences lead him to defend what I deny: the existence of a single, principled way to distinguish the tolerable from the intolerable and to justify the restrictions on liberty that follow or not. They also generate fundamentally different conceptions of virtue. For Forst, tolerance is the capacity for self-restraint that accords with moral reasons, moral principle. It resides in the reason, not in the will, and it acts alone, not among (and with the assistance of) other virtues. Aquinas would call it a craft, the capacity to generate an outcome in accord with an antecedently determined principle (*ST* I-II.57.3–4). Forst will probably call my account of tolerance indeterminate and arbitrary. He will reject my claim that determination comes, not as a principle of practical reason is applied, but rather as tolerance and the other moral virtues are acquired and exercised. He will probably consider it hopelessly circular to argue, as I do, that virtue terms are properly applied only as reasons are traded, corrected, and revised in exchanges that already exhibit, in some measure, the perfection of judgment and desire that the moral virtues provide. For my part, I find the relationship he assumes between practical reason, its principles, and the demands of morality untenable, and so too the central claims that follow from this assumption, including his account of tolerance as a virtue. As I said, our differences regard basic matters in ethical theory. They need to be resolved at that level, in a different kind of book.

lead. Or, as is more likely, appeal to principle will bring resolution only as
unjust violence is brought to bear against one collection of goods and loves
on behalf of some other. Still, it is not exactly clear what it means to say
that tolerance (or any other virtue for that matter) is natural, that it somehow emerges from our humanity and is somehow fitted to human life. At
the very least, it remains to be seen what kind of metaphysical apparatus we
are obliged to take on as we make this claim or what kind of moral commitments follow from the apparatus we eventually adopt. So too one wonders
whether that apparatus is compatible with the metaphysical commitments
we already have and whether the moral commitments it recommends com-
ports with those judgments about the good and the right, the virtuous and
the fine, that we cannot image forsaking.

In the end, it is this latter concern that will determine whether talk of natural virtue makes sense. Most of us have little control over the metaphysical
commitments that we happen to have or the basic moral judgments we are
inclined to make. Some deliberate revising is possible here, some recasting
there, but not much. If it turns out that talk of natural virtue makes sense only
as we adopt a collection of commitments that is in fact incompatible with the
other things we happen to believe about how the world hangs together in the
most general way, or if the moral judgments that follow from that collection
conflict with our most basic hunches about the just and the unjust, then we
will simply have to abandon that talk. Here I can only speculate, but I suspect
most of us will not find ourselves in this circumstance. Or, at the very least, I
have reason to hope that most will find the account of nature and virtue that
I develop below with the assistance of Aquinas and Wittgenstein both metaphysically manageable and morally palatable. No doubt, some will wonder
whether this hope can be sustained in the cultural context we find ourselves
in. Moral and metaphysical disagreement abounds and divisions among us
are considerable. Some of us are skittish about metaphysical commitment;
others are not. Some of us want to keep those commitments few and insubstantial, while others cannot imagine an acceptable account of human
nature that is not theologically rich and metaphysically robust. Given this
diversity, one wonders whether an account that satisfies one side of this divide
could avoid alienating the other. By the same token, one wonders whether
the moral commitments that follow from any particular account of human
nature, any specific collection of theological and metaphysical commitments,
could satisfy all comers. Disagreements about basic moral matters are common in societies like ours, and though they tend to be less substantial and
divisive than some have assumed, they remain nevertheless and what remains
tends to track our metaphysical and theological differences.

Given this context and these doubts, it is unlikely that my account of nature and virtue will satisfy all. How could it? Metaethical matters are conten-
tious and theological commitments are diverse and divisive. Those that regard

tolerance are no exception. Herman's efforts make this plain. Still, the aims
that I hope to achieve do seem to place certain constraints on contention and
division, or more precisely, on the measure of contention that can accompany
success. Since I hope to show that tolerance is a natural human virtue, that
most of us have good reason to think that it is, and that the problems it addresses tend to show up everywhere and always, it would seem that my efforts
can succeed only as my conclusions cross various moral and metaphysical divides. If tolerance shows up in human life naturally, then a truthful account
of its basic conceptual content, its essential ends, and ordinary actions ought
to be compatible with whatever moral and metaphysical commitments human beings happen to have, at least for the most part. This is, I admit, a rather
weighty demand upon success and a somewhat unfashionable aspiration to
have, but my confidence here has two sources.

First, the moral commitments that follow from the account of human
nature that I propose are largely grammatical. While they have substance
enough to be called commitments they are general enough to function most
prominently as rules that govern the use of certain moral terms, in this instance justice and tolerance. The claim is not simply that these terms show
up in some form everywhere and always, but that they appear only as certain moral commitments are made about the just and the unjust, the tolerable and the intolerable. Because these commitments are general, their
principal function is to specify what these concepts regard by marking
the outer boundary of intelligible use. The commitments do not specify
what will be said as these terms are employed within that boundary, nor
do they determine the particular judgments that will be made when they
are. Rather, they set the truth-conditions for meaningful speech, for basic
conceptual mastery. To make intelligible use of these concepts, to speak
about the specific matter that each regards, one must assume certain commitments and consider them true. If it happens that you do not, even as you
make noises about the just and the unjust or the tolerable and the intolerable, then the rest of us will wonder whether you have in fact mastered
these concepts. If you continue to make these noises in spite of our objections and in the absence of these commitments, we will have to cast about
for some other explanation for your behaviors. Perhaps you have mistaken
one concept for another and you are talking nonsense without knowing
it. Or perhaps the failure is ours, not yours. It could be that you are applying the concept in novel ways, and it could be that your novel application
loads conceptual content into the concept that makes it difficult for us to
see that you are in fact using a concept we share. This would be a failure of
our imagination. But the point remains the same: using a concept entails
taking on a certain collection of commitments that governs basic use. Failure to take on enough of that collection casts doubt on basic conceptual
mastery, and this applies to both novel and traditional applications. Novel

applications assume some continuity in basic commitment with traditional applications. Without that continuity we would not be able to recognize a novel application of the *same* concept.

On the metaphysical and theological side of the ledger, confidence comes from the fact that I solicit aid from both Aquinas's treatment of the natural law and Wittgenstein's account of what he calls *Gnade die Natur*, nature's grace. One offers a theologically robust description of the humanity we share, the other a metaphysically minimalist one, and yet both assume that a disposition to act in certain ways and to acquire and exercise certain virtues follows from that shared humanity, as does a tendency to make use of certain moral concepts. What matters at this point is the fact that these common consequences follow from such dissimilar sources. Nothing will be done to sort out these differences, and no effort will be made to uncover the warrants that might justify commitment to one source or the other. I have no interest in resolving the differences in assumption and judgment that divide these quite different metaphysical and theological points of view. In fact, I'm not certain what a resolution would look like or accomplish, and so I propose nothing exhaustive in this dual appeal. Other accounts of our shared humanity are certainly imaginable and so long as they generate something like these common consequences, my aims are satisfied.

That Wittgenstein's account of our common humanity is in fact metaphysically minimalist, few dispute. That Aquinas's account, embedded in his remarks on the natural law, has substantial theological content is something that some twentieth-century Thomists have tried to disregard, at times even to deny. Most have assumed that those remarks constitute a prescriptive ethical theory, one that specifies the basic moral principles that human beings ought to recognize but too often don't, that ought to govern our agency even as we too often refuse their rule. Guided by this assumption, too many exegetes have either ignored the theological content in Thomas's description of those actions and habits characteristic of our kind, or misidentified the anthropological motives that (in part) generate the description. There have been varying degrees of complicity in this mistreatment of Thomas, and some interpreters have done a better job than others in acknowledging the theological commitments at work in his remarks. Nevertheless, their aims have been largely shared: to take what is, in Thomas's hands, a description of divine jurisdiction over the internal sources of human action, of reason and will, and turn it into a moral theory in the modern mode. The hope is to locate a collection of moral principles that can be used in a regime of public reasoning and that can garner respect from secular moral philosophers, all under the cover of nature's authority.[26]

26 For an account of the emergence of Thomism in the modern period, see Hittinger, "Two Modernisms, Two Thomisms." For a history of the natural law tradition that puts Aquinas at the

The success of these efforts can be noted in the textbooks and histories of moral philosophy, where Thomas's remarks on the natural law are invariably included in moral theory's canon, and in the various schools of contemporary Thomism, where natural law theory holds sway.[27] By insisting, as I do, that Thomas's treatment of the natural law is more theological anthropology than philosophical moral theory, that its norms do not tell us how our agency ought to be governed but describe how it is, everywhere and always, ruled by God's judgment and ordered by God's command, my own efforts work against this tradition of interpretation. By arguing that this theological anthropology generates a kind of grammar and that the natural law's fundamental precepts are best regarded as basic rules of rationality in action and of intelligibility in speech about moral matters, my interpretation of Aquinas's remarks on the natural law is novel, and somewhat unusual.[28] Nevertheless, I hope my interpretation can be made plausible, perhaps even compelling, as those remarks are set against Wittgenstein's efforts. His account of the judging and acting that "is the substratum of all [our] enquiring and asserting" (*OC* 162) place him in roughly the same corner of the natural law tradition that Aquinas occupies, or so I argue.[29] Reversing the exegetical vectors, I claim that the relationship between the natural law's primary and secondary precepts, left artfully vague by Aquinas, can be spelled out in terms borrowed from Wittgenstein's treatment of conceptual mastery and material commitment. Both efforts involve what Richard Rorty calls rational reconstruction.[30] Both figures are treated as victims of time, training, and habit, as thinkers

---

center and that regards natural law theory as a hedge against tyranny, see Rommen, *Natural Law*. Rommen's views were widely shared among mid-twentieth-century European Thomists in North American exile. For doubts that Aquinas's remarks on the natural law can be teased apart from his theological commitments and then distilled into something equivalent to a moral theory, see Brock, "Legal Character of Natural Law" and Hittinger, *First Grace*.

27   For recent examples of natural law Thomism, see D'Entrèves, *Natural Law*; Finnis, *Natural Law and Natural Rights*; Grisez, "First Principle of Practical Reason"; Lisska, *Aquinas's Theory of Natural Law*; McInerny, *Aquinas on Human Action*; Porter, *Nature as Reason*; and Rhonheimer, *Natural Law and Practical Reason*. Notable exceptions to this consensus include Hall, *Narrative and the Natural Law*; Nelson, *Priority of Prudence*; and Rogers, *Aquinas and the Supreme Court*.

28   By "moral matters" I mean what Thomas does: matters that regard human action as such. Citing Ambrose, he says that as "morality is said properly of man, moral acts properly speaking receive their species from the end, for moral acts are the same as human acts" (*ST* I-II.1.3).

29   I make use of Wittgenstein, *On Certainty*, hereafter *OC*, and *Philosophical Investigations*, hereafter *PI*. Texts and translations are listed in the bibliography.

30   Rorty, "Historiography of Philosophy." In Brandom's idiom, when we interpret their words, the views we *ascribe* to them given their epistemic context are not always the views we *undertake* given our own. Brandom, *Tales of the Mighty Dead*, 94–106.

who might have put their remarks differently, in a new and improved vocabulary, had they been aware of what we know now. Rorty's examples of rational reconstruction look backward Whiggishly: Strawson on Kant, Bennett on the British Empiricists.[31] The conceptual content implicit in the views of the mighty dead is made explicit by situating those views in our own epistemic context and recasting them in a more recent idiom. But there is no reason why we cannot reverse the historical vectors as I do when I recast certain Wittgensteinian themes in Thomistic terms. At times the more recent can be reconstructed and improved by a past it did not know but would have benefited from knowing.

Benefit comes to us as well. These reconstructions allow us to see that both Aquinas and Wittgenstein reflect on the conduct, virtues, and moral concepts that distinguish our humanity and that find their origin in the form of life we lead according to our kind. Above all, reading them together, as members of this shared tradition of reflection, enables us see how justice can be regarded as one of those virtues, how it emerges in human life naturally, and how tolerance accompanies justice as one of its parts.

ACTION AND INTELLIGIBILITY

Pick up almost any history of moral philosophy and you will find a story about the natural law that goes something like this. In the beginning, Aristotle offered scattered remarks about the connections that obtain between our nature and our most basic moral obligations. Later, the Stoics tried and failed to gather together those remarks and spell out those connections. In the third century Ulpian made advances but left the task unfinished. Only in the hands of Thomas Aquinas did this project find its proper conclusion and this tradition its zenith. Soon after the death of Aquinas the tradition began to decay, and putrid it remained until the early modern period when it was revived by Suarez and Vitoria and updated by Pufendorf, Hobbes, and Locke. While the members of this long tradition disagree about the details of a successful natural law theory, they nevertheless share a common aim. They look to nature for moral guidance. They hope our common humanity will specify and then justify our most basic obligations. Nature, they insist, can tell us what we should do and why we should do it.[32] Indeed, it was doubts about these basic obligations, doubts elicited by the political crisis in Europe, that precipitated the revival of natural law theory in the

---

31 Bennett, *Locke, Berkeley, Hume*; Strawson, *Bounds of Sense*.

32 For a recent installment, see Schneewind, *Invention of Autonomy*, 17–36. For a more nuanced story about the natural law in the early modern period, see Brett, *Changes of State*, 11–114.

mid-twentieth century. In the words of perhaps the greatest of the revivalists, Heinrich Rommen, "the natural law doctrine became willy-nilly the ideological basis of the struggle against totalitarianism."[33] One turns to the natural law in order to answer skeptics and thugs with the authoritative call of nature.

Pick up almost any recent treatment of Aquinas's account of the natural law and you will find this story confirmed. Most exegetes agree that the first precepts of the natural law, spelled out in *ST* I-II.94.2, provide a general outline of the human good from which specific obligations can be derived and the skeptic's challenge met. But textbook histories can be unreliable and exegetical consensus often masks complacency. In this instance, both hunches are confirmed, or so I will argue. For reasons spelled out in this section, we should not think that Aquinas offers theoretical comfort to the morally anxious, to those who can doubt our most basic moral commitments, their character and warrants. We should not think that he provides a moral theory of this sort or has interests that would require one. Skeptical doubts about basic obligations did not trouble Aquinas, and they did not take on their modern form until Montaigne's essays and Hume's *Treatise* shaped a quite different intellectual culture, one that placed quite different burdens on its philosophers and critics.[34] The burdens Aquinas bears are principally theological. He offers his remarks about the natural law and its first precepts in order to say how human action and its internal principles, reason and will, are created by God and governed by providence. All things fall under divine jurisdiction, even human action, reason, and will. The difficulty, the task Thomas takes up, is to say how our agency is created and ruled even as it remains our own.

Once we locate Aquinas's efforts in theological context, the interpretation that follows should constrain our rational reconstructions of those efforts. We can, of course, reconstruct the views of our favorite philosophers and theologians as we please, and most of us do. Most of us want our contemporary puzzles addressed by our long dead heroes. Still, some rational reconstructions are more plausible than others, and in this instance contextualized interpretation sets the constraints. When textbooks and Thomists insist that Aquinas's remarks on the natural law are designed to address skeptical worries, we should insist that they have confused rational reconstruction for contextual exegesis, commitments undertaken by us for commitments properly ascribed to him. Once those remarks are properly contextualized and ascribed, we can see why they are difficult to reconstruct as a response to skepticism. We can see that Aquinas is best regarded as incapable of thinking that the skeptic's doubts about obligation deserve an

33   Rommen, *Natural Law*, 135.

34   From Augustine (*c. Acad.* II and *Trin.* 10.10.14), Aquinas was acquainted with ancient skepticism, but he never took up its concerns.

answer. It is an alternative reconstruction of his efforts that generate this conclusion, but one more plausible than the reconstructions of the exegetical consensus precisely because it begins where contextual interpretation leaves off.

That interpretation, in brief outline, goes like this.[35] Agency specifies being, and law governs agency. Everything is what it is and not some other thing because of the character of its agency, because of the ends it pursues and the manner in which it pursues them. Law governs agency—it rules and measures what is done—by specifying these ends, determining this manner, and binding the agent to them. On this rendering, a law is nothing but a deliverance of practical reason, a dictate of a ruler. It determines the ends and actions of those within its jurisdiction, and it commands their obedience (*ST* I-II.90.1–4; 91.1). With these assumptions in hand, Aquinas treats the ends that we apprehend and will naturally as effects of God's eternal law. The fallout is an account of creation and providence as they pertain to human beings and human actions (*ST* I-II.91.1–2).

Creation regards the individuation of things, providence their governance. Both follow from God's practical judgment about the ends that a creature should pursue and the way it should pursue them (*ST* I.22.1).[36] Since a law is a "dictate of practical reason", an authoritative judgment about actions and ends, Aquinas maintains that God creates and governs all things by framing laws (*ST* I-II.91.1; 93.1). The eternal law is the collection of those dictates and creation's diversity and multiplicity follow from the diverse ways that God's many creatures participate in that law "from its being imprinted on them" (*ex impressione eius*) (*ST* I-II.91.2). Everything is what it is and not some other thing because it participates in the eternal law in one way and not another, directed by God's judgment and bound by God's law to act for the sake of some ends but not others (*ST* I-II.91.2; *SCG* III.4–5). A swallow, for example, is the creature that it is, not an eagle, fish, or slug, precisely because it participates in God's eternal law as only swallows do.[37] Its actions and passions are directed toward certain ends, such as nest building, by certain means, with mud and grass, not sticks and stones. And a swallow becomes a perfect instance of the sort of thing that it is, a good swallow according to its kind, when, by virtue of its swallow-like participation in the eternal law, it acts in swallow-like ways and secures its proper ends. It flourishes as swallows should

---

35   What follows is an abridged version of Bowlin, *Contingency and Fortune in Aquinas's Ethics*, 121–127.

36   Aquinas considers providence akin to prudential judgment, but there are differences. The prudent take counsel, while God has no need of "an inquiry into matters that are doubtful." Nevertheless, counsel concludes in "a command as to the right ordering of things towards an end," and this is the work of providence (*ST* I.22.1.1).

37   The example is Aquinas's. See *De vert.* 24.1.

when it acts as swallows do, in ways that are perfective of its nature, a nature created and governed by God's law.

The creation and governance of human beings follows a similar pattern. God's practical judgment directs us to apprehend certain ends, to consider them good, and to be inclined toward them in accord with that knowledge. We tend to these ends naturally, which is to say necessarily, and this particular collection of ends—knowledge, friendship, survival, and so on—is one of the things that distinguishes our agency (*ST* I-II.10.1; 94.2). The other is the knowledge with which we act (*ST* I-II. 91.2). Acting with knowledge entails knowing the ends we will naturally and necessarily in a manner that permits deliberation over the means (*ST* I-II.6.1–2). And since the ability to deliberate, to compare one course of action with another, assumes a certain indeterminacy of agency, we are not bound by God's eternal law to intend any one of the ends that we will naturally or choose any particular means to any particular end we come to intend (*ST* I-II.10.2; 14.1). It is precisely because knowledge of this kind mediates our participation in the eternal law that we are able to act voluntarily and in all sorts of particular ways. And it is precisely because swallows act without deliberative knowledge of the ends characteristic of their kind that their actions are neither voluntary nor diverse. Instead, they have a small repertoire of actions that they must perform insofar as they are swallows. So too, our ability to act knowingly explains why we are rational creatures and they are not (*ST* I-II.6.1–2; 91.6). For when pressed for an account of what we have done, we can provide reasons in defense of our intentions and choices, reasons that refer to ends and means that are known to be good and pursued because of that knowledge.

Aquinas sums up this difference by saying that rational creatures, those who participate in God's eternal law by knowing its demands, act according to the natural law. "The natural law," he insists, "is nothing else than the rational creature's participation of the eternal law" (*ST* I-II.91.2). Other creatures participate in the eternal law, but not in a rational manner and therefore it cannot be said that the actions characteristic of their kind, their natural actions, are performed in response to its normative demands. "A law is something pertaining to reason," and thus strictly speaking it can rule and measure those subject to it only as they know its demands (*ST* I-II.90.1; 91.2 and ad 3). Because providence makes demands upon rational creatures by giving them natural and habitual knowledge of the ends characteristic of their kind, what Aquinas calls *synderesis* (*ST* I.79.12; I-II.94.1.2), they participate in God's practical judgment—in God's eternal law—by becoming provident themselves, by making their own practical judgments as they direct their own actions.[38] And since a law is nothing but a dictate of practical reason,

---

38   Regarding operations, habits are twofold. Perfectly and essentially, a habit disposes a power to act in this way or that. But the term "may also be applied to that which we hold by

our participation in God's practical judgment is called the natural law in us, whereby we become provident over the actions characteristic of our kind by sharing God's judgment about our proper ends (*ST* I-II.91.2; I.22.1).

Thus to say, as Thomas does, that human beings act in accord with the natural law is to say something about human agency as such, created by God and governed by providence. It is to say, on the one hand, that knowledge generates our natural inclinations, knowledge of those ends "naturally apprehended by reason as being good," and that this knowledge moves us to act in ways that are characteristically human (*ST* I-II.94.2). On the other, it is to say that human actions are rational precisely because of this knowledge, this judgment we share in common with God about our good. It follows that every human action, whether good or evil, participates in the eternal law and accords with the natural law in some minimal sense (*ST* I-II.91.2.1).[39] Every human action is done knowingly and for the sake of a specific instance of one of the ends to which we are inclined naturally, one of the goods that we will simply and absolutely.[40] It might also be done to avoid the loss of one of these goods, but no matter. In all that we do, the first precept of the natural law is fulfilled, the most basic requirement of rationality in human action is satisfied. Some human good is pursued or some evil is avoided (*ST* I-II.94.2), and it is knowledge of the human good, natural and habitual, that generates both our desire to act and the reasons we offer in defense of what we do.

Notice how little determinate moral guidance this account of the natural law's first precepts provides. Concrete obligations receive neither specification nor justification. The content of right reason in specific cases is neither outlined nor defined. Instead, Aquinas maps the full range of human agency, rational and voluntary, both good and evil, as he describes "all those things to which man has a natural inclination, are naturally apprehended as good, and consequently as objects of pursuit" (*ST* I-II.94.2). "Actions" that fall outside of this range will be unnatural in the most basic sense: they will not be

---

habit," and in this sense *synderesis* is a habit. It is not a habit by which we are disposed to know the first precepts of the natural law. Nor are those precepts the habit itself whereby they are held. Rather, we hold these precepts habitually, such that sometimes they are "considered by reason actually, while sometimes they are in the reason only habitually" (*ST* I-II.94.1). It is in this sense that *synderesis*, "the law of our mind," is also a habit (*ST* I-II.94.1.2).

39   This is true of the passions as well. Insofar as they are, in some minimal way, ruled by reason, they also belong to the natural law (*ST* I-II.94.2.2).

40   Even actions done in weakness or ignorance, insofar as they are actions—which is to say rational and thus voluntary—are done for the sake of some end that is known to be good. In these cases, it is not the right end, the *bonum honestum*, the good that right reason would pick out in that particular circumstance, but it nevertheless remains good in some way. Ignorance and weakness are sources of erroneous judgment about the human good, not absolute alienation from it.

human, indeed they will not be actions. They will not be done for the sake
of one of the ends that distinguish our agency, our humanity. They will not
be rational and intelligible precisely because they will not be ordered to an
end that is known to be good by the agent who acts, an end that can be offered as a reason in response to doubt or puzzlement about what was done.
Thus Aquinas insists that, "the precepts of the natural law are to the practical reason, what the first principles of demonstrations are to the speculative
reason" (ibid.). Just as the principle of noncontradiction is assumed in all
human knowing, so too the first precepts of the natural law are assumed in
all human action. Consistent failure to reason and judge in accord with the
principle of noncontradiction yields, not false belief, but something more
fundamental: basic alienation from the ordinary human capacity to reason and judge, to believe and know. In the same way, consistent failure to
act knowingly for the sake of the human good, for the sake of one of the
ends specified by the primary precepts of natural law, yields, not unjust action, but something more fundamental: nothing that can be recognized as
human action. It would be unintelligible *as action*, more akin to madness
than to rational agency.

If this interpretation is sound, then Aquinas is hardly the sort of natural
law theorist one finds in the textbooks and histories. Nor is Wittgenstein for
that matter, and yet if Aquinas is a natural lawyer of some sort, so too is Wittgenstein. Like Aquinas, he has no interest in defending a moral theory that
will tell us what we are obliged to do.[41] Rather, like Aquinas, he hopes to
mark the boundary between sense and nonsense, between intelligible human action and madness. He wants to describe those necessities that specify
the human character of our acting in the broadest possible terms. And like
Aquinas, he wants to say what's given in human life, what is natural to us in
judgment, inclination, and conduct.

For the sake of argument I will assume that Part I of the *Philosophical
Investigations* generates something like the following conclusion. We have
been held captive by a certain picture of language. We have assumed that
language is a medium of expression and representation. In fact, it is not—
meaning is neither an intention expressed in language nor a state of affairs
represented by language. Truth is neither accurate representation of the
world, nor faithful expression of internal states. Rather, language is a tool
that helps creatures like us get on in the world doing this and that. One grabs

41 Aquinas does make judgments about specific courses of action, and some of those judgments are conclusions derived from the first principles of the natural law. But we should not
think that he refers to the natural law's first precepts in order to justify those conclusions,
as if they were in doubt. As I shall argue in the next section, the relation between primary
precepts and proper conclusions regards the grammar of certain moral concepts, not the
justification of basic moral judgments.

hold of a concept—one understands how to use it well—only as one comes to understand how it contributes to the success of some activity, to the pursuit of some collection of ends.

Imagine I want to teach my one-year-old son how to understand the word "spoon."[42] Picking up a large wooden spoon, pointing to it dramatically, and saying "spoon!" in my most authoritative voice will do little good. It will not help him grasp the concept. He might imitate my voice and expression, but when I hand him the spoon he will most likely use it to swat the cat, or dig in the mud, or terrorize his older brother. "No, no, no I will say, it's a spoon, it's a spoon, don't you see. We use it for eating, like this," as I thrust my spoon into a bowl of oatmeal and take an exaggerated bite. "You do it," I'll say, "give it a try." And of course, he will try; only he will use the spoon to lift oatmeal out of his bowl and on to the floor. Then he will try the same trick on the oatmeal in his brother's bowl. And finally, he will lift the spoon high over his head while making unintelligible noises. Oh well. The truth is, at this juncture, he does not see the point of using a spoon as I do, and it is precisely this inability that prevents him from using the concept. He simply does not know what a spoon is. If, however, after much training, practice, correction, and imitation he does come to see the point of acting as I do, then he will also come to understand the word as I do. Wittgenstein's insight—captured in his famous image, *Sprachspiel*—is that these are related matters (*PI* 7). One grasps a concept only as one comes to see the point of certain activities and concedes the truth of certain moral and empirical judgments. My son will grasp the concept "spoon" only as he acknowledges that eating in certain ways is good, presumably with utensils and not with one's hands, and that the human community made possible by using a spoon for eating is more desirable than the fleeting pleasure one receives in flinging oatmeal and attacking cats with spoon-like implements. In addition to these judgments about the goodness of certain ends and activities, he must also assume the truth of a vast collection of claims about the world that circumscribes the activity of using spoons for eating. Spoons do not disappear and reappear by magic. People do not disappear when they pick up spoons. Spoons do not bite. His own hand picks up the spoon. His father, the spoon master, does not have sawdust where his brain should be, and so on (*OC* 159, 207).

The conclusion we should draw regards the foundation of our linguistic~~✗~~ *world* practices. At bedrock are certain ways of thinking and acting that presuppose certain moral and ontological commitments. ~~These~~ commitments are given. They are not chosen, but accepted and trusted in advance of all utterance and activity. We are justified in undertaking these commitments, not because good reasons warrant them, but rather because none are more

42   I once had a son of this age, two of them in fact, but now they are grown. See chapter 3.

certain. Our epistemic confidence in these commitments is so high that they function more as rules of linguistic usage than as bits of knowledge (*PI* 251; *OC* 124, 136). Returning to my example, one cannot use the word "spoon" as we do without first conceding that spoons do not bite and that food is worth having. How do we know that they do not bite? Well, they just don't. How do we know that food is worth having? Well, it just is. And if you are uncertain here, about these matters, it is not clear how we can respond. Why? Because these doubts indicate that your grasp of the concept is insufficient for ordinary conversation about spoons (*OC* 126). In fact, if you press your strange doubts, it is likely that the rest of us will respond by discounting either your sincerity or your basic rationality (*OC* 154–155, 219–220).

Here a distinction is needed. The moral and ontological commitments that help constitute our linguistic practices are of two kinds. Some are conventional. They are shared by the inhabitants of some linguistic communities, but not all. Thus, for example, in my linguistic community spoons are used principally for eating food, not digging dirt, not swatting cats. Nonetheless, other linguistic communities are perfectly imaginable, communities in which the word "spoon" or its equivalent finds its meaning in the garden, not at the breakfast table. On the other hand, some of the moral and ontological commitments that constitute our linguistic bedrock are given, not by convention, but by nature. They are judgments that form the foundation of all our linguistic practices, all human speech and conduct (*OC* 558). Judgments of this sort mark the outer boundary of what Wittgenstein calls the *Lebensform* that we share by virtue of the fact that we are a creature of one sort but not another, a creature that does some kinds of things but not others in the world as we find it.

Return again to eating. To participate in this activity, to understand its goals and make use of its concepts, one must accept certain judgments. Food stops hunger. Satisfying hunger is good. Food sustains life. Life is good, and so on. The person who doubts these judgments cannot self-consciously participate in the activity we call eating. She cannot speak of food and hunger, of pain and relief. And, insofar as she cannot speak sensibly about these matters or offer reasons that make her actions intelligible by referring to these goods, we will be hard-pressed to confirm the rationality of her speaking and acting. And since doubting is an activity pursued by rational human beings, it is not exactly clear how her "doubts" fall under that activity. One can have doubts about a particular account of how food stops hunger, sustains life, or ranks among other goods. About these matters, disagreement is common and nature is silent. About these matters, doubt is both possible and possibly rational. And, as rationality goes, so too goes the ability to sustain real doubt. But the person who "doubts" that food stops hunger cannot speak, act, and give reasons for acting in matters related to food as rational human beings do. This, in turn, calls into question her basic rationality, if not in general, then at least with respect to this corner of human life.

Wittgenstein puts the matter this way in *On Certainty*:

> 154. There are cases such that, if someone gives signs of doubts where we do not doubt, we cannot confidently understand his signs as signs of doubt. I.e., if we are to understand his signs of doubt as such, he may give them in particular cases and may not give them in others.

> 155. In certain circumstances a man cannot make a mistake. ("Can" is here used logically, and the proposition does not mean that a man cannot say anything false in those circumstances.) If Moore were to pronounce the opposite of those propositions which he declares certain, we should not just not share his opinion: we should regard him as demented.[43]

The point is this: the shared linguistic competence that comes packaged with our common humanity depends on our acceptance of a collection of moral and ontological commitments, a collection of judgments about the goodness of certain ends and the truth of certain empirical propositions. Those judgments set us about pursuing certain activities, some of which are given with our humanity. They are the kinds of things that we do in the form of life we happen to lead and in the world we find ourselves inhabiting. Like the first precepts of the natural law, these judgments and activities mark the outer boundary of rational speech and human conduct. That boundary is simply "there—like our life" (*OC* 559).

Here it should be noted that some interpreters resist this conclusion, this effort to find Wittgenstein concerned with the connection between our common linguistic capacity and our shared natural history. Most find Wittgenstein defending the existence of multiple human languages embedded in multiple human forms of life. On this interpretation, a form of life is largely equivalent to a culture or a conceptual scheme. Its boundaries are set by convention, not nature. Its consequence is a language used by some human beings but not all. This view has become a kind of orthodoxy in some quarters, and yet I think it is mistaken.[44] There is little evidence that Wittgenstein thinks in these terms. When he speaks of *Lebensformen*, his attention is typically fixed, not on the diversity of human cultures and conventions, but

---

43   See also *PI* 288.

44   Other dissenters include Cavell, *Claim of Reason*, 86–128; Incandela, "Appropriation of Wittgenstein's Work"; and Lovibond, *Realism and Imagination in Ethics*. Support for the view of language assumed by the dissenters can be found in Davidson, "On the Very Idea of a Conceptual Scheme."

rather on the differences that divide human beings from other animals. His concern is with those features that distinguish our life from theirs, above all those features that make language possible. His remarks are designed to describe the collection of activities, powers, frailties, and judgments that specify our humanity and generate our most basic linguistic practices. Apart from that collection, we would not be kind of animal that we are, and we would not speak and act as we do.

Consider the following remarks, the first three from the *Philosophical Investigations*, the remainder from *On Certainty*.

19. And to imagine a language means to imagine a form of life.

25. It is sometimes said that animals do not talk because they lack the mental capacity. And this means: "they do not think, and that is why they do not talk." But—they simply do not talk. Or to put it better: they do not use language—if we accept the most primitive forms of language.—Commanding, questioning, recounting, chatting, are as much a part of our natural history as walking, eating, drinking, playing.

384. You learned the *concept* 'pain' when you learned language.

357. One might say: "'I know' expresses *comfortable* certainty, not the certainty that is still struggling."

358. Now I would like to regard this certainty, not as something akin to hastiness or superficiality, but as a form of life.

359. But that means I want to conceive it as something that lies beyond being justified or unjustified; as it were, as something animal.

360. I know that this is my foot. I could not accept any experience as proof to the contrary.—That may be an exclamation; but what *follows* from it? At least that I shall act with a certainty that knows no doubt, in accordance with my belief.

475. I want to regard man here as an animal; as a primitive being to which one grants instinct but not ratiocination. As a creature in a primitive state. Any logic good enough for a primitive means of communication needs no apology from us. Language did not emerge from some kind of ratiocination.

The remarks from the *Philosophical Investigations* highlight the connection between acting in human kinds of ways, mastering certain concepts, and speaking as human beings do. The remarks from *On Certainty* highlight the connection between acting and speaking as human beings do and conceding the truth of certain judgments. Both sets of remarks accent the natural character of certain activities and judgments in the form of life human beings happen to lead. Both are designed to show how language is embedded in our nature and how our nature is distinguished by a certain collection of actions and judgments that form the bedrock of our language.

At this point, I hope I have said enough to justify my hunch that Wittgenstein's remarks about the natural history of our linguistic practices have a striking resemblance to Aquinas's account of the first precepts of the natural law. Both efforts are designed to specify the necessities that constitute our humanity, the actions and judgments that distinguish our human form of life from the life that nonhuman creatures lead. This much seems plain enough. At the same time, one might wonder whether Wittgenstein offers a *natural law* account of our common humanity. A law, according to Aquinas, is a dictate of practical reason, a command that something be done, that some end be pursued. It is a dictate designed to bring about right relations among persons, and it is promulgated by one who has authority to make this command and set right these relations. Aquinas can say that our nature is created and governed by law precisely because he believes in a God who creates and governs all things, even human actions and relations. Wittgenstein, by contrast, does not assume the existence of this kind of God. Still, he knows that the necessities he describes—the judgments we must maintain and the ends we must desire—give the appearance of being the effects of a lawgiver's command. Consider the following remarks from *On Certainty*.[45]

> 172. Perhaps someone says "There must be some basic principle on which we accord credence", but what can such a principle accomplish? Is it more than a natural law of 'taking for true'?

> 361. But I might also say: It has been revealed to me by God that it is so. God has taught me that this is my foot. And therefore if anything happened that seemed to conflict with this knowledge I should have to regard *that* as deception.

> 505. It is always by nature's grace that one knows something.

> 670. We might speak of fundamental principles of human enquiry.

I do not want to make too much of what is said here. In Wittgenstein's hands the natural law has no theological substance. At the same time, he clearly uses the image of a divine lawgiver, of one who imprints certain necessities

---

45   *OC* 505 reads: "Es ist immer von Gnade der Natur, wenn man etwas weiß." I have altered Anscombe's translation, rendering "Gnade" as "grace," not "favor."

upon our intellect and will, in order to signal the necessity of believing certain things and desiring certain ends in order to speak and act as we do, as the creatures that we are. When set against Aquinas's efforts, this image does acquire a certain power and vitality.

"Is it more than a natural law of 'taking for true'?" In the remarks that come before and after this one, Wittgenstein cajoles us into conceding that our ability to provide explicit justification for what we believe comes to an end in certain activities. These activities come packaged with certain judgments that we consider true because we trust certain authorities (OC 159–161). When we resist and ask for some prior principle that we could use to assess the credibility of the authorities we trust, Wittgenstein responds with more cajoling. If language cannot be used without accepting certain judgments on authority, judgments that give our concepts substance, then no principle of credibility can escape this dependence upon trust. At best, such a principle could do no more than point out that language-using creatures like us must take certain judgments for true (OC 191, 205–206). Nature requires no less.

"God has taught me that this is my foot." In the remarks that precede this one (OC 357–359; noted above, p. 88), Wittgenstein speaks of the beliefs we must accept and the actions we must pursue if we are to speak and act human beings do. Here, remarkably, he uses the image of a divine lawgiver's authority over our knowing and willing to describe these necessities. This could be Aquinas speaking, but with credulity. God imprints certain judgments about the good upon our hearts by gentle persuasion. God constitutes our nature as he instructs the intellect and courts the will, not like a tyrant, but like a teacher who "orders all things sweetly" (*disponit omnia suaviter*) (*ST* I.22.2 *sed contra*; II-II.23.2; 165.1).[46]

"It is always by nature's grace that one knows something." This remark weds the language of natural necessity and external cause to the language of grace. We know certain things and act in certain ways because we are creatures of certain sort. Not chosen, not earned, our human way of knowing and acting is given. The proper response is gratitude, and gratitude begins with the simple recognition that the internal sources of human action have external causes. Aquinas would put it this way: the knowing and acting that distinguish our nature and that generate the speaking and doing characteristic of our kind are unmerited gifts, real evidence of God's self-giving love for us. What we know and do by nature are the first effects of this divine help, this first grace (*ST* I-II.109.1–2).

---

46   The image regarding providential rule comes from Book of Wisdom 8:1. From the Latin Vulgate: *adtingit enim a fine usque ad finem fortiter et disponit omnia suaviter* ("She reaches therefore, from end to end mightily, and orders all things sweetly").

And finally: "We might speak of fundamental principles of human en-quiry." Here, Wittgenstein refers to those moral and ontological commit-ments that one must accept in order to speak, act, and enquire as human beings do, which is precisely how Aquinas regards the natural law's basic precepts. A principle is, for Aquinas, a rule or starting point of action. When it is determined and dictated by one party, known and accepted by another, it is a law. The natural law provides rules of action, precisely because its pre-cepts are known and accepted by us as principles that guide all our thinking and speaking about acting.

NATURAL JUSTICE

Suppose Wittgenstein's remarks about the natural history of our speaking and acting can be brought together in this way with Aquinas's remarks about the natural law's first precepts, shedding mutually useful light. Suppose we conclude that both Aquinas and Wittgenstein attend to what is given in human life, to what is antecedent to all thinking, speaking, and acting, while refusing to look to what is naturally given for concrete moral guidance. Put another way, suppose both assume that nature's grace is always at work, its moral reality everywhere present, there to be acknowledged. How might the exegetical consensus reply? Perhaps by pointing out that Aquinas appears to break ranks when he notes that we derive a small collection of *conclusiones* "from the general principles of the natural law" (*ST* I-II.95.2). He mentions the prohibitions against harming, killing, stealing, lying, and the like (*ST* I-II.100.1). Given this observation, one might reasonably ask how can it be said, as I do, that Aquinas has no interest in answering the moral skeptic. How can it be said that he refuses to locate and justify our most basic ob-ligations when he appears to do precisely that as he derives secondary pre-cepts of the natural law from the first?

Well, the first thing to note is that Aquinas lived largely untouched by skepticism's challenge. He never had to decide whether the moral skeptic de-serves to be answered or ignored. Since Wittgenstein *did* have to decide, and since I am reconstructing Aquinas's views in conversation with his, the objec-tion can be addressed to each. Why do they think that skepticism about fun-damental moral matters is not a real option, at least not for most of us? Why do they think that worries of this kind are best bypassed, not answered? Well, imagine Wittgenstein and a moral skeptic cross paths. How might Wittgen-stein reply? Perhaps as he does in *On Certainty*. Pick a basic moral judgment, any one will do. Torturing children for fun is cruel and horrific. Killing the innocent is unjust. When the skeptic asks for reasons that warrant these judg-ments, we should respond as we did to Herman. The reasons we might offer in reply and the moral theory we might propose when pressed—whether a natural law theory or some other variety—would be far more dubious than the judgments they are asked to justify. And if this is right, if no precept or theory can address doubts about the justice of torturing children or killing the innocent, then there is little reason to offer a reply. At some point, justification must come to an end (*OC* 204).

To be sure, this conclusion leaves the skeptic's doubts unanswered, but no matter. There is little reason to think that they are genuine, even if the temptations they pose are real.[47] As before it is Wittgenstein who points the way. When the skeptic asks whether it is just to torture children or kill the innocent, we should reply by asking whether he knows what "justice" is, whether he knows what the concept entails. It is a reasonable question. If someone holds up his hand and wonders out loud whether it is *his* hand, we will most likely dismiss the doubt. He must be joking or hallucinating or speaking in code because if he persists, and if his rationality and sincerity remain intact, then we will be compelled to ask whether he knows what a hand is. His failure to assume the truth of certain basic judgments about hands casts doubt upon his basic understanding of the concept. If he doubts that the hand attached to his arm is in fact his own, and if we assume sincerity in what he says, then it is unlikely that he knows what "hand" means. It is unlikely that he knows how to make proper use of the concept (*OC* 369–370). Wittgenstein spells out the proper conclusion: in certain instances "the *truth* of my statements is the test of my understanding of these statements" (*OC* 80). Confronted with glaring falsehoods or unimaginable doubts, we cast about for an explanation that saves the linguistic competence of our interlocutor. "He doubts that it is his hand!! Well, he must be teasing or intoxicated or play acting or something, for if it turns out that he's serious, well, in that event, we will have to conclude that he does not understand what he is saying, that he does not know what a hand is. We will have to conclude that his doubts are, in fact, confusions" (cf. *OC* 81).

Returning again to our moral skeptic, he will likely reply that he knows what "justice" means, that he has sufficient acquaintance with the concept to press his doubts. He is not a fool, he will insist. He understands that justice involves giving to others the good they are due by right. He simply wants to know why we should think that torturing children and killing the innocent fail to deliver that due. He wants to know whether these actions represent basic transgressions of justice, or not. But this can't be right. If he has basic grasp of the concept, then he has accepted a collection of judgments about particular instances of just and unjust conduct, judgments that he considers true, that he cannot doubt without losing sight of the concept. Included

---

47   For an account of those temptations and for Wittgensteinian sources of resistance, see Cavell, *Claim of Reason*, pt. 3.

in that collection we will surely find the judgment that torturing children for fun is vile or that killing the innocent is unjust. Or, if not these, then we will find some other short list of moral banalities that give "justice" its conceptual form, banalities that most of us concede and that find expression in much of what we say, do, and feel in response to human relations set right by just acts or deformed by injustice.

Note well the tight connection between judgments assumed, concept deployed, and the capacity to act and feel in certain ways. In some measure, all three arrive as nature's grace. If concepts are embedded in activities, then basic mastery of "justice" not only requires taking on certain commitments about the just and the unjust but also participation in a collection of activities that express and bear witness to these commitments. Fail to take on those commitments and you can't make use of the concept. Consistently fail to participate in those activities or to act and feel in accord with those commitments, and it is unlikely that we can assign the concept to you. The point regards basic concept mastery not perfection in virtue. Most of us know how to use the concept precisely because we participate in the activities that just actions perfect: exchanges, promise making, distributions, and all equivalent matters that mediate our relations with each other and that configure the communities in which we reside. So too, most of us manage to give to others the good they are due by right most of the time and to feel outrage at the most obvious injustices and horror at the most grievous. Consistently fail in this—in participation, exercise, or passionate response—and it's unlikely that we can assign the concept to you. Succeed in this and the concept will be in evidence but not necessarily the virtue. For the latter, we will need to know whether you act justly in the most difficult circumstances, where goods conflict and losses mount, and whether you exhibit passions of the right kind and intensity in response to many instances of just and unjust conduct. We will also need to gauge your commitment to the goodness of justice itself, to the intrinsic value of its acts, principles, and outcomes.

From all of this it follows that our skeptic is either someone who knows not what justice is, who needs to be taught before he can produce real doubts about concrete cases, or, as is more likely, someone who trades in false doubt, who has grasped the concept well enough to be expected to know that there can be no uncertainty in *these* particular cases. In that event, he is also someone who can be expected to know that *warranted* uncertainty about *other* cases requires confidence here. He can't have *real* doubts about the justice of particular actions or real disputes about basic application of the term without having first acquired the concept, and he cannot acquire and deploy the concept without leaving certain judgments about the just and unjust beyond dispute, at least for now. However we diagnose his condition or interpret his remarks, he deserves no theoretical effort in reply.

Aquinas, I suggest, would justify his disregard for the skeptic's doubts in roughly the same terms, and it is precisely these terms that can help us understand the notoriously obscure relation between the natural law's primary and secondary precepts. There are ironies here. The exegetical consensus finds Thomas's reply to the moral skeptic in precisely this relation. But in fact, his reply is hard to locate, the need for it hard to see, once his treatment of the natural law's primary precepts has been situated in theological context and once his account of its secondary precepts has been reconstructed in these Wittgensteinian terms.

Like Wittgenstein, Aquinas thinks that most of us understand "justice" well enough to use the concept competently and to speak about it intelligibly. If we have acquired a human language, act and feel as human beings do, and live among others in a community of some sort, we will know what justice is, at least in broad outline, and a good portion of what we know will be shared in common with most human beings. And like Wittgenstein, he assumes that concepts are acquired only as certain judgments are accepted, judgments that give a concept its basic form. It follows that for Aquinas, as for Wittgenstein, the ability to speak intelligibly about justice and to apply the concept competently in ordinary cases precludes global doubt about its most basic features. If we understand what justice is we cannot doubt those basic judgments about obligation and entitlement that constitute the rational form of the concept we claim to understand.

These are empirical claims. Aquinas finds human beings using the languages of justice whenever and wherever they craft a life together. He also finds considerable agreement among us. When asked about justice, about human relations set right, we tend to say and do similar kinds of things. No doubt, we have always disagreed about the specifics of just exchanges and relations and the details of commutations and distributions. All this is well known and frequently noted. Less obvious, and often ignored, is the fact that disagreements of all kinds take place against a broad backdrop of agreement in concept and judgment, meaning and truth. So, for example, my neighbor and I cannot disagree about the proper location of the fence that will divide our properties without sharing a whole collection of concepts and judgments that set the terms of the dispute. If it turns out that he does not know what fences are for, then our disagreement is more apparent than real. If the specific judgments that give substance to his concept "property" are substantially different from mine, then it is not disagreement that divides us, but confusion. Disputes about just distributions, exchanges, and relations will proceed in the same way. They will presuppose basic agreement about "justice," about the specific judgments that give the concept substance and the specific examples that identify its proper use. To those who wonder whether this agreement in judgment and use actually obtains Aquinas has little to say. He can point out that the desire to render to each the good that each is due by right can be found in all human communities, and he can remind us that we could neither recognize this fact, nor share this desire without finding considerable overlap between our account of justice, with its specific material content, and every other. But this is not much of a reply. It is, rather, an invitation to go and look.

Look around and we will notice that human beings are creatures of one sort and not another, that we act in ways characteristic of our kind precisely because we know and will a small collection of ends naturally and necessarily. We will also notice that each end marks a sphere of human conduct, an order of deliberation and choice, and that one such sphere regards our life together, our natural desire for human society (*ST* I-II.94.2). Look around again and we will find human beings in all times and places concerned with justice, with relations set right among those with whom they share some sort of society, set right through distributions and exchanges (*ST* II-II.57.1; 58.3). We will also find that all human beings concede the truth of a small set of precepts that regard right relations, a small collection of prohibitions and prescriptions that specify the basic shape of the concept (*ST* I-II.95.2; 100.1).

These are related matters. Justice comes packaged with society and concepts come packaged with commitments. If our nature inclines us to form social and political relationships, then it must also incline us to care about justice, about right relations among persons and about the common good that is shared when relations are set right.[48] And if it inclines us to care about justice, to acquire basic mastery of the concept, then it must also command assent to those basic commitments or precepts that give the concept substance. No doubt we will also find some difference of opinion about those commitments and precepts, but this should neither surprise nor worry us. Secondary precepts of the natural law are conclusions derived from its primary precepts "with very little consideration" (*cum modica consideratione*) (*ST* I-II.100.1; cf. 100.3), and in some few cases (*ut in paucioribus*) some human beings may consider things differently (*ST* I-II.94.4). Some might even make basic mistakes. On Caesar's authority (*BGall.* vi.16), Thomas tells us that the Germanic tribes beyond the Danube had not derived the prohibition against theft from the first and most general principles of the natural law (*ST* I-II.94.4). Still, these differences cannot go all the way down without losing sight of the concept we share. All of us must concede the truth of some basic *conclusiones* about right relations among persons in order to make use of the

---

48   These are also related matters. The proper object of justice is right action or work that mediates relations between persons, that sets their relationship right (*ST* II-II.57.1–2; 58.2). This is what justice is properly about. So too this relationship set right and shared in common among those who are party to it is the common good that justice principally regards, especially in political relationships (*ST* II-II.58.9.3). Both remarks concern the grammar of the concept "justice."

concept "justice," and we can recognize that the concept is used across our species precisely because of our substantial agreement in *conclusiones*. No doubt we will also notice considerable disagreement about what particular *conclusiones* themselves amount to. If the prohibition against unjust killing follows at once and after very little consideration from the first precepts of the natural law, surely agreement about definitions and cases does not. Concrete instances of just and unjust killing will have to be distinguished, and while some agreement in judgment about specific cases must be assumed in order to identify what is actually being prohibited, there is no reason to think that all times and places will agree about every case or distinction. Indeed, we cannot even expect this kind of agreement among the inhabitants of any one particular time and place. Aquinas concedes these facts and accepts these tasks.[49] He knows that this kind of moral diversity is both expected and beside the point. What matters are the facts on the ground. Our agency has a certain shape and range because we are inclined to know and will a certain collection of ends, naturally and necessarily. From the fact that we know, will, and act as human beings do, certain secondary precepts follow "by way of conclusions" (*per modum conclusionum*) (*ST* I-II.95.2). These secondary precepts will be abstract enough to make disagreement about them unavoidable, but concrete enough to give substance to the moral terms we all employ, "justice" above all.

We can easily imagine Aquinas saying that "justice"—the concept and concern, not the virtue—is there, like our life, that it comes to us as nature's grace. We can also imagine him insisting that the commitments that give it substance are the rules that govern its use. Like all grammatical rules, these commitments do not tell us how the concept must be employed "in order to fulfill its purpose, in order to have such-and-such an effect on human beings" (*PI* 496). That wisdom, he thinks, comes only as our use of the concept and the operations that it regards are perfected by good habits, by virtues that we either acquire through imitation and repetition or receive by God's grace. This is what it means to say, as Aquinas does, that the most basic precepts of the natural law, the precepts that specify the basic rationality of our acting, speaking, and feeling, are the *seminalia virtutum*, the seedbed of the virtues, justice among the rest (*ST* I-II.51.1). And this is what it means to say that justice is a human virtue, a perfection indexed to our humanity (*ST* I-II.58.3; II-II.58.3). "Virtue is natural to man inchoately," Thomas tells us, and "this is so

---

49   His treatment of killing and murder (*ST* II-II.64.1–8) offers a good example. He begins with a secondary precept, the prohibition against murder, a specific kind of injustice. He then spells out the content of this prohibition by distinguishing just and unjust killings across a number of concrete cases and against the backdrop of disagreement in his own time and place.

in respect of the specific nature, in so far as in man's reason are to be found instilled naturally certain naturally known principles of both knowledge and action, which are the nurseries of intellectual and moral virtues, and in so far as there is in the will a natural appetite for the good in accord with reason" (*ST* I-II.63.1).[50] And note, it is precisely because the goods that we know and will by nature are general, because specific instances of them are many and diverse, and because action always regards specifics—it is because of all this—that our natural loves must be "set in order by virtue" (*ST* I-II.55.1.4). We might be inclined by nature to love the goods that we know by nature, and yet these loves need to be further and more determinately "inclined, by means of a habit, to some fixed good of the reason" (*ST* I-II.50.5.3). This further inclination, made determinate in habit, is a virtue of the will—in this instance, justice.

In this way, justice comes with our humanity. As concept, concern, and inchoate virtue, it comes naturally and necessarily. We might say that justice begins in love, our love for the basic outlines of the human good. We might say that love always precedes justice.

NATURAL TOLERANCE

Consider at last how tolerance emerges from this account of nature, concept, act, and virtue. By natural necessity, we are disposed to exercise certain powers of apprehension, appetite, and sensation, to know and love certain ends, to act in certain ways, make use of certain moral concepts, care about certain moral matters, and acquire certain virtues. This is a good portion of what it means to be a human being, rational and self-moving. These dispositions have "a certain latitude" (*quandam latitudinem*), as Aquinas puts it in his discussion of natural habits (*ST* I-II.51.1). Our nature does not tell us how to exercise the powers it provides or how to regard specific instances of the ends that we apprehend and love according to our kind. So for example, we are naturally inclined to know the truth about things and to think that

---

50   Thomas clarifies this claim by drawing a distinction (*ST* I-II.51.1). The inchoate virtues that come packaged with our humanity, so that no human being can be without them, are different from those virtues that are natural to a person on account of his or her individual nature. Thus, for example, while all of us are disposed by our specific nature to acquire courage in some measure, some are more courageous than others by virtue of individual temperament. By the disposition of their bodies, they might be more spirited, and thus disposed to acquire courage with greater ease. Alternatively, they might have the virtue created in them by an external principle, as is the case with infused courage (*ST* I-II.63.3–4). For an excellent account of Aquinas's treatment of natural virtue, see Decosimo, *Ethics as a Work of Charity*, 98–103.

knowledge is good and thus desirable (*ST* I-II.94.2). Yet the world is full of "many and various things" that might be known (*ST* I-II.50.5.1), many bits of wisdom that might be had, more than any human being could ever seek or grasp. So too, our shared humanity does not specify what we will know and love in particular, and it offers little guidance as to what we should. Compared to the specific natures of other creatures, ours holds us lightly in its grip. It provides neither specific direction nor concrete perfection. Combine this substantial indeterminacy in the sources of our agency with the diversity of the human good and the need for moral judgment emerges quite naturally, as does our disposition to acquire habits of apprehension and appetite, habits that give our judgments and desires some measure of determinacy, our actions some measure of immediacy and ease (*ST* I-II.49.4; 50.5.3). Combine all of these features together—this indeterminacy and diversity, this need and disposition—and the whole moral enterprise comes into view: acquiring habits of mind and affection, employing concepts and applying rules in concrete cases, making explicit our commitments and revising them as needed, distinguishing true and apparent virtues, and so on.

As we have already noted, this enterprise does not proceed without constraints. Certain general ends will always be judged good, certain moral concepts will invariably be employed, and certain virtues will be cultivated and praised in every imaginable human life and social relationship. But these constraints are loose. Talk of justice will show up everywhere and always, but the concrete judgments that determine the concept's material content will show some variation across time and place. Thus when Agamemnon insists that it would be unjust of Menelaus to spare Adrestus, thrown from his chariot and now begging for his life, I can understand the point even as I disagree with some of the judgments about honor, enemies, and mercy that determine his particular account of the just and the unjust.[51] Given the cultural and tem-

---

51   As Adrestus's "pleas were moving the heart of Menelaus," Agamemnon intervenes and puts the matter this way:

> "So soft, dear brother, why?
> Why such concern for enemies? I suppose you got
> such tender loving care at home from the Trojans.
> Ah would to god not one of them could escape
> his sudden plunging death beneath our hands!
> No baby boy still in his mother's belly,
> not even he escape—all Ilium blotted out,
> no tears for their lives, no markers for their graves!"

It is shameful injustice, this mercy that Menelaus considers, or so Agamemnon assumes, and it is shame that turns his heart once again. "And the iron warrior brought his brother round—

> rough justice, fitting too.
> Menelaus shoved Adrestus back with a fist,
> powerful Agamemnon stabbed him in the flank

poral distances that divide our age from the Bronze Age my dissent hardly surprises. That Homer shares my dissent, as some exegetes assume, might give us pause, but then again, why should it?[52] He finds disagreement about this matter in his own time as well. He pits Menelaus's soft heart against Agamemnon's rough justice in order to give these differences their due, to exhibit the commitments that animate them, and to encourage reflection, criticism, and perhaps even revision. Whether they come to us across deep divides of history and culture or across the skins and characters that separate one human being from another, disagreement about the rank and merit of particular goods, about the determinate character of specific virtues, and about the real substance and proper application of certain moral concepts is an inescapable feature of human life. As Augustine points out in his litany of our temporal sorrows, they come willy-nilly in every imaginable human society: among friends, family members, and fellow citizens, and between cities and peoples.[53]

There are remedies for this woe. There are, as Thomas puts it, external sources of internal order (*ST* I-II.90.prologue). There are the various regimes of positive law and human custom that direct us to know and love certain things and thus to act in certain ways (*ST* I-II.95.1, 97.3). There is also divine help given gratuitously, or so Christians will confess, a grace that perfects action for the sake of the good that is natural to us and that enables us to know and love the good that transcends our nature's reach (*ST* I-II.109.2–4). When these external sources in-form our souls, they can, in the best circumstances, create shared judgments, loves, and passions, shared virtues, actions, and lives (*ST* I-II.92.1; 95.1; 113.1), and these shared effects certainly contribute to "the sweetness of peace that all men love."[54]

But these sources are inconstant, circumstances are rarely best, and this sweet peace is hardly the norm. Some societies lack the just "discipline of laws" that they need in order to harmonize their members in judgment, love, and action.[55] In others, the external sources of internal order are present as they should be, and yet disagreements and dissents remain nevertheless. Some of these are ordinary and welcome. They bear witness to the sacred individuality of persons. But some generate conflict and strife, and this hardly surprises. Custom cannot specify every judgment, love, and action,

---

and back on his side the fighter went, faceup.
The son of Atreus dug a heel in his heaving chest
and wrenched the ash spear out." (Homer, *Iliad* 6.59, 63–76)

52 See Bernard Knox's introduction to Fagles's translation, especially 59–63.

53 Augustine, *civ. Dei* XIX.5–10.

54 Augustine, *civ. Dei* XIX.11. For Aquinas, it is precisely this sweet fellowship, this civic friendship, that human law hopes to create (*ST* I-II.99.2).

55 *ST* I-II.95.1.

and human law cannot rule with this kind of specificity without disregarding the bounds of its jurisdiction and inflicting grave injustice upon the governed. Human law, Thomas tells us, regards those external actions and exchanges that mediate our social and political relationships. Ideally, its precepts prescribe and prohibit certain actions and exchanges in accord with the norms of justice. It sets these relationships right and secures this common good for those who participate in them (*ST* I-II.96.3; 100.2). At the same time, some actions fall under the jurisdiction of human law but cannot be governed by precept without doing "away with many good things" and hindering "the advance of the common good" that is both the effect of justice and the necessary ground of "human colloquy" (*conversationem humanam*) (*ST* I-II.91.4).[56] When this concern for justice and jurisdiction is taken seriously, the precepts of positive law will not—or at least, ought not—prohibit every vicious act, prescribe every virtuous choice, or compel perfect unity among the governed. Even in the best regimes of law, some differences in judgment, love, and passion will remain, some injustices will go unchecked, and some substantial disagreements about the good and the right will persist.

For Thomas, there is a sense in which the natural law that rules and measures all that we do also prescribes every act of virtue and a sense in which every act of virtue accords with the natural law. At the same time, there is nothing concrete in the way of judgment and desire that follows from either of these senses and thus little reason to think that a sweet unity of judgment, love, and virtue follows from our shared subjection to the natural law. He puts the point this way:

> [T]o the natural law belongs everything to which a man is inclined according to his nature. . . . Since the rational soul is the proper form of man, there is in every man a natural inclination to act according to reason: and this is to act according to virtue. Consequently, considered thus, all acts of virtue are prescribed by the natural law: since each one's reason naturally dictates to him to act virtuously. But if we speak of virtuous acts considered in themselves, i.e., in their proper species, not all virtuous acts are prescribed by the natural law: for many things are done virtuously to which nature does not incline at first. (*ST* I-II.94.3)

Put another way, if the natural law is nothing but our rational participation in God's judgment about the human good expressed in the eternal law (*ST* I-II.91.2), if basic participation specifies our humanity (*ST* I-II.91.4.1), and if our perfection in being, and thus our participation in God's judgment, can be more or less complete according to the measure of our virtue, then of course

---

56 Cf. *ST* I-II.96.2–3. Aquinas draws on Augustine's authority for this conclusion. See *lib. arb.* i.5–6.

every act of virtue is in accord with the natural law. So too, if the natural law's basic precepts order the apprehensions and inclinations characteristic of our kind, then indeed there is a sense in which the natural law prescribes the acts that perfect those powers. But this kind of perfection is not given with our humanity. The moral and intellectual virtues must be acquired, and yet, as we noted above, their acquisition is uncertain and their distribution irregular, even in the best regimes of positive law and settled custom.

So too, for Christians there is a sense in which the moral precepts of the Divine law prohibit every sin and prescribe every act of virtue (*ST* I-II.91.4; 100.2), and yet Thomas tells us that those precepts were delivered to Israel on Sinai precisely because, as we just noted, human law cannot punish or forbid every evil deed or command every act of virtue. "In order, therefore, that no evil might remain unforbidden and unpunished, it was necessary for the Divine law to supervene, whereby all sins are forbidden" (*ST* I-II.91.4). On this rendering of God's motives, the old law is not given in order to create a perfect union of apprehension, affection, and action among God's people in time. Rather it is assumed that there will be no such temporal union, that law and custom cannot produce it, and that sinful departures from perfect virtue must be forbidden by general prohibition nevertheless.

Here then are the claims about human nature, action, habit, and law that must be gathered together in order to see that tolerance comes with our shared humanity as concept, act, and potential virtue.

- There is the relative indeterminacy of the internal sources our agency, the diversity of the human good, and the whole moral enterprise that results.
- There is the concern with justice that emerges from these sources, a concern that is natural to us as concept, act, and inchoate virtue.
- There is the small collection of material judgments, the thoroughly general prescriptions of virtue and prohibitions against vice, that give this concept its specific form.
- There are the substantial constraints placed on the scope of positive law and human custom, on their ability to set human relationships right, to unify conduct, judgment, and love, and to restrain injustice in any particular time and place.
- And, last, for Christians, there is the utterly gratuitous character of God's grace, which is dispensed variously and received imperfectly.

Gathered together, these claims generate two conclusions: the unity of peace we hope to secure in the various communities we happen to inhabit will always be imperfect and this imperfection is an inescapable deliverance of our humanity. No doubt, some measure of judgment united and love shared is equally inescapable, but, given the kind of creature that we are, perfect measures are unimaginable. Look around and more often than not we find human beings working to maintain this imperfect peace in spite of the differences and disagreements that divide them. Given the ordinary ubiquity of these efforts, it's natural to include them among the activities we are disposed to pursue according to our kind, if not immediately and in every actual society, then for the most part and after a bit of reflection. They constitute a portion of the moral enterprise that accompanies our nature. And of course, if these activities come packaged with our humanity, then so do the habits that perfect them, not actually but inchoately, not the full fruit of virtue, but its nursery (*ST* I-II.51.1; 63.1).

Experience bears this out. In most times and places we find the virtuous praised for their willingness to bear the burdens of those with whom they share some sort of society, praised for their ability to endure at least some disagreement and dissent for the sake of that shared life. No doubt we also find considerable variation in judgment about the disagreements and dissents that deserve a tolerant response and about the duration and circumstances of its exercise, but these differences do not go all the way down. They couldn't, not without losing sight of the concept we share, disregarding the concern with enduring difference that turns up almost everywhere, and discounting our ability to see goodness in this act. Look around again and we find that in most times and places the virtuous consider themselves obliged to act in this way, to respond with patient endurance to at least some of the objectionable differences posed by friends, family members, coalition partners, and fellow citizens. We find them determined to render this due with a constant and perpetual will. When they forsake this obligation, we find others calling them to account. When they take up its tasks and their efforts succeed, we find them grateful for the imperfect peace these actions help them maintain in the company they keep and for the autonomy they secure with respect to the differences in dispute. When their patient endurance delivers this due and yet fails to achieve these ends, we find them consoled by the expression of this excellence, by the good embodied in the act quite apart from its success (*ST* II-II.58.1).

Some will note the paradox in this. Societies of every sort can survive their imperfect unions of judgment and desire and maintain bearable measures of imperfect peace only as their members are joined in praise of tolerance and united in their determination to encourage its act and cultivate its habit. But the trouble here is merely apparent and the paradox dissolves across the divide between imperfect and nonexistent unions. In most societies there is enough unity of judgment and desire to generate a collection of shared virtues and moral practices, if not in fact at least in aspiration, and enough disagreement and difference to find tolerance and its acts in the collection.[57]

---

57   At the very least, most societies have enough agreement in judgment and desire to generate debate about which virtues and practices deserve praise and cultivation. If the argument so far is sound, then, in most societies, tolerance will be an object of debate.

Placed in theological context, these pieces, taken together, confirm what Christians typically confess: that a perfect union among judgments, wills, and affections follows from God's gracious redemption of our fallen nature, or not at all. It is largely an object of eschatological hope, not of moral striving. Its temporal manifestations are infrequent and imperfect. To think otherwise is to deny the current condition of our humanity. At the same time, the virtues of this life are geared to its imperfections, some in our souls, some in the world, some in the societies we inhabit. On this side of the eschatological horizon, coping with these imperfections is one of the things that those with temporal virtue do. They also pursue the goods of right reason, but in this life, those goods can be had only as various imperfections are addressed. When they are addressed well—promptly, willingly, with judgment and passion in right order and with the ease of habit—we can say that soul's imperfections have been transcended by virtue. Yet even when the virtues flourish and the soul is set right, the imperfections that abide in the world remain: not only disagreements and differences of various kinds, but all sorts of difficulties and dangers, all kinds of violence and injustice. The point is not that these imperfections can, at times, prevent the virtuous from achieving their aims. Nor is it that virtue's transcendence of the soul's disorder can be tragically undone as the world lurches about in this way and that, distorting passion and corrupting judgment. The point is not, in other words, that the temporal virtues are defeasible in act and fragile in substance. Rather, the point is that everywhere and always imperfection frames the context of their work and existence. In Thomas's useful shorthand, the temporal virtues are always about the difficult and the good, which is to say, among other things, that the good the virtuous desire is pursued in the face of various difficulties and that some of these difficulties remain even as virtue's good is achieved.[58] Consider again the courageous. When confronted with serious difficulties or dangers, they typically respond well, with passions and choices that accord with reason's better judgment. When their actions succeed and justice is done, relations are set right in one corner of the world.[59] Still, all of this takes place in the context of difficulties and dangers that require a right response and in spite of the soul's tendency to flirt with disorder. For the courageous, these imperfections remain intractable aspects of the soul regardless of virtue's measure and persistent features of the world in spite of their efforts to set right its affairs.

There is, in other words, something utterly mundane and unheroic in the virtues that come packaged with our humanity. No doubt, there is also something marvelous, something beautiful and powerful. Those who manage to act at the limits of their natural powers with the ease of habit, who

---

58 *ST* II-II.129.2.

59 See *ST* I-II.65.1 for Aquinas's treatment of the unity of the virtues.

reproduce in action a likeness of that habit, and who set right some corner of the world as a result of that action—they certainly deserve our admiration and praise.[60] Recognition is required; honor is their due. But the point is that their virtue is difficult to recognize apart from the imperfections that afflict human life, and these deficits remain largely untouched even when the right is done and honor is given. Even at their best, the virtuous do little more than cope with imperfections and labor against difficulties. Muddling through remains their ceaseless work, the ironic substance of their perfection, and traces of that work remain even as their virtues shine through with a kind of transcendent glory. It was, after all, sweat and gore that John Lewis, Jim Zwerg, and others wiped from their necks and limbs after their patience and courage met racist violence in Selma and Montgomery. So too, in a quite different moral context, it is the wise ruler who, according to Augustine, fights just wars for the sake of just peace and yet feels sorrow at the close of the day, who "reflects with pain upon such great evils, upon such horror and cruelty."[61] In each case, virtue's goodness comes into focus only as virtue's difficult work is acknowledged.

On this account, tolerance is a perfect instance of its kind, of the natural moral virtues, precisely because it begins and ends in imperfection, because its attitudes are thoroughly unheroic, and its acts utterly mundane. Responding well to disagreement and difference, usually with an act of patient endurance, this is what the tolerant do. When others resort to coercion or contemplate exit, they stay put and muddle through—all for the sake of social peace and mutual autonomy. While they certainly transcend certain deficiencies in their souls, certain imperfections in judgment and desire, the tolerant do not overcome the imperfect unity of judgment and desire that divides the communities they inhabit. Nor do they necessarily hope or intend to. They doubt this corner of the world can be set right, that justice can be done and civil peace secured, as outrage is unleashed, autonomy crushed, and unity compelled. They suspect that justice can be achieved only as some of these differences

---

60   *ST* II-II.123.7.

61   *Civ. Dei* XIX.6. There are differences that divide Aquinas and Augustine here. Both insist that the temporal virtues regard the difficulties and imperfection of this life, and yet Augustine denies that the virtuous in any way transcend these conditions. Their actions always follow from deliberate and arduous self-control, never with the prompt ease of habit. Aquinas disagrees. By his lights, to say that there are those among us who exhibit justice and prudence (for example) is to say that some act justly and wisely with ease and delight, with neither resistance nor struggle. At the same time, he knows that virtue's transcendence escapes most of us much of the time, that we struggle to act among the virtuous more often than we would like. So too he concedes that even those with virtues in full measure can be undone by tragedy, that there are difficulties and imperfections that they cannot transcend. There's no reason to resolve this dispute here, but the facts on the ground seem to favor Thomas's cautiously hopeful assessment of temporal virtue.

and disagreements remain unresolved, as civil peace bears certain kinds and measures of imperfection, and as tolerant actions and habits are cultivated and praised. In many instances, they know it would be unreasonable, if not unjust, to hope for something more.

That there might be an act of endurance that includes this hope, that emerges from love and thus longs for union, for overcoming the conditions that call for its act—this possibility will be considered in chapter 6. In the meantime, we need a better understanding of the endurance that belongs to tolerance. If the argument so far is sound, then tolerance is natural to us as concept, act, and inchoate virtue. Fair enough, some might reply, but what more can we say about tolerance as an actually acquired virtue? What is the object of its act, the matter that it regards, and what ends do the tolerant seek by means of this act? What judgments must they make, what passions affect their actions, and how is tolerance related to the other moral virtues? I have said that it is a potential part of justice, but how exactly is tolerance related to justice and what follows from insisting that it is? And finally, given the conclusions of this chapter, how is it that some societies recognize tolerance and encourage its cultivation, while others apparently do not? If our nature disposes us to make use of the concept, to find goodness in the act, and to acquire the virtue, then why is tolerance cultivated and praised in some times and places but not all? And this puzzle about distribution becomes all the more puzzling when it is Thomas's account of justice and its parts that we use to locate tolerance among the virtues. Thomas agrees that acts of toleration can be good. In some circumstances and with respect to some ends, its patient endurance can be due another; it can be a requirement of the relationship in which it is exercised. But he does not identify a virtue that perfects resort to this act. He does not theorize tolerance. He does not list it among the potential parts of justice. The same applies to love's endurance, to forbearance. He assigns it to charity as one of its works, but he says nothing at all about its origin in a virtue of its own. It is to these questions and puzzles that we now turn.

CHAPTER 3

AMONG THE VIRTUES

Tolerance is a moral virtue. It belongs to justice as one of its parts, and it acts in the company of other virtues. This is what I will argue in the account that follows. The account is indebted to the treatment of the moral virtues that Aquinas develops in the *secunda pars* of his *Summa theologiae*, and this debt should give us pause. As I noted at the close of the last chapter, Thomas regards acts of toleration as right and due in some circumstances with respect to some ends, but he does not theorize a virtue that perfects resort to this act. Tolerance does not show up on his list of the potential parts of justice (*ST* II-II.80). Since it shows up on mine, I will eventually have to account for this difference. For now, I begin as Thomas does, by defining the terms, drawing the distinctions, and making the inferences we need in order to say that tolerance is a virtue annexed to justice and dependent upon the efforts of a small collection of other virtues.

DEFINITIONS AND DISTINCTIONS

Tolerance is a moral virtue and moral virtues are habits (*ST* I-II.58.1). Habits are, as Aristotle says, dispositions whereby the subject in which the disposition resides is disposed well or ill, and this "either in regard to itself, that is to its nature, or in regard to something else, that is to the end."[1] Moral virtues are habits that dispose us well in both of these ways. They perfect our passionate responses to the world and our desire for the good that is known, and when exercised together with right reason about things to be done

---

1 The text is from Aristotle (*Metaph.* v.20, 1022b6), cited by Aquinas (*ST* I-II.49.3).

(prudence) and knowledge of the self-evident starting points of practical reason (understanding), these perfected appetites dispose us to good action (*ST* I-II.56.4, 6; 58.2, 4; 60.2). In general, this is what habits do. They always have some sort of relation to the things they inhabit, and, as "operation . . . is the end of nature," this relation typically involves actions and ends (*ST* I-II.54.1). As each thing is what it is and not some other thing because it is ordained to some ends but not others, it follows that habit "implies relation not only to the nature of a thing, but also, consequently, to operation, inasmuch as this is the end of nature, or conducive to the end" (*ST* I-II.49.3).

As the soul is a principle of operation through its various powers (*ST* I.77.1–2), through its different capacities to act, its various habits reside in those powers that can be the subject of habits.[2] Not all can be. Some powers of the soul are ordained to one thing, to one act according to their natures, and these cannot have their operations disposed by habit. The powers of exterior apprehension for example—sight, hearing, and the like—cannot acquire habits because they are "ordained to their fixed acts, according to the disposition of their nature" (*ST* I-II.50.3.3). Consider hearing. There are not many ways to hear, and thus no indeterminacy in this power that a habit might reduce, fix, and so dispose us to hear in this way but not that. There is no perfection that can be brought to this power, no potency that a habit might complete. We simply hear, or not.[3] By contrast, a power that "acts at the command of reason" (*ST* I-II.50.3) and is thus "capable of determination in several ways and to various things" can acquire a habit that disposes it "to one of those things to which it is in potentiality" (*ST* I-II.49.4). The power will be the subject of the habit, the "matter in which it exists" (*ST* II-II.55.4), and the habit will be the active principle that in-forms the power and disposes it to act (*ST* I-II.54.2). Once a power has been so disposed, it will act in certain ways with the consistency of habit, and its habit will be available for deliberate use.

The point has two parts and is well known. A habit both determines and enables action. With an operative habit in place, one can act consistently and

2 Two points require clarification. First, not all of our habits reside in the soul's powers or regard operations. Some, like health, reside in the body and dispose it well or ill with respect to its proper function as determined by its form, by the soul. Since my concern is with actions, I will concentrate on Thomas's treatment of operative habits. Second, if habit is something superadded to nature and its operations, something that disposes its potencies in this way or that, then the soul cannot be its subject. "For the soul itself is the form completing human nature." It is responsible for the powers and potencies that habits are superadded to. That said, the virtues that grace infuses have the soul as its subject, precisely because it is the soul's essence that grace re-forms as these virtues are infused (*ST* I-II.50.2). For a detailed account of Thomas's treatment of habit, see Decosimo, *Ethics as a Work of Charity*, 72–105.

3 There are, of course, habits that generate attention to aspects of what we hear, that encourage us to listen more intently to this or that, but these are powers of reason and will that generate the desire to attend to what has been heard and the command to do so (*ST* I-II.50.3.3).

with ease in accord with the habit's particular determination (*ST* I-II.49.3). Habit also "implies a certain lastingness." Once a habit resides in a power and disposes it to act in certain ways and with a certain stubborn regularity, it is, as everyone knows, difficult to dislodge (*ST* I-II.49.2.3). This is what it means to say that habits inform the powers they inhabit and bestow those powers with a kind of second nature (*ST* I-II.54.2; 58.1). That's the first point. The second is this: a person can make use of her habits (*ST* I-II.50.5). She can use them—prowess with a fly rod, mastery of ancient history, capacity for outrage at injustice, and so on—when she acts for the sake of the ends she intends. This is the twofold meaning of Thomas's insistence that habits regard operations. They dispose us to act in certain ways with consistency and ease, and we make use of them when we act for the sake of the ends we have.

Those powers of the soul that "may be variously directed to act" (*ST* I-II.50.5) and that can be disposed by habit in various ways can also take on various habits (*ST* I-II.54.1 and ad 1). Powers of this sort have this potential when their acts can be directed to several distinct ends. A specific difference in ends "entails a specific difference of acts," and this formal difference holds even when the acts themselves are materially identical (*ST* I-II.54.1.1; 18.6). So, for example, while it is one act, materially speaking, to give money to someone, it is an act of charity if it is done in love for the neighbor who belongs to God but an act of justice if done in order to pay a debt. The diversity of intended ends generates specifically distinct chosen acts, giving alms versus paying debts (*ST* I-II.54.2.3 and ad 3). Since virtues are concerned, above all, with this internal source of action, this internal orientation of act to end, a specific difference of ends generates a specific difference, not only of acts, but also of the habits that cause them (*ST* I-II.54.1.1; II-II.47.11). Thus charity is different from justice and yet both reside in the will. When this happens, when different virtues reside in a single power, there can be different parts or kinds of one principal virtue when they are united by a common subject matter and yet distinguished by their ends. Prudence, for example, resides in the practical reason and regards taking counsel about actions in relation to ends (*ST* II-II.47.2, 5). Its specifically distinct parts regard this common subject matter, and yet they are distinguished by their different ends. Thus *prudentia oeconomica*, which is directed to the common good of the household, is different from *prudentia politica*, which is directed to the common good of the political community (*ST* II-II.47.11).

Now consider justice. Justice is a *moral* virtue, which is to say that it resides in an appetitive power (*ST* I-II.58.1). Courage and temperance are also moral virtues, but they reside in the sensitive appetite and perfect its response to goods that can be sensed by infusing that response—our various passions—with reason's judgment (*ST* I-II.56.4; 59.4). Justice, by contrast, resides in the rational appetite, the power of the soul that responds with desire for the good that has been apprehended by the intellect (*ST* I-II.56.6).

Since rational desire for the good characteristic of our kind is the source of those actions that distinguish our humanity, rational and free (*ST* I-II.6.1), it follows that justice regards actions, what Thomas calls operations. They are as it were the "matter about which it is concerned" (*materia circa quam est*) (*ST* I-II.60.2), and not actions of just any sort, but only those ordered to ends that we desire knowingly and pursue with some difficulty.[4] These are few. The will's object is the good apprehended and proposed by reason, and, more often than not, the will responds with desire for the specific good that is actually apprehended and proposed. This is, after all, the kind of thing that the will does given the kind of power that it is. But note, there is no necessity in this. So long as the object apprehended and proposed falls short of the perfect good—so long as it is not good in every respect and thus indispensable for the perfect happiness we all desire no matter what our proximate ends happen to be (*ST* I-II.1.6)—it need not be desired by the will even as it is apprehended and proposed by the intellect (*ST* I.82.2). Some other object, good in some other respect, and thus bearing some other connection to our last end might also be apprehended and proposed, and it might intervene and trump the first (*ST* I.82.2.1). Because the human good is diverse in kind and number, and because the intellect can take note of this diversity, it's no surprise that this proposing, trumping, ranking, and reranking of the will's objects goes on all the time. As we have already noted, it is this relative indeterminacy in the rational appetite and this diversity of the good that makes the will "variously directed to act" and thus a potential subject of habits (*ST* I-II.50.5).[5] At the same time, Aquinas points out that there are certain objects

---

4   All of the moral virtues have good operations as their effect or product (*ST* I-II.60.2). Courage, for example, perfects the irascible appetite's passionate responses to difficulties and dangers. It elicits anger, fear, and daring of the right intensity and duration in response to the right objects and in the right circumstances. Yet the effect of this right response is a good operation, a courageous action. Without irascible passions of the right kind and intensity there would be no such actions. Even so, operations are not the matter about which courage regards. Its proper matter is the courageous person's passionate response to those difficulties, dangers, and actions. Justice, by contrast, has operations as its proper matter. It perfects those operations such that through them our relations are set right with another. The key point is that actions and so too the relationships they mediate are different from the passions that respond to them (ibid.). This difference marks the need for distinct virtues, some that perfect operations, others that perfect passionate responses.

5   Caution is required at precisely this point. Some might conclude that this relative indeterminacy at the start of moral reflection implies that the will's choice is the principal source of human action, choice determined by nothing but itself. But this would discount Aquinas's most basic claim about the relationship between intellect and will: the intellect moves the will by "presenting its object to it," and "the will tends to its object according to the order of reason" (*ST* I-II.9.1; 13.1). The proper inference is this: when the intellect picks out one of the will's potential objects, and when that object has been judged best, moral reflection comes to an end, not in indeterminate choice, but in choice determined necessarily by judgment, by the weight and order of reasons (*ST* I-II.14.1).

that we have difficulty willing either because their goodness cannot be apprehended by us, as is the case with God's goodness, or because we consistently misapprehend their relative goodness, as is the case with the good of others (*ST* I-II.56.6). It is this latter difficulty, associated with this latter good, that justice regards. When justice informs the will, we are inclined to intend our neighbor's good with the constancy of habit and we are less likely to disregard that good—by misapprehension, self-deception, or weakness—and tend to some other, lesser good.[6]

So justice brings perfection to the rational appetite, which in turn enables the just to desire goods of the right kind in the right circumstances, above all the good that our neighbor deserves, a good that cannot be willed consistently without virtue's assistance (*ST* II-II.58.1.3). The operations that justice regards are just these: actions that mediate our relations with others, relations given a determinate shape by those actions and by those things that we make use of when we act (*ST* I-II.60.2; II-II.58.2, 8, 10). This is what the virtue justice is about (*ST* II-II.58.9). It perfects those operations, it makes good use of those things, which in turn brings good to our neighbors as it sets right our various relations with them (*ST* II-II.57.1; 58.2). When those relations have been set right by a person whose actions originate in "a constant and perpetual will" to render to each the good that each is due by right, we say that she does what is right from habit, because she is just (*ST* II-II.58.1). Across a number of cases and relations, the fallout is a kind of equality, where she is well disposed toward all precisely because she treats all equally (*ST* II-II.58.10). The point is not that the just person delivers the same good to each, at least not materially, but rather that she provides a portion to each that equals what each is due by right, due from her and owed to them. "Each man's own is that which is due to him according to equality of proportion," and this is precisely what the just person provides to each (*ST* II-II.58.11). When she receives the same in return, she lives at peace with the company she keeps, enjoying the common good of a relationship set right. As Cicero points out, maintaining this peaceful life, this common good, in societies large and small is the principal point of justice (*Off.* I.7; *ST* II-II.58.2 *sed contra*). It is the distant, external end that the just intend to achieve regardless of their proximate ends and specific acts and

---

6   Since Aquinas insists that there is nothing in the will that is not first in the intellect, it is the intellect's misapprehension of the relative goodness of the will's objects that brings disorder to its acts. And of course, a good portion of the intellect's trouble here follows from distortions in judgment precipitated by disorder in the passions. The fallout is at least twofold. This cascade of trouble and difficulty confirms what Aquinas says about the unity of the virtues (*ST* I-II.65.1), and, unlike the other virtues, justice does not have a unique difficulty that it alone regards and addresses.

independent of the size and character of the social relationships their virtue helps perfect (*ST* II-II.58.6–8).

Justice informs the will's intentions and helps generate the actions that set these relationships right. By habit, the just *tend* toward these rightly ordered relationships, and in specific circumstances they intend to have them by means of specific actions. As our relationships with others can take different forms, so too there are different kinds of justice that can perfect the will's act, each distinguished by the different proximate ends of these distinct social relationships. So, for example, legal justice regards the relations that obtain among those who share a political community of some sort. It safeguards the common good of that community, which includes civil peace but also its source: the right relations among members that just actions create and sustain (*ST* I-II.58.7). Legal justice secures this good by perfecting the rational appetites of both ruler and ruled, by directing their actions and interests to this end (*ST* II-II.58.6). Domestic justice, by contrast, orders and perfects relations within households. When those who share a household have wills informed by domestic justice, they are disposed by habit to deliver to each what each is due in accord with the role each plays: wife or husband, parent or child, brother or sister, and so on. When this occurs with the consistency of habit, they maintain the shared goods that are the substance of that life, above all their rightly ordered relationships (*ST* II-II.58.7.3). Finally, there is particular justice, which perfects our various private affairs and relations (*ST* II-II.58.7). When present in the will, it enables the just to secure the particular good of those with whom they share some sort of common life, activity, or friendship. Particular justice regards the mutual dealings that go on between persons and the equality that ought to obtain between them (*ST* II-II.61.1–2), but it also regards the just distribution of those common goods that accrue in their common life (*ST* II-II.61.1.4).

While each of these virtues exhibits the *ratio vero iustitia*, "rendering to another his due according to equality" (*ST* II-II.80), only legal and particular justice are integral parts (*ST* II-II.79.1). Just as "wall, roof, and foundations are parts of a house" and diminish its perfection when absent, so too the integral parts of a virtue must be present for the perfect exercise of its act (*ST* II-II.48). Legal and particular justice are integral parts precisely because justice regards our relations with *another* (*ST* II-II.58.2), with a neighbor who must be simultaneously regarded as an individual and as a member of a political community (*ST* II-II.58.5). Perfect acts of justice deliver the good the neighbor is due by right insofar she is a *neighbor* and also the good that is due the political community of which she is a part. The first due is the concern of particular justice, the second, the concern of legal justice. And of course, just as a house without a roof is still somewhat a house, so also justice that lacks one of these integral parts is still true justice but now imperfect. Thus, the person who does right by his neighbor but not by the community they share (or vice versa) is just, but not completely so.[7]

Of these two, legal justice is the principal virtue, the one that exhibits most plainly the perfection that justice brings to the rational appetite and its acts. Aquinas writes, "the legal due is that which one is bound to render by reason of legal obligation; and this due is chiefly the concern of justice, which is the principal virtue" (ST II-II.80). Those perfected by legal justice act in harmony with the laws (concordat legi) (ST II-II.58.5). They are disposed by habit to render to others the good specified by just legal precept and to direct their other acts and virtues to this same end (ST II-II.58.5–6). This end will always regard the common good of the political community precisely because legal precepts, by definition, ordain human actions to public ends and relationships (ST I-II.90.2). For Thomas, it's this order to the common good that, in part, explains the priority of legal justice, for the common goods of political life are, he thinks, the finest of temporal goods (ST I-II.19.10; II-II.58.5). But more basically, it's the conceptual connections that obtain between the precepts of the law and the demands of justice that give legal justice its priority. Law and justice regard similar matters, and not just human actions and social relationships. The connection is tighter than that, or so Thomas thinks. Something can be determined by law only insofar as it belongs to justice, only as it is an operation that delivers to another a good they are due by right (ST I-II.99.5.1), and the actions that are the chief concern of justice are precisely those specified by legal precept (ST II-II.58.5).

This connection between law and justice is mediated through the ratio debiti, the "idea of duty," that Thomas finds embedded in each. For "it is most evident (manifestissme) that the notion of duty, which is essential to a precept, appears in justice, which is one towards another" (ST II-II.122.1). Now the notion of something due implies necessity (necessitatem importat) (ST II-II.80). It conveys the idea that "something should be done" (aliquid faciendum) (ST I-II.99.5), that one is bound to do it (adstringitur) (ST II-II.80), that one is obliged to deliver some good and act for the sake of some end. All of this is implicit in the idea of law. When a practical dictate comes from one authorized to rule, it binds those subject to it, binds them to act in certain ways, for the sake of certain ends, and restrains them from acting in others (ST I-II.90.1). When one falls under the jurisdiction of this law, one is obliged to act in these ways. Since law regards human actions and since human actions bear on our relations with others, on the life we share and the goods we hold in common, its binding dictates have the "character of duty" and are properly called praecepta (ST I-II.99.5; 100.2 ad 2). They specify actions that deliver what is due in accord with the norms of the relevant

---

7   Thomas doesn't tell us, but presumably domestic justice is not an integral part precisely because not all of us live in households.

social relationships. An action specified by legal precept gives to another the good she is due as a member of some political community. No doubt, the just will be disposed to render this due out of the "rectitude of virtue" (*ex honestate virtutis*) (*ST* II-II.80), and since the notion of something due implies necessity, they would act in this way regardless, without the determination of law (*ST* I-II.99.5.1). But when the law's precepts determine specific acts as right, certain goods as due, the just respond in harmony with that determination, and they set right a public relationship as they deliver that due. And it is precisely their attention to this public relationship set right, their settled desire to secure this good held in common, that exhibits the chief concern of justice (*ST* II-II.58.5).

Aquinas uses this account of the essence and chief concern of justice to identify and distinguish its potential parts. These are virtues annexed to justice because they share the matter about which justice is concerned, operations that set right our relations with other persons (*ST* I-II.60.2). They are *potential*, not integral, parts, because they exhibit the essential character of justice imperfectly, either "by falling short of the aspect of equality," or "by falling short of the aspect of due" (*ST* II-II.80). Religion and piety, for example, belong to justice insofar as they regard the relations of one person to another, and yet they fall short of its perfection and land among its potential parts precisely because they regard debts that cannot be repaid in full. God gives us life, as do our parents, and both are due honor and worship in return. Yet our efforts never rise to the task. The religious offer prayers and sacrifices to the powers they considers divine and the pious worship their parents, but in each instance these honors fall short. They do not equal the portion that is in fact due. They do not fully provide what is owed; they do not set the relationship fully right. They can't; nothing could. When we consider God's singular excellence as creator and governor of all things, and when we regard our parents as the proximate sources of our life and well-being, anything we might give in return would be insufficient (*ST* II-II.81.3–4; 101.1).

Other virtues can share the essence of justice but not its chief concern. They can regard common goods that are not public relationships and obligations that are not legal. In these circumstances, they dispose us to render to another the good that is due morally speaking. By *debitum morale*, Aquinas means nothing more than a due that follows from the demands of virtue, not from the precepts of law, a due that regards individuals, their shared goods and social relationships, not a political community and its common welfare (*ST* II-II.80). So for example, "vengeance consists in the infliction of penal evil on one who has sinned" and is an integral aspect of justice when the sin in question involves the violation of legal precept, when the one who seeks vengeance has authority to render justice in the political community, and when his or her intention is directed chiefly to its common weal (*ST* II-II.108.1). At the same time, vengeance is a virtue annexed to justice as one of its potential parts when the wrong done is to a private good and the punishment of sin is ordered to the satisfaction of individual right (*ST* II-II.108.2.1). In this sense, the virtuously vengeful person "resists harm by defending himself against wrongs, lest they be inflicted on him, or he avenges those that have already been afflicted on him, with the intention, not of harming, but of removing the harm done" (*ST* II-II.108.2). By the same logic, gratitude, "whereby we give thanks to our benefactors," answers to a legal due in some settings, to a moral due others (*ST* II-II.106.1). In the standard cases, one gives thanks in order to repay a benefactor for a good given and this falls under legal precept "when it is specified that so much be paid for so much" and when the end sought by the act is to uphold the just peace of the political community (*ST* II-II.106.1.2). In this event, the repayment made belongs to justice *in se*. If, however, the favor is a private matter, then "the beneficiary is under a moral obligation to bestow something gratis in return" (*ST* II-II.106.6) and the recognition of this due and the performance of this act fall under the special virtue, gratitude, a potential part justice (*ST* II-II.106.1).

At this point, enough has been said about justice to consider what it might mean to say that tolerance resides among its parts. But before we take up that task, we need to consider two final matters, both indispensable for thinking about tolerance as a virtue. The first regards what Aquinas call *iudicium*, the judging that precedes willing and the willing that precedes judgment, while the second regards the precepts that circumscribe just conduct. *Iudicium* will appear repeatedly in our discussion of toleration's special difficulties, while the precepts of justice will help us specify the outer boundaries of the tolerable.

Turning first to judgment, Aquinas's treatment assumes his carefully drawn account of the relations between reason and will. He insists that these powers move each other to their respective acts, but not in the same way. There is mutual causation, but not of the same sort. The intellect moves the will by specifying its object, while the will moves the intellect by making use of its act. Neither power acts without the other. On the one hand, there is nothing in the will that is not first in the intellect precisely because the will's object is the good apprehended and proposed by reason (*ST* I-II.4.4.2; 9.1.3; 19.3). This is a portion of what it means to say that the will's appetites are rational. There are, he admits, certain exceptions to this rule, certain moments in the Christian drama of salvation that compel him to imagine a will that moves itself quite apart from reason's judgment about the good that is best, but these moments are few.[8] More often than not, the intellect's determination precedes and causes the will's desire. On the other hand, "the will moves the

8 For a discussion of these moments, see Bowlin, "Psychology and Theodicy in Aquinas."

intellect as to the exercise of its act" precisely because the intellect's object—
the truth about this or that—is a good that falls under the will's intention.
The intellect seeks the truth only as the will intends to have it and only
as the will uses the intellect's act in order to get what it intends (*ST* I-II.9.1
and ad 3). And of course, the will intends to have the truth about something
in particular only as the intellect has determined that this particular truth
is good and deserves pursuit. So goes the formal character of their mutual
causation.

When we turn to justice, to things that have to be done in order to secure
the good that is due another by right in accord with the norms of a determinate social relationship, Aquinas concedes what all us of know: that there
is often uncertainty here and that judgments about the good and the right
cannot be made well without prior inquiry. Counsel must be taken and reflections made before a judgment can be rendered and before the will can
choose the just course (*ST* I-II.14.1). Put another way, acts of intellect and
will are ordained to one another in a "decision and determination of what
it just" (*ST* II-II.60.5), and as such, right judgment in any matter requires the
collaboration of two virtues that Aquinas gathers under a single heading. One
belongs in the intellect, the other in the will, and yet both belong to *iudicium*.
Lumping them together in this way is, I take it, Thomas's way of acknowledging the unity of the soul and its acts. Reason and will might be different
powers, different sources of action. Prudence and justice might be different
perfections of those sources. Yet it is *persons* who act and their actions that
matter, not the powers that produce them. The first of these virtues is the
part of prudence that enables the practical intellect to judge rightly and decide what is just. Judgment is, after all, "an act of reason, because it belongs
to the reason to pronounce or define" (*ST* II-II.60.1), and presumably the just
person pronounces judgment only after counsel has been taken and various uncertainties about the good that is due another have been put aside
(*ST* I-II.14.1). The other virtue is "the disposition of the one who judges, on
which depends his aptness for judging aright," and "this proceeds from justice" (*ST* II-II.60.1.1). Justice is, after all, the habit that disposes us to desire the
good of another with a constant and perpetual will, and it is this good will
that in turn disposes the just to "pronounce according to the right ruling of
prudence" (*ST* II-II.60.2). The point is that the practical intellect's judgments
cannot be right unless its starting point is, and "the starting point of reason
is the end of the thing to be done, to which man is rightly disposed by moral
virtue," by justice above all (*ST* I-II.65.1). It follows that "judgment is an act
of justice in so far as justice inclines one to judge aright and of prudence in
so far as prudence pronounces judgment" (*ST* II-II.60.1.1).[9]

---

9   The part of judgment that belongs to prudence is preceded by reason taking counsel and
deliberating over the means (*ST* I-II.14.1; II-II.51.1–2) and followed by reason's command,

Finally, recall what Aquinas says about the precepts of justice and consider where he places those remarks. We noted in chapter 2 that these precepts follow at once and after very little consideration from the primary precepts of the natural law and that they provide material content to "justice," to the concept that all human beings share. In Wittgenstein's idiom, they are the grammatical rules that govern our use of the concept, which is to say that failure to concede the truth of more than a couple of these precepts casts doubt upon basic mastery of the concept, basic capacity to apply it in ordinary circumstances. By placing his discussion of those precepts at the conclusion of his account of justice, in the last question of the treatise, Aquinas gives expression to precisely this point (*ST* II-II.122). He does in the order of explication what the precepts themselves do in act. The precepts themselves mark the outer boundary of justice as concept and activity, and his discussion of them brings his account of justice to a close. It specifies those commitments that have been assumed all along, those grammatical rules that have governed all that has been said up to this point and that form the threshold of the sayable with respect to justice. It is as if he declares to his reader: "here, as we cross from one inquiry to another, let us also take note of the grammatical rules that have governed our speech and that have made our talk of justice intelligible."

ENDS AND INTENTIONS

With these preliminaries behind us, we now turn to tolerance. I have said that it is a moral virtue annexed to justice as one of its parts. Like justice, it perfects an internal source of external actions, actions that mediate our relations with others. It requires right judgment about acts, ends, and circumstances, and it depends upon the assistance of a small collection of other virtues. We are now in a position to unpack these claims.

To say that tolerance is a moral virtue is to say that it specifies, orders, and (as virtue) perfects our appetites and does so with the ease and constancy of habit. To say that it is annexed to justice is to say, among other things, that it resides in the will and perfects those appetites that follow from a right rational apprehension of the human good. It is also to say that it regards human actions that bear on the good of another, actions that set right our relations with them. In general, this is the matter about which justice and its parts are concerned (human actions) and the end to which they tend (rightly ordered relations among persons). To say that tolerance resides in the will with

---

which "consists in applying to action the things counseled and judged" (*ST* II-II.47.8). Reason commands the power of the soul that regards the means chosen (*ST* I-II.17.3), which is followed by the will's use of that power in order to execute the choice (*ST* I-II.16.4; 17.3.1).

other virtues, other parts of justice, is to say that it has a distinct matter about which it is concerned, a special kind of human action that it regards, and a distinct collection of ends to which it tends, above all a special kind of rightly ordered relationship.

Thomas puts the point this way: "All the moral virtues that are about operations agree in the one general notion of justice, which is in respect of something due another: but they differ according to various special notions" (*diversas speciales rationes*) (*ST* I-II.60.3). The special *ratio* of tolerance follows from the special character of the relationship it regards, the special due it delivers, and the distinct ends that it seeks by means of this act. The relationship it regards is one divided by an objectionable difference of some sort. The due it delivers is a right response to this difference, and it regards only those responses that can be ordered to its distinct ends: to the peace and well being of the society that the tolerant share with the tolerated and to the autonomy that each enjoys with respect to the difference in dispute. Finally, to say that tolerance is annexed to justice as a potential, but not an integral, part is to say, on the one hand, that tolerance has the essential character of justice insofar as its act renders to others some good that is their due according to equality. It is to say that the truly tolerant set right their relationship with the tolerated as they deliver the good that is in fact due, that is equal to what is actually owed. On the other, it is to say that tolerance can, in certain instances, fall short of the perfection of justice precisely because it can regard ends that are shared but not public, relations that are social but not political, and acts that are not specified by legal precept. It is to say that in some times and places, in some circumstances and relationships, tolerance is an integral part of justice, while in others it is not.

All of this follows from the definitions and distinctions that we have borrowed from Aquinas. At the same time, a number of matters remain opaque and clarity will come only as we consider some objections and attend to some of the inferences that follow from our definitions. It is to these that we must now turn.

Tolerance shares the essence of justice, but not its perfection. What does this essential identity and specific difference amount to? The just, Thomas tells us, are disposed by habit to render to others the good that is their due with a constant and perpetual will. It's a fair enough definition, but what does justice involve in act? Well, for starters, consider the fact that the human good is diverse in kind and number, and so too the various social and political relationships that human beings might inhabit, identities they might have, roles they might play, and offices they might occupy. Consider as well the various contingencies of time, place, and circumstance that frame human action. And finally consider the fact that these various diversities and contingencies intersect in all kinds of ways in any given circumstance and that the just invariably attend to each of these variables. They must. By habit they are disposed to discover what the good of another actually is in this or that circumstance, to think that they are obliged to make this discovery, and to realize that neither disposition can be fulfilled without attention being paid. Since it is human relations that justice regards and sets right, relations mediated through external actions and things, it is not any and every good of another that we are obliged to provide in act but only the good that is actually due this or that person given their specific relation to us in this or that circumstance. Determining what the good of another amounts to is one thing. Concluding that this particular person is due this particular good from us in this specific circumstance is another thing altogether. Each of these determinations requires *iudicium* and presumably the just act tolerantly when their habitual disposition to offer the good that is due in response to disagreement and difference elicits sound judgment about the character of that response. They act tolerantly when they conclude that *this* particular response to *this* particular objectionable difference is what *this* particular person is due in *this* particular circumstance.

So far so good, but other matters remain murky. For example, what does it mean to say that a paradigmatic act of tolerance—the patient endurance of another's objectionable difference—is good, that it delivers *their* good to them, something they are due by right? Well, if tolerance is a virtue, then as habit and act it must be, like the other moral virtues, a mixed good, both good in itself and an instrument that helps the tolerant achieve other ends, other goods. This is what it means to say that a virtue confers not only aptness to act in this way or that, "but also the right use of that aptness." And it is because a virtue has this dual aspect that it "makes its possessor good, and his work good likewise" (*ST* I-II.56.3). On this rendering, the instrumental aspect of the virtue's goodness seems easy enough to make out. The tolerant endure the objectionable differences of another in order to maintain the society they share, the peace that abides between them, and the autonomy each enjoys with respect to the differences in dispute. The tolerant conclude that these ends are worth having, that they have a certain intrinsic goodness of their own, and that they can be had in this particular instance by resorting to this particular act. By habit, the tolerant tend toward these rightly ordered relations when confronted with these particular differences. No doubt, the tolerant will bring benefit to *themselves* as these ends are achieved and these goods had. After all, when a just act achieves just ends it sets a relationship right, and a rightly ordered relationship is a common good, one that is shared and enjoyed in common by those who participate in the relationship. But to say that tolerance belongs to justice is to say that the tolerant intend to achieve these ends, to enjoy this common good, not only for themselves but also and principally for the neighbor who is the source of the difference in dispute. It is to say that tolerance, like justice, sets a relationship right and that the relationship set right is the end that the tolerant hope to achieve, the common good they hope to secure for and share with the person they tolerate.

As with justice itself, this can be done in more than one way, in more than one social setting. If the society in question is a political community, then the tolerant achieve these goods for a specific member of that community indirectly, through the mediation of the laws. Their patient endurance of another, of her actions and attitudes, is specified by legal precept and directed immediately to the common good of all. She is due this act only insofar as she is a member of that polity, and she receives its benefit only insofar as she shares in that good. This same logic of intention applies in domestic and civil settings, but without the command of law. The tolerant intend to achieve the common goods of family life or civic association for all who participate in these societies, and the tolerated receive these benefits only insofar as they are members. In each of these cases—political, civic, domestic—the good that is due the tolerated by right is the common good *for the* that she shares with all others. She is tolerated for the sake of that good and *take of.* enjoys its benefits only as all others do as well.[10]

This logic helps us account for three different cases, three different attitudes toward the person tolerated and the common good shared with them. In the first two cases, the tolerant endure an objectionable difference in order to maintain the well-ordered and peaceful society they share with the tolerated. In both, the tolerated receive this benefit precisely because (and only as) they are members of that society. But in the first case, the tolerant actually desire these benefits for the tolerated, and they hope that the tolerated will remain in the society they share. The tolerant want to secure the common goods of that society, but they also want the person they tolerate to enjoy these goods and share in that society. They hope, in other words, that the tolerated will continue in their company, in the society sustained by their patient endurance. In the second case, this latter hope is absent. The tolerant want to secure the common good of a well ordered social relationship for the person they tolerate, not because they want him to remain a member, but because for now he *is* a member, and because the common good of the society as a whole cannot be had without recognizing that he is and providing what he is due in accord with his standing.

---

10   For the most part, Thomas uses *bonum commune* in order to refer to goods had and enjoyed in common within a political community, above all the common good of a rightly ordered political relationship (*ST* II-II.58.6). Less strictly speaking, he uses the phrase to refer to rightly ordered relationships in other kinds of associations. Domestic prudence, for example, is "directed to the common good of the home or family" (*bonum commune domus vel familiae*) (*ST* II-II.47.11). I will use the phrase even more loosely to refer to any rightly ordered relationship shared by the participants of a social relationship of any scale or kind, from friendships to cosmopolitan communities.

Consider Uncle Halvor. Prone to racist innuendo and cruel bigotry across the holiday dinner table, you tolerate him nonetheless. You can't avoid him by refusing your mother's invitation or breaking off relations with the family. The first would be unjust, and the second just isn't possible. As Albert Hirschman reminds us, families are not easily exited, even when relations deteriorate, and this fact tends to stimulate voice.[11] But perhaps not here. All things being equal, Halvor certainly deserves to be publically corrected if not roundly denounced, not endured in silence, but the circumstances give you pause. You know that correction won't work, it might even egg him on, and you suspect that a denunciation will push gloomy Aunt Hildegard into ever deeper depression and destroy the already fragile society you share with your mother's family. Moreover, you know that the young people in the room already despise Uncle Halvor's racism, so their moral formation is not at risk. To avoid scandal, you may want to pull them aside after the fact and explain why you kept your mouth shut, but this is easily done. So tolerance is the better course. You endure Uncle Halvor. You might try to redirect the conversation to a topic less likely to prompt his racism, but in the end you tolerate his presence and his odious remarks for the sake of the society you share with him in the company of these others. You secure this common good for *him* insofar as he *is* a member, but you would shed no tears if Aunt Hildegard would leave him and if he would depart the family. So it goes. In some instances, the tolerant person endures another in the hope that the common goods secured by this act and due this other will be shared with him. In other instances, the tolerant provide this due and intend these ends but without this hope.

In the third case, the society in question extends no further than the relationship that abides between two individuals, and the tolerance that perfects that relationship belongs to particular justice and proceeds according to a different logic of intention. When the tolerant act, their patient endurance of objectionable difference secures both fellowship with the tolerated and peace in that fellowship directly. In this case, there is no Uncle Halvor scenario, no divide between the good intended for the society and the good desired for the tolerated. There is no chance that I might tolerate another for the sake of the common good of the society we share but without directly intending to secure that good for them.

It is precisely because we can imagine the tolerant pursuing their ends in each of these social settings and relationships that tolerance is a potential, not an integral, part of justice, that some of its acts fall under legal precept and some do not, that some are chosen for the sake of a common good that many might share while others are chosen for the sake of a relationship that is shared in common by none other than the tolerant and the neighbor they

11   Hirschman, *Exit, Voice, and Loyalty*, 97–98.

tolerate. It is to say, as I have said, that tolerance can share the essence of justice but not its perfection. But the real point is that in every social setting, every kind of relationship, the tolerant act justly. They respond to the objectionable differences of their neighbors as they should and when patient endurance is due they choose this act for the sake of those ends, those common goods that they intend to secure *for* the neighbor who deserves this endurance. And this good can be secured for the tolerated in one of two ways: either directly, when tolerance is a species of particular justice, or indirectly, when it is part of legal, civic, or domestic justice. In the first way, tolerance delivers this good to the tolerated through direct intention. In the second way, it delivers this good to the tolerated through their membership in the society that the tolerant intend to maintain by means of their act. A response to difference that does not intend to secure these goods for the tolerated in one of these two ways cannot be an act of true tolerance.

Some may find this account of tolerant ends and intentions odd, if not misleading. They might point out that more often than not the tolerant endure the objectionable differences of others in order to secure civil peace and social stability for themselves. By these lights, the tolerant would prefer to intervene against their neighbor's objectionable difference but find they cannot without forsaking the peaceful society that they love. So they endure this difference, but not because they hope to secure this peace for that neighbor, but rather because they fear the loss of this good for themselves were they to intervene as they would like.[12]

But this can't be right, not if tolerance belongs to justice. If it belongs to justice, then it delivers to others those goods they are due by right, in this instance the goods secured by tolerant acts. These goods are had and enjoyed in common by all who participate in the relevant relationship; they are aspects of that relationship set right. But this means that one cannot act tolerantly without intending to secure *these* goods *for* another, and one cannot intend to secure these goods for another while erasing oneself, while denying oneself the same, that same relationship set right. Indeed, if you deny yourself the good of that relationship set right, a relationship that cannot exist without your participation, then, by definition, you will fail to deliver to the other that same good, that relationship set right. Indeed, you will fail to act justly.

Of course, it may well be the case that many who act *among* the tolerant, who replicate their patient endurance but not their just intention, in fact

---

12   It's an objection of this sort that leads Nicholas Wolterstorff to doubt that a eudaemonist rendering of action and virtue can generate a convincing account of justice. By eudaemonist lights, an agent always acts for the sake of an end that she considers good, a good that she lacks and that will contribute to her happiness. Wolterstorff doubts that an act with *this* intention can be just, if only because the just, by definition, intend to deliver a good to *another*, the good *they* are due by right. The good of the person who acts justly is beside the point. See Wolterstorff, *Justice: Rights and Wrongs*, 149–179.

hope to secure the ends of the tolerant principally for themselves, just as it is certainly the case that many of those who admire and defend mutual tolerance assume that this self-regarding intention exhausts the disposition and justifies our resort to its act.[13] But why should we think that an account of what most of us do and intend as we act among the virtuous tracks the truth about virtue? If, by definition, a virtue is a habit that resides in a power of the soul and perfects its acts, and if perfection involves acting at the limit of that power for the sake of some good and in spite of some difficulty, then it should come as no surprise when Aristotle notes that action at this limit is rare and the truly virtuous few.[14] And if this is right, then it is likely that those of us who manage to act among the virtuous often fall short of virtue's perfection, in this instance by failing to intend as the virtuous do. So for example, surely some of us might manage to act among the courageous from time to time, coping with dangers to life and limb as they do and in their company, and yet not because we intend (as *they* do) to secure the good that is due another, but rather because we fear looking cowardly, or because we hope to win honors, or because we wish to avoid reproaches and legal penalties. Aristotle calls this variety of false courage "the bravery of citizens" and places it on top of his list of the virtue's semblances, presumably because public life provides abundant opportunity to pose in courageous company for the sake of other than just and courageous ends.

The same can be said of tolerance. Its false image appears repeatedly in our actions and in our philosophical portraits of the virtue, presumably because, as with courage, our lives provide numerous opportunities to act among the tolerant for reasons of our own. Disagreement and difference confound the various societies we inhabit, acts of toleration offer a useful solution to the problems of association that follow in turn, and these conditions provide those of us weak in virtue with sufficient reason to take up this solution and act among the tolerant. We want those problems of association solved and we want to enjoy the peace and autonomy that toleration's solution affords. That we intend these ends for ourselves alone, that we regard them as private possessions not common goods, denies us standing among the just, but then, one might reasonably ask why we should care about the loss of virtue's privileges. Civil peace and social survival are sought and acts of toleration emerge, not for our neighbor's sake of course, but why should this

---

13   That *acts of toleration* appear in response to fear and self-interest should hardly surprise. For an example of their appearance in early modern Europe, see Hill, "Toleration in Seventeenth-Century England." Nor should we discount the possibility that these actions actually deliver what is due, that they track the right, even as they fall short of true virtue, of right endurance done for the sake of tolerant ends. One can always do the right thing for reasons that fall short of the right.

14   Aristotle, *NE* 1156b25.

matter? If something like mutual toleration flourishes among those attentive to their own interests, and if this attention and this act in fact deliver to all what is right and due—both the endurance of their difference and the social peace and shared autonomy that this endurance yields—then why should we lament the less-than-virtuous intentions of those who participate in this regime? Given these salutary consequences of false tolerance, what difference does this deceit actually make? There might indeed be a difference between true tolerance and this particular false image, but it is not at all clear that it's difference that makes a difference. And if this is right, then why should we bother to distinguish false image from real perfection? Why praise and cultivate the latter when the former seems to serve the common good just as well and with far less moral effort? Why, in other words, should we care that tolerance is a virtue that belongs to justice?

Well, begin with the fact that an action acquires formal specification—it becomes this act and not that—by the end that the agent intends when she acts (ST I-II.1.3). The end tells us what she did and should govern our description of her deeds. Thus, for example, one might steal for all sorts of reasons, all sorts of ends, and those ends do more to specify the act than the theft itself. This means, on the one hand, that "he who steals that he may commit adultery is, strictly speaking, more adulterer than thief" (ST I-II.18.6; cf. NE 1130a29–33). On the other, it means that two acts of thieving done for the sake of formally different ends are strictly speaking, two different actions. The same applies to tolerance. Two acts of patient endurance done for the sake of different ends are, strictly speaking, two different acts. A person does one kind of thing when she endures an objectionable difference in order to secure peace and stability for herself in the company she happens to keep. She does something quite different when she acts in order to achieve these goods for the members of the society she inhabits, herself included, but principally for those persons whose difference she endures. Although she performs the same material act in each instance, formally her actions are quite distinct, and, presumably only one of them, the second, belongs to justice, which by definition regards the good of another. Let's call this latter variety an act of true tolerance, and the other, "ordinary toleration." Now that we have distinguished these acts by their ends, let's reframe our opponent's question this way: why should we prefer true tolerance to ordinary acts of toleration when the effects of true virtue—the right is done and the good achieved—are hardly distinguishable from the successes of its semblance?[15]

15   Following Aristotle's lead, I assume here a political context and consider the variety of tolerance that is annexed to legal justice and the semblance that mimics this variety. The variety of tolerance annexed to particular justice has a similar semblance, its own potential disorder with respect to its ends.

It's a sensible question and yet there are a couple of reasons to resist its suspicion of virtue. The first regards the inconstancy of the semblance, while the second regards our ability to describe its acts and effects truthfully. Both reasons begin with the fact that those who perform acts of ordinary toleration regard these effects as private goods. If you treat social peace and individual autonomy in accord with this regard, then you intend to secure these goods for those with whom you share some sort of society precisely because you think that this is the best way to secure them for yourself. You don't want these goods for yourself in their company as common members of a common society. Rather you intend to secure these goods for yourself and you will secure them for these others as a means to this end.

Notice the temptation that accompanies this intention. If there is some other way to secure these goods for oneself on one's own terms, then presumably one will. One endures patiently because the circumstances of the act offer no other options, no other way to secure the peace that one loves for oneself. But this means that one will resort to means less painful and demanding once circumstances improve. There are, after all, other ways to cope with objectionable differences and other ways to secure a peace of one's own. Given access to those other ways, one will likely abandon the regime of mutual toleration as soon as one can. Where this leaves the rest of us depends on what one does. Replacing mutual toleration with coercion will obviously affect our lives in unwelcome ways. Replacing it with tactical withdrawal from our objectionable company might leave the rest of us relatively untouched, but then again, it might not. When the wealthy and the powerful retire to their enclaves, to gated communities and private schools, they tend to take their talents and resources with them, which surely leaves the rest of us diminished. But the real point is that the person who tolerates others in this ordinary way does not actually want civil peace *for us and with us*, even if it is our right. He resorts to actions that generate this public benefit only as he must in order to secure it for himself, and he is likely to forsake those actions whenever he can secure a peace of his own by some less burdensome means.

Consider what follows, or rather, what doesn't. For of course it's not exactly clear whether the arrangements that emerge from this particular semblance of tolerance can in fact be called a society. According to Augustine's minimalist definition, a society is "an assembled multitude of rational creatures bound together by a common agreement as to the objects of their love" and it is not at all clear that ordinary toleration manages to generate a multitude of even this minimalist sort, which brings us to the second reason to resist its charms.[16] Once again trouble comes from the fact that those

---

16 *Civ. Dei* XIX.24. According to his more robust definition, a society is a multitude united in fellowship by common agreement about what is right (*civ. Dei* XIX.21).

who perform ordinary act of toleration treat common goods as though they were private, which of course, they're not. Social peace and individual autonomy can neither be secured and nor enjoyed on one's own. They can only be had as others have them. No doubt, they can be *treated* as private goods, just as one can treat the local public park like one's own backyard—digging up its shrubs, ignoring its curfews, letting the dog do his business on its paths, and so on. But there is a kind of self-deception in this. You can treat a public park as if it is your own, but of course it isn't, and treating it as though it is doesn't make it so. By the same token, social peace and individual autonomy are common goods, and they remain so even when the intentions that produce acts of ordinary toleration deny this fact about them. There is a fundamental incompatibility between the regard this variety of false tolerance has for these goods and their actual moral reality, and this incompatibility should be enough to convince our imaginary opponent that the distinction between true tolerance and this particular semblance matters, that the former is worth having and the latter worth avoiding. Ordinary toleration encourages this deception about the moral facts on the ground, and few of us want to be so deceived. Still, the real trouble here has more to do with consequences than with truth. That is, in the end, there is something fundamentally self-defeating about an appeal to ordinary toleration in order to secure the common goods of a social or political relationship. Why? Because the person who offers ordinary toleration in order to acquire these benefits for herself does not consider herself a participant in a common social enterprise. She does not think that peace within a social relationship and autonomy among members are goods that must be pursued and enjoyed in common with others, and she does not suppose that her interests and prospects depend in every instance upon those particular shared pursuits and common enjoyments. Put simply, her regard for these goods, her willingness to cast them under private intention, undermines the society of shared loves that has emerged in response these goods.

Notice the fallout. If you reduce tolerance to this semblance, this imposter, and then propose it as a solution to the problems of association posed by disagreement and difference, then you invariably undermine what you hope to secure. Why? Because a society cannot be maintained and its welfare secured as one encourages its members to regard its common goods as private possessions. If enough people regard these goods in this way and their actions in these terms—and ordinary toleration does indeed encourage this regard—then it's not at all clear that it's a society that they share. Better to say that their resort to this particular semblance of tolerance bears witness to its absence and to their despair, to the fact that a life of shared loves for goods held in common is no longer an object of their hope. By contrast, one cannot regard a good as common, as belonging to oneself only as it belongs to others, without regarding these others as in some way one's own, without sharing some sort of society with them and hoping that this shared life can be sustained in spite of the disagreements and differences that divide them.

It follows that the person who is truly tolerant is distinguished, at least in part, by her habitual willingness to endure the right sorts of objectionable differences for the sake of the peaceful society and individual autonomy that she shares with others, and she intends to secure these goods and that society by this act for herself (no doubt) but principally for those with whom she shares this society. She intends to secure this good for the person she tolerates, which implies, as we have said, that the truly tolerant person acts justly. She endures the objectionable difference of some other in order to secure for them the common good that is their due, in this instance the society she shares with the one who offends, the peace that sustains what they share, and the autonomy that abides among members across this particular difference. And presumably, she could not act in this way for the sake of these ends, if she did not participate in that society of shared goods and common loves from the start and if she did not hold that society dear. When it is threatened by difference and disagreement, she tolerates those who offend, at least in part, because the shared society counts more than the offense. It is this peaceful sociality with them that she wants, and she tolerates their objectionable differences in order to secure this good for them and with them.[17]

Recall that this can be done with two quite different attitudes toward the tolerated. In some instances, the tolerant person hopes that the tolerated will remain in her company and enjoy the common goods of that fellowship in spite of their differences and disagreements. It as if she says to those she tolerates, "let us not allow this difference to sunder the society that we share, unsettle the peace that we love, or cause us to forget what we owe each other." This is the hope built into her tolerant acts and a version of this hope infuses our praise of this version of the virtue. We desire the habit and praise its act, in part because we want to sustain the relationships we care about, and in part because we hope that new social relations might be possible and that new depth might be had in those we already have. Indeed, this is

---

17   Tolerance regards actions objectionable in some way, dispositions and passions that generate those actions, and persons disposed to act in those ways. Why then do I speak of tolerating actions and *things*? Because tolerance is a part of justice and justice regards and perfects human relations that are mediated through external actions, but also things. At times, our tolerance of another is mediated through something. So, for example, we might say that I tolerate my sister's meatloaf, and I suppose in a way I do. It *is* objectionable, and when she serves it I do endure it. That said, the community I share is with my sister, not her meatloaf, which means that if it was not *hers*, I would not tolerate it. Strictly speaking, I tolerate my sister and her cooking, not the meatloaf, even as my tolerance is unintelligible apart from that objectionable thing.

one of the reasons parents want their children to be tolerant: so that social relations of various kinds might be possible for them. In other instances, the tolerant person acts without this hope. She wants to secure the peaceful sociality that the tolerated are due as members, but she would rather that they depart than remain. This is the tolerance that she offers to those whose words and deeds are gravely unjustly and who are unlikely to change their ways. Racist Uncle Halvor is one example, but there are others. When abortion providers are endured by those who consider their actions unjust and their commitment to the injustice unshakable, the tolerance offered does not necessarily come with a desire to retain the company of the tolerated. For some, these acts might express a desire to maintain the shared life that is already present, to secure its peace, and to deliver these common goods to all members, even to those whose company the tolerant do not, all things considered, hope to keep.

It matters then, that we regard tolerance as a part of justice precisely because it matters that we regard its ends truthfully and because justice insists that we do. After all, the just can't act without a truthful account of what others are due by right. The tolerant recognize this requirement of justice and manage to fulfill it, at least in part, as they treat common goods as common and work to deliver those goods to those who deserve them.

This conclusion helps us better understand the resentment directed toward tolerance in the modern period. More precisely, it casts doubt on a collection of assumptions that tend to encourage complaint with both tolerance and modernity. As we noted in chapter 1, it is widely assumed that tolerance emerged in the wake of the wars of religion that followed the Protestant Reformation and that as practice and act it expresses modernity's moral commitments, above all its high regard for individual choices that serve private interests. For some, this collection of assumptions captures what they consider most admirable about tolerance: its attention to the lives and interests of individuals. But for others, these assumptions merely confirm their suspicions about tolerance and goad their desire to expose its swindle. For them, tolerance cannot be counted among the virtues, precisely because it protects modernity's most harmful excess, its reckless individualism. The fact that philosophers tend to reduce tolerance to its self-interested semblance, where the act itself expresses this recklessness and harm, only confirms this suspicion and authorizes this complaint.

But this can't be quite right. If tolerance is in fact a virtue annexed to justice, then neither these assumptions nor these inferences capture all that must be said about it. As we have seen (and as we shall see in the pages and chapters that follow), there's no disputing the fact that the tolerant want their patient endurance to preserve autonomy, but nor can we say that they desire this good for themselves alone. Indeed, like social peace, they assume that autonomy is a common good, that it can be had only as others have it.

So too, there's no denying that a certain variety of tolerance emerges in the modern period, one with a generous account of those actions and things that fall under autonomous choice. Since each period seems to corrupt true virtue in its own way, in accord with its own distinctive excesses, it may well be that hyperindividualism and reckless self-interest are the principal sources of this variety's decay in our time and place. And, in any case, as I have said, virtue's semblances abound, and it may be that one or more imposter is more prominent in modern life than true tolerance itself. It may be that the "tolerance" with which we are most familiar is nothing but this self-interested semblance, nothing but tactical endurance dressed in virtue's garb. Even so, we should not be duped into complaint against real virtue by the excesses and prominence of its imposters. Nor should we conclude, as so many critics have, that this particular semblance, so common in an age that accents private choice, exhausts what tolerance might be. It's a conclusion that enables these critics to cast doubt on both the virtue itself and the modern period altogether, but as we have seen and as we shall see, it also turns on a couple of confusions—on the failure to distinguish true and apparent virtue, no doubt, but also on the failure to imagine equivalents of our own virtues and vices appearing in the lives and practices of another time and place.

These are related confusions; they compound each other. If one mistakes a semblance for a virtue, and if one assumes that the semblance exhausts what the virtue might be and distinguishes the age one happens to inhabit, then, chances are, one will consider that age corrupt, its virtues bankrupt, and its moral isolation from other ages unbridgeable. One will conclude that true virtue resides elsewhere, but not here. If, by contrast, one attends to the differences that divide virtues and semblances, if one thinks that real virtues matter even as their semblances abound, and if one does not exaggerate the moral divide between this time and that place, then it is unlikely that one can muster complaint against the virtues of one's age. Or, more precisely, it is unlikely that one will be able to cast complaint against the semblances of virtue that appear in one's own age in the language of global resentment and wistful longing. Resist these temptations and forsake these resentments, and one might still lament the scant distribution and ragged condition of the moral virtues in one's own time and place. One might despair over the prospects for rectifying these imperfections. But these responses regard the conditions of true virtue not its reality, and every age should care for the former while resisting the temptation to confuse the semblances of virtue for the real coin and the imperfections of true virtue for its semblances.

We have already noted how frequently discourse about tolerance bears witness to these conceptual confusions and exaggerated complaints, and we have seen how difficult they are to sustain once we find tolerance among the virtues that come packaged with our human form of life and annexed to justice as one of its parts. Spelling out what it might mean to find tolerance in this company is the task before us. Now that its ends have been considered, we must look to its object and act. We have not considered every imaginable end that an act of patient endurance might have, but then how could we? Surely one can endure the objectionable differences of others for the sake of all sorts of ends, more than one could catalogue without tedium, and surely the semblances of tolerance are at least as numerous as those sorts. At the same time, an act can fall short of virtue's perfection in more than one way. As we have seen, it can be disordered with respect to its end, but disorder can also come to the act itself, regardless of its end. Our next task is to consider a tolerant response to disorder of this kind.

ACT, OBJECT, AND CIRCUMSTANCES

Consider the following example of the tolerance that perfects familial relations, the tolerance that belongs to domestic and particular justice. Why begin here? Because Augustine is surely right when he insists that the virtues emerge in the smallest societies and the most basic, unavoidable associations, and that larger societies and political associations are perfected by virtues that bear traces of these beginnings.[18] This is certainly true of tolerance, which typically begins at home, in families and among coworkers and neighbors.

Homework complete, chores done, my ninth grader retires to his room to listen to music that I despise. He's a good kid, respectful of others, so he keeps the door closed and the volume low. Still, from where I sit (in the living room most likely) there is nothing much to admire about the music he loves. All beat and no melody, all posture and no substance, all rage and no craft, all dissonance and no harmony—if music affects the souls of the young as Plato contends, then my son's soul will soon be ill-formed. Exaggerated fears or not, what is to be done? Well, I could cast aside my reading, leap out of my chair, storm down the hall, burst into his room, unplug the device, and rant. I could toss him my dog-eared copy of the *Republic* and insist that he read books II and III. "No book report, no dinner!" I could dash into my study and download the music that would save his soul: Mozart and Bill Monroe, Palestrina and Charlie Parker, Bob Wills and Fats Waller. I could make threats and issue pronouncements. I could, in other words, use my paternal office to coerce his conduct in the hope that his taste in music might follow.

18 Augustine, *civ. Dei* XIX.14, 16.

Or, alternatively, I could cultivate a settled indifference to this thumping offense that resounds down the hall. It's not that bad really, and even if it is, why bother? Why be troubled by Platonic worries that are, quite frankly, anachronistic at best, and dripping with snobbery at worst? And why fall under the spell of those contemporary interpreters of Plato who accent his account of disordered music and damaged souls in order to disparage democracy? Why allow my overwrought parental anxieties to corrupt my judgment, equal parts philosophical and practical? Why indeed? And if, after all of these mental gymnastics, the music still offends, well, then perhaps I should just get the boy some proper headphones. It would kill two birds with one stone: his pleading for this purchase would cease and I could return the house to quiet and my soul to peace, untroubled by what I cannot hear.

Or, if I am unwilling to abandon him with indifference, I suppose I could go native and get hip. I could learn to love what I once loathed. I could sashay down the hall, plop down on his bed, and listen in. I could become his initiate. I could learn the beats, the rhymes, and the moves. I could become what I despise: the tuned in dad, the Peter Pan papa who tempts the contempt of his child. I could, in other words, accept the music that I was at first inclined to dislike.

Any one of these options, or some combination of them, is available to me, but chances are, I'll just stay put, keep quiet, and endure what I dislike. I'll suffer this noise, this insult to the soul, his and mine. I'll object to what I hear but tolerate it nevertheless. Fair enough. But suppose I am pressed to justify this response, how might I reply, what would I say? More to the point, how do I know that my patient endurance of this particular objectionable difference is in fact an act of true tolerance, of real justice? How do I know that this act is the good that my son is due from me in this instance, the good that justice demands, the good that is his by right? Could it be that something else is owed, that he deserves some other act, whether coercion, indifference, or acceptance? Could it be that my virtue is false, that my act of toleration is in fact callous and inattentive, cowardly and unjust?

Well, we might be tempted to say that my patient endurance is just and good, that it deserves to be called true tolerance because of the intentions I happen to have, because the end I intend to achieve with this act has a goodness that trumps all others, and because the act itself is well ordered to that end. It has a good chance of achieving the peaceful society and shared autonomy that I want for my son with my son. But this can't be right, or at the very least, this reply ducks the question. We are not asking whether this act is ordered to an end that is just and good, and, in this instance, without peer. Rather we are assuming that it is so ordered and that the goodness of this end is, for now, beside the point. Indeed, it must be if it is the goodness of the act ordered to the end that concerns us here, for these are different matters. The intended end might fix an act in its species considered formally, but the end does nothing to alter its material substance (*ST* I-II.18.6). As we have already noted, an act has no matter "of which" (*ex qua*) it is made, but every act has an object, a "matter that it regards" (*materia circa quam*), and some objects have moral substance apart from the end they are ordered to achieve (*ST* I-II.18.2.2). Returning for a moment to Aquinas's example, while it may well be the case that "he who steals in order to commit adultery is more adulterer than thief," this fact changes neither the material substance of the act, nor its moral status. The act was still thieving, and theft, like a handful of other acts, is evil in its species, which is to say that its object, "to appropriate another's property," is, by definition, in "disaccord with reason" (*ST* I-II.18.5.2). Presumably Aquinas means that its object is unsuitable to right reason, to our better judgment, and presumably it is because the object specified by right reason comes loaded with moral content in sufficient measure that we are able to consider theft evil in its species. Thieving is not just taking what another has, for of course, not all takings involve theft. Borrowing, repossessing, reclaiming, taxing, and so on are certainly takings, but they are not equivalent to thieving, at least not always. Thieving, by contrast, always involves taking what rightfully belongs to another, and thus by definition—by the kind of act that it is as specified by its object—theft is always evil, always unjust, always a violation of right. One cannot steal without violating this right, without doing this harm, and these facts specify the moral reality of the act even when it is done for the sake of an end that is itself just and good.

Notice what follows. While theft is unjust in its species, taking what another has is not. This does not mean that borrowing, repossessing, reclaiming, taxing, and so on can't be unjust, that they can't be theft, but rather that sometimes they are and sometimes they aren't. In Thomas's lingo, they are indifferent in their moral species at the start of moral assessment (*ST* I-II.18.8). With actions of this sort, deliberation about what to do and evaluation of what others have done require right reason's judgment. The local sheriff takes my neighbor's cow and my neighbor cries "thief!" Is he right to do so? Assume for now that the sheriff's intentions are impeccable, that she acts in service of the common good, and that she intends to secure this good for the members of our society by means of this act and through the mediation of the laws. Assume as well that she has kept watch over the circumstances of the act and that none of them vitiate what was done (*ST* I-II.18.10). In that event, the act will be fixed in its moral species—that is, we will be able to say whether it is just or unjust, good or evil—once we know what its object is, and we will know what its object is once we have determined the cow's rightful owner. If it turns out that my neighbor is in arrears on his taxes, that the tax codes are just, and that the civil magistrate who has rightful authority over these matters has determined that this debt must be set right by transferring ownership of this cow and removing it from this field, then neither the transfer nor the taking was theft. Neither involved taking what rightfully belongs to another, precisely because, in this instance, the cow did not belong to my neighbor, even as it grazed on his grass and found shelter in his barn.

Is toleration's patient endurance like theft? Does its moral substance come packaged with the act itself? No, but then, most acts are nothing like this. Most are like "taking what another has" or "walking across a field," where the moral species of the act remains undefined even as its object is known. We might know, in general terms, what was done and yet remain uncertain about its moral substance until we situate the act in its circumstances and take note of the end that it has been chosen to achieve (*ST* I-II.18.9.1; 20.1). Apart from these findings, we won't know whether the act was good or evil, just or unjust. In Aquinas's language, it will remain in its natural species (*ST* I-II.1.3.3), and an act of patient endurance is like this. If we assume that it was chosen for the sake of a tolerant end—for the social peace that is shared with the tolerated and mutual autonomy with respect to the difference in dispute—then it will be the circumstances, the who, what, where, and how of the act, that determine its moral substance.

So then, suppose someone objects to something about another, something said or done or embodied in the other's life, and suppose she responds with toleration's act, its patient endurance. Is this act good and this good due this person? Is this an act of true tolerance? Well, it depends on a couple of things. First, is the difference in dispute in fact objectionable, or at the very least, does the person who finds it so have good reason to think that it is. Some differences are in fact objectionable, some are not, and some are thought to be so even when they are not. So for example, we often hear of the need for tolerance in response to racial differences, and I suppose this was a sensible goal for some to have in the early days of the American civil rights movement. White racism and privilege were entrenched in all sorts of institutions and political arrangements, all sorts of practices and lives, and racial differences were used to justify inequalities of power, status, and recognition. While it might have been easy to imagine the speedy transformation of at least some of these realities by the force of law, as we know, the institutional sources and regimes of power that reproduce white racism have been slow to change, and so too many hearts and minds. Participants in the movement knew this. They assumed that real progress would take years, perhaps generations, and they disciplined their hopes to this reality. Dr. King wanted the humanity of African Americans acknowledged, and he wanted them admitted to the promise of American life from which they had been excluded. He hoped that the movement would eventually yield reconciliation and civic friendship, and yet he did not expect immediate love or welcome from those who benefited from their whiteness.[19] He assumed that many of his fellow citizens would object to the African Americans with whom they would eventually share a social and political life. No doubt, he considered these objections false and repugnant, but the fact that he gestured toward toleration indicates that he also considered them inevitable. He was, after all, trying to transform a time and place where power and privilege tracked racial difference and where white racism and regional resentment were taken in with every breath, perched on every corner, and buried deep in every plot and field. In these circumstances, finding racial difference objectionable might be difficult for some to avoid even if they were obliged to avoid it. Here, the call for patient endurance might well make sense.[20]

But does it make sense now? Well, can we imagine someone in our day, on this side of the civil rights struggle, who, given everything else he believes and is obliged to know, has good reason to find racial difference objectionable? Can we imagine him acting in accord with his epistemic rights as he concludes that racial difference is a proper object of toleration? Well, maybe. Maybe a child raised in a white supremacist compound, removed from the rest of us on a rural mountaintop. But apart from cases of extreme moral and epistemic isolation, most of them imaginary, it is actually quite difficult to find someone from our time and place who has good reason to consider racial differences objectionable. Because, of course, they aren't and most of us are obliged to know as much and to realize that toleration's endurance cannot be a just response to those racial differences that continue to matter

19   King, "Experiment in Love," 17.

20   As far as I can tell, Dr. King never spoke of tolerance directly. He did, however, distinguish a desegregated community from an integrated, blessed commonwealth in a way that provides for an intermediary regime of toleration. By integration he meant a change of heart, by desegregation the restraint of the heartless. The former requires eternal grace, the latter temporal law. "Desegregation will break down the legal barriers and bring men together physically, but something must touch the hearts and souls of men so that they will come together spiritually because it is natural and right." Presumably, in the meantime, toleration must flourish (King, "Ethical Demands for Integration," 124). Would it be true tolerance that emerged in these circumstances, acts of real virtue? No. The act regarded differences that are not in fact objectionable, that could have been judged differently, and it was very likely ordered to ends that fall short of the right. It might have been difficult for some to avoid finding racial differences objectionable, but it would also have been difficult for most to ignore the moral resources, some close at hand, that would have challenged this finding. And regardless, it's unlikely that acts of toleration offered begrudgingly would be ordered to just ends, to relations set right across lines of racial difference. Better to assume that those who offered toleration feared legal penalties and public reproaches in the new American republic that the civil rights movement was bringing about. Still, as Dr. King seemed to realize, begrudging endurance is better than violent exclusion. It might even offer persons and communities a first step toward moral transformation.

in American life. If this is right, then what is that just response? Well, if the truly tolerant are those who proceed in the world with a habitual desire to render to others the patient endurance they are due, then presumably *they* will know. Rendering this due with the consistency of habit will require that they respond justly to differences and disagreements of all kinds, and this ability will be the principal mark of their virtue. With the constancy of habit, they will single out those differences that are in fact objectionable and treat them differently from those that are not. They will distinguish those objectionable differences that are intolerably harmful from those that are harmlessly disagreeable, and they will know how to respond to each, dispensing coercion, correction, prophetic critique, and patient endurance in accord with these judgments and as circumstances warrant. And they will determine which unobjectionable differences deserve our acceptance and recognition, if not celebration and admiration, which deserve our indifference, if not apathy and inattention, and which deserve both responses— sometimes the one, sometimes the other. In contemporary America, racial differences bear witness to such a long history of injustice, resistance, and overcoming and inscribe so many divergent meanings and attitudes that all of these responses may be required, not all at once, but across a variety of circumstances and relationships. Race not only matters, but its complexity and significance generate precisely those special difficulties that require a virtuous response, one that expresses genuine justice, humility, and courage.

So, then, some differences cannot be considered objectionable and thus cannot be treated as proper objects of the patient endurance that we typically associate with tolerance. If, as is often the case, tolerance is nevertheless proposed as a proper response to those differences, then we should seek clarification. Is it a paradigmatic act of toleration that is in fact being proposed, objection united with patient endurance? Or, as is so often the case, is it an altogether distinct attitude, perhaps one that produces an image of toleration's paradigmatic act, something like indifference or acceptance, or perhaps something positive such as respect or recognition? This lack of clarity is relatively common. Consider, for example, the many organizations that say they are committed to promoting tolerance among peoples of different races, ethnicities, religious commitments, and gender identities. Their work is important and their goals just, and yet more often than not their declarations mislead. It's not acts of toleration they hope to promote, not the patient endurance of objectionable difference, but recognition, respect, and equal standing across various lines of difference, status, and power.

Teaching Tolerance, the web project of the Southern Poverty Law Center, offers a good example of this trouble.[21] On its pages, tolerance talk is really about these other matters, these other attitudes, which are terribly difficult

21   See http://www.splcenter.org/what-we-do/teaching-tolerance (accessed July 7, 2015).

to instill, particularly in those who consider the unobjectionable differences of race, religion, ethnicity, and sexual orientation objectionable nevertheless. We can hope that they will put aside their intolerant attitudes, but until they do we will most likely encourage *acts of toleration*. We will encourage them to endure the differences they find objectionable but in fact are not, and we will hope that this imperfect internal act succeeds in setting an external relationship right. Given this divide between aspiration and expectation, I suppose there is something sensible about this imprecise talk. It cuts the difference between internal act and objective right. So why then call it trouble? Most virtue terms bear this kind of conceptual complexity and we should not be surprised that tolerance does as well. As we have just noted, the term can denote these other attitudes precisely because they fall under virtue's perfection. The truly tolerant will accept and respect those differences that deserve recognition and understanding, disregard those that deserve indifference, and so on. So it might appear that there is little reason to tighten up this loose talk with a more precise vocabulary.

Except there's this. If the aim is to encourage recognition and respect across lines of racial difference, then there is something self-defeating about resorting to the language of toleration. Two reasons stand out, reasons that point in opposite directions. The first has to do with power and the creation of subjects who need to be tolerated. The second has to do with resentment and the hope that toleration will be offered by those who cannot recognize and respect what they should. First, as Wendy Brown points out, if the differences in question are identities or statuses, if they are created by institutions, practices, and discourses that sustain unjust inequalities of power and standing, and if they are (nevertheless) regarded as natural and fixed, then a plea for toleration will simply reinforce these differences and inequalities and encourage this regard. It will mask the arrangements of power that create certain identities as appropriate objects of toleration, as persons and lives that embody differences that are thought to be objectionable in some way and must be endured. And it hardly matters whether the call for toleration expresses a desire for something other than patient endurance, for mutual recognition and genuine respect. When it is taken at face value, when it is included in regimes of education and formation, it will likely contribute to the creation of marginalized subjects who are regarded as essentially different and so require endurance. The recognition and respect that are desired will be compromised by the misplaced appeal to toleration.[22]

The solution, some might say, is to take this appeal at less than face value. When recognition and respect are desired and yet toleration is proposed, we should accept the fact that this talk is loose. But this won't do either. Some

---

22 Brown, *Regulating Aversion*, 25–47, 149–175.

of our fellow citizens will contest the significance of these identities and statuses. They will deny that fields of power create them. They will refuse to offer respect and recognition to those who embody them. And they will fail to acknowledge the sorrows and joys of those who struggle to transform a marginalized identity into a site of sacred value, into a source of vitality, beauty, and community. We will no doubt try to change their minds and, if necessary, restrain their violence, and yet following Dr. King's lead, we will also encourage them to offer acts of toleration. Until real change comes, this is all we can expect. At the very least, these acts will set the relevant external relationships right. But here the second problem with loose tolerance–talk emerges, for it is precisely these necessary acts that it discredits. A plea for toleration that is really a request for recognition and respect has a good chance of being resented by those who are unable to honor the request. They will assume that it comes tainted with hypocrisy, with the desire to dissemble and manipulate. "They say they want us to endure what we despise, but truth be told they want us to forsake our objection. If pressed, they will admit as much. They don't want us to endure and muddle through. No, they want us to abandon our judgment and accept what we despise. Well, if that's what tolerance amounts to, then why bother, why recommend it? Why call this moral slight of hand a virtue in the first place?"

A dangerous and confused point of view, no doubt, but hardly surprising given the linguistic muddle that precedes it. If you make a plea for toleration when you mean to encourage acceptance and respect, then those who disagree with your specific judgments about the tolerable, the intolerable, and the acceptable will most likely express their disagreement by denouncing every resort to toleration's endurance. This loose talk only encourages this outcome, this doubt about rightful acts of toleration that genuine virtue might produce, and this doubt about tolerance the virtue undermines our ability to endorse its act in response to differences that actually require it. If loose talk threatens to produce this unwelcome yield, then we had better bring some precision to what we say.

Suppose we do just that, and suppose we confront some action or thing that is in fact objectionable. Suppose further that we have sufficient reason to think that it is. Does this justified objection oblige us to act tolerantly, to endure patiently? Is this what justice requires? Is this act from us the good that is rightfully due another in this instance? Well, again, it depends. As I just said, in some instances, when faced with some kinds of objectionable difference, toleration's patient endurance would actually be an unjust response, if only because some differences are, quite literally, intolerable, and more often than not we are obliged to know that they are. Imagine my teenage son was using his bedroom, not as a music sanctuary, but as a meth lab and a drug lair? Suppose I knew what was afoot. Suppose I objected to the criminality of these activities, lamented their spiritual sources, feared their physical consequences, and yet tolerated them nevertheless. ("What can I do? If I play it tough, crack down on his reckless behavior, and banish his friends, he'll just take his operation to some other home, to some greasy garage or moldy basement where I have no access, no way to protect him. At least this way I can keep watch over his activities and keep him safe in my own house. And besides, his self-esteem is so fragile, if I come down hard on him, who knows what would happen?") I suspect we would say that I was tolerating the intolerable, that my patient endurance of this danger- ous activity was more transparent vice than semblance of virtue. We would say that I was a coward and that my unchecked fear of my son's anger and my disordered desire for his love have prevented me from giving him the good that he is due in this instance, not patient endurance but something altogether different, something like determined coercion and wise correc- tion mixed with attentive, unconditional love. And doesn't this viciousness, this cowardly and unjust endurance of what ought not be endured, appear on every corner of every ward and precinct? Isn't it an ordinary response to those low-grade injustices that seem to pop up everywhere: racial slights at the office, sexist remarks in the classroom, class snobbery on the play- ground, religious bigotry in the boardroom, and so on? And it's precisely because this moral flabbiness is so frequently defended on appeal to real virtue, to the praise that tolerance typically receives and the scorn that intol- erance is always thought to deserve, that toleration's critics howl, and with good reason.

Still, it is worth noting that both the morally flabby and the resentful critic make the same mistake, and here we see its source. Both succumb to the dif- ficulty associated with the moral specification of toleration's act, and, as a re- sult, both collapse true tolerance into one of its semblances, the one to justify an injustice, the other to denounce the virtue defended in that justification. As is the case with every other virtue that involves operations, true tolerance is difficult to distinguish from its semblances precisely because its principal action—patient endurance of objectionable difference—is, at least at first, in- different morally speaking. Fixing that act in its moral species—ordering it to an end and nesting it in a collection of circumstances—is a challenge the tolerant address well. With wise counsel and sound judgment, it is a task they complete with the ease of habit. For the rest of us, it's a trap that we either avoid with hard work that replaces virtue's ease, or stumble into despite our best efforts. And it is precisely because tolerance regards the difficulties as- sociated with specifying the moral substance of its act that deceptions and manipulations so frequently and so easily confound our account of the virtue, our resort to its patient endurance, and our assessment of its merit.

With this in mind, consider another circumstance. Let's leave drugs and return to rock and roll. My son's music *is* objectionable. At the very least, *I* find it so. *I* can't be indifferent to this noise and I suspect that I have good reasons to protest. My son would probably dispute the objective merit of my aesthetic judgment, but I doubt he would find it surprising. Indeed, I suspect he would admit that he expects me to object and that the music becomes all the more powerful and pleasurable for him as I do. So it goes with teenage sons and stodgy fathers. But does my son deserve my endurance in this instance? Must I tolerate his music? Indeed, why not resort to coercion instead? Why not delete his playlist and replace its angry and ugly sounds with something just and beautiful? Why not cultivate his taste by force and so his save his soul?

Well, not because these efforts wouldn't necessarily work. Augustine's famous reply to Donatist complaints should convince us that loves can be compelled, not directly but obliquely, through the offices of the intellect. Attention can be focused and judgment transformed, and, for the most part, as the intellect goes, so goes the will's desire.[23] And of course, if medicinal coercion managed to make our musical loves unite, if it enabled the beautiful to captivate us together, then surely harmony would come to the society we share. So the uncertain efficacy of force has little to do with my resistance to this rough resort. With enough patience and determination on my part, it too might secure the peaceful fellowship that I desire for my son with my son. No, if I am truly tolerant, I will shun coercion precisely because this act itself denies my son the good that he is due in this instance. Regardless of its consequences, it would be unjust, we might say, precisely because he doesn't deserve to have his musical tastes pushed around by his father. Rather, he deserves tolerance because he deserves autonomy in this, and he can't have autonomy in this unless those with whom he shares his life are willing to suffer some of his objectionable choices. If the music he loves causes him harm along the way, well, I will have to trust that other choices will diminish its effects, some of them his, some of them mine. At the very least, I doubt that he will deliberate well and choose wisely, either in this setting or in others more weighty, if I deny him experience in choosing in these lighter venues.

So he chooses the music that he likes, while I, disliking what he chooses, tolerate what I hear as best I can. I can't be indifferent. The music *is* terrible and possibly harmful. I suppose I could try to sympathize with what I despise. There may be something sublime and important in this music, something that he hears and that I don't. If taking him seriously is a portion of what I owe, and if my tolerance is an expression of my valuing and respecting our relationship, then this effort to understand must surely accompany my endurance.[24] And certainly it is tolerance—my patient endurance of what

23   For an account of Augustine's efforts, see Bowlin, "Augustine on Justifying Coercion."
24   On the expressive character of virtuous action, see Adams, *Finite and Infinite Goods*, 214–228.

I currently dislike and his acknowledgment of it—that will provide the time and space we need for mutual recognition to come, understanding to grow, and for transformed selves to emerge.[25] There's no guarantee that I will succeed in this, and I can't act as though I have when I haven't. That would be false and transparent, a vile attempt to manipulate my son's affections, one that deserves the contempt that it would undoubtedly receive. If pressed for a response other than toleration's endurance, I suppose I could try to redirect his attention, contest his taste, and complicate his loves. I could take him to symphony concerts, blues festivals, and opera houses, all in hope that he might be seduced by things that are truly beautiful, truly sublime. But prospects for success in this are slim. Indirections of this kind, especially the not-so-subtle sort, rarely succeed with fifteen-year-olds, in part because teenagers see through the ruse too easily, in part because the ruse offers too little assurance that disagreement does not bleed into disrespect.

So I tolerate.[26] I don't pretend that I like what I loathe, but nor do I rant. And note, there is little passivity or inaction in this course, little disregard for my son's welfare. Once I have chosen a tolerant course of action, once I am deliberately tending toward tolerant ends, the object of my concern is not so much the harm that might result from the music, but rather the possibility of autonomy that I hope to secure for my son as I tolerate his choice. Teenagers typically desire what their friends do and thus it's not always autonomy that gets expressed in their choices. Unreflective mimesis tends to get in the way. If this is right, and if it's autonomy that my son deserves as the end of my tolerance, then it's unlikely that patient endurance *alone* will get him *what* he deserves. Other actions will also be required.

---

25   This is one way to describe Barbara Herman's mistake. She pits tolerance against the attention that might generate sympathy and understanding across lines of difference. This contrast might hold if tolerance is reduced to mere indifference, but not if it's a virtue. True tolerance assumes the just attention that Herman endorses. It also creates opportunity for the *opportunity* effects Herman desires, but without assuming they can be had without the time its patient endurance provides. I am grateful to Molly Farneth for helping me see this point.

26   Will tolerance be mutual here? Will my son tolerate my response to his music? Well, if he finds this difference in musical taste objectionable, if he has good reason to think that it is, and if the virtue resides in his soul, then yes, I suppose he will. But there's no guarantee in this. One or more of these conditions might fail to obtain, and if so, my tolerance might be met with some other response: indifference, anger, contempt, and so on. So it is with justice and its parts: although geared to goods shared in common, at times they work alone. Still, it's our shared life that my tolerance regards, and I have to assume that he too will contribute to the maintenance of that life. I have to assume that he will tolerate me as difference, objection, and justice demand. At the very least, I have to hope that he will come to tolerate as I do, or at least aspire to. (It's this hope that justifies our talk of tolerating the colicky cries of an infant.) Indeed, if it happens that I proceed without this hope and expectation, then it's not exactly clear that it's a society that we share or tolerance that I exhibit. And note, my hope is that he will tolerate as he is tolerated, not that he will share my taste in music.

Real autonomy comes with the ability to judge and desire knowingly, as Aquinas would put it, with the ability to make reflective assessments about one's own judgments and desires (*ST* I-II.6.2), presumably in response to the right sorts of challenges from those with the right sort of authority. One might hope that the potential for this kind of reflectiveness emerges willy-nilly with maturity and experience, but too often it doesn't and certainly in teenagers it needs to be cultivated and encouraged. In this instance, a little Socratic questioning might help. So can exposure to other sorts of music, other kinds of beauty, as can the wisdom that comes in knowing how to make the music that offends. Good garage bands tend to love good music of all kinds, and their members tend to be reflective about the good in the music they love.

At this point, some might say that this talk misleads. They might insist that to speak of autonomy as something due, as the end my tolerance seeks for my son, fails to account for the fact that, as his father, it's possible that I want this good for myself. I want him to be autonomous precisely because *his* autonomy is a portion of *my* happiness, and thus it's not *his* right that ultimately occupies my attention but my flourishing. But this can't be right, or at least, it can't be if it's true tolerance that I exhibit as I act. Two reasons stand out. First, tolerance regards actions that others are due regardless of the benefits that may or may not accompany them. I owe my son patient endurance of his objectionable music, full stop. It's this endurance that he is due regardless of the good that may come as a result of this act. This is a portion of what it means to say that tolerance belongs to justice, that it attends to the right. Second, as tolerance does in fact belong to justice, its acts will always be ordered to just ends, to a relationship set right by its act and to goods had and enjoyed in common. Autonomy is certainly one of those goods. The moral reflectiveness that genuine autonomy assumes, reflectiveness about the merit of the various ends we intend and means we chose, is something that one acquires and exercises in the company of others, in response to their challenges and counterclaims. Moreover, one can't intend to lead this or that life, pursuing this or that collection of ends, apart from a shared social context that makes certain pursuits possible and that provides for choice among them. It follows that if I am truly tolerant, then I will want this autonomy for my son with my son. I will want to partake of this good with him. He can't have it without sharing it with me and I can't want it for him without desiring it, as least indirectly, for myself. So it is with common goods and so it is that tolerance works.

If patient endurance of his difference is in fact a good that I owe my son in this instance, and if it's a certain measure of autonomy's reflectiveness that I hope to achieve with this act, then I need to do various things to deliver what I owe and achieve what I hope. And notice how these efforts and obligations emerge from our relationship and its roles, to the fact that he is my son and I am his father and that we share a certain sort of life together. Patient endurance is the good that he is due, the good that I am obliged to provide, in part because certain privileges come with that relationship and certain duties attach to these roles. Suppose my neighbor's boy listens to music of the same sort. Like my son he's a good kid. He doesn't play his music all that loud or late at night, but still, there he is, washing his mother's car in the driveway with that noise thumping from the speakers. Dozing in the hammock next door, I can't resist finding it objectionable, at least at first, and yet in this instance my dis-ease is different. It's not what I feel when I hear the same music coming from my son's bedroom. Why not? Surely it's because I don't worry as much about its effects on his soul. He is not my son after all, and I am neither authorized nor obliged to care for his welfare in quite the same way. Nor am I concerned with the harm that our disagreements about music might do to the community we share or to the neighborly peace that we both desire. In fact, I doubt our disagreement about *this* can generate these harms. Neighborhoods are not families and most do not depend for their survival on the substantial union of loves that families tend to have. Not that neighborhoods survive without shared loves of some sort, but rather that the loves shared among neighbors are neither as broad nor as deep as those that bind families. Without this more substantial union and love, there is less chance that any particular disagreement can disrupt. For the most part, divergent judgments about music and souls, about the beautiful and the sublime, do not threaten the peace that I share with my neighbors, and nor should they, so there is little at stake as I object in this instance and little reason to offer patient endurance in response to this particular difference. If, despite all this, I conclude that I must remain in his company and endure what I despise, then clearly I have not assessed the circumstances of the act as I should. I have not paid sufficient attention to my relationship with the person who is the source of the difference that offends. Indeed, if I respond in this way, it's plain that I don't understand what kind of community this neighborhood is or what sorts of disagreements might actually threaten its union and require just endurance in reply.

But what should I do? I can't be indifferent to what I hear; the music is too harsh and ugly for that. Nor can I coerce his conduct with threats and penalties, for this requires a kind of authority over his affairs that I do not have. I suppose I could ask him to turn off that racket, and being a good kid, he would surely comply. Still, as long as he keeps the decibel level acceptable and the hour reasonable, one wonders why he can't listen to the music he prefers in his own driveway. Why deny him this obvious good? So, chances are, if I am truly tolerant, I will banish myself to the quiet of the living room and the comfort of its couch. Keeping things separate, this removed from that, is, after all, one of the tasks that the just take up and manage well. As participants in this task, the tolerant act justly when, as circumstances warrant, they keep certain objectionable actions and things separate from those who happen to object. In most instances, the intent is not to terminate the society the parties happen to share, but just the opposite. The intent is to sustain that society justly, to give to each the good that each is due in these particular circumstances without denying the differences that divide them and without allowing those differences to subvert the relationship.

In the end, it is the quality of love that distinguishes these different social relationships and justifies these different responses. I owe my son patient endurance of his difference in part because he is my son, because of the love I have for him, the society I share with him, and the union that I hope to retain despite our differences. I owe him a certain kind of sympathetic attention, and a certain hope to understand what I currently dislike and now endure, because my love for him expresses desire for union with him. My endurance of his difference is caused by this desire and ordered to this end. The neighbor boy is owed something else, in part because my love for him is quite different, as is the society we share. In chapter 6 I will consider this intersection of love, justice, and tolerance in greater detail. Here I simply point to its existence, which should come as no surprise. In the previous chapter we noted that love precedes justice precisely because it creates the social context within which the concept emerges, care for the just takes hold, and the habit begins to operate. Here we see that the same applies to tolerance. Apart from those we call our own and with whom we share some sort of society—apart from loves that bind these beloveds—tolerance would have no chance to emerge as an idea, no arena to operate, and no reason to take hold among the other virtues.

DIFFICILE ET BONUM

Suppose the tolerant reflect on the object of their actions in cases like these in roughly this way and suppose they act in accord with their reflections. No doubt, the truly tolerant in our time and place might judge and act somewhat differently than I suppose, but this is largely irrelevant. So too is the fact that the concern in these cases—domestic differences in taste—is not all that important, not all that far-reaching. Tolerance quite obviously regards tolerable differences, but this is to say that its patient endurance bears on those actions and things that land between the indifferent and the acceptable, not that these actions and things are always insubstantial or that the social relations that the tolerant perfect with this act are always local. Indeed, as we shall see in the next chapter, tolerance might begin at home in response to ordinary disputes about the simplest things, but it extends to larger associations, to the market and the city, and in these settings its patient endurance often regards disagreements about first things and disputes about basic justice.

At this point in the argument, what matters is that we take note of the reflections that the tolerant must pursue and the judgments they must make if they are to choose just courses of action, if those from whom they are divided by some objectionable difference are to be given the good they are due, and if the peace and autonomy that they hope to secure for these others with these others has any chance of being achieved. Everywhere and always, in cases trivial and profound, these are the labors that the tolerant take up in accord with their habit. And, since habitual effort of this kind, wise judgment of this sort, and predictable success in cases like these distinguish the virtuous, surely we must count the tolerant in their company.

But imagine a tolerant act fails to achieve its tolerant ends. Returning to the previous example, suppose my son mistakes my just endurance for heartless indifference and takes offense. He hardly notices my efforts on behalf of his autonomy and he has nothing but contempt for the actions and outcomes that he thinks he does see. In his eyes, my so-called tolerance does nothing to protect the peace of our little society and everything to undermine its substance. Inspired by some of the books he has pulled off my shelves, by some of toleration's critics, he has come to conclude that this subtle virtue masks hidden vice. In his mind, tolerance is just an excuse to forsake life with others for a life alone, one that appears blameless and upright but in fact is not. Every pious defense of the virtue's intrinsic merit and happy consequences is in fact cowardly, hypocritical clap-trap, just as my tepid response to the music he loves is actually an expression of my indifference to *him*, to his deepest longings and fears. It lays bare my secret desire to live at a distance from his emotionally messy teenage soul. Having come to this conclusion he quite sensibly replies with his bedroom door open wide and the volume turned up high. And, if that were not trouble enough, suppose my neighbor notices that *his* son's music has made me forsake my relatively public hammock for my absolutely private couch, and suppose he feels the snub of snobbery in this change of venue, not the respect that neighbors are due, not the tranquility of peace that justice typically yields.

Imagine, in other words, that virtue fails to achieve virtue's ends. Failure of this sort is hardly uncommon. In the case of justice and its parts, failure tends to follow from the fact that these virtues regard those actions and things that mediate our relations with others, not actions and things *in se*, but only as due, and thus only as they fall under a certain description, one that fixes the act in its moral species and casts it among those goods that by right belong to another. As any particular action or thing can always be cast under multiple descriptions, it is always possible to disagree about what was done, about its object, end, and circumstances. And of course, an action due another by right but received as neither right nor due can hardly secure the peaceful relations that the just hope to achieve as they act. As with justice, so too with tolerance: its actions can fall flat when they are not recognized for what they are, and right recognition is difficult. Indeed, it is unlikely without some measure of the virtue had and expressed by the recipient of virtue's act.

But will we say that something worthwhile was done nevertheless? In spite of its failure, will we insist that the act and its cause (the habit that informs the will, orders its desire, and encourages right judgment about concrete cases) are good regardless? Well, if tolerance is a virtue, then indeed we must. As we noted above, a virtue and its actions are mixed goods. They are useful instruments for achieving virtuous ends, and they are good in some measure regardless of their success. But what exactly warrants this insistence? Put another way, what makes the tolerant think that simply acting tolerantly, simply giving expression to their virtue in act, is one of the ends that they ought to intend whenever they act in accord with their virtue? No doubt, they will also intend to secure ends external to the act itself, but what makes them think that the act itself is good and desirable quite apart from its actual successes and failures with respect to its ends?

The short answer is this: their virtue makes them think in these terms. It is their virtue that brings this complexity to their judgments and desires and it is this complexity that distinguishes their agency. It sets them apart from those who fall short of true virtue and yet nevertheless manage to act as the virtuous do. The courageous, for example, respond to the gravest difficulties and dangers with the right measures of fear and daring, which in turn makes it possible for them to intend just ends and choose just means in spite of these threats to life and limb. Their courage also enables them to regard their habit and its act as good in themselves, to take quiet delight in each, and to intend "to reproduce in action a likeness of [their] habit." This is the immediate end of their actions: simply acting courageously. The proximate end is the just state of affairs that they hope to secure as they act in accord with their habit (*ST* II-II.123.7). And the courageous intend both ends simultaneously, in part because they see the causal connection between them, but also because they see goodness in each. For Aquinas, it is this stereoscopic apprehension of virtue's good and this dual intention ordering virtue's act that distinguish the courageous. Those who fall short of virtue's perfection might very well choose to act as the courageous do for the sake of that proximate end. They might consider that just state of affairs worth having and choose accordingly, coping with difficulties and dangers along the way and moderating their irascible passions. But when the world's unexpected twists and turns bring their efforts to naught, they are unlikely to respond as the courageous do. They will be hard-pressed to see the good that has accrued as their efforts reproduce a likeness of the soul's perfection in act. They will not take delight in the act of virtue itself (*ST* II-II.123.8). And, crucially, the fact that they do not see goodness in the act itself is the surest sign that they do not possess a full measure of the virtue, one that can generate a full complement of its good.

The delight the courageous take in the act itself will be of a *certain sort*. It will be *tempered*. But why and how so? Well, recall what was said in chapter 1. It would be obscene, and thus no part of courage, to take delight in the circumstances that demand courageous acts. Courage, after all, regards the most fearful dangers and the most pressing difficulties, and who in their right mind desires these? Right desire comes as the courageous perform a second volitional two-step. They regard their act as good, both in itself and for the sake of the end they hope to achieve. They take delight in the act itself, and if it succeeds, they welcome the end it secures. If it fails, they count the act good nevertheless. *At the same time*, they have a negative will toward the circumstances that require the act. They won't welcome them, don't want them, and would avoid them if they could. In Thomas's terms, the subjunctive state of their will, their velleity, is negative toward these circumstances (*ST* I-II.13.5.1). Looking back, the courageous recognize that those circumstances could have been different and that different circumstances would not have demanded their act. Of course, they know that it's impossible for things to be different now. What's happened has happened, and they concede the necessity in this. Given this necessity, they have no desire to act differently than they did.[27] Still, they wish that the world had not presented these circumstances and that these circumstances did not demand their courage. They don't *resent* what the world has presented or the need it creates for a virtuous response; indeed this would be incompatible with the regard they have for their act and the delight (tempered by their negative velleity, yes, but delight nevertheless) they take in it. But nor do they welcome without reserve what the world *has* brought. Thus, their negative velleity.

If this is right, if the courageous are distinguished by the complexity of their intentions, by their response to just actions that fail to achieve just ends, and by their negative velleity toward the circumstances that they find themselves in, then surely the tolerant understand their virtue and frame their intentions in much the same way. Surely these states of mind and affection

---

27 In this respect, the virtuous, whether courageous or tolerant, are different from the persevering and the tolerantly self-restraining that we considered in chapter 1. Their negative velleity regards the circumstances of their act and has a counterfactual character. It indicates what they *would* have willed and done had those circumstances been different. By contrast, the preserving and the tolerantly self-restraining are distinguished by what they *actually* will. They actually will two incompatible ends, and their negative (indeed resentful) response to the circumstances that they find themselves in follows from their recognition of this incompatibility.

distinguish their souls as well. Even so, we might reasonably ask what they might say in defense of their commitments and intentions. Why is it, exactly, that they find intrinsic worth in tolerant acts? Surely these acts are useful for coping with disagreements and dissents of a certain sort, but why do the tolerant think that goodness accrues even when their efforts fall short, when the due they had hoped to deliver to another is not received, when the relationship they had hope to maintain comes apart, and when strife replaces peace in the society they share with those they tolerate? Why, in other words, do they regard tolerant acts as evidence of the will's perfection quite apart from success or failure with respect to tolerant ends?

Well, it's likely that the tolerant would respond with disregard for the question and exasperation with the questioner.[28] "Of course, a tolerant act is good and desirable in itself. How could it not be? It gives to another what is rightfully theirs. How could this not be good? Indeed to say that tolerant treatment belongs to another by right is to concede that the good secured in that treatment is best. All other goods that might be intended in this instance fall short, and it is precisely this judgment that distinguishes genuine virtue, true tolerance. If those who are owed this treatment from us fail to regard this act as it is—as both due and eminently desirable—well, this is unfortunate, but why should it diminish the merit of what was done? Indeed, *your* suggestion that it might gives us pause. The just and the tolerant describe actions and things as they are, which is precisely what you seem incapable of doing."[29]

So might the tolerant reply.[30] If pressed again, this time for reasons, they might respond with more caution. The reflective among them might speak, as Thomas does and as we did in the previous chapter, of the largely inde-

---

28   Virtue can come with contempt for vice, for its base wickedness, of course, but also for its doubt about virtue's merit, doubt that can justify the resort to vice. For a defense of this attitude, see Davis, *Warcraft and the Fragility of Virtue*.

29   For the just, virtue's demands trump all other considerations, but not all demands are identical. There are two sorts precisely because "a person establishes the equality of justice by doing good, i.e., by rendering to another his due: and he preserves the already established equality of justice by declining from evil, that is, by inflicting no injury on his neighbor" (*ST* II-II.79.1). Thus we are not only obliged to deliver to others the good they are due by right, whatever that might be, but we are also obliged to "resist against an instigation to do evil" for the sake of some other good (*ST* II-II.79.1.2). "Doing good is the completive act of justice," while resisting evil is its necessary condition (*ST* II-II.79.1.3). The tolerant do good and thus establish the equality of justice insofar as they deliver to another the patient endurance they are due. But they also resist evil insofar as they refuse to take up an unjust response to difference, a response that would secure some other good.

30   Would this be an intolerant reply? Not necessarily, not if tolerance is a virtue and not if virtue is expressed in these remarks. Better to recall that the virtues strike reason's mean. Just as the courageous will sometime tremble and retreat, so too the tolerant will, at times, speak critically and forcefully.

terminate character of the human will, of the diversity of the human good, of the intellect's ability to apprehend that good in all of its diversity, and of the many loves and lives that result in turn, with their various conflicts, imperfections, and incompatibilities. Given these features of our humanity and given the fact that tolerance, both the habit and its act, comes tightly packaged with them, the reflectively tolerant would probably reply that intrinsic goodness attaches to the whole package. Deny the intrinsic merit of tolerance and the other human virtues and one casts doubt on the inherent worth and indisputable dignity of our humanity. Discount the intrinsic goodness of just acts, tolerance among the rest, and you deny the sacred value of human life.

Annexed to justice, tolerance emerges as justice does, from our natural inclination to form social bonds and to recognize value in a life shared with others. There are, of course, social lives of various sorts, and yet every actual sort must instantiate minimal measures of justice. A society whose members consistently fail to render to each other those actions and things that each deserves and where justice, the virtue, did not perfect their souls in some measure and set right their relations in some degree, is literally unimaginable. It can hardly be called a society. Its common life would likely collapse in virtue's absence. If, by contrast, we live among those who are disposed to render to others the actions and things that each deserves with a more or less constant will, then it is likely that we will also discover that justice is done in this society only as frequent resort is made to the patient endurance of the tolerant, to their characteristic response to objectionable difference. Given the unavoidable features of our natural history that we considered above, the circumstances that compel this resort are likely to be many and thus it should hardly surprise us when the just have a constant and perpetual will to this particular act of justice, this particular specification their neighbor's good. And, as this good cannot be willed habitually or this act chosen consistently without coping with a special collection of difficulties, we should expect a special virtue to emerge in the souls of the just. As Aquinas likes to remind us, "virtue is about the difficult and the good; and so where there is a special kind of difficulty or goodness, there is a special virtue" (*ST* II-II.137.1; cf. *NE* 1105a9–14).

It is both a special good—a right response to objectionable difference, one that is ordered to social peace and individual autonomy within a relationship—and a special collection of difficulties that account for the existence of tolerance among the virtues. Some of these difficulties we have already considered, principally those associated with locating an act of patient endurance in its moral species. There is the difficulty of identifying and willing the proper end of this act, and there is the difficulty of determining whether this or that collection of circumstances make this particular act (and not some other) both good and due this particular person. The tolerant address each of these difficulties as they exercise the right judgment that comes packaged with justice and that infuses each of its parts. As we noted earlier in this chapter, this involves both an act of will and an act of right reason, both an aptness to judge aright and the ability to judge rightly (ST II-II.60.1). The tolerant are disposed by habit to act tolerantly, to will this act and its benefits for those with whom they share some sort of society, and to do so only when it happens that this act and these benefits are in fact owed this or that person in this or that instance. This in turn disposes to them determine when and where that might be, to judge aright in each circumstance of choice. And the tolerant make a right judgment when, on the one hand, they determine which differences are in fact objectionable and which are not, and when, on the other, they distinguish those objectionable differences that are tolerable, and so require our patient endurance, from those that are literally intolerable and that demand some other response altogether, perhaps coercion, perhaps exile or withdrawal. These determinations and distinctions are difficult to make because of the many and changing circumstances of choice that the tolerant find themselves in. For this reason, the tolerant cannot activate their settled will to act tolerantly without right judgment about ends and circumstances, and they cannot consistently judge aright without the perfection that prudence provides.

Will this reply do, this account of the intrinsic goodness of tolerant habits and acts? Yes and no. For many of us, there's nothing more to say. This reply will have to stand. For those who concede what Thomas does about God, grace, and the unity of the good, this reply must be qualified with certain hesitations. They may concede that tolerance has an intrinsic goodness that cannot be denied given the facts of our natural history and our life in this world, and yet they will doubt the necessity of at least some of those facts. By their lights, we were made to be transformed by grace, to be gathered up into a different sort of life, and to be perfected by a kind of virtue that does not tether moral goodness to difficulty. For them, the intrinsic goodness of tolerance as habit and act cannot be asserted without qualification. Its goodness remains only as our life in this world does, and, as we shall see in chapter 6, those who share Aquinas's theological commitments will yearn for the transformation of that life, for the overcoming of certain features of that world. Even now they see hints of that hope fulfilled in an endurance that begins and ends in God's love.

SUFFERING VIRTUE

Theological qualifications aside, it should now be apparent that the mixed goodness of tolerance—part instrument of external ends, part intrinsic worth all its own—cannot be conceived apart from the difficulties posed by the diversity of human goods, the conflicts that emerge among our loves and lives, and the desire for peace and stability in the various societies we inhabit and for autonomy with respect to at least some of the differences that divide us. Gathered together, it is precisely these features of our lives that make right recognition of those differences, persons, and circumstances difficult and contested. And it is precisely these difficulties that are addressed by tolerance in the will and by prudence in the practical intellect.

At the same time, the difficulty we have acting tolerantly often has less to do with the rigors of judgment or the constancy of will than with the turmoil of passion. That is, the truly tolerant person judges well—she places toleration's act in its proper moral species despite the many circumstances and competing ends that threaten to confound her—in part because she is disposed by habit to will right relations across difference, in part because prudence informs her practical intellect, but also because she responds as she should, with passions of the right kind and intensity, to the rather unpleasant straights she finds herself in. The differences she must endure may not be intolerably harmful, but nor are they harmlessly benign. She may consider some genuinely unjust, others seriously vile. She acts tolerantly nevertheless because this is what justice demands, because the peace, security, and autonomy that she hopes to secure are owed to the company she keeps, and because she values and respects this company. Still, when she acts in this way she finds herself sharing her life with those from whom she is divided by the differences she tolerates. Her virtue leaves her cut off from them; it leaves these differences in place. Her alienation from them is, no doubt, partial and tolerable, as it must be if her endurance in fact succeeds in preserving the society they share. Every society is founded on shared commitments and common cares of some sort, and yet the need for tolerance indicates that her society's foundation has weakened. She preserves the society she loves only as she accepts its partial decay and takes note of its real fragility. Surely this unsettles her soul, and surely her alienation from those she tolerates causes her sorrow.

Sorrow is, on Aquinas's useful rendering, a species of pain (*ST* I-II.35.2), and pain requires two things—contact with some evil, with some action or thing that defeats some good, and apprehension of this contact (*ST* I-II.35.1). It also comes in two varieties—pain simply, which is caused by an apprehension of external things, and sorrow, which is caused by an interior apprehension of thoughts and feelings. A tolerant response to objectionable difference causes sorrow precisely because it generates contact, often extended contact, with an evil that cannot be sensed but can be conceived: the partial but persistent alienation of the tolerant from those they tolerate. It's a passion that acquires its mood and content from the good lost in the difference that divides. What's lost is the ability to recognize one's loves and commitments in the society one inhabits—in the lives of its members, in the norms of its social practices, and in its familiar orders of solidarity. And this loss might also generate fear. The objectionable commitments and practices that the tolerant endure may, over time, move the society they share with the tolerated in a direction they despise. Their tolerance may even encourage this transformation, a prospect that elicits their fear.[31]

Here we see how the passions that the tolerant tend to suffer threaten the constancy of their action. Fearing the transformation of their society in accord with the differences they tolerate, the tolerant might be tempted to forsake their virtue, ignore the just due of others, and save their society, or rather, save the version of their society that they prefer. It is, after all, their tolerance that sets the stage for the transformation they fear, or, if this exaggerates its influence, then at the very least their actions leave that stage set as it is. Their tolerance does nothing to diminish its threat. In a different state of mind, one more attentive to other effects of their virtue, the tolerant might also find themselves full of sorrow over the alienation they must endure from their society as a consequence of their tolerance. Lamenting this alienation and hating these fears, they might be tempted to forgo tolerant attitudes and actions. They might resort to paternal power, either to purge the society of the differences they fear or seek that more perfect unity of loves that coercion promises.

If these passions intensify and the tolerant succumb to these temptations, it will be because a certain weakness afflicts them. They will fail to consider actually what they know habitually. They know that tolerance is an instrument of social peace and individual autonomy. They know that its principal act, the patient endurance of objectionable difference, is a good they often owe the persons they live among. And, by the offices of sound judgment, they know that toleration's endurance is in fact due *these* particular persons in *this* particular instance. At the same time, they know that this just act will, in some degree, leave them alienated from these same persons. Hearts and minds will be divided by the differences tolerated. So too they suspect that their own society would become intolerable were it to be transformed in the image of what they must endure. These reflections generate sorrow first and then fear, and these can distract and distort the judgment that is needed to sustain tolerant attitudes and acts. When these passions distort judgment, the tolerant come to believe what is in fact false: that their patient endurance would not be the best response to this particular difference. When these passions distract, the tolerant are prevented from deliberating and concluding in light of their virtue's wisdom about the good in general and in accord with their better judgment about the particular good, the patient endurance that is due in this instance. With their reason fettered by fear, they argue instead from their conviction that certain social transformations

31 For an account of tolerance that takes this fear seriously, see Scanlon, "Difficulty of Tolerance."

are intolerable, and they conclude that this particular objectionable differ-ence ought to be checked before it transforms the society they love in ways they cannot tolerate.[32] Or, if it is their sorrow that gets the better of them, they begin with the assumption that a society of shared loves and common convictions is superior to one divided by difference and conclude that it would be better, all things considered, to secure that union of hearts and minds by coercive means. If these sorrows and fears persist and this failure to act tolerantly becomes habitual, the virtue that they once possessed as second nature will decay and eventually disappear, perhaps to be replaced by intolerance, its opposing vice.

Given these threats and failures, we might be tempted to encourage these poor souls to strengthen the virtue they have, to buck up and do what they can to become more tolerant in spite these sorrows and fears. But this won't work, largely because tolerance perfects willed action and here the trouble regards passionate response. If they are to act as they should and remain as they are, the tolerant will need assistance from virtues that perfect precisely these responses. This hardly surprises. The moral virtues are, as Aquinas re-minds us, connected. They come packaged together. The successful exercise of one virtue typically involves the exercise of others. We have already seen how justice and prudence come packaged together in *iudicium* but there are other examples of this mutual support among the virtues. One cannot delib-erate well and make prudent choices under the influence of disordered pas-sions and wayward desires. They will send you traipsing off after some false end, some lesser good. In a similar way, one cannot have passion infused with right reason and desire tutored by sound judgment without a practical intellect that has been perfected by prudence (*ST* I-II.65.1).

So the tolerant need a full complement of the moral virtues to act in accord with their character, above all patience and perseverance, two virtues that belong to courage. Courage enables us to endure dangers to life and limb that are present and unavoidable and that would be unwise or impossible to attack or confront. It moderates those fears that would otherwise have us flee these circumstances, and it enables us "to stand immovable in the midst of [these] dangers," not attacking, but not retreating or cowering either (*ST* II-II.123.6). On Aquinas's rendering, courage, like justice, has parts, virtues an-nexed to it. Some are so integral to its work that the courageous cannot act as they should, with the perfection that distinguishes their character, without the assistance they provide (*ST* II-II.128). Others are potential parts because they regard certain minor hardships. Not all dangers are deadly, nor every difficulty extreme, and yet these lesser troubles must also be confronted, not with the full perfection of courage, but through the offices these lesser parts.

---

32   Here I follow Aquinas's treatment of moral weakness, *ST* I-II.77.2 and ad 1–5.

It is here, among these second string perfections, that we find the patience and perseverance that tolerance requires (*ST* II-II.128; 136.4.1; 137.1–2).[33]

Following Augustine, Thomas contends that patience regards sorrow caused by some hardship or evil.[34] The patient person endures this hardship and bears this evil with, as Augustine puts it, "an equal mind," one that is not disturbed by excessive sorrow "lest he abandon . . . the goods whereby he may advance to better things."[35] With help from Aristotle, Aquinas spells out this logic a bit more. The patient person endures "arduous and difficult things for the sake of virtue or profit" lest the mind be "broken by sorrow, and fall away from its greatness, by reason of the stress of threatening evil."[36] This captures quite nicely what the tolerant must do as they cope with some of the differences and disagreements that confound the various societies they inhabit. These differences and disagreements are evils of this precisely sort. They threaten the union of love and conviction that every society assumes in some measure, and they tend to generate sorrow over the

---

33   Thomas concedes that, at times, the courageous must endure and persevere in order to respond well to deadly dangers and extreme hardships. For this reason, we will also find patience and perseverance among the integral parts of courage (*ST* II-II.128 and ad 4–5).

34   Aquinas refers to the acquired cardinal virtues as natural, political virtues. "Since man is by nature a political animal, these virtues, in so far as they are in him according to the condition of his nature, are called political virtues; since it by reason of them that man behaves himself well in the conduct of human affairs" (*ST* I-II.61.5). The same can be said of those virtues annexed to these as parts. But now consider the Apostle Paul's famous remark from chapter 13 of his letter to the Corinthian church: "Love is patient" (1 Cor 13:4). For Thomas, the implication is obvious. Perfect patience requires charity. It accompanies the love for God and neighbor that God's grace makes possible. With its aid one endures evil and bears sorrow for the sake of supernatural goods to come, principally fellowship with God and the blessed. Thomas assumes these goods transcend love's natural reach and so he doubts this patient endurance can be exercised apart from God's gracious re-creation of the will and intellect (*ST* II-II.23.2 and ad 1–3; 136.3). It is a patience that accompanies the gracious forbearance that we will consider in chapter 6. By contrast, the patience that is imperfect by comparison, that is "commensurate with human nature," and whose work is indexed to goods and hardships of this life—*this* patience is a natural, political virtue. It can exist "without the help of sanctifying grace," and its act can be ordered to ends that are not supernatural (*ST* II-II.136.3.2). The independence asserted here is relative. For Aquinas, no good work of any kind can be done without some sort of divine assistance, and thus the patience that is geared to the goods and hardships of human life must depend upon other kinds divine aid. Aquinas notes two such dependencies. There is the first grace of God the creator, through which we are able "to do or wish any good whatsoever" according to our nature. And there is the healing grace of God the redeemer, through which we are healed of sin's effects and thus enabled to act more fully, more perfectly in accord with the nature we have been given (*ST* I-II.109.2).

35   *ST* II-II.136.1. Here Thomas quotes from Augustine, *pat.* ii: "Patientia homini, quae recta est atque laudabilis et vocabulo digna virtutis, ea perhibetur qua aequo animo mala toleramus, ne animo iniquo bona deseramus."

36   The first remark is from Cicero *Inv.* II.54, cited by Aquinas at *ST* II-II.128 and accompanied by his own additions, captured in the second.

estrangements they cause. When tolerant acts leave these differences and disagreements in place this sorrow remains. When the difference endured is an injustice of some sort, this sorrow is compounded by the realization that the tolerated will receive neither punishment nor deterrence.[37] These estrangements and sorrows tend to threaten the persistence of toleration's act, and yet among the tolerant who are also patient this act persists. They endure this estrangement and bear these evils as they moderate the sorrow that accompanies their actions. In the words of David Harned, they "wait upon the good," and in this context they wait upon the social peace and stability that comes only as differences are tolerated, estrangements endured, and sorrows of various kinds suffered with an equal mind.[38] It will not come to those who are impetuously intolerant of these differences or unable to endure these estrangements or moderate these sorrows.

Notice the mutual causation of action and passion and the curious doubling of their acts. The tolerant who are also patient endure an effect of toleration's act, of their own patient endurance. This act causes estrangement from those they tolerate. This estrangement elicits their sorrow, and this sorrow requires the moderating influence of their patience. With sorrow moderated, they can endure the estrangement from others that their act of toleration allows and so persist in this act and tend toward its ends. Notice as well how perfection in the passions enables perfection in chosen act. Virtue in one power enables virtue in another.[39] Following Aristotle, we might say that the patient endure hardship by moderating sorrow, and they do so for the sake of

---

37 They might be rebuked and challenged; they might be prophetically denounced or politically opposed. As we will see below, and then again in the next chapter, there's nothing about tolerance that prevents this kind of contestation with the tolerated. In fact, tolerance and contestation quite often come packaged together. Still, until verbal contest succeeds, the difference remains, in this case, an injustice. If exit and coercion are refused, then tolerance must be the response.

38 Harned, *Patience*, 80–106.

39 Sorrow and pain regard present evils, and the passions that regard good and evil belong to the concupisciple appetite. Why then does patience, which perfects the capacity to suffer sorrow, belong to courage, which perfects the passions of the irascible appetite? Thomas replies: the annexing of virtue to virtue regards common formal matter, not shared subject. The sorrows that temperance perfects regard the body and its pleasures. They arise from abstinence, and perfection comes to the concupisciple appetite when they are moderated along with the desire for pleasure. By contrast, the sorrows that patience regards arise from evils inflicted by other persons. Here, perfection comes to the concupisciple appetite as these sorrows *alone* are moderated and the good of virtue is not forsaken. Courage resides in a different subject, the irascible appetite, and yet it regards this same formal matter (evils inflicted by another) and this same formal perfection (holding fast to the good). It differs from patience in that the evils it regards are the greatest (dangers of death) and its passions regard these evils as either future (fear) or present (sorrow). It is in this latter sense—when sorrow is caused by present evils inflicted by another, sometimes evils of the greatest sort, sometimes not—that patience belongs to courage (*ST* II-II.136.4 and ad 1–2).

virtue and profit—in this instance, for the sake of the tolerance that is due the tolerated and for the social peace and individual autonomy that the tolerant hope to secure for those they tolerate and for themselves in this company.

Caution is required here; there are temptations to avoid. We might be tempted to say that the tolerant who are patient, who endure the sorrow of estrangement from those they tolerate "for the sake of goods to come" (*ST* II-II.136.3.1), are in fact waiting for the objectionable difference to pass. We might say that the good they hope to secure is the union of hearts and minds that now escapes them. Returning for a moment to my son's objectionable music, we might say that I am able to endure patiently precisely because I am confident that this too will pass, that with time musical maturity will come, our tastes will converge, and my need for tolerance will fade. On this rendering, patience encourages the tolerant to wait upon those conditions that will make their virtue irrelevant. This is their hope. This is the arduous good they desire.

But this can't be right, not in every instance. This hope is often unreasonable, this good often impossible to secure. Many of the differences and disagreements that divide us one from another will remain indefinitely. There is little reason to think that they will pass or to stake our tolerance on the expectation that they will. This is a portion of what it means to say that tolerance belongs to justice. Justice assumes a shared collection of judgments and loves, a collection that creates the social and conceptual context of its act. But this collection need not be perfect. One need not be united with another in every judgment or love in order for justice and its requirements to emerge, and the just are not required to heal every breach of judgment or failure of love. Justice is offered to some at a cool distance, with no desire for a better union, to others with a warm heart, with hope that union might increase as a consequence of its act. Tolerance is much the same. In some instances, with respect to some persons and differences, it amounts to nothing more than enduring some difference, forsaking coercion, and not exiting the relationship. In other instances, it also includes the hope that persuasion and time, contestation and correction, will collapse the divide that difference creates. Still, the tolerance offered as these efforts proceed does not depend on this hope—not on its existence, not on its fulfillment.[40] Indeed, the lines of dependence run in the other direction. One can proceed with these efforts to contest and persuade only as one tolerates the differences

---

40   The matter regards reasonable hope, not theoretical possibility. It is one thing to conclude that it would be unreasonable to hope for *these* differences to be set aside and disagreements resolved at *this* time among *these* persons. It is quite another thing to assume that some differences and disagreements are tragically intractable. The conclusion does not depend on the assumption, which is to say that a satisfactory account of tolerance does not require commitment to the view that some disagreements are in principle unresolvable.

that one opposes, only as one endures the differences one hopes to transform. This may seem somewhat counterintuitive, and yet every attempt to
challenge or persuade that is not in fact an attempt to coerce ("Accept these
reasons and change your ways or else!") bears witness to the ends that true
tolerance intends: the sociality that abides between the parties and the autonomy each shares with respect to the difference in dispute. Verbal contestation and rational persuasion assume these ends, and until they succeed, it
is tolerance and its acts that must secure them.[41]

But more to the point, in many instances, it would be *unjust* to hope for
certain differences to pass and *false* to endure them because of that hope.
What my son deserves is my patient endurance, period. In this instance, it
is his right, his just due, and my act will fall short of true tolerance if I ignore this right and proceed instead with the hope that time will heal his
judgments and bring his loves into accord with mine. Maybe it will, maybe
it won't. The point is that these possibilities are irrelevant. They regard the
consequences that may result from the act, not the tolerant act itself that is
due, not the intended ends that this act is ordered to achieve. If my attention is fixed on these possible consequences, if their reality is the good that
I hope for and wait upon, and if my son's difference is endured because of
that hope, then it is not tolerance that I have exhibited, but a semblance of
its act. Nor is it patience that I have, for in this instance, my waiting upon
the good has been divorced from the just act that, in true patience, precedes
the waiting and requires its response.[42]

41   If this is right, then we should regard David Hume's *Dialogues Concerning Natural
Religion* as one of great modern works on tolerance. The *Dialogues* don't discuss the concept,
but they do put it on display. Philo, Demea, and the rest disagree about some of their deepest,
most important commitments. They contest and persuade across the day, and then they go
home, some in new agreement, some still divided, and yet all determined to endure the differences of all for the sake of the sociality and autonomy that made their spirited debate possible. No swords are drawn, no permanent exits made or expulsions threatened. We can easily
imagine them returning for another day of tolerant contest. See Herdt, *Religion and Faction
in Hume's Moral Philosophy*. Hume's explicit remarks on tolerance are mostly in his *History of
England*. For an interpretation see Sabl, "Last Artificial Virtue."

42   The same applies to the case of Uncle Halvor. In each instance, endurance is offered in
response to something truly objectionable but without the expectation that things will improve. Does this, as Hirschman suspects, turn the loyalty that tolerance assumes into irrational faith (Hirschman, *Exit, Voice, and Loyalty*, 78–79)? Hardly. Instead it accents the reasons
that love's loyalties provide. One refuses exit and tolerates some objectionable difference without hope of remedy precisely because the antecedent union that this act assumes is worth
having, its common good worth retaining, or so one concludes. This union and its goods
provide reasons for staying put, even in the absence of that hope. This may be difficult, and
yet the tolerant are disposed to overcome this difficulty as they are moved by these reasons.
To his credit, Hirschman, recognizes loyalty's pull when common goods are at stake (100–105),
but he fails to consider how tolerance might respond to that pull when a society or organization deteriorates.

So the tolerant wait upon the good, yes, but they are not moved to act by their expectation of that good. Rather, they are moved by their judgment that a particular difference ought to be endured. This is the good that is owed this person in this instance, or so they conclude. When they judge and act in this way, the need for patience follows, but only as the deed is done, time passes, and the tolerant wonder whether the society they share can survive the difference endured. They wonder whether their union of loves now diminished and their diminished union now tolerated can be sustained nevertheless. They wonder whether the company they keep will remain. It's upon this company that they wait and for this society that they hope, and in a way, this implies that they wait and hope upon the other. In effect they ask, "Will you retain my company as I do yours even as this difference divides us? Will you suffer this difference with me and so remain?" With patience they await a reply.

Now consider perseverance, which, like patience, helps the tolerant cope with an unwelcome consequence of their restraint, in this instance, the chance that the tolerated will transform the society they share in the image of the difference that the tolerant dislike and yet endure. As this chance remains as long as the tolerant persist in their act, fear of this transformation will be constant and unavoidable. Those who are tolerant but do not persevere might resist this fear and persist in this act, but not indefinitely, and that's precisely the problem. As we have just noted, the tolerant need not assume that the tolerated will change, that the difference in dispute will be resolved by anything that might be said or done. The reasons they might offer in defense of the actions, commitments, and sentiments they endorse leave the tolerated unconvinced, unmoved. Given this state of affairs, the tolerant must assume that these differences will remain permanent features of the social landscape they share with the tolerated, as will the endurance they must offer to maintain it. And yet how can they endure endlessly when doing so puts the society they love at permanent risk of being transformed by the differences they despise? This nagging thought generates fear, if not today, then certainly tomorrow, which in turn tempts the tolerant to abandon their virtue and forsake its endurance. Such is the likely outcome of those who attempt toleration's long and difficult act without a full complement of the virtues. If, by contrast, their tolerance comes packaged with perseverance—with the habitual capacity to moderate their fear of toleration's consequences—then it is likely that they will persist in their endurance as long as objectionable difference divides and tolerance is due.

As with patience, there is a temptation to guard against as we assign perseverance to the tolerant. We are tempted to say that the tolerant must persevere *principally* because of the long delay in accomplishing the good they hope to secure with their act. But, as before, this is a temptation to avoid.

The perseverance that accompanies and assists tolerance does not chiefly regard the long delays between act and outcome, if only because this is not the chief difficulty that the tolerant confront on account of their endurance. As I have said, *they* fix their attention on the act that is due and only then on the end that the act might yield. It follows that the perseverance that assists tolerance must enable the tolerant to "persist firmly in good against the difficulty that arises from the very continuance of the act" (*ST* II-II.137.3), and the act itself is difficult to continue precisely because it leaves differences in place that the tolerant abhor and that, with time, may dominate the society they share with the tolerated. This is what they fear. The tolerant who are also persevering moderate this fear and thus "persevere to the end of the virtuous work," which, in this instance, is nothing but persistence in this act in spite these fears (*ST* II-II.137.1.2). If asked to provide reasons that justify their perseverance, the tolerant would no doubt speak of their virtue's object, of the patient endurance that it delivers and that is due this or that person in this or that instance. But if asked for the reasons that motivate and justify the moderation of those fears that accompany their persistent act, they might very well speak of the society they share with the tolerated, of the commitments they hold in common and the practices they pursue together, and of the fact that succumbing to those fears and abandoning this act would yield an intolerable result—loss of sociality and alienation from one's own.[43] It's as if the persevering say, "They are ours and we are theirs. This is why our acts of patient endurance are due *them* and not some other, and this is why failure to moderate our fear of what they might do to the society we share and refusal to tolerate them and their differences is, quite literally, intolerable. It would shatter our life with *them* and this we cannot bear. So instead we check our fears, bear their burden, and remain in their company. We are divided by our differences, no doubt, and yet we tolerate what we despise in order to remain united with them, with our own."

Taken together, these reflections on the passions and virtues of the tolerant accent the suffering in their endurance, the loss it requires. As with any sacrifice, theirs mixes activity and passivity. All things considered, they do not want to endure the differences they find objectionable or accept the unhappy transformation of their society that their endurance makes possible. They would forsake this action and avoid this outcome, even as they know they cannot. Given the tolerant intentions they actually have, the means at their disposal, and the circumstances they find themselves in, they can do no other. They must endure these particular differences and then suffer the consequences that come. And so they act, knowingly and willfully. At the same time, there is also a kind of passivity in what they do, a pain in their endurance, and something oddly fearful in their willingness to withstand

---

43 Scanlon, "Difficulty of Tolerance," 231–232, develops this insight.

what they loath.[44] We have noted various objections to tolerance, various doubts about its place among the virtues, and here another source of complaint comes into view. Suffering differences we dislike is neither easy nor enjoyable, at least not for most of us, and we certainly don't like being told that we are *obliged* to suffer in this way. Yet, as before, there is nothing here that distinguishes tolerance. All of the moral virtues involve suffering of some sort, either directly according to their objects, as is the case with courage, temperance, and the like, or indirectly, as a consequence of their acts, as is the case with justice, tolerance, and the other virtues that regard operations. In each case, the suffering endured combines passivity and choice. In some cases, one chooses to sacrifice some good because it is due another. In other cases, the losses are neither intended nor chosen, but accrue as consequences of what one does. In both cases, the losses arrive unwelcome and the suffering comes willy-nilly. Indeed, no one can be said to sacrifice a good with an undivided heart or to endure an unhappy consequence without resistance to the loss. In Aquinas's useful idiom, their sacrifice comes with a negative velleity toward the act and its unintended effects.

Such are the ordinary sacrifices, losses, and sorrows of a virtuous life and presumably the virtuous among us cope with these difficulties well. They suffer as they should, with passions of the right kind and intensity, and they act with ease in spite of these difficulties and with joy that tempers these pains. Still, as we noted in chapter 1, tolerance stands out among the virtues in at least one respect. When confronted with its special difficulties, less than perfect tolerance can decay into a semblance that nevertheless produces something like a tolerant act, and this in turn makes it easy to confuse the semblance for the virtue. When true tolerance requires suffering, and when patience and perseverance are imperfect or absent, this decay becomes more likely, this confusion more common. Some will accept what deserves to be opposed; others will cultivate indifference. Both responses diminish suffering even as they generate actions that resemble what the tolerant do. This, in turn, makes it easy to think that the attitude that produces the act—the weak vice disguised as strong virtue—is all that tolerance amounts to. The relative scarcity of true tolerance, of virtuous sources of its act, only confirms the hunch.

Here the tasks of philosophical explication and the need for virtue converge. We need tolerance and its attendant virtues to cope with the disagreements and differences that confound the various societies we inhabit, and we need a truthful account of these virtues to avoid the collapse of tolerance into its semblances and ourselves into resentment. So too, we need to recognize that the actions and passions of the tolerant depend upon something prior, on the common commitments and loves, the shared practices and activities, and the fellow feeling and mutual identification that in some measure animate every healthy social relationship, every flourishing political community. As we have noted before, as love precedes justice so too a community of shared loves precedes tolerance.

We tolerate our own. Our tolerance allows us to remain in their company, to stay put and stay with. It's a finding that follows from a good portion of what has been said so far. It is also an odd and somewhat surprising conclusion in at least this respect: it contradicts what many assume about tolerance. Many assume that tolerance is principally about our relations with strangers, that it helps the tolerant keep the tolerated at a distance, and that it flourishes in modern, liberal societies where (it is assumed) strangers are many and distance is encouraged so that liberty might flourish. If the inquiry so far is sound, then we will have to put aside these assumptions. We will have to admit that tolerance, like justice, is a creature of social relationships. Those relationships, threatened by differences and divisions, are its matter, right relations its concern. Even strangers become objects of tolerance only as they are included in this matter and connected to us in some way as participants in some kind of social order. In the standard cases, we tolerate what we find objectionable about a stranger only as we find her among us, only as she occupies the social role reserved for strangers, and only as justice demands tolerance of those who occupy this role. Our tolerance emerges against the backdrop of these antecedent roles and relationships. Without them, it would not emerge.

Put aside these false assumptions and replace them with the conclusions reached so far, and we will have to reconsider what liberal tolerance amounts to. If it is one species in a broader genus, then what distinguishes it from other varieties and what encourages these false assumptions about its character? We will take up these questions in chapter 5, but only after we have paused in chapter 4 to catalogue the terms we have used to talk about tolerance. It is to this task that we now turn.

A VIRTUE'S VOCABULARY

Tolerance is a moral perfection, a virtue annexed to justice as one of its parts, or so I have argued. On the way toward this conclusion, I have used a number of the concepts that, until now, I have left largely unpacked. I have assumed a collection of inferences and distinctions that have remained (again, until now) largely implicit. At this point, it's time to unpack these concepts, specify these distinctions, and make explicit these inferences. It's time to take stock and regiment our vocabulary for the sake of precision and clarity. Anticipating a theme from the next chapter, I resort to a list.

1. **An action in its natural species and that same action in its moral species.** The distinction between an action in its natural species and an action in its moral species regards *us* not the action itself. It regards our access to a description of the action that is specific enough to allow moral assessment of it. It bears witness to the fact that in some instances, with respect to some actions, a description can be specific enough to identify what was done and distinguish the act from other possible doings, but not specific enough to judge it good or evil, right or wrong.

So, for example, I might know just enough about an action to describe it as an instance of promise making. I can identify the act and distinguish it from making a claim, making a tackle, making a deposit, and so on, but without being able to say much more. I know that the person who made the promise intended to do so, but beyond that, the order of action to ends remains opaque. I know that she made the promise yesterday, but apart from that, I can say little about the circumstances that frame the act. Given this rather vague description, I cannot say whether this particular act of promise making was just or unjust, good or evil. In Thomas's shorthand, my description locates the action in its natural species, not its moral species.

Notice what this distinction assumes: (a) that every human action tends to some end that the agent who acts has judged good and has desired because of that judgment;[1] (b) that an action in its natural species is morally indifferent (*for us*) until we identify the end to which it is ordained and circumstances in which it resides; (c) that an action that is initially indifferent can, depending on its end and circumstances, occupy different moral species—it can be good or evil, just or unjust; and (d) that every human action that is morally indifferent (again, for us) has an end and a collection of circumstances that, when accurately described, will situate that action in its proper moral species, thus canceling our perception of its indifference.[2]

   2. An act of toleration. By an act of toleration, I mean the act of patiently enduring some objectionable difference, a difference assigned to some action, attitude, or arrangement of things by the person who endures. I mean an action that has a natural specification, one that is indifferent in its moral species at the start of moral assessment.

   To say that an act of toleration is offered in response to some action, attitude, or arrangement of things that is, in some way, both different and objectionable is to say that it assumes a departure from some norm, presumably a norm endorsed by the person who makes this assumption and acts in this way. This person finds some aspect of the world in a condition she dislikes or despises, different from the norm she endorses, and it's this normative difference that is the object of her act, the matter about which it regards.[3]

---

1   Here I concentrate on human actions that proceed from a deliberate will and tend to an end that is known while ignoring those actions (e.g., thoughtless chin-scratching) that human beings perform but are neither deliberate nor end-directed. Thomas considers the first properly human actions (*actus humani*). The second are not. They are merely human doings (*actus hominis*) (*ST* I-II.1.1).

2   The distinction drawn here is, I think, widely assumed, even if the terms used to draw it are not. Aquinas's treatment of the distinction (*ST* I-II.1.3.2; 18.6, 8–11) includes a discussion of actions that are *never* morally indifferent (*ST* I-II.18.2, 5). These latter actions are good or evil in their species, which is to say that one cannot identify the action and assign it to an agent without also recognizing that something good (or evil) has been done. No doubt, the ends and circumstances of these acts must be included in a complete moral specification of them, but the point is that we know something about their moral status quite apart from these considerations.

3   This somewhat formal way of identifying the object of toleration's act is needed in order to accommodate those cases in which it is apparently sameness, not difference, that is both objectionable and endured. Suppose you live in a community that is homogenous—racially, ethnically, and religiously. Everyone is the same, and, given a cosmopolitan ideal, it's this sameness that you find objectionable and that you endure nevertheless. How is it, then, that your act of toleration has objectionable *difference* as its object? Answer: the difference regards the departure from a norm, in this instance, from the cosmopolitan heterogeneity that you prefer but that is nowhere in evidence. It's this departure, this difference from normative principle, that you find objectionable and that you tolerate. I am grateful to Alda Balthrop-Lewis for pushing me to make this clarification.

To say that an act of toleration has a natural specification is to say that it can be identified and distinguished by a description that nevertheless fails to locate the act in its moral species. It is to say that, in principle, it is possible for us to know that some difference has been endured with patience, but without knowing much at all about ends (proximate and distant) or circumstances (who, what, where, how, and so on). Without this additional information, we will be unable to locate this act of toleration in its proper moral species. We won't be able to say whether the difference in dispute is in fact objectionable and in what way, and we won't be able to say whether this particular response to this particular difference is right and good or wrong and vile. It could be either. Some acts of toleration are right; some are not. Some are ordered to just ends and situated in the right circumstances; some are not.

Unlike making a promise, taking what another has, or walking across a field, patiently enduring the objectionable differences of another is an internal act of the will. Like hoping and intending, it tends toward ends that are external to it, and yet like them it remains within the agent. In some instances, this act is sufficient to achieve those ends. Recognized as just and good, received with gratitude, and (in the right circumstances) returned in kind, it sets a relationship right, secures its peace, and guarantees autonomy with respect to the differences in dispute. But in other instances, the action alone is insufficient to achieve these ends. Others must be performed as well, some deliberately chosen. Some will be negative: not coercing the person, exiting the relationship, or expressing disregard for either. Some will be positive: offering assurance that disagreement does not imply disrespect, confessing the need for mutual endurance, and acknowledging the possibility that judgments might change. And some will regard the perfection of virtue: seeking autonomy within the relationship by encouraging real reflectiveness about the differences that divide and that require toleration's internal act. Quite often, it is through reference to these other actions, some of them external, that we recognize this act and ascribe it to another.

3. **Rightful acts of toleration and tolerant actions.** An act of toleration is *right* when it delivers to one person the patient endurance that is in fact due from another. Full stop. If the person who is tolerated acknowledges this act and so receives this due, this response to the difference she expresses or embodies, then things are set right between her and the person who objects and yet endures. This is what matters, this objective arrangement of persons and things. The character of the intention that generates the act and rearranges the world is another matter, and, for the identification of the act as right, beside the point. By contrast, a *tolerant action* delivers this due, it sets things right across a divide of difference, and yet it is done for the reasons that the virtuous happen to have, reasons that motivate the truly tolerant. These reasons *identify* this particular act of patient endurance as due, they pick out certain ends, and

they help *generate* the desire to deliver this due and secure these ends by means of this act. It's precisely these reasons that I considered in chapters 2 and 3.

The distinction drawn here is between objective right and just motive as they regard our response to objectionable difference. The distinction is ordinary and well known: one can deliver the good that is due by right for all sorts of reasons, some virtuous, some not. In this instance, one can deliver to another the patient endurance she is due while acting for reasons that the truly tolerant do not have.

4. Tolerant actions: three varieties. Tolerant actions come in three varieties. All three are acts of patient endurance that in fact set things right across a divide of objectionable difference, and all are done for the reasons that the virtuous (the truly tolerant) happen to have. At the same time, an action in accord with these reasons can have different sources in the will. Most of us who act in this way, who respond to these reasons, do so without a settled will to generate this response. In some cases, the person simply lacks a habitual love for the goods identified by these reasons. In others, she must resist a habitual love that *opposes* precisely these reasons, a settled will to do otherwise. By contrast, the truly tolerant produce this act by habit, by a settled disposition to will in accord with these reasons, to make use of the virtue we call tolerance.

In each case, we have the same external action, the same collection of reasons at work, and yet in the end we have three distinct causal histories. In the first, the act can be traced to tolerant reasons that do nothing more than elicit tolerant desires and generate a tolerant act. In the second, the act arises from reasons that not only cause tolerant desires and generate tolerant acts but also, simultaneously, discount the reasons and desires of a contravening habit. In the third, the act arises from tolerant reasons that are encouraged and confirmed by a habitual and wholehearted love for the goods specified by those reasons.

Notice three things. First, tolerant actions that emerge apart from habit appear to be acts of real virtue, but in fact they are not. The same can be said of many (but not all) *rightful* acts of toleration and many (but not all) acts of toleration whose moral specification remains uncertain. Perform any one of these actions, and you can appear to stand among the virtuous without actually being one of them. Second, the appearance on display *here* is *not* captured by the distinction between a virtuous action and one of its semblances—between a real moral excellence and a vice in virtue's drag—but rather by the distinction between a virtuous action and one of its imperfect antecedents. By imperfect antecedent, I mean an action that, while not virtuous, can nevertheless contribute to the development of a virtuous habit. In this instance, the person whose desires are formed by tolerant reasons and whose actions follow from those desires is on her way to becoming truly tolerant. How do we know? Because repeated action in accord with those reasons is likely to produce a habitual love for the goods specified by them. Third, the distinction between the tolerant actions of the truly virtuous and those actions that come only as judgment opposes a contravening habit is analogous to the distinction that divides the actions of the truly temperate from those of the merely continent. In each case, the latter act as the virtuous do but only as they control themselves, only as they restrain their habitual desire to pursue some other end and so to forgo this act. By contrast, the former act from habit and thus without divided desire or the need for self-restraint.

5. Acts of acceptance or indifference as tolerant actions. An act of toleration, of patient endurance, is not the only imaginable response to objectionable difference. There are others, and of these, acts of indifference or acceptance resemble acts of patient endurance in three key respects. First, each generates external actions that resemble the external actions generated by each of the others. Each regards a difference of some sort that divides one person or community from another. Each allows this difference to stand, and each act can be ordered to the welfare of a social relationship or political community, to the persistence of its shared life and common goods. Upon closer inspection, these external resemblances will reveal their different internal sources; these are, after all, distinct acts of the will. Still, even up close, their external resemblances remains.

Second, the moral specification of these actions, their status as right or wrong, good or evil, depends on their order to some end and their place in a collection of circumstances. When we observe these acts without grasping these details, they will appear in their natural species, as indifferent in their moral species. Once these details are known, this indifference will pass and we will know whether this particular response to some particular difference is just or unjust, and of course, it could be either. Combine this uncertainty with the simple fact that these details are often difficult to know, stir in the shared appearance of these external acts, and the potential for confusion about their identity and moral status is obviously substantial, as is the opportunity for resentment among the confused. As we noted in chapter 1, it's precisely this confusion and resentment that confound discussions of toleration, that make accounting for its substance and merit so difficult, and that the truly tolerant tend to avoid.

Third, like acts of patient endurance, acts of indifference and acceptance belong to tolerance, the virtue annexed to justice. Each belongs to tolerance because each act is offered in response to differences that are in fact objectionable in some way, at least initially so, and because differences of this sort are the matter about which tolerance regards. Tolerance is the virtue that informs and perfects these responses. It orders each of these acts to its proper end, and in each instance its act is right, it delivers what is due in response to the morally relevant circumstances. Sometimes patient endurance is the right response to the differences in dispute; sometimes its act delivers the good that is due, but not always. Sometimes indifference is best, sometimes acceptance, and the virtuous, the truly tolerant, are those who consistently know which act is best and habitually will in accord with that knowledge. They object to the right differences, intend the right ends, take note of the right circumstances, and respond with the right actions, all with the ease of habit.

In this respect tolerance is like courage. Courage has a single material concern (the most pressing difficulties and dangers) to which the courageous respond well with a hodgepodge of passions (anger, daring, sorrow, fear, hope, and the like) that help generate a diversity of actions (fighting, fleeing, standing firm, and so on).[4] These many passions fall under the authority of this one virtue because they share its material concern and because each can generate actions that can help or harm the right relations and common goods of some society, presumably the one threatened by the difficulties and dangers. Courage perfects these passionate responses, orders these acts to its ends, and so secures these right relations. At the same time, few regard flight as the principal act of courage, the paradigmatic expression of the perfection it brings to the irascible passions. While flight can certainly *be* courageous, it is not what comes to mind when we imagine the courageous and their acts, and the reason follows from a basic fact about the virtues in general that we have already considered. The virtues are about the difficult and the good, and thus a virtuous action that regards greater measures of each will likewise embody greater measures of virtue's perfection. Thus standing firm in the face of the most threatening dangers, not fleeing, not fighting, is the paradigmatic act of courage precisely because of the greater difficulty of this act when compared with these others.[5]

---

4   There are, of course, *differences* between tolerance and courage, and not just the obvious ones. Like every part of justice, tolerance regards human actions that mediate our relations with others. *These* are its most general material concern. In particular, it regards actions that respond to the objectionable differences of others. Courage, by contrast, regards irascible passions; *they* are the matter about which it is concerned. It follows that we can speak of courageous actions (fighting, fleeing, and so on) but only as *effects* of the perfection that courage brings to the passions. Fear, daring, and hope perfected by courage help elicit right actions in difficult and dangerous circumstances—at the very least, they don't get in the way of right action as unperfected passions tend to—and yet the principal causes of these actions lie elsewhere: in rational desire and practical reason, each perfected by their respected virtues, by justice and prudence. By contrast, we can say that tolerance is the principal cause of tolerant actions precisely because operations are the matter that it regards, operations in response to difference and disagreement. See *ST* I-II.60.2.

5   The argument is Aquinas's (*ST* II-II.123.6), which he borrows from Aristotle (*NE* 1115a25–28; 1115b12–14) but with a caveat. Both regard standing firm in the face of deadly dangers as the paradigmatic act of courage, and yet Aristotle insists that the greatest acts of courage involve standing firm against the threat of death in public war. He has in mind those acts of courage that are honored by cities and monarchs (*NE* 1115a30–36) and involve fighting while

The same logic applies to tolerance. It perfects those actions that fall under its material concern—actions in response to objectionable difference—and the tolerant choose among those actions in order to secure the right relations and preserve the common goods of some society, presumably the one threatened with disruption by disagreement and dissent over some objectionable difference. Just as the courageous respond with the right passions and actions when confronted with the most serious difficulties and the gravest dangers, so too the tolerant respond with the right intentions and choices when confronted with the most divisive disagreements and stubborn differences. Just as there are many acts that the courageous can choose, each in a distinct natural species until it is situated in the right circumstances and ordered to the right ends, so too there are many acts that can count as tolerant, each in a distinct natural species until chosen in the right circumstances and ordered to tolerant ends—to the peace and preservation of the society and to autonomy with respect to the differences in dispute. Just as flight can be a courageous act in response to dangers, so too acceptance or indifference can be tolerant acts in response to difference. And, just as standing firm is the principal act of the courageous, not attacking or fleeing, patient endurance of objectionable difference is the principal act of the tolerant, not indifference or acceptance.

Two reasons account for its rank above these others. The first regards the eclipse of objection in acts of acceptance or indifference. When the tolerant take up these acts, the difference that was initially judged objectionable no longer is. The disagreement that was once troubling no longer vexes. In the standard case, the tolerant object and oppose but only at first. As reflection proceeds, they come to the conclusion that their initial reaction is unwarranted, that some other response would be right. If it's indifference that would be best, then the disagreement and difference remain, but the specific matter they regard is now considered unimportant, or, if not that, the specific difference with regard to this matter is now considered trivial, no longer a threat to common life and shared peace. If, by contrast, acceptance would be the right response in this instance, then the difference remains, as does its importance, but it is now welcomed, perhaps even celebrated. In each case, the difference that was objectionable at the start is recast, its divisiveness di-

---

standing firm. Thomas does not deny that courage is "properly about dangers of death occurring in battle," but he clearly accents "private combat, as when a judge or even private individual does not refrain from giving a just judgment through fear of the impending sword, or any other danger though it threaten death" (*ST* II-II.123.5). One stands firm in order to contest an injustice with words and signs, not attack it with deeds and arms. The dispute here turns on the ends, social relationships, and moral exemplars that matter most. Aristotle has in mind the warrior who fights to preserve the common goods of temporal politics, while Aquinas refers us to the martyr who bears witness to Christ and the common goods of a heavenly city (*ST* II-II.123.5.1).

minished, if not eliminated altogether.[6] And note, unlike the recasting that we considered in chapter 1, this variety is virtuous, not vicious. It follows from the recognition that objecting to this difference in this instance would be unjust, and it is motivated by (and ordered to) the just ends that the tolerant desire—autonomy with respect to the differences that divide us and social peace in spite of those difference—ends that they hope to secure for (and share with) the person who expresses or embodies the difference.

The second reason that patient endurance of objectionable difference is the principal act of tolerance follows from the simple facts of relative difficulty. Patiently enduring what one finds objectionable is far more difficult than abandoning one's objection and responding with indifference or acceptance.[7] No doubt the truly tolerant will choose this endurance and execute this act with the ease of habit that distinguishes the virtuous, and yet the difficulty that they must transcend in order to will in this way, acquire this virtue, and secure this ease is indeed substantial. It is precisely this substantial difficulty that picks out patient endurance as the principal act of the truly tolerant.

6. Acts of coercion. Among those differences that are in fact objectionable, that *deserve* our doubts and protests, there are some that should not be endured with patience but resisted, some with acts of coercion. Assume for the sake argument that coercion can be deployed justly, not in every instance but in some, and not only to frustrate the objectionable act, but also to compel attention, transform judgment, and thus diminish the will to act in the objectionable way. Here, the point is more basic and less controversial: just acts of coercion cannot be tolerant acts. This should be obvious, or so it would seem, and yet one might take the preceding remarks about endurance, indifference, and acceptance to imply that coercion belongs in their company. After all, each is an act in response to objectionable difference, and responses of this sort are the material concern of tolerance. Since tolerance perfects these responses and since coercion is one of them, why not consider just coercion an act of true tolerance? If we assume, as I do, that coercion is an action that can reside in a natural species, that it can be morally indifferent until it is ordered to some end and situated in a collection

---

6 I am grateful for helpful comments from Cécile Laborde on this point.

7 Could the judgment that precedes acceptance, the coming to understand a difference well enough to recognize that it deserves to be acknowledged and respected, turn out to be more difficult than the one that precedes endurance? Yes, in a particular case, but not in general. In general, the tolerant are disposed by habit to respond well to those commitments and actions, those persons and lives, that are objectionable precisely because they depart from some important norm. In every instance, a right response—whether acceptance, endurance, or some other—will require sympathetic attention to those persons and lives. It will require the hard work of coming to understand those commitments and actions in relation to this norm. In this, endurance and acceptance are on equal footing.

of morally relevant circumstances, then why not conclude that, like indifference and acceptance, coercion can be fixed in its moral species by tolerance and counted among its acts? Paradoxes aside, why not?

Well, recall what I said about the material object of tolerance, the matter about which it is concerned. Tolerance is concerned with actions that respond to objectionable difference, but not *all* such actions. It concerns only those actions that can be ordered to each of its principal ends: the society that the tolerant hope to retain with the tolerated despite the differences that divide them; the peace that animates this society; and the autonomy that its members share with respect to these particular differences. Killing, cursing, and banishing are all possible responses to objectionable difference, no doubt, but none can function as means to these ends. They cannot deliver these goods to those who bear this difference. Coercion, by contrast, is an ordinary means of securing peace and stability in certain kinds of social and political relationships threatened by certain sorts of differences. This is well known. Less obvious, but no less certain, is the fact that autonomy can emerge and flourish in any conceivable social context only as words and deeds are constrained by recognized norms and only as normative constraint is at times coercive.[8] That said, the resort to coercion in response to some particular objectionable difference cannot be a tolerant act precisely because it cannot secure autonomy with respect to *this* particular difference, at least not directly. This resort might secure social peace and stability, but no matter. Since it does not guarantee the autonomy of the other across the difference in dispute, it cannot be considered a tolerant act, and its response to difference must be perfected by some other virtue, presumably justice.

Better to say, then, that coercion marks a limit, that it brings tolerance to an end. Better to admit that tolerance and its acts provide a significant but not an exhaustive portion of our just response to objectionable difference. Since tolerant actions are a portion of that response, we can assume that the tolerant will know where this limit lies. They will know, better than most, when their tolerance must come to an end, when the difference in dispute requires something other than a tolerant act as right and due. Mastering the concept "tolerance" includes understanding this entailment, and acting in accord with this entailment is a good portion of what this virtue involves. In this respect, it's fair to say that the tolerant will at times coerce, not tolerantly, but justly.

7. **Tolerance and contestation.** Some objectionable differences cannot be offered easygoing acceptance, regarded with blithe indifference, honored with respect, or combated with coercion. Given the social relations at stake and the circumstances in play, each of these responses would be unjust, or so the tolerant will at times conclude. But let's also assume that they doubt

---

8   See Brandom, "Freedom and Constraint by Norms."

these particular differences should be endured patiently, not in these circum-stances and relationships, not at the start of the day. Rather, their first response should be to oppose them, persuade others to forego them, and protest those institutions and practices that sustain them. While refusing resort to physical and verbal violence, they will nevertheless correct and contest, challenge and dispute, sometime publically, sometimes in private, and there is no reason to think that these acts fall under tolerance. They are, no doubt, responses to objectionable difference, but, as we noted with respect to coercion, not every such response be can be included in the material object of tolerance. Those responses that cannot be ordered to each of its ends cannot be counted among its acts, and contestation is precisely one of those responses.

Suppose you are committed to some belief or activity that I consider seri-ously unjust or entangled in some custom or institution that offers access to undue privilege or unaccountable power. Your commitment might be tacit or not, your entanglement blithely ignorant or deliberately chosen. Recall the discussion of racial and ethnic differences from the previous chapter. I said these differences are improper objects of toleration precisely because there is nothing objectionable about them. The same should be said of differences in gender or sexual orientation. But a regime of political power or social recognition that tracks these differences is a different matter alto-gether. Surely *this* difference, this departure from equality's norm, is not only objectionable but plainly intolerable. Commitment to it should be con-tested, the institutions that sustain it should be overturned, and the persons and communities that benefit should be exposed.

Now suppose you are one of those persons, a member of one of those com-munities, and I try to persuade you to abandon your commitment and dis-entangle your life. And suppose that I resort to a collection of agonistic means: prophetic challenge, immanent critique, public satire, political con-test, organized confrontation, and so on. Suppose further that I make this re-sort without discounting the good in the society we share or the autonomy we have with respect to our differences. Indeed, I contest these differences precisely because they threaten our common life and undermine its ideals, or so I believe. My aim is to sustain our sociality, preserve these ideals, and respect your standing in the relationship by contesting your commitment to these departures from moral norm, your entanglement in these unjust differentials of power. And while I might forgo resort to coercive force for any number of reasons—effective means are unavailable, the harm done would be disproportionate to the good achieved, the hope that coercion will work is unreasonable, and so on—I do value the autonomy we share, and I do want that autonomy preserved. I want *you* to revise certain beliefs, quit certain practices, and to take on certain others. I want to persuade you to make these revisions, and I want *you* to be persuaded and to do the re-vising. The reasons that persuade and motivate might regard self-interest, goods held in common, or the demands of justice. But regardless, I want them to be *your* reasons, reasons that give expression to your autonomy. This desire is an expression of the respect I have for you.[9]

At the same time, contest, correction, and confrontation will certainly unsettle the society we share. They will disrupt and destabilize, indeed intentionally so. I want our sociality retained, but not cross this normative divide, this particular difference, and I contest in order to change the terms of our relationship. It is for precisely this reason that my efforts do not belong to tolerance.[10] Like those who contest and persuade, the tolerant want to retain sociality and preserve autonomy, and yet they pursue these ends, not by resisting these differences, but by enduring them. These differences deserve to stand, or so they conclude, and this relationship will have to proceed on these terms, at least for now.

As we noted in chapter 3, in this respect, the patient endurance of the tolerant is sacrificial. It includes a willingness to live among the differences despised, and, in some instances, to proceed without the hope for moral transformation that distinguishes contest and persuasion. Still, this willingness carries with it a negative aspect that inclines the tolerant toward those who contest, and those who contest justly cannot entirely forgo tolerant acts. While the tolerant are willing to allow certain objectionable differences to stand, they remain ill disposed toward what they allow. All things being equal, they would prefer these differences to pass. The subjunctive state of their will with respect to these differences, their velleity, we noted, is negative even as they concede the justice of enduring patiently and the necessity of willing in accord with this concession.[11] So too, those who contest and confront at the start of the day must tolerate at the close. They must endure the differences they oppose and hope to overcome. What else can they do? Unless they forsake persuasion for coercion, insurrection, or exit, they must

9   My concern is with tolerance the virtue, a moral perfection, and so here I describe *just* contestation, *just* persuasion, even as I admit that these activities are frequently vitiated by twisted motives and unjust means. In many instances, those who contest care nothing about the autonomy of those they oppose or the welfare of society they share with them. The difference in dispute fills them with hatred and spite, and they contest in order to dominate the other and undermine their standing. Resort to unjust coercion might be checked by fear of its cost, and this fear might generate a reluctant patient endurance at the close of the day, but this act of toleration, although objectively right, is clearly not a tolerant act.

10   We might say that here toleration has reached a limit. For an account of toleration limited by the need to correct and contest in the context of early modern religious disagreement, see Bejan, "Bond of Civility."

11   Aquinas puts the point this way: "The perfect act of the will is in respect of something that is good for one to do. Now this cannot be something impossible. Wherefore the complete act of the will is only in respect of what is possible and good for him that wills. But the incomplete act of the will is in respect of the impossible; and by some is called *velleity* because, to wit, one would will [*vellet*] such a thing, were it possible" (*ST* I-II.13.5.1).

endure with patience as they wait for their hopes to be fulfilled.[12] Until then, toleration must remain a portion of their response to the differences they contest, and we will ascribe it to them as we do any other interior act of the will, by referring to the other actions they perform or forsake and by attending to the ends they appear to have. No doubt, the person who contests may insist she feels nothing but intolerance toward what (or whom) she opposes, and she may resist the ascription on account of this feeling. But these feelings can mislead. Toleration's patient endurance is not a passion, but an action. It might arrive with negative feelings for the difference endured—hatred for its injustice or sorrow over its persistence—but so long as its ends are sought and its alternatives set aside, toleration's interior act remains a portion of their response even as they contest its object.[13]

This combination of contestation and tolerance is a central feature of democratic political life. Laws are passed, elections held, policies put in place, and court opinions handed down. Some regard important matters, others trivial, but in each case there are winners and losers, those who support the outcome and those who do not. Some of these larger losses and significant differences may be intolerable, or so some of us may conclude. If they cannot be recouped by democratic means—if the voice these means assume is no longer effective and the loyalty they demand no longer possible—then some of us may contemplate insurrection (John Brown) or exit (James Baldwin). But all other losses, all other differences in love and commitment, policy and practice, that divide us from our fellow citizens, and all other sources of sorrow over the inability to recognize ourselves in the political society we inhabit—all of this will require precisely this combination of contestation and tolerance, of voice and challenge combined with a willingness to endure the persons and differences one opposes.[14] This combination

12   Adding tolerance to the vocabulary that Albert Hirschman develops in *Exit, Voice, and Loyalty*, we can say that voice always comes packaged with loyalty, hope, and tolerance, while tolerance comes packaged with loyalty, but not always with voice and its hope.

13   "Roughly speaking, a man intends to do what he does." Elizabeth Anscombe's dictum can be reversed: a person does what he intends to do. When an intended end is identified through reference to external acts done and omitted, we can ascribe to the agent those internal acts of the will that are also necessary in order to achieve that end. We may even make this ascription against the agent's protests. Actions can be cast under multiple descriptions and disagreements about what a person is doing or has done are perfectly ordinary. When disagreements arise about what internal act to ascribe to another, first person reports must be taken into account but they are not decisive. As Anscombe points out, the agent's authority to refuse our ascription has limits. Some refusals have to be themselves refused, most certainly when the agent professes "not to have had the intention of doing the thing that was a means to an end of his." Anscombe, *Intention*, 11, 44.

14   Tolerance and contestation, insurrection and exit—these possibilities require standing of some sort in the relevant social and political relationships, but also the capacity for effective agency. Some human beings live in conditions of extremity so severe, under necessity so

is not easily had or exercised. It is a democratic ideal but difficult to achieve. The need for virtue, for tolerance, emerges just here.

8. Tolerance and its semblances. Strictly speaking, a semblance is a vice that resembles a virtue in *both* habit and act. It is a habitual disposition that (to the untutored eye) appears to be virtuous precisely because it causes actions that appear to be just or wise or courageous but in fact are not. In fact, they are vicious. Speaking less strictly, a semblance can regard action alone. It can be an action that resembles what the virtuous do, that is evil despite appearances, and that is *not* caused by a vice. The person who produces the action has no settled disposition to do so. Her fraudulent goodness emerges, not from malicious habit, but from other sources: culpable ignorance, disordered passion, self-deception, and so on.

The distinction between the strict and the less strict regards causal history not external act. As external actions, the two sorts of semblances can be identical, and both can resemble and yet fall short of true virtue in three different ways. The first regards virtue's ends, the second regards virtue's acts, and the third regards both. Returning to tolerance, there are those rightful acts of toleration (or acceptance, indifference, and so on) that are nevertheless done for the wrong reasons, presumably for the sake of some unjust end. Semblances of this sort deliver to another the good they are due by right, and yet at the same time this act and its outcome are ordered to the denial of some other due. Like the person who gives alms for the sake of vainglory, the person who endures the objectionable difference of another in order to dominate or deceive cannot be said to have acted virtuously. The first is not charitable; the second is not tolerant. Second, there are acts of toleration (or indifference, or acceptance) that fail to deliver to another the good they are due by right. Given the circumstances of the act, given the difference in dispute, the action chosen—whether patient endurance, blithe indifference, or easygoing acceptance—is itself unjust. It might resemble true tolerance, it might be ordered to tolerant ends, but no matter. It remains unjust. And finally, there are acts of toleration (or indifference, or acceptance) that fail to deliver to another the good they are due by right and that are ordered to ends that are not just, not tolerant.

OBJECTIONS AND DOUBTS

So goes my list of definitions and distinctions. It's a demanding list, somewhat tedious in detail, and it may encourage some to object. If these con-

---

cruel, that neither requirement is met. Tolerance, it is said, has a limit. It comes to end. Its action is replaced with some other. But for some, it doesn't even begin. I am grateful to Clifton Granby for this qualification.

ceptual demands must be met in order to count tolerance among the virtues, then why take the trouble? If these details must be mastered, then why bother? Or rather, who among us will be able to care enough about these definitions and distinctions to master and deploy them? If this is what it takes to count tolerance among the virtues, then who among us will have what it takes?

It's a reasonable objection, and yet I'm inclined to think that it fails to grasp the basic claim. Tolerance stands *among* the other moral virtues, which is to say that the definitions and distinctions one needs in order to consider it a habitual moral perfection apply to these others as well. The comparison with courage that I have used to draw these distinctions and unpack these definitions is designed to make this relation explicit. If these definitions and distinctions are too much trouble, then it's not only our talk of tolerance that must be abandoned, but all talk of moral virtue. And yet, for the most part, we are committed to this talk. We speak of courage and justice and the rest as virtues, of persons and actions distinguished by degrees of moral perfection, and most of this talk assumes the distinctions I have just drawn and the terms I have just defined. At the very least, most of us assume something like the distinction between an action in its natural species and that same action in its moral species. In a reflective moment, most of us can see that, as object or effect, each moral virtue regards a distinct collection of actions in their natural species and that the virtuous are those who consistently choose the right actions in the right circumstances and order them to the right ends. My claim is that tolerance should be regarded in the same way and spoken of in these same terms. In the three previous chapters, I have argued that tolerance is a natural virtue indexed to the form of life that human beings happen to lead and annexed to justice as one of its potential parts. I have said that confusion about its character can be cleared up and resentment toward its act defused once we think of tolerance in this way, situate it among the other moral virtues, and distinguish it from its semblances and imperfect antecedents. And, finally, I have spelled out what it means to say that tolerance is a virtue that belongs to justice; what due it regards, difficulties it addresses, and passions it elicits.

Fair enough, these same critics might say, but on a practical level isn't there something strangely self-defeating about this effort? Surely we want true tolerance to flourish wherever differences and disagreements threaten the peace and stability of our social and political arrangements. We want those differences that are in fact objectionable to be distinguished from those that are not and we want those objectionable differences that deserve patient endurance to be set apart from those that deserve some other response, whether indifference, acceptance, coercion, or exit. And surely we want the patient endurance of the tolerant to be given because it is right and due, because just acts of this sort are good and desirable in themselves, and because the social peace and stability that the act is designed to achieve belong to the tolerated in the company of those who tolerate. And certainly, we want the passions that typically accompany tolerant acts and threaten their constancy to fall under the moderating authority of patience and perseverance. At the same time, this is a lot to want, perhaps too much. Indeed, one suspects that the difficulties that the tolerant address well and that make our talk of their virtue intelligible also make their perfection exceed our moral reach. The virtues are about the difficult and the good, no doubt, but acts of true tolerance may well be too difficult for most of us to exercise with any regularity. And of course, without regular exercise, acquiring the habit will be unlikely. Cast these doubts about our meager moral capacities against our obvious need for something like rightful acts of toleration and it appears that our praise of virtue has painted us into a moral corner. Insist that tolerance is a virtue that comes packaged with a few others, encourage its exercise and applaud its cultivation, and strangely enough you doom the societies that demand its act.

So goes a second objection.[15] It's a specific version of a more global complaint about any account of the moral life that accents the virtues and distinguishes them from their semblances and imperfect antecedents. The virtues are perfections, after all, and few of us are perfect. Whatever virtues we happen to have are typically secured with great difficulty and maintained with little constancy, and it's this fact about our moral prospects that leads some to doubt that the virtues deserve special attention or to think that they can be reliable sources of the actions we need, actions that set relations right within the societies we love. By contrast, semblances and imperfections of virtue are almost always within our moral reach, they are often sources of action that approximates the right, and as such there is no reason to discount the good they deliver or the happiness they yield. These acts might emerge from imperfect sources and be ordered to less than virtuous ends, but insofar as they secure, more or less, what another is due by right, why complain? Indeed, when we attend to the facts on the ground, more often than not we find that virtue's counterfeits and half measures rule our relationships, rarely virtue itself.

Thus Christopher Hill argues that toleration in response to religious difference did not emerge in seventeenth-century England as a consequence of theoretical labor or moral exhortation, not as "a gradual victory of reason and common sense over irrational prejudice," and certainly not as a result of virtue's flowering. Rather, it emerged then and it will emerge now "only when men become indifferent to the issues involved. If those issues ... [are] serious, then the virtue of tolerance is the result of the vice of indifference."[16]

---

15   On different occasions John Kelsay, David Levinson, Graham Burnett, and Jacob Howland have each pressed me to address this objection.

16   Hill, "Toleration in Seventeenth-Century England," 27, 37.

And indifference grows only as the parties to a dispute exhaust themselves and their options and come to the realization that their foes cannot be brought around by force.[17] Bernard Williams, we have noted, speaks in similar terms. The practices of toleration become a live political option as external necessities and mundane interests converge, not from the routine exercise of an impossibly difficult virtue. In some settings, these practices might be supported by "Hobbesian considerations" about the fruitlessness of force when power meets power and when fear of reprisal generates anxiety about one's own intolerance. In others, toleration might be encouraged by "skepticism about religious and other claims to exclusivity, and about the motives of those who impose such claims." Combine this skepticism with the cruelty of intolerance and "the evils of toleration's absence" and a basis for toleration's act emerges that is predicated not on the just conduct of citizens but rather on their fear of fanaticism and their hatred of bloodshed.[18]

Given these indisputable facts and this sober hope, talk of the virtues in general and of tolerance in particular is either reckless or irrelevant. What's needed instead is an account of action and flourishing geared to the life we actually lead, one more sympathetic with our moral limitations and more hospitable to right action produced by less than virtuous means. If moral mediocrity is all that we can expect, all that we should, and if it is rightful *acts* of toleration that we need in order to get along in spite of our differences, then we had best stake our hopes on something other than true tolerance. Other sources of its act will have to do the trick; some combination of mutual fear, power checked by power, and contempt for coercion's cruelty.

So goes the second objection in a bit more detail. Much of its substance is obviously quite sensible. Count tolerance among the virtues, and you will have certainly set the moral bar fairly high. So too, there is no denying that acts of patient endurance can come from virtue's semblances and imperfect antecedents or that those who wish to generate these acts will at times stake their hopes on these less than virtuous sources. But surely we can admit these facts without concluding that our ordinary moral mediocrity makes our praise of true tolerance beside the point. If it did, then presumably that same mediocrity would encourage us to forsake our praise of every other moral virtue—justice, courage, and the rest—and quite obviously it has not.

Consider again courage. We have noted that external *acts* of courage frequently follow from one of its semblances or antecedents, not from the virtue itself. And yet this fact hardly deters us from speaking of courage, distinguishing it from these imposters and imperfections, and preferring the

---

17 Ibid., 42.
18 Williams, "Tolerating the intolerable," 73–75.

real thing, even as we admit that quite often we manage to act courageously only as we pose among those who exhibit real virtue.[19] When Agamemnon offers his troops a chance to cut and run after nine fruitless years of war, Odysseus and Nestor use words that shame and humiliate in order to stay the dash to the beaches and the ships. It's not true courage they hope their words will elicit, but certain passions and actions that mimic the real thing. Wise Nestor and cunning Odysseus know exactly what they are doing. They know that real virtue surpasses most of their men, that something like courageous acts are needed nevertheless, and that provocations and insults might do the trick. At the same time, they know that true courage exists in the souls of some and that it's worth having and admiring despite its relative scarcity. So in addition to shaming the men into standing fast against the Trojans, they also concoct a scheme that will help Agamemnon distinguish those who are in fact courageous from the many who are merely ashamed to flee.[20]

The reasons that warrant this ordinary talk of the virtues and their semblances and that justify our preference for the real coin are easy enough to locate. When we speak of doing the right thing for the right reasons, of choosing virtuous courses of action both for their own sake and for the good they deliver to another, and when we praise the strength and constancy of the act that comes from habit, we express some of our deepest moral commitments and bear witness to some the most unavoidable features of our of humanity. We convey our understanding of what the best kind of human life is like, of the goodness and beauty it instantiates, not just in external right and successful act, but also in habit and motive. These features come packaged together. In a cool and untroubled hour, most of us will admit that virtuous habits and actions are good in themselves, quite apart from the ends they achieve; indeed most will confess that they are among the most choiceworthy goods we can imagine. And, in that same hour, most will admit that when the virtuous succeed, secure the right, and achieve the ends they intend, the combination of goods that accrue, both internal and external, is undeniably best when compared with all other combinations.[21] All others fall short.[22] And it

---

19 *NE* 1116a17–1117a29. The insight is Aristotle's, who, at the same time, admits that an army of those with imperfect courage and many needs might be best, for men of this kind "are ready to face dangers, and they sell their lives for small gains" (*NE* 1117b19–20).

20 *Iliad* 2.116–438.

21 As Thomas put it, "the will is not perfect, unless it be such that, given the opportunity, it realizes the operation," and thus, "it is better that man should both will the good and do it in his external act" (*ST* I-II.20.4; cf. 24.3).

22 Thomas contends that some virtues are better than others, some more perfective of our humanity: the wisdom (*sapientia*) that enables contemplation of divine things (*ST* I-II.66.5), the theological virtues that perfect love for God and neighbor (*ST* I-II.66.6), and the virtues of those holy men and women who are on the way (*virtutes transeuntium*), who are tending

is precisely this reflective assessment of habits, acts, and outcomes that elicits our praise of virtuous persons and our desire to emulate them: Bonhoeffer and Trocmé, Merton and Day, Heschel and King.

At the same time, we recognize that in some circumstances the virtuous actions we praise threaten other goods that we love, some of them important and thus difficult to forsake. When confronted with unhappy conflicts of this sort, most of us lose our cool. Most of us find it difficult to maintain our judgment that virtuous actions and ends are best or to act in accord with that judgment when we maintain it nevertheless. When the conflict passes and a cool hour returns, most of us will admit this as well, and it's precisely because we do, precisely because we share this sober assessment of our moral capacities, that we praise the habitual perfection of the soul's powers of reason, desire, and emotion. Why? Because this perfection enables the virtuous to generate just and courageous actions in circumstances like these, circumstances that prevent those of us with imperfect or counterfeit sources of virtue's act from acting among the virtuous for other than virtuous reasons. In circumstances like these, most of us either fail to concede the merit of virtue's act, or we make this concession but find that we cannot (in this instance) act in accord with virtue's demands. Our cares are fixed on the good that is lost in the act, not on good in the act itself. Either way we cannot produce the virtuous actions that most of us judge best once those circumstances have passed, a cool hour returns, and our better judgment is restored.

And note, there's a kind of necessity in this high regard for the virtues. Returning again to our attitude toward courage—at the deepest level, we praise courageous habits, actions, and ends because of the creatures we are and because of the just relations that, in a cool hour, we cannot but love. If we were a creature of a different sort—not subject to pain and death, not prone to anger and fear, not bound together by friendship and love—then we would have no reason to say that just relations are good, that courage is required to maintain them, or that courageous habits and actions are fine— good and beautiful in their own right. That we concede the truth of these commitments and the power of these natural realities and yet act in accord with them only as easy circumstances allow does nothing to diminish their merit. Indeed, (as should now be obvious) it is precisely these realities and weaknesses that the virtues, at bottom, regard. Along with our inclination toward certain goods, they provide the very conditions out of which the virtues emerge and to which we appeal as we explain their existence, justify our commitment to them, and speak of their beauty.

---

toward God, and that are called the perfecting virtues (*virtutes purgatoriae*) (*ST* I-II.61.5). These last two, he insists, come as gifts of God's grace.

Our talk of tolerance and our preference for the real thing emerge from similar realities, weaknesses, and commitments. Acting as the tolerant do, with their judgments, passions, and intentions, is difficult, and thus true tolerance is rare. When we encounter rightful acts of toleration, they often have less than tolerant sources. Those who hope to encourage these acts will, like Nestor and Odysseus, typically ignore virtue and look to its semblances and imperfect antecedents. This is the course that Hill and Williams endorse. And yet, when confronted with the most demanding circumstances, those who rely on semblances and imperfections typically fail to produce rightful acts of toleration. When the persons and differences that deserve our tolerance are difficult to identify, when the consequences of the act are difficult to accept, or when a response to difference that fails to deliver the right offers temptations that are difficult to refuse, those without real virtue typically fail to produce virtue's external act. None of this should surprise us. At the same time, the ordinary facts of pluralism, as I have called them, make disagreements and differences among us constant and the need for rightful acts of toleration inevitable and frequent. It's this combination of difficulty and inevitability that makes it impossible for us to forsake our talk of tolerance, our praise of the tolerant, or our discontent with the semblances and imperfect antecedents that we (the morally imperfect) cannot do without. Such are the ironies of virtue this side of true perfection.

Next objection. If tolerance is a natural virtue, if it emerges from our human form of life, then why is it counted among the virtues in some times and places but not in others? Why, for example, does it turn up on my list of the potential parts of justice but not on Aquinas's? Why is it considered an indispensable virtue in societies like ours—liberal, pluralist, and democratic—even as it was largely ignored in thirteenth-century Latin Christendom?[23] It's an obvious question. I have made repeated use of Aquinas's accounts of nature, law, agency, and virtue in order to spell out what it might mean to say that tolerance is a natural virtue that belongs to justice. Crucially, I have said that Thomas recognizes the special goodness in acts of toleration offered in response to the limits that justice imposes on the reach of human law. As it would be unjust for human law to prohibit every action contrary to virtue, it leaves "permissible" (*permittenda*) to the majority of human beings many things "which would be intolerable in a virtuous man" (*quae non essent toleranda in hominibus virtuosis*) (*ST* I-II.96.2). It is precisely these many permissible things that a just human government and its citizens will rightly tolerate.

---

23   Largely ignored, but not entirely so. As Cary Nederman notes, there were discourses and practices of tolerance in medieval Europe. Most were designed to temper the well-established power of ecclesiastic elites to constrain dissent and of secular rulers to coerce dissenters. Paternalism was the rule, tolerance the exception. Nederman, "Discourses and Contexts of Tolerance in Medieval Europe."

For similar reasons, Thomas concludes that toleration must be granted to the rites of some unbelievers in some circumstances, certainly when prohibition by law would fail to safeguard the common good. In circumstances like these, those who exercise political authority "rightly tolerate certain evils (*recte aliqua mala tolerant*), lest certain goods be impeded or greater evils incurred" (*ST* II-II.10.11). Insofar as unbelievers fail to give due worship to the triune God, they sin in their rites, or so Thomas assumes. Yet their injustice may be tolerated either for the sake of some good that ensues or because of some evil avoided. He gives an example of each possibility. Like Augustine, Thomas thinks that ancient Jewish rites prefigured the central truths of the Christian faith, and even now these rites bear witness to that faith *in figura*. For the sake of this witness their observances should be tolerated (*in suis ritibus tolerantur*) (ibid.).[24] By contrast, the injustices committed in the rites of other unbelievers provide no equivalent witness and therefore should not be endured, although there can be exceptions. Legal toleration should be offered in those circumstances when proscription by law is likely to scandalize the weak in virtue, jeopardize civil peace, or hinder the chance that particular unbelievers, left unmolested (*sic tolerati*), might convert (ibid.).

We might not accept the relationship between civic life and religious rite that Thomas assumes in these examples, and we might not endorse the distinction he draws between the tolerable and the intolerable or the warrants he provides in defense of his judgment. I certainly don't. But for my purposes, what matters is that he recognizes the importance of the judgment and the moral significance of the act. He knows that toleration's patient endurance can be good, that in certain circumstances it can be right and required. Why, then, doesn't he follow his own rule and use the special goodness in these acts of toleration to identify a virtue that perfects resort to them?[25] Thomas discusses many virtues, some in great detail, and yet his list is neither exhaustive nor meant to be. There are unnamed virtues at work in our lives that our theoretical efforts to date have overlooked and about which we are insufficiently attentive. Thomas admits as much and identifies a few.[26] But why doesn't he identify this one, tolerance?

---

24 For discussion of Augustine's views, see Fredriksen, *Augustine and the Jews*.

25 Recall his dictum: "Since virtue is directed to good, wherever there is a special kind of good, there must needs be a special kind of virtue" (ubi occurrit specialis ratio boni, ibi oportet esse specialem rationem virtutis) (*ST* II-II.114.1).

26 So, for example, daring (*audacia*) is a passion that must be moderated according to reason *and* a vice that names habitual immoderation. Thomas explains the verbal confusion by referring to the solution commonly offered to fact that "some vices are unnamed, and so also some virtues." To confirm the fact, he cites Aristotle's authority, who has no name for persons insensitive to pleasure (*NE* 1107b5–8), or for holding ordinary honors in right regard (*NE* 1125b25), or for the person who is neither ingratiating nor quarrelsome but who manages to

Here we must speculate. Begin with the slogan that Aquinas borrows from Aristotle: "Virtue is about the difficult and the good" (*ST* II-II.129.2). It abridges much of what he has to say about nature, virtue, and agency. We have already unpacked some of its content and entailments, but there's more to be said and some of it bears on the historical range of tolerance. If tolerance emerges as a perfection because its paradigmatic act, patient endurance, enables us to respond well to certain kinds of differences and disagreements in the various societies we inhabit, then it is unlikely that it will become a prominent response when there are other, equally effective and less painful ways to cope with these difficulties. Coercion is the obvious alternative. As a means of coping with difference and disagreement, it obviously comes packaged with its own labors and pains. And yet, it can be an effective means, in certain circumstances its resorts can be just, and for those who take up its labors (leaving aside for a moment those who are subject to them) its pains are often less odious than the difficulties associated with toleration's patient endurance. The good that just and measured coercion seeks—a union of loves within a shared life—is also difficult to deny. Its sweetness is hard to forsake, especially when toleration's alternative involves enduring differences that, to some degree, divide us from our own, from those with whom we would rather be united. Thomas's slogan implies that the virtues of our life in this world do not emerge without difficulties to confront. But this means that a specific virtue will not emerge at all—and tolerance is a good example—if, in a given context, there is some sensible way to secure its ends while dodging the difficulties that attend its act or some obvious way to cope with those difficulties through less arduous resorts.

This insight brings needed precision to the account of natural virtue defended in chapter 2. In the strictest sense, a virtue is a natural feature of our shared humanity when its principal act regards a specific matter found in every human life, when this act helps us achieve specific instances of a general end that all human beings consider good and desirable, and when its constancy with respect to this act helps us overcome the difficulties that must be addressed whenever this end is intended and pursued. Regular and unavoidable resort to the act, consistent success in the achievement of its end, and recurrent overcoming of those difficulties—these will eventually generate our recognition of a virtue. We will come to see that the habitual performance of this act in the face of those difficulties is in fact a moral excellence, a perfection of our agency and thus of our humanity. In this strict sense, a natural

---

strike the mean between them (*NE* 1127a7–12). The solution is to allow certain passions to designate certain unnamed vices and virtues. Thus hope and love name certain virtues, passions, and actions (*ST* II-II.127.1.3). In this same way, *audacia* can designate the unnamed vice of those who respond to arduous evils with habitually immoderate measures of the passion itself (*ST* II-II.127.1).

virtue is a necessary virtue. It emerges in some form in every minimally flourishing society, in every imaginable human life and relationship. It is both unavoidable and ubiquitous. Quite often, it is depicted in story and art and cultivated in households and cities. Its sources and norms become explicit in theory. Here one thinks of justice, courage, and the other cardinal virtues.[27]

Tolerance, by contrast, is a natural virtue in a somewhat looser sense. Human life in the world we inhabit is indeed the seminary of this virtue. That life in this world constitutes the conditions for its emergence and growth, conditions that we considered in chapter 2. At the same time, those conditions cannot by themselves generate the virtue. They are necessary but not sufficient. Other conditions must be added to the mix. In particular, circumstances must arise that favor toleration's act as a sensible and useful response to an important collection of disagreements and differences, circumstances that make the labors associated with that act unavoidable and the pains bearable. If these circumstances are regular occurrences in human life and history, as I think they are, then we can say that tolerance is a virtue that comes packaged with our humanity, not because it emerges with hard necessity everywhere and always, in every society and relationship, but rather because it occurs regularly and repeatedly, in most times and places but not all, in some social arrangements but not others. It is an unavoidable and recurrent, but not ubiquitous, feature of the human form of life we happen to lead.

As a natural, inevitable, but not ubiquitous virtue, tolerance will become prominent in those times and places, in those relationships and circumstances, that make dodging the difficulties associated with its act more troublesome than taking them on. Historians tend to put the point negatively. Acts of toleration emerge as last resort. Praise for tolerance develops only among the singularly defeated or the mutually exhausted.[28] But this understates the positive case. Not every objectionable difference can be coerced with violence or controlled by law, not actually, not justly. Acts of toleration will appear when their labors are not only sufferable but also indispensable for the life we lead in the circumstances we find ourselves in and for securing the peaceful society that we love and cannot imagine doing without. In circumstances like these, need for the act will eventually generate recognition of the virtue, at first tacitly, among those who benefit directly, and then explicitly, among all who share in its good.

By this logic, tolerance will be neither recognized nor praised in those circumstances that favor some other response to the most pressing problems of association posed by disagreement and difference, some other collection

---

27   Aquinas is explicit about this relation between the goods we cannot but love and the cardinal virtues we cannot do without. On his rendering, the first precepts of the natural law specify those goods and those goods are the seminaries of these virtues (ST I-II.94.2–3; 63.1; 63.2.3).

28   See Garnsey, "Religious Toleration in Classical Antiquity," 25 and Pettegree, "Politics of Toleration in the Free Netherlands," 198.

of actions, and here the most important variable is not the distribution of power but the kind of society that difference threatens to unsettle. Societies with tightly drawn and vigilantly monitored boundaries, relatively strict membership criteria, carefully sorted rank hierarchies, and a rich collection of socially significant symbols and distinctions might very well take up defensive responses. Objectionable differences might be expelled, quarantined, or coerced out of existence. By contrast, societies with relatively loose boundaries and membership criteria, on the one hand, and a relatively free-floating collection of symbolic resources on the other, tend to accommodate difference with either acceptance or indifference.[29] As tolerance strikes the mean between these responses, it seems likely that it will emerge and take on special prominence in those societies that have boundaries and membership criteria that are substantial but subject to dispute and revision. It will appear in those societies whose symbolic resources and significant distinctions are abundant but neither universally shared nor indisputably fixed. Above all, it will appear when membership in the society in question is decoupled from at least some of its symbolic resources and significant distinctions, when authoritative interpretation of at least some of these is up for grabs, and when commitment to any one interpretation is uncertain and inconstant.

Every society has boundaries of some sort, membership criteria of some substance, and a collection of symbols and distinctions that mediate relations among members and between the society and the world beyond its boundaries. When these social structures are threatened by disagreement and difference, the response of first resort tends to be some kind of paternalistic coercion, if not in fact, then at least in threat. When coercion unifies the loves that matter and resolves the disagreements that threaten tranquility, when its use is selective and restrained, and when the peaceful society that all desire can in fact be secured through its offices, then it's unlikely that tolerance will appear on the list of virtues that are cultivated and praised. In a society of this kind, in circumstances like these, tolerance will remain inchoate, a potential perfection of these social relations, but not an actual one. Or, as is more likely, it will languish as a relatively minor virtue. Theoretically underdeveloped, it will either address insignificant disagreements and differences, or perfect relatively inconsequential social relations.

If we assume that these circumstances are common and that paternalistic coercion is often the first resort made in response to the disagreements and differences that do matter, then we should expect resort to toleration's act to emerge sporadically. Heydays of toleration will come and go. In each instance, the members of the society in question will find that some of the most important differences that divide them cannot be overcome by coercion, that for some reason crucial loves and commitments cannot be compelled

---

29 The best account of these matters remains Douglas, *Natural Symbols*, 20–68.

together, and that any such attempt would destroy the life they share, the peace they hope to bring to that life, and the autonomy they desire with respect to these differences. This discovery is often long in coming and typically preceded by repeated attempts, often violent and futile, to make coercion work.[30] When it becomes obvious that it will not, some combination of two things must happen: the membership criteria of the society in question must be revised and the socially significant symbols and distinctions must be recast. The list of commitments and activities that determine membership must be either expanded or rethought. New items must be added to it, or old items must be removed and replaced with others, presumably with vague generalities. So too, the symbols and distinctions that mediate the relevant social relations must be altered, presumably in a way that diminishes their importance for how those relations are structured. With this done, membership will no longer depend upon acceptance of certain contested items and relations among members will no longer be structured so carefully, so tightly, by certain symbols and distinctions. Stability in this newly constituted society and peace among its members can now be secured, at least in part, by toleration's patient endurance. After enough time has passed and enough discussion of this act and its merit has transpired, the members of the society in question may come to regard its attitudes and acts as indispensable features of justice. Left to their differences by an abandoned paternalism, they may come to the realization that they have no choice but to recast their affairs in this way, praise toleration's patient endurance, and cultivate its habitual sources. Over time, they may even admire the habit itself quite apart from its ability to achieve tolerant ends. They may add it to their list of virtues. And yet, even as they come to count tolerance among the virtues—even as they see goodness in its constancy and beauty in the perfection it brings to our agency—most will admit that it's the act they want, regardless of internal attitude. Most will settle for less than virtuous sources of that act, for self-control that nevertheless generates rightful toleration ordered to genuinely tolerant ends. In a weak moment, some may even endorse responses to difference that fall short of the right but that nevertheless secure those ends. As we have seen, many will mistake these half measures and impostures for the real thing.

None of this implies that tolerance excludes coercion, that the two cannot coexist in the same social circumstances. They always do. The list of tolerable actions and things is always finite; it is never a Borges book. It always come to an end, even in those societies we are inclined to call tolerant.[31]

---

30   For one such heyday's progression from coercion to toleration, see Digeser, *Making of a Christian Empire* and Drake, *Constantine and the Bishops*.

31   In this story, a fictional Borges acquires a book with an infinite number of pages. Try as he might, he can turn neither to the first, nor to the last page. The pages just keep coming. Borges, *Book of Sand*.

Eventually a page is turned and we come to a new list, to those intolerables that must be coerced, banished, or quarantined before they harm the society that nevertheless tolerates what it can. At the same time, no society can coerce, banish, or quarantine every objectionable difference. Those that do, or at least try to, don't last long, which is to say that all societies this side of tyranny, even those that we are inclined to call paternalistic, tolerate some actions and things.

Nothing in these remarks should surprise. The real complication comes when societies with overlapping memberships have competing lists. If acts of toleration become a sensible response to objectionable difference only as our humanity conspires with social circumstances of the right sort, and if a virtuous resort to this act can be recognized and praised only as time has passed and its special goodness comes into focus, then it may very well happen that individuals with multiple social memberships will find that they offer that response and praise that virtue in some settings and in relation to some actions and things, while forsaking them, perhaps even denouncing them, in others. In liberal democracies inhabited by immigrants from illiberal lands and by citizens with hyphenated identities, this complicated relation between a virtue term and its application tends to be the norm, and the drama that plays out across the hyphen has a certain formal consistency.[32] The public square will have its own lists of the tolerable and the intolerable, its own collection of virtues and demands, its own ways of coping with difference and disagreement, while the illiberal home and local community will have competing lists, collections, and ways. Caught up in this drama, most individuals experience some measure of moral dissonance and conflict. In most cases, the norms of one social setting will eventually trump the norms of the other, participation in one society eventually preventing full and untroubled participation in the other. It's a familiar American story, but it makes sense only if we assume the persistent but irregular career of the act and its virtue, of their unfailing appearance and undeniable importance in societies of a certain kind and in circumstances of a certain sort, and their relative insignificance, if not absence, in others.

So far so good. But notice how this account of the uneven but persistent distribution of tolerance across our species and its relation to our shared humanity generates a final objection. The worry goes like this. If tolerance is a recurrent but not a necessary feature of our natural history, and if it appears in those circumstances that make paternalistic coercion an unworkable response to the threats posed to social peace by disagreement and difference, then (as we have seen) there is no denying that it grants greater measures of autonomy to the tolerated or that its intrinsic goodness assumes the special

32   For a discussion of hyphenated identities in liberal, immigrant societies, see Walzer, *What It Means to Be an American*.

value of autonomy itself. We have already seen how this relation between tolerance, autonomy, and intrinsic goodness plays itself out in the reasons that might encourage a parent to tolerate a teenager's choice of music. Yet this relation seems to cast doubt on the natural character and historical recurrence of tolerance. It seems to confine the virtue to modern, liberal societies and to reassert its standard history. Why? Because there is a tradition of reflection on toleration that runs roughly from John Stuart Mill to some of the most important contemporary accounts, a tradition that considers the act good in itself and caused by a virtue but only as its connection to autonomy is assumed.[33]

Here we need a distinction. So far, when I have spoken of the connection between the goodness in an act of toleration, the autonomy made possible with this act, and the virtue that perfects resort to it, I have regarded autonomy as the power or capacity to determine which actions to perform, which ends to pursue and activities to take up. It is this capacity the tolerant person hopes to secure with respect to the difference in dispute—secure it for and with the tolerated. Strip away coercion and manipulation, bracket circumstances where choice is impossible because necessity rules, assume a basic level of intellectual and physical prowess, cultivate reflectiveness about the relative goodness of the available options, and the capacity to act autonomously will emerge. Tolerance and its act, I have said, will assist its emergence.

Here, however, in this objection, autonomy refers to the ideal of a freely chosen life, a life that one chooses for oneself. It is a life in which the capacity to act autonomously is exercised consistently across a significant number of good and morally serious options.[34] It is, in the words of Alon Harel, "the ability of individuals to promote their own life projects, to pursue their own conceptions of the good, and to live in accordance with self-chosen goals and relationships."[35] Since the inhabitants of liberal societies do indeed count this ability among the goods that must be found in the flourishing life they hope to lead, and since the inhabitants of other sorts of societies in other times and places typically do not, some will argue that the tolerance associated with this ideal determines what the virtue can be. Tolerance will appear in liberal societies alone and be counted among the virtues only as liberals do the counting, or so the objection goes.[36] By these

---

33   I am referring to the tradition that runs from Mill's "On Liberty" to Raz's *Morality of Freedom*.

34   For a discussion of the distinction between the capacity and the ideal see Raz, *Morality of Freedom*, 369–390.

35   Harel, "Boundaries of Justifiable Tolerance," 115.

36   In each instance, I assume a relatively widespread and untroubled consensus about the ideal of autonomy, and in some cases this assumption misleads. Some societies are divided over autonomy's merit and some disputes generate hidden transcripts among dissenters from

same lights, it would seem that we could track the history of tolerance, its origin and subsequent career, by following the progress of autonomy as a capacity linked to an ideal life, follow it from the emergence of that ideal in the early modern period to our own day. If this collection of inferences follows from the conceptual connections that obtain between tolerance and autonomy, then it would seem that the argument we have followed to this point is misleading. Put simply, we cannot count tolerance among the virtues that come with our humanity. Rather, we must concede what most do: that tolerance has causes that are entirely local and contingent. As virtue and act, it comes with the life that the inhabitants of liberal societies actually lead, with the goods they tend to love and the ideals they typically have, autonomy above all.

Given this objection and puzzle, what's needed, or so it seems, is a better account of the conceptual connection between tolerance and autonomy, and in particular, a better account of the kind of autonomy that liberal tolerance assumes. With that in hand, we should be able to assess these inferences and conclusions, and we should be able to say whether the connection to autonomy prevents us from finding tolerance among those virtues that come packaged with our humanity. It is to these tasks that we now turn.

---

the dominant point of view. In a hidden transcript, decisions about the good of autonomy, the range of autonomous action, and the extent of the tolerable are spoken in whispers and heard on the margins, not proclaimed in official summaries of doctrine. For an account of hidden transcripts, see Scott, *Domination and the Arts of Resistance*.

CHAPTER 5

LIBERALISM AND LISTS

Consider the difficulty we have describing the variety of tolerance found in contemporary liberal democracies. Consider, for example, Alon Harel's attempt to characterize this virtue by specifying its limits. We must begin, he says, with the conception of human flourishing that liberals assume. A flourishing life must include autonomy, by which he means the ability of individuals to live in accord with their "freely made choices."[1] Without autonomy there can be no flourishing as liberals would have it. From this it follows that the liberal state must do a number of things to secure this good. It must be largely impartial with respect to individual choices and life projects. Within certain limits, it must also protect the choices that individuals make against undo interference from others. And, as "individual choice is always made within a particular social context," the liberal state must "sustain and reinforce a social context conducive to individual choice" (115). Although autonomy regards the choices of individuals, it is not something that individuals exercise on their own or in a context of their own making. Rather, as Harel quite sensibly assumes, it is our participation in a community of shared activities, judgments, and loves that makes autonomy possible, for it is only in a community of this kind that certain options are made available, certain others are excluded, and certain choices are made meaningful. Does this imply that the liberal state must *create* social contexts conducive to choice? No, at least not by Harel's lights, but it does imply that the liberal state must do what it can to support the contexts that already exist, and this obligation gives Harel a novel angle on a puzzle that has long

---

1 Harel, "Boundaries of Justifiable Tolerance," 115. Hereafter page numbers are cited in the text.

vexed liberal theory: when should liberals tolerate illiberal intolerance and when should they intervene on behalf of those denied autonomy in the social context they happen to inhabit?

AUTONOMY AND TOLERANCE

Harel's reply is roughly this: those of us who inhabit liberal societies should tolerate intolerant judgments, practices, and institutions when they are integral features of a shared way of life that is otherwise conducive to choice and when that way of life is, on the whole, a good one (117). So for example (it's Harel's), some varieties of Orthodox Judaism assume a comprehensive worldview that includes, perhaps even encourages, intolerance of gays and lesbians. No doubt some Orthodox Jews will resist this characterization, but for now, let's ask their forgiveness and proceed as if Harel's assumption is largely correct. In some Orthodox communities, a certain kind of intolerance prevents gays and lesbians from exercising the measure of autonomy that most inhabitants of liberal societies consider indispensable for a flourishing life. Within these communities, gays and lesbians cannot pursue certain activities; they cannot take up certain life projects. What should the citizens of liberal political societies do in reply, if anything? When should they tolerate this illiberal intolerance of autonomous choice and when should they intervene in defense of autonomy?

Harel answers as one might expect, with reasons that put autonomy first. Orthodox Jews share a way of life that is, on the whole, good in itself precisely because it nurtures the capacity to choose autonomously. It is a life that makes certain ends and activities available for choice and it gives meaning to those options that are actually chosen as it places them in a framework of judgment and rank among other options and within social practices of assessment and revision. As the "condemnation of so-called 'unnatural' sexual practices" forms a piece of the worldview that helps sustain this life, and as this piece is not easily teased apart from the whole without damaging what remains, Harel concludes that there should be a liberal presumption in favor of tolerating this bit of illiberal intolerance (117–119). Liberals must endure this local and limited affront to autonomy for the sake of the autonomy that they hope to secure for all. It's a conclusion that sounds paradoxical, but in fact it isn't. If autonomy requires a social context for its exercise and if every social context has a boundary marked (in part) by judgments about things intolerable, then autonomy will thrive only as this boundary is recognized and autonomy confined.

There are, of course, limits to this limit and constraints on this conclusion and for Harel they are specified by the unwelcome "spillover effects" that the tolerance of intolerance may have on the broader political community (122). Returning to Harel's example, when those of us who inhabit liberal political societies tolerate local, circumscribed intolerance of same-sex relations, when we leave this objectionable response to difference in sexual preference unchallenged, we may leave our fellow citizens who happen to be gays and lesbians uncertain about their standing in the larger community. Our limited tolerance of local homophobia, justified by our commitment to preserving one of autonomy's social contexts, may cause these fellow citizens to doubt our commitment to the equal treatment of all in the broader political community, which in turn may diminish *their* autonomy. Uncertain about their standing in the broader community and somewhat guarded as they proceed among its members, their capacity to choose the life they prefer may be pinched by their doubts and hesitations. If we are committed to the good of autonomy, we may consider this outcome intolerable. It may, Harel thinks, compel us to change course, forsake our tolerance of Orthodox intolerance, and intervene in the affairs of this local community (120–121).

Harel admits there are competing commitments here that are not easily reconciled, but the difficulty comes from the terms he employs, from the role autonomy plays in the argument, not from the moral challenges of the case. For my part, the case isn't all that challenging. I consider discrimination against gay and lesbian persons unjust and intolerable regardless of whether its emerges from ideas about gender and family, covenant and law, ideas that are otherwise good and that support a social context conducive to choice. The spillover effect this discrimination may have on the autonomy of others, while important to consider, is beside the point. In fact, it's not clear that the matter is best regarded in terms of competing autonomies. To see how this might be, consider the option that Harel does *not* propose. He does not suggest that the liberal state come to the rescue of those who bear the brunt of local illiberal intolerance—those who inhabit a minority community and have their autonomy diminished as a result—and perhaps his example encourages the omission. Many Orthodox gays and lesbians wouldn't want rescue. They would consider state action an unjustified incursion into local affairs.[2] But suppose we change the example. Suppose we are confronted by an immigrant community that forms a recognizable social niche in a broader liberal society and that also happens to practice radical female circumcision on its adolescent daughters. How might the argument go? Well, following Harel's lead, we might say that, while objectionable, this practice is a portion of a distinctive and valuable way of life that constitutes an important

2   Those who resist the thought of rescue may nevertheless want legal pressure as a sign of support. See Greenberg, *Wrestling with God and Men* and Rapoport, *Judaism and Homosexuality*. For the analogous case regarding women's rights and standing, see Manning, *God Gave Us the Right*.

social context of autonomous choice. As individual autonomy is the good that matters most, and as this practice cannot be altered without harming that life, we might conclude that the threat to autonomy posed by this practice, the threat these girls must bear, is, in fact, tolerable. So long as the spillover effects are negligible, we might tolerate this practice among a small collection of our fellow citizens for the sake of the autonomy that we desire for all.

Well, we might, but I doubt it, and I doubt that our hesitations would follow from whatever worries we might have about spillover possibilities and effects. Rather, I suspect that many of us would argue that this practice is an intolerable injustice and that the liberal state should take action against it. Some will refer to its cruelty, some to the unaccountable power relations it assumes, and some to the equal dignity of all that it violates. But however its injustice is regarded, I suspect many of us support state intervention even if it harms the distinctive way of life that the members of this community lead, even if it undermines the social context of their autonomy, and even if most of the girls would rather submit to this practice than suffer the effects of our interventions on their standing in the community. In this instance, and in those like it, I suspect that liberals make paternalistic moves against injustice long before they worry about local intolerance spilling over and threatening the autonomy of others.

Notice what follows. If this hunch is sound, then it casts doubt on the account of tolerance and autonomy that Harel and others who trade in liberal theory assume. Harel contends that the inhabitants of liberal societies are willing to tolerate some of the beliefs and practices that they abhor because they think autonomy is good. But if autonomy is regarded as Harel does, as the ability to choose one's own course of life, then two problems trouble this account of liberal tolerance. First, as the female circumcision example makes plain, some choices are simply intolerable, even for the inhabitants of liberal societies, autonomy be damned, spillover effects or no, and this fact should provoke misgivings about the object that they are said to tolerate. In the textbooks and treatises on liberal theory, it's said that they tolerate autonomous choice, its contexts, content, and consequences, but in fact they appear to tolerate something else altogether. They tolerate specific courses and lives, specific activities and attitudes, and not all of them, but only some. The second problem confirms this suspicion in the first. If we insist that the inhabitants of liberal societies tolerate the choices that individuals make regarding the course of their own lives, then we assume that choice actually sets that course, and this overestimates what it can actually accomplish. For most of us, choice is not the only, and frequently is not the principal, cause of the course we happen to be on. Many of the most significant features of our lives are given to us by sources that transcend autonomy's reach. They are an inheritance of parents and providence, nature and circumstance, community and culture. On reflection, we might come to endorse what we have inherited, to love what we have been given with enough self-consciousness to call it our own, but this is not exactly choosing one's inheritance. Moreover, many of the features of our lives that we do manage to choose are made available for choice by that same inheritance. We might choose this or that, but not the options put before us. On this rendering, we clearly have less power over the course of our lives than liberal theorists tend to assume, and if this is largely correct, then once again, the conclusion seems to be that, regardless of what they say, it is not so much autonomous choice that the inhabitants of liberal political societies actually tolerate but certain courses and lives, certain activities and attitudes, whether chosen or not.

Given these problems, it would be better to say that liberal tolerance accents the multiplicity of options made available in liberal societies, whether chosen or not, not choice itself. The emphasis is on the relatively long list of courses and lives that liberals are willing to tolerate, not on the importance of actually choosing one's own.[3] By these lights, "choice" and "autonomy" are placeholders for that relatively long list, for the collection of attitudes, activities, and lives that the inhabitants of liberal societies tend to endure with patience, regard with indifference, or accept without complaint. The emphasis is (or rather ought to be) on the concrete moral judgments that constitute that collection, not on the philosophical abstractions that abridge those judgments and whose conceptual content is, in broad outline, determined by them.[4] Confusion comes when liberal theorists like Harel *say* that autonomy and choice distinguish their account of tolerance and justify their preference for it; it comes, in other words, when emphasis is misplaced and undue attention is given to these philosophical abstractions. And (no surprise) this confusion tends to compound as it encourages mischief among the friends and foes of liberal tolerance.[5]

---

3   It is *better* to put the point this way, but, as we shall see below, it's also somewhat misleading. The number of items on a liberal society's list of tolerable actions and things does indeed help specify the liberal variety of the concept, but so does the *significance* of those items.

4   This conclusion lines up quite nicely with the Wittgensteinian account of moral concepts developed in chapter 2.

5   Joseph Raz does not make this mistake, and I suspect it is because he recognizes two senses of autonomy—the capacity to choose and the ideal of a life freely chosen. The ideal requires the capacity, but they are distinct and it's the ideal—along with the range and significance of the options it assumes—that distinguishes liberal toleration. On Raz's rendering, liberal toleration is not a virtue, even if he calls it one. It is, rather, self-restraint of an "inclination which is itself desirable . . . because it is a reaction to wrongful behavior." So too, for Raz, liberal toleration exhausts what toleration can be. He never imagines other social and political circumstances of the act or other varieties of its perfection. *Morality of Freedom*, 402.

Foes, of course, will be tempted to regard this talk of autonomy and choice as hypocritical nonsense and so dismiss liberal conclusions about tolerance. When the virtue is defended on appeal to autonomy, its foes will complain of its incoherence precisely because there are autonomous choices that liberals are quite obviously unwilling to tolerate. That liberal moral theorists typically reply to this complaint by tinkering with their talk, by adding epicycles to theoretical epicycles, only confirms what these foes suspect: that liberal tolerance is a hoodwink, a philosophical masquerade, nothing but hypocrisy packaged as theory.[6] Changing the metaphor, foes will suspect that tolerance is a philosophical Trojan horse that liberals load with the normative commitments they prefer but are unwilling to defend with ordinary argument, commitments they hope to foist upon the rest of us under the cover of theory and its abstractions. "Everyone is in favor of autonomy and choice, right? Then everyone must be in favor of tolerance too." But this isn't an argument; it's just special pleading for liberal versions of these notions, versions that come packaged with certain judgments about the concrete lives and commitments that the inhabitants of liberal societies are willing to tolerate, or not. In these societies, one can apply these terms only as one accepts these judgments, these lists of actions and things tolerable and intolerable, which means that those who refuse a specific item on the list of tolerable actions and things will very likely find themselves cast among the intolerant foes of autonomy and choice.

It's this kind of talk—where philosophical abstractions are used to assert false universality and complicate dissent—that can tempt those who refuse certain key items on these liberal lists to toss out the virtue with the theoretical bathwater. But this won't do either. If the arguments of the preceding chapters are sound, then it's unlikely that tolerance can be tossed aside without ignoring the form of life that human beings lead and the virtues that come packaged with that life. So this temptation is best avoided. Or, rather, given the form of life that we actually lead, this temptation proposes what cannot be done. The special goodness of toleration's act offered in response to at least some objectionable differences cannot be denied, nor the virtue that comes as this goodness is recognized. And if this is right, there's no way to avoid talk of autonomy and choice; they are among the ends that tolerant acts must seek. At the same time, there's no denying the truth that motivates the temptation. Some friends of liberal tolerance do indeed resort to a theoretical sleight of hand in order to both affirm and deny the concrete judgments that give substance to their favorite concepts. These concepts can't be applied without tacitly assuming those judgments and the friends of liberal tolerance surely assume them. At the same time, they tend to defend theories of tolerance

6   For an account and criticism of "autonomy-based" defenses of liberal tolerance and of the theoretical epicycles offered in reply, see Mendus, *Toleration and the Limits of Liberalism*.

and autonomy that ignore the relation between concrete judgment and conceptual content. Harel makes a defense of precisely this kind. In his account, whatever conceptual content liberal tolerance and autonomy happen to have, it does not come from the list of specific actions, commitments, and things that the inhabitants of liberal societies typically judge tolerable or from the list of activities and lives they cannot endure.

It's this failure of attention, this acting as though conceptual content is one thing and concrete judgment another, that enables the friends of liberal tolerance to use these abstract ideas in their social criticism. They refer to tolerance and autonomy to find fault with those who reject certain items on these lists and to encourage the conclusion that one cannot in any way deploy these concepts or exhibit this virtue without accepting these items. At times they use this ploy to recast these lists, shifting new items on or off and thus subtly transforming the conceptual content of these ideas and altering the lives and practices that they help legitimate. And yet, if "choice" and "autonomy" are placeholders for items already on these respective lists, for the judgments assumed by those who make use of these concepts, then simple appeal to them should not be mistaken for argument. Nor should it compel those who do not share certain contestable judgments into transforming their own lists, forsaking their use of these concepts, or abandoning their commitment to the ideals that come packaged with them. Indeed, if all we can say is that this or that controversial action or thing should be tolerated because autonomy demands it, then we have said very little. We have asserted that our list of tolerable actions and things ought to be revised, that a new item ought to be placed among those actions and things that autonomy regards, but we have provided no reasons that might warrant these revisions.

MULTIPLE LISTS

Given these dynamics, it's no wonder that the debate between friends and foes of liberal tolerance tends to generate so much acrimony. Nor should it surprise us that both sides are content with the standard history. If it is assumed that tolerance emerges in the modern period as a response to the wars of religion that followed the Protestant Reformation, then there is reason to believe that the liberal variety exhausts what the virtue might be. And, if this is so, then friends of liberal tolerance will be disposed to think that doubts about this variety in fact regard tolerance *in se*. Foes will be inclined to agree. As tolerance is, by these lights, a deliverance of certain historical contingencies, there is no reason for its foes to consider it an unavoidable virtue. If the liberal variety is fitted to the life many of us lead and if there is reason for complaint with that life, then foes of this variety will be disposed to think that tolerance can be bypassed, that it's an accidental virtue of an unfortunate time. Combine these assumptions about the history of tolerance with the self-serving hypocrisy that these same foes find in its philosophical defenses, and it's no surprise that they doubt the virtue's merit and usefulness.

But again, this won't do, not if there is reason to think that as concept, act, and inchoate virtue tolerance arrives with our humanity. In that event, it can neither be confined to the modern period nor bypassed and ignored by those dissatisfied with its liberal forms. So too, if the conclusions of chapter 2 are sound, if conceptual mastery is less a matter of grasping definitions than of conceding judgments about concrete matters—judgments that one must consider true if the concept is to be employed with even the most basic competence—then it would seem that when we speak of tolerance, liberal or otherwise, we need to accent those judgments. When we speak of the philosophical ideas that accompany our talk of tolerance—autonomy, choice, and the rest—we need to resist the thought that these ideas do something more than abridge the judgments that are the real substance of that talk. Discipline ourselves to these tasks and we should be able to give a truthful rendering of the dispute between friends and foes of liberal tolerance and a useful diagnosis of the persistent assumption that the virtue emerges in the modern period but not before, in liberal societies but not elsewhere.

The argument follows from what we know. As concept, attitude, and act tolerance is natural to us, to the human form of life that all of us lead. Given the diversity of our judgments, loves, and activities, given the social character of our existence, and given the moral imperfections that we cannot avoid—given all this, some measure of disagreement and difference will always trouble our social and political relationships and all of us will resort to toleration's patient endurance in response to some of this trouble. We will make this resort in order to set these relationships right. Some of us may even come to speak of a habit that perfects this resort. Since social relations come in every shape and size, the frequency and character of this resort will vary. In fact, this variation is so great in kind and degree that we are tempted to say—and the standard history encourages us to believe—that some times and places exhibit tolerance and the capacity to act autonomously while others do not, but this is a temptation to avoid. Better to say that different societies have different items on their lists of actions and things tolerable, intolerable, indifferent, and acceptable. Every society that uses these concepts will resort to these lists. The items on each list—the judgments considered true by the linguistic community in question—give these concepts substance and determine basic application. They specify the shape and range of each society's account of tolerance and autonomy. In philosophical shorthand, meaning always comes packaged with truth. The concept of autonomy that we happen to have always comes packaged with a list of options that we consider tolerably choiceworthy. But this means that societies can be distinguished and their responses to difference identified by the lists they happen to have, by the concrete judgments they make, judgments that give these concepts both their general form and a portion of their determinate content. Attend to these judgments and lists, take note of their differences across time and between places, and identify the local interests and forces that shape them and we should be able to say how these concepts change and yet stay the same. Identity and difference in application and range should be easier to see. Exaggerated differences and facile similarities should be easier to discount.

Some will object to this reduction of moral typology, history, and diversity to the cataloguing of lists. Some might contend that these lists, while important for the purpose of comparing conceptual use across time and place, are secondary. What matters, what is indispensable, are the metaphysical warrants that justify this or that collection of judgments, this or that list, and that govern right application of the relevant concepts. Some societies speak of eternal law and divine command, some of human dignity and natural rights, some of primordial chaos and mythical forces of order. Regardless of its metaphysical content, all of this talk is designed to provide reasons that distinguish those items, lists, and applications that have contingent and customary causes from those that emerge from some kind of necessity—some unavoidable feature of our humanity, some hidden logic of the cosmos, or some consequence of God's will. And surely we should look to these warrants as we distinguish the different ways that societies respond to difference. Others, like Richard Rorty, will turn the argument on its head and insist that it's not the metaphysical warrants that matter but their absence. Given philosophy's metaphysical Babel of confusion—its well-documented failure to reach consensus about any particular metaphysical prop, on the one hand, and its equally well-known success in exposing the weaknesses of every prop proposed, on the other—these critics encourage us to proceed without metaphysical delusion. We should forgo every appeal to transcultural criteria and speak only of random forces of history constituting utterly contingent lists, concepts, and applications.[7]

But if the conclusions of chapter 2 are sound, then neither of these options can be quite right. If certain moral concepts come packaged with our humanity and certain judgments with those concepts, then contingency can't go all the way down. There are limits. If our humanity compels us (ever so sweetly, as Aquinas would put it) to speak of justice and tolerance, to make use of these concepts in our various social relations, then we can expect a certain constancy in the judgments that give them substance. Those judgments will not be endlessly diverse. Regardless of time and place, some generalities will

7   Rorty, "On Ethnocentrism," 208.

be shared—not all, but some. Some will show up on many lists of things just and unjust, things tolerable and not, and certain others will show up on many more. At the same time, concrete specification of these generalities does not come with our humanity. Or, put another way, our nature does provide us with lists of concrete judgments, judgments that would make our shared concepts fully determinate. Specificity of this kind follows from the contingencies of history, or if you like, from the cunning of reason, from the wisdom of providence, or from our gracious re-creation. For of course if these moral concepts do not emerge from our humanity fully determinate, nor do they come packaged with a theoretical account of their emergence and subsequent development. One might go metaphysically minimalist as Wittgenstein does, or theologically maximalist with Aquinas. Those concepts might be deliverances of nature's grace or the secondary precepts of a divine lawgiver's command. About this, our humanity is silent.

What's needed, then, is attention to the different lists of different times and places, regardless of their metaphysical packaging. A society with relatively few, and mostly insignificant, items on its list of actions and things tolerable, similar numbers on its lists of actions and things indifferent and acceptable, and (not surprising) many and important items on its list of actions and things intolerable will give little attention to the virtue and it's unlikely that we will call its inhabitants tolerant. Too many disagreements and differences about too many actions and things fall under coercion's purview, too few under endurance and restraint, and too little autonomy remains at the end of the day. Even so, it is unlikely that as concept, attitude, and act, tolerance will be unknown to the members of such a society. They will tolerate some actions and things, but not many. Their list will be short, but the point is that it will not be empty, and some of the items found on their list will also appear on ours. Some agreement in judgment and list must obtain, for without it we could not assign the concept to them as we interpret their actions and utterances. As conceptual form follows from judgments about concrete matters, complete absence of agreement would prevent us from recognizing their utterances as being *about* the tolerable and the intolerable. No doubt, in this instance, the agreement in judgment (and thus the overlap in lists) will be partial and the concept we assign to them will be significantly different from our own, and yet it will have to be similar enough for us to conclude that their concern regards objectionable difference and that their sentences refer to actions and things that deserve something like patient endurance.

By contrast, a society with many, significant items on its list of actions and things tolerable and a comparatively short list of actions and things intolerable will most likely accent the attitude and act. Its inhabitants might even insist that their application of the concept requires talk of justice and virtue, of an act that is right and due and of a habit that is its cause. Will we be inclined to call them tolerant? It depends. If we attend to the details of their lives and epistemic contexts, if we look at what they are capable of knowing and loving, what they are within their rights to infer from what they know, and what they are obliged to infer nevertheless, and if, after all that, we find them justified in having these particular items on their respective lists, then we will probably count them among the tolerant. If many of the items on their lists show up on ours—or if not many, then at least the items that matter most to us—then we surely will. At the same time, there might be items on their list of actions and things intolerable that we cannot imagine placing on ours. These items could be deliverances of choice, nature, or inheritance. They could show up on our list of things tolerable, indifferent, or acceptable. For the moment, these distinctions are irrelevant. What matters is that this society considers intolerable what we cannot, and this will give us pause. Why? Because it is not the *number* of items that a society considers tolerable and intolerable that *alone* determines our assessment of its character. The significance of these items also matters and in this instance the numbers are sufficient but not every item of significance falls on the right list.

If this account is sound, then it would seem that we cannot assess liberal tolerance by reference to numbers alone. The significance of the items found on liberal lists will also matter. No doubt, liberal societies tend to have a comparatively short list of intolerable actions and things and relatively more items divided among the tolerable, acceptable, and indifferent. And surely the tolerance that we find in liberal societies is distinguished, in part, by this distribution, by the plurality of things tolerated and by the effects of this pluralism. Many items are reserved for individuals, for the choices they make and the lives they inherit, many that illiberal societies do not. But it matters which items fall where, and this is the real sticking point. If the inhabitants of a certain society are divided by disagreement and difference over actions and things that matter both to us and to them, and if a majority are tempted by coercion's appeal to cast these actions and things among the intolerable, then I doubt we would call this society tolerant or give unqualified praise for the scope it reserves for autonomy. I suspect our doubts would remain even if we discovered significant overlap in our respective lists of things tolerable, indifferent, and acceptable. So it's not pluralism alone that distinguishes liberal societies, the autonomy they grant their members, or the tolerance that governs their affairs. Indeed, I doubt we would call a society liberal and tolerant that left most things to individual choice and endorsement, but not some of the most important matters—one's religion, marriage partner, or vocation.

Once again the point follows from the tight coordination of meaning and truth, of concept mastery on the one hand and the judgments one considers indubitably true on the other. The rules that govern the use of a concept are judgments that regard certain concrete matters. We considered this relation between judgment, rule, and use in chapter 2's discussion of justice. Suppose someone says that he knows what "justice" is, that he has mastered the concept well enough to use it in ordinary conversation. At the same time, he insists that torturing children for fun is just. If, in response to our request for clarification, he repeats what he said, then I suspect that we would grant him either the concept or the judgment, but not both. That is, I suspect that we would conclude either that he believes what he says about torture and thus cannot have mastered the concept "justice" well enough to use it competently, or that he knows what "justice" is, knows how to use it as we do, and is simply confused about "torture." He doesn't know how to apply the concept; he can't be counted on to identify the horrendous evil of the act, to see its fundamental injustice. Now imagine a person who not only considers certain racial and ethnic differences objectionable but who also refuses to endure with patience those who embody them. For this person, these differences are quite literally intolerable. Those who embody them must be controlled, quarantined, or expelled. This judgment is obviously false and these responses plainly unjust—indeed they are vile and contemptible—and yet suppose this person insists that she understands "tolerance" and "intolerance" as liberals do. She knows what these concepts involve, knows how to apply them, and understands what values they pick out—or so she says. Would we believe her? Would we assign these concepts to her? Well, again, I suspect that we would grant her either the concepts or the judgment, but not both. Just as we don't quite know what to think of persons who say they know what justice involves and yet doubt that torturing children for fun is unjust, so too we are puzzled by persons who say that racial and ethnic differences are objectionable and intolerable and yet insist that they know what liberal tolerance entails. In each case, failure in judgment encourages doubt about their mastery of the concept and their commitment to the ideals it embodies.

Again, if this account is sound, this treatment of concept and judgment, tolerance and lists, then we cannot distinguish liberal tolerance from other varieties on appeal to the relative open-endedness of liberal lists. Richard Rorty makes the appeal this way: "Our bourgeois liberal culture . . . is constantly enlarging its sympathies. It is a form of life that is constantly extending pseudopods and adapting itself to what it encounters. Its sense of its own moral worth is founded on its tolerance of diversity. The heroes it apotheosizes include those who have enlarged its capacity for sympathy and tolerance. Among the enemies it diabolizes are the people who attempt to diminish this capacity, the vicious ethnocentrists."[8] But this can't be right, or at the very least, it cannot, on its own, help us pick out the variety of tolerance praised in liberal societies. That is, it may well be the case that Rorty's variety of Whitmanesque liberalism is characterized by its openness to nov-

---

8   Ibid., 204.

elty and that liberals of this stripe are "connoisseurs of diversity," who relish the findings of our "specialists in particularity," our "agents of love"—"historians, novelists, ethnographers, and muckraking journalists."[9] But this disposition distinguishes this variety of liberalism, not liberalism per se, and not liberal tolerance in particular. The point is not just that there are liberals of other stripes or that some of them, Oakeshottian liberals for example, are less willing to experiment with experience in the hope that new items might be added to our list of tolerable actions and things. Rather, the point is that a disposition to recast the lists one happens to have can hardly be called liberal if it generates revisions that are not. Add, remove, and reshuffle certain items in certain ways and liberals of every stripe will cry foul. Tinker with the basic judgments that govern liberal use, and they will lament the demise of tolerance. A precedent is not hard find. After all, Whitmanesque liberals share their openness to difference and their disposition to revise with Nietzsche and his progeny, and these latter reside uneasily among the liberal and tolerant. Here the difference lies in the concrete commitments that give substance to the kind of tolerance that liberals admire and that Nietzsche resisted, commitments that liberals cannot forsake without losing the ability to make use of the concept and that Nietzscheans cannot adopt without becoming liberal and tolerant.[10]

And finally, if this account of liberal tolerance is sound, then we can explain the persistent assumption that tolerance—not just its liberal variety, but tolerance per se—emerged in the modern West. We can do so by referring to these lists. While this assumption misleads, we can note that many are nevertheless disposed to speak in these terms precisely because of the dramatic, at times violent, and no doubt significant transformation of Christendom's lists that occurred in the early modern Europe. Tolerance did not emerge as a result of this transformation. Rather the conceptual content of the idea was substantially altered as items of great importance for the identity and legitimacy of Europe's political societies were moved from one list to another. Locke's famous *Letter Concerning Toleration* is best regarded in these terms. It is his attempt to say how Christendom's lists had already been recast on the ground after 1640 in the ecclesiastical practices and theological convictions of English dissenters and why there was no going back to the old lists even after the Restoration of 1660 made it possible for some to imagine a return. It is also his attempt to offer reasons that might justify those practices and convictions and that might reinforce this recasting of lists.

But as we noted in chapter 1, many readers, both in Locke's day and in ours, have found his justifications wanting, his recast lists impossible to accept,

9   Ibid., 206–207.

10   That there might be hybrids, Nietzschean liberals of some sort, I will leave for others to decide. See Redhead, "Debate," and Strong, *Friedrich Nietzsche and the Politics of Transfiguration*.

and the consequences of his efforts unhappy, if not dangerous. He says that his proposals are utterly "agreeable to the Gospel of Jesus Christ, and to the genuine Reason of Mankind," that these authorities justify his reshuffled lists, and yet one hears special pleading in his proposals. His lists will hardly secure the agreement of all who consider themselves faithful or who stake their affairs on reason's judgment.[11] His intolerance of Catholics and atheists makes this much plain.[12] It also exposes the sources of the reshuffling he proposes in his dissenting and Calvinist sympathies.[13] And if this special pleading were not trouble enough, we have already noted that, whatever its sources and justifications, his recast account of the tolerable and the intolerable constrains the authority of religious elites only as it provides civil magistrates with potentially unlimited power over all things that do not fall under the inwardness of true religion. These are standard complaints with Locke's *Letter*. They have merit, or so it seems to me, and yet I mention Locke, his efforts, and his critics, not to discount his achievement but rather to insist that the great works on tolerance from the early modern period (Williams's *Bloudy Tenent of Persecution*, Locke's *Letter*, and Bayle's *Philosophical Commentary*), like those from the European Enlightenment (Voltaire's *Philosophical Letters* and Lessing's *Nathan the Wise*), are best regarded in this rather mundane light. The theological argument might be dense and the philosophical firepower substantial, and yet in the end no discovery is made. No new concepts emerge that regard our various responses to disagreement and difference, certainly not something uniquely modern called "tolerance." Rather, in each instance, a medieval inheritance is updated and an established collection of concepts is transformed as the judgments that give them substance are recast, their respective lists reshuffled, and the relevant membership criteria reformed.

No doubt this recasting was substantial, this transformation great. At the same time, those who are tempted to speak of the intolerant Middle Ages ought to avoid concluding, as Gibbon does, that tolerance was unknown in the fourteen centuries between Theodosius's assault on the easygoing pluralism of pagan Rome and the Enlightenment's undoing of Christendom.[14]

---

11   Locke, *Letter*, 25.

12   For Locke, Catholics ought not be tolerated because they insist that "Dominion is founded in Grace" and thus deny the tidy distinction between civil and religious affairs that Locke assumes. Atheists ought not be tolerated because they doubt the existence of a gracious God and thus cannot be counted to honor "Promises, Covenants, and Oaths." Ibid., 50–51.

13   For the development of Locke's theological commitments, see Marshall, *John Locke*. For an interpretation of Locke's *Letter* that accents the coordination of religious and civil loyalties, see Perry, *Pretenses of Loyalty*, 102–142.

14   Gibbon contrasts Theodosius's intemperate zeal for persecution (Gibbon, *History of the Decline and Fall of the Roman Empire*, chap. 28) with Julian's wise and measured policy of universal toleration (chap. 23).

Rather, we can explain the temptation by referring to the consequences of this great transformation. The concept of tolerance that emerged—the one familiar to readers of Bayle's *Commentary* and Lessing's *Nathan*—is indeed quite different from its medieval antecedent, which is to say nothing more than that our lists of actions and things tolerable and intolerable contain items that they could not imagine, could not endorse. Might we nevertheless speak (as most do) of medieval intolerance? Certainly, but only as we resist the temptation to confuse substantial transformation of the concept for its utterly novel emergence and only as we forsake the assumption that the societies of medieval Christendom should have shared our version, our lists. Better to begin with humility about the sources of our own moral concepts and charity about the substance of theirs. Better to assume that, for the most part, the judgments that give our concepts substance have causes that outstrip our control—history lurching this way and that, customs and practices that we inherit, the unexpected appearance of moral geniuses, prophets, and reformers, and so on. No doubt we want the effects of those causes—our judgments, lists, and concepts in use—to be justified by reasons that warrant our commitment to them, reasons that take into account the strengths and weaknesses of alternative judgments, lists, and uses. And yet the reasons available to us and the alternatives we might consider are also accidents of history, circumstance, and inheritance. What follows (or at least, ought to) is not skepticism about all reasons and effects but, as I said, humility about those we happen to have. We should assume that our ancestors will be subject to causes that we know not, resort to vocabularies that are unavailable to us, and offer reasons that we cannot imagine. We should assume, in other words, that their judgments and lists will be somewhat different from our own and so too the shape of the moral concepts they employ, tolerance and intolerance among the rest. The same applies to our medieval predecessors. The causes converging on them, the reasons made available as a result, and the vocabularies at their disposal were different from those that helped constitute our own judgments, lists, and concepts. And yet, on the whole we have good reason to count them justified in maintaining the lists they happen to have and in making use of the concepts specified by those lists.[15]

EXAGGERATION AND RECOGNITION

Suppose this account of tolerance, history, concept, and list is largely correct, and suppose we live in time and place that finds itself actively debating which items belong on which lists. When the items up for grabs are many

---

15   Here I follow Stout, *Democracy and Tradition*, 231–234.

and significant, when competing reasons are offered in defense of competing lists, and when reasons give out and violence steps in, then we find
ourselves in a heyday of discourse and dispute about tolerance. Locke and
Bayle lived and worked in one such heyday. Today we find ourselves in another. Critics of liberal tolerance think that liberal lists of actions and things
tolerable, intolerable, acceptable and indifferent need to be recast. By their
lights, too many items show up on one list, too few on another, and, regardless of numbers, the most important items appear on the wrong lists. In
times like these, debate tilts toward rhetorical excess. Exaggeration abounds.[16]
Those who think that too many items of too great a significance have been
taken from our list of intolerable actions and things and distributed reck-
lessly among the indifferent and the acceptable are tempted to speak in apo-
calyptic tones of relativism, nihilism, and tolerance that has decayed into a
vice.[17] In much the same way, those who think that our list of intolerable actions and things is unreasonably bloated are tempted to speak of the bigotry
and intolerance of those who think otherwise. But, as I said, this kind of talk
distorts the terms and stakes of the debate. Societies that have lively disputes
about the tolerable and the intolerable, the indifferent and the acceptable,
rarely consider the virtues and vices of tolerance itself, even if some participants insist that they are. Rather, they are trying to determine which items go
on which lists, which is another way of saying they are trying to specify the
material content and the right use of those moral concepts that regard objectionable difference. And, since mastery of these concepts (however they
are finally specified) and commitment to their right use (whatever that ultimately entails) are roughly equivalent to perfection in one's response to
difference, objectionable and otherwise, we can also say that these debates
regard the shape and range of a virtue, of those actions and attitudes that it
perfects. We can say that the participants in these debates are simply trying
to determine the scope and significance of tolerance.

   In societies like ours, one fears exaggeration of this kind precisely because
one hopes these debates about the tolerable and the intolerable will proceed democratically and, for want of a better term, ethnographically. Debate
proceeds democratically when no one is denied standing in the relevant
discursive community arbitrarily, when members hold each other accountable for what they say and do by asking for reasons that might justify words
and deeds, when each defers to the authority of each in the right circumstances and for the right reasons, and when no person or claim is thought
to deserve deference by default.[18] It proceeds ethnographically when the
reasons traded back and forth and the differences explored in debate are

---

16   See Stout, "Spirit of Democracy and the Rhetoric of Excess."
17   See Geertz, "Anti-Anti-Relativism," 47–48.
18   Stout, *Democracy and Tradition*, 209–213.

taken seriously: not dismissed as irrational, impossible, or inhuman, not do-mesticated by false familiarity, not disregarded by our moral narcissism.[19] It involves a certain mixture of empathy and reserve, a certain "imaginative entry into (and admittance of) an alien turn of mind" that is (nevertheless) tem-pered by the recognition that one cannot embrace all that one might come to grasp and respect.[20] And it requires a certain willingness to understand the reasons internal to a different frame of mind and to follow an argument in its conceptual vernacular.[21] One hopes that debate about the tolerable and the intolerable will proceed in these ways, that one's interlocutors will be regarded as neither nihilists nor bigots. Neither can be expected to offer rea-sons that can be taken seriously or to exhibit lives that one might want to imagine as alternatives to one's own. And, as in Locke's day, when rhetoric becomes excessive and serious reasons go missing, some will conclude that other means—threats, manipulations, and violence—are both needed and warranted. Locke, after all, wrote his letter in exile, having fled England for the Continent after his efforts on behalf of toleration in the early 1680s brought persecution to his door. In the 1960s it was the radical, disgruntled left that took up these means. In more recent decades, it has been the radical, alienated right. In each instance, violence replaces reasons that have been discredited, in part, by exaggeration.

Rhetorical excess tends to shut down democratic debate about the toler-able and the intolerable before it can begin and to suffocate ethnographic sympathy before it can emerge. This is a source of trouble that emerges from *within* a political community, but there might also be external sources. Imagine a community trying to determine whether it will tolerate logging in an old-growth forest, or the denial of drug benefits to veterans, or the demolition of an historic building. Most consider these actions objection-able. But are they tolerable, and if not, on which list do they belong? Well, if tolerance belongs to justice as one of its parts, and if justice is, as Aquinas contends, attentive to the common weal of the community, then, at least in part, the question here turns on the relation between these objectionable actions and that shared life. If there are certain goods held in common that the community holds dear, certain ends that it cannot imagine forsaking,

19   It's this domestication that Stanley Fish captures so effectively in his essay "Boutique Multiculturalism."

20   Geertz, "Uses of Diversity," 82, 87.

21   The language in this sentence comes from Akeel Bilgrami, who thinks this desire to "reach each other" across a normative divide by attending to the internal reasons assumed by each is incompatible with the disapproval that tolerance assumes. It isn't. Rather, it's this desire that makes debate about the tolerable and the intolerable go well and its outcomes just. As in any disagreement, it may turn out that differences remain despite mutual attention to internal reasons, and in that event, resort to toleration seems unavoidable, and so too its perfection by virtue. See his "Secularism: Its Content and Context," 54–55.

and if these goods cannot be had as these objectionable actions and things are tolerated, then it is unlikely that they will be. At the same time, there's no predicting in advance how these judgments will go. Actions and ends can be assessed in different ways and so too judgments about the tolerable and the intolerable. This should hardly surprise us. What matters is how the debate proceeds. It ought to proceed among *members*, not only those who have recognized standing in the community, but also those who ought to even as they are now excluded. It ought to include all those who have a stake in its shared goods and rightly ordered relationships and who make the sacrifices that sustain them. In many communities, the legal membership criteria fail to identify all who deserve recognized standing, and even when they do, debate will too often proceed under the influence of forces external to the community, its members and interests. So, for example, in our day, it is too often global markets and multinational corporate interests that determine whether old-growth forests are logged, not the local communities affected by the decision. In much the same way, it is too often insurance companies and health care managers who specify the ends of medical practice and who determine the normative contours of a healthy life, not real and potential patients, not health care providers, not those who actually care for the sick. When this happens, judgments about tolerable and intolerable distribution of drug benefits will not be made by those most affected by them, and they will not be assessed by the particular standards of excellence implicit in these local practices.[22]

Such are the difficulties that corrupt democratic debate about a just response to objectionable difference, difficulties that the moral virtues—tolerance and judgment, patience and perseverance—are obviously designed to address. Or, more precisely, a capacity for these virtues has to emerge before these difficulties *can* be addressed. In addition, we need a collection of political practices, institutional arrangements, and governmental regulations that specify the domain in which these virtues operate, that do not hinder their cultivation, and that protect us from those external forces that might preempt debate and compel an outcome. And note, these are not entirely different matters, this hope for virtue's success and this need for a collection of institutions and practices that mark the domain of its exercise.

Consider how these debates conclude. Actions and things will be distributed among the various lists, and some members of the moral community will rest content with the way things stand. Others will not. Certain items that end up on one list belong on another, or so they think. What will they do? Well, if the debate that preceded this outcome went as it should, if it was neither corrupted from within by rhetorical excess nor manipulated from without by alien interests, then we can assume that the dissenters will tolerate

---

this loss, these lists, and those who commend them. At the very least, they will know that their loss emerged from within the life they share with those they must now tolerate, a life that they love in part because it allows for democratic debate of precisely this sort. If, by contrast, their loss has little to do with the life they share with these others, if external powers, alien interests, and corrupt institutional arrangements determined this outcome, then it's unlikely that these dissenters will endure patiently. Why should they? A regime of tolerance and a collection of lists will have been imposed upon them, presumably in accord with the interests of those they are now asked to tolerate. In these circumstances, it's unlikely that these dissenters can regard themselves as participants in a common moral and political enterprise with these others. The shared life that provided both social framework and moral warrant for their mutual tolerance will now seem less than shared. Some of these dissenters will exit. Among those who remain, we should not be surprised to find the emergence of less than democratic social forms and other than tolerant responses to objectionable difference.

In the end, it's shared membership and mutual recognition in a flourishing moral and political community that matters most, that makes the patient endurance of objectionable difference possible, and that enables a regime of tolerance to survive the disappointment of dissenters. Undermine that community and you threaten its regime of tolerance. Expand its boundaries and you extend the reach of its endurance. This latter possibility emerges directly from disputes about items and lists. When the items in dispute define membership in the community that tolerates and when revised lists alter the opportunities for mutual recognition, then the dispute is at least as much about who deserves standing in that community as it is about the proper objects of its tolerance. This is what we should expect from a virtue that belongs to justice, that regards right relations among persons. When we ask about the just extent of our patient endurance we are often asking about the just boundaries of the community. Who belongs in its give-and-take of tolerance? Who deserves standing, and who has been unjustly denied? Who receives recognition, and who does not but should? Settle these matters and quite often the question of tolerance answers itself.

CHAPTER 6

LOVE'S ENDURANCE

Like justice, tolerance is a creature of social and political relationships. Its patient endurance delivers the good that is due in response to some difference that divides one person from another. It sets their relationship right across this difference—sometimes on its own, sometimes accompanied by other actions—and it does so in accord with the roles they occupy and the requirements of that relationship. Since most of us occupy many roles and since differences can divide each of our many relationships, tolerance is needed across our lives. As citizens of a political community, as members of a household or congregation, as partners in a political coalition or opposition movement, as colleagues on the job, and as strangers thrown together in all sorts of haphazard ways—in each of these relationships we must give and receive toleration's patient endurance in accord with virtue's norm. It's this give-and-take that helps set these relationships right and that allows the common good of right relationship to be enjoyed by all.

But now consider two possibilities. Any one of these relationships can have features that resemble friendships, and friendships might emerge among members in any one of these relationships. In both scenarios, a good delivered in act can be offered as gift, not simply or only as due. It can come as an instance of friendship's love, of its well-wishing and desire for union, not as a requirement of justice. Once delivered and received these acts of love do not set the relationship right, at least not principally. Rather, they deepen the bond that unites the friends and that distinguishes their life together.

These possibilities return us to forbearance, which we encountered in chapter 1, in Christian complaint with tolerance. Forbearance was pitched as true virtue, tolerance as imposter. Love for another was said to be the only source of virtuous endurance; just tolerance, it was assumed (or implied), will always arrive as virtue's semblance. If the argument so far is sound, then tolerance cannot be dismissed as fraud or forbearance regarded as the only virtuous response to objectionable difference. At the same time, we should not allow Christian efforts to strip this moral landscape of everything but love's forbearance and the semblances of virtue to discount the important truth in the mistake. As habit and act, forbearance is as different from tolerance as love is from justice. So too, the forbearance that abides in ordinary friendships is different from the kind that the Apostle Paul commends to "those who belong to Christ" in "the household of faith" (Gal 5:24; 6:10), the kind that, on his account, recapitulates God's gracious forbearance of humanity's sin (Rom 3:23–26; 15:1–6), that begins and ends in God's love, "bears all things" (1 Cor 13:7), and so "fulfills the law of Christ" (Gal 6:2).

Here three different virtues come into view: (1) tolerance annexed to justice and acquired by natural means; (2) forbearance as a perfection of friendship's love; and (3) a forbearance that, by Christian confession, comes by grace, expresses God's love, and participates in God's life. Three different virtues, each one *specifically* distinct from each of the others.

So too, tolerance referred by love beyond its own ends to those of friendship is different from tolerance alone, and Christians will insist that *both* of these are different from tolerance that has been healed and elevated by grace, its act referred by charity beyond its own ends to friendship with God and neighbor. Unlike the first, this latter collection of three virtues does not include distinct *species*. Each is an instance of tolerance despite the fact that in two cases its act is elevated by love and referred to love's ends. The pattern is reproduced with respect to forbearance. It is one thing by nature, a virtue that abides in ordinary friendships and acquired by ordinary means, and it remains specifically the same virtue when its act is elevated by grace to union with God and neighbor. What holds these virtues together in a single family—both the specifically distinct and the different instances of the same kind—is the fact that each regards the same act in its natural species, an act of patient endurance in response to some objectionable difference. In each case, a virtue perfects that response, but not as the others do: not always with the same formal specification of the act, with the same ends in view, or within the same collection of social circumstances and relationships.[1]

This family of virtues has members that some readers will obviously not recognize. Virtues that arrive by grace alone or whose acts are elevated by divine love, these will be acknowledged only as certain theological commitments are assumed. Since some readers will not assume them, what justifies

---

1 Put in the terms we have borrowed from Thomas, these virtues share the same object considered materially but are distinguished by different formal specifications of this object (*ST* I-II.54.2.1; 63.4). A virtue's material object that has been specified by some form is its *materia circa quam*—the specific matter about which it is concerned (*ST* I-II.55.4).

attention to these virtues? Simply this: these commitments and virtues provide the resources we need—the concepts and moral imaginary—to theorize love's response to objectionable difference, whatever its source, and to consider its relation to the just endurance of the tolerant. Love's endurance has gone largely unnoticed among secular political theorists. Moral theologians have ignored its relation to tolerance. Both disregard an important feature on the moral landscape. We need to do better.

Aquinas offers some assistance here, but only some. He refers to *acts* of toleration and forbearance. He knows they are *distinct* acts of patient endurance in response to objectionable difference, and he recognizes that both can be good. But he never asks whether the special aspect of goodness embodied in these actions requires a corresponding virtue, and he never reflects on the identities and differences that might obtain across their shared material object, their common act in its natural species. His failure is ours also. He doesn't consider tolerance and forbearance together or count them among the virtues, and, for the most part, nor do we. My efforts in this book are designed to correct this lapse, and so far I have borrowed and adapted some of the concepts and distinctions that Thomas deploys in his account of the moral virtues in order to locate tolerance among them. I now turn to those resources again, this time to spell out the sibling relations that obtain within this family, to identify the work that love's endurance might do, and to see how secular and theological discourses in response to difference might illumine each other.

AQUINAS ON FORBEARANCE

Thomas treats forbearance in his discussion of fraternal correction.[2] Fraternal correction is an external act or effect of charity that is also a kind of alms, which is itself a kind of beneficence (*ST* II-II.31.prologue). On Thomas's rendering, charity is a virtue of the will (*ST* I-II.56.6). Like justice, it inclines us toward another, toward a relationship with them mediated by the will's act, but here the inclination is toward a friend and the act is love's well-wishing and desire for union (*ST* II-II.23.2–3). Because charity's inclination always generates its act, and because its act always achieves love's end, its union of friend with the friend, of love with love (*ST* II-II.27.2), Thomas insists that charity simply is friendship (*ST* II-II.23.1, 5). The friendship resides in the will so inclined, not just between the friends in their

2 Here we have additional evidence that tolerance and forbearance are siblings. Both perfect resort to acts of patient endurance in response to objectionable difference, and both are accompanied by acts of correction and contestation that are themselves perfected by either justice or charity.

shared life and affections.[3] Above all, it is "the friendship of man for God," a friendship made possible by the Holy Spirit's re-formation of the will, a re-formation that expresses God's love precisely because it enables us to love God in return (*ST* II-II.23.1–2). Once transformed in this way, we will not only love God, but all those who belong to God and who might share in charity's friendship for God with us—even sinners, strangers, and enemies (*ST* II-II.23.1.3; 25.1). Among love's external acts, fraternal (and presumably sororal) correction is the work of charity that extends to the neighbor who is delinquent in some way and is offered as remedy for his sin (*ST* II-II.33.1). It is an act of charity, of love's mutual well-wishing, because it is directed to his amendment and because "to do away with anyone's evil is the same as to procure his good" (ibid.). It is a species of alms giving, a kind of mercy, because it is designed to address his spiritual needs (*ST* II-II.32.1–2). And it is distinct from the correction that belongs to public authority, that includes punishment and coercion, and that regards those sins that are seriously harmful to others (*malum aliorum*) or in some way detrimental to the common good of the political community. Its aim is not to safeguard that good but rather to bring benefit to the sinner—to wish him well, to help him see his sin and amend his ways, and to show him that this sin, whatever its magnitude, does not prevent friendship with him (*ST* II-II.33.1). Indeed, the more one loves him, the more zealous one will be in moving "against everything that opposes . . . [his] good" (*ST* I-II.28.4).

As an act of friendship's love, correction of this kind will invariably require conversation with the sinner, an exchange of points of view, of reasons for action and for amending one's ways.[4] And presumably the one who takes up this work must be willing to take time. Sinners are not easily amended, and those who correct must be willing to be corrected in turn. No one is without spot or wrinkle, and, depending on the rank and position of the parties involved, the corrected may be authorized to point out, with due humility, the faults of those who correct (*ST* II-II.33.5). For Thomas, it follows that fraternal correction must be paired with forbearance, another act of spiritual alms deeds (*ST* II-II.32.2). He admits that this pairing may at first seem odd (*ST* II-II.33.1 ad 3), but in fact it isn't. In fact, mutual forbearance makes mutual correction possible. A friend can become a burden on account of his sin, "an annoyance to those who live with him" (*gravantur*

---

3   I am grateful to Adam Eitel for this insight.

4   Friendship for Thomas always includes *communicatio* and *conversatio*. It requires a communication of goods bestowed upon each other, above all the exchange of love that simply is the friendship (*ST* II-II.25.2.2). Quite often, as with fraternal correction, friends communicate this good by means of conversation or rational exchange. The conversation bestows love and so communicates love's goodness. *ST* II-II.23.1.1; 25.3; 25.10.3.

ei conviventes) (*ST* II-II.32.2). We may be inclined to exit his company, to leave him bereft of our well-wishing and mercy. We may forsake all hope for a better, deeper union with him. Forbearance allows us to stay, to endure his company and help him bear (*portate*) the burden of his sin and so fulfill the law of Christ, the law of charity (ibid., cf. *Gal.* 6:2). It also allows us to retain the relationship we share and so too the good it instantiates. And it is precisely this staying put that enables correction. "For a man bears with a sinner (*Intantum enim aliquis supportat peccantem*), in so far as he is not disturbed against him, and retains his goodwill towards him: the result being that he strives to make him do better" (*ST* II-II.33.1.3). His love's zeal for the friend makes both the correction and the forbearance possible. Citing a gloss on John 2:17 ("Zeal for thy house will consume me"), Thomas writes, "a man is eaten up with good zeal, who strives to correct whatever evil he perceives; and if he cannot, bears with it and laments it (*tolerat et gemit*)" (*ST* I-II.28.4).[5]

Given the specifically distinct character of this act, both according to its object (the patient endurance of objectionable difference determined by divine rule and offered as love) and its ends (maintaining and deepening union with the person befriended for God's sake and securing a certain autonomy within that union with regard to the differences in dispute), and given the "special aspect of goodness" (*specialis ratio bonitatis*) that it embodies (*ST* II-II.109.2), we can say that forbearance, the virtue, corresponds to it. Annexed to charity as one of its parts, we can say that forbearance generates habitual performance of this act and habitual attention to these ends, especially when friends are divided by the gravest differences, by sins against God and neighbor. Since Thomas develops important aspects of his account of charity by adapting what he finds in Aristotle's treatment of friendship, we can say that the gracious forbearance that begins and ends in God's love has a sibling, naturally acquired forbearance, the virtue that perfects resort to love's endurance within temporal friendships.[6]

These are not conclusions Aquinas reaches.[7] Charity, he insists, is a virtue without parts precisely because its two objects, God and neighbor, do not

5   I am grateful to Adam Eitel for directing me to this remark. The implication is that forbearance must remain an aspect of charity, a portion of its work, even when correction must be abandoned on account of its ill effects upon the corrected or because of its potential for public scandal (*ST* II-II.33.6–7; *DFC* I and ad 3).

6   Other sources for Thomas's treatment of charity as friendship come from Augustine, Boethius, Dionysius, and the gospel of John. For an account of these sources and for a superb interpretation of Aquinas on love and friendship see Eitel, "*De Beata Vita*."

7   For Thomas, charity is both virtue and friendship. It is a habitual perfection of our loves that enables the person befriended by God and transformed by God's love to respond to that love and love God in return. In this, he tells us, it is distinct from ordinary friendships. In these, love responds to the friend's virtue, but it is not a virtue itself (*ST* II-II.23.3.1). My ad-

generate two, specifically distinct acts. The neighbor is always loved in relation to God, loved because she comes from God and in the hope that she might abide in God with the one who loves.[8] It follows that an act of charity directed to a neighbor has the same intentional content as that same act directed to God. In each case, the act is ordered to a single end, the goodness of God, which is loved for its own sake, and a single communion, which is fellowship with God and with those who belong to God (*ST* II-II.23.5; cf. *DC* 4 and ad 2). When neighbors are loved out of charity, it is *propter Deum*, because of God. It is because they belong to God, because they are already beloved of God, and because, by grace, the goodness that accrues to them on account of that love elicits our desire for union with them in God (*ST* II-II.23.5.1; 25.12).

True enough. But I am not suggesting that the forbearing regard God and neighbor under formal descriptions that are *altogether* distinct. Nor am I suggesting that they have intentions that can be specified without reference to union with God. Put another way, do I think that their patient endurance of objectionable difference is offered as love for a neighbor but not for God or because of God. Rather, following Aquinas, I assume that a neighbor can be offered charity's friendship only as she is regarded as belonging to God and beloved of God, that goodness accrues to her on account of that belonging, and that God is loved when the neighbor is (*DC* 4). One loves the parent when one loves the child (*ST* II-II.23.1.2–3). The forbearing love God when they love the neighbor who belongs to God, when they endure her objectionable difference for the sake of union with her in God, and when they recognize that a temporal participation of this union can be had only as it includes autonomy with respect to the differences endured. At the same time, I think acts of forbearance have a formal aspect, a *formalem rationem* (*ST* II-II.25.1), and an intentional structure that are distinct from other acts of charity. Aquinas does not.

Yet I think he could have. He concedes that the one, divine good that charity regards is "related to God in one way, and to our neighbor in another" and that as a result "charity must have diverse modes for its primary and secondary objects" (*habeat diversum modum*) (*DC* 4.5). This difference in mode with respect to charity's good follows from the fact that the neighbor must be loved *as neighbor* even as she is loved *propter Deum*, a fact that forbearance puts on sharp display. After all, it is the *neighbor's* objectionable differences that are endured in love, not God's, and this places her in a different relation to charity's good. She will not be loved as God is, not exactly, not with precisely the same act or for the sake of the same proximate ends,

---

dendum is this: in each case, friendship's love needs to be perfected by virtue in order to sustain its response. Thus forbearance.

8 "Ratio autem diligendi proximum Deus est, hoc enim debemus in proximo diligere, ut in Deo sit" (*ST* II-II.25.1).

and forbearance compels us to take note of this difference. It brings the neighbor into focus as a distinct object of love, as a creature different from God who nevertheless belongs to God, whose objectionable differences call forth an act of love that can be offered for God's sake but never directly to God. Here the crucial point comes into view. Forbearance can be an act of love *for God* only as it extends *to a neighbor* whose differences require endurance. In this, forbearance exhibits the conditions of divine love in time, conditions that God's grace meets but does not deny, conditions that account for the special goodness of an act of patient endurance offered in love *propter Deum*. It is precisely this special goodness that makes forbearance a virtue that belongs to charity as one of its parts. And note, the claim is that forbearance is a *potential part*. It *belongs* to charity, and as part it is deficient when compared with the whole. Its act of love is offered across the differences, disagreements, and sins that divide us from each other and thus from God. Charity's perfect act makes no such crossing; it assumes no such deficiency. As habit and act, forbearance has something in common with charity, and yet it assumes a deficit in human relations that charity need not. In this, it falls short of charity's perfection.

NATURAL SIBLINGS

It should now be obvious that tolerance and forbearance, like siblings in a family, resemble each other in important ways. Both assume a shared society of some sort and both act in response to members or to those, like strangers, who lack full standing and yet nevertheless occupy a designated role within the society. Both are virtues that regard operations. Both produce acts of patient endurance in response to objectionable difference, both accent the goodness of this act, the value and respect it expresses apart from its effects, and both offer this act for the sake of the society shared with those endured and the autonomy enjoyed with respect to their differences. At the same time, these are distinct perfections; tolerance belongs to justice while forbearance either belongs to divine charity or resides in ordinary friendships. However they are to be distinguished, we should begin with this fact.

I will begin by distinguishing the tolerance we have considered so far, the virtue annexed to justice, from the forbearance that resides in ordinary friendships. With this done, I can distinguish both of these from the forbearance annexed to charity, to the friendship for God and neighbor that, by Christian confession, comes by God's grace alone. Then I mix things up. I soften the distinction between the endurance that belongs to justice and the kind that belongs to love by considering (1) the effects of friendship's love on tolerance and (2) the effects of divine charity on the naturally acquired versions of *both* tolerance and forbearance.

The temptation is to draw the first distinction on appeal to the difference between gift and due. Tolerance, a part of justice, generates acts that are due the tolerated by right, while forbearance generates love's endurance that arrives as gift from another. But this account of these virtues and acts, while accurate in outline, misleads in various ways. While it is certainly true that tolerance generates acts of justice and that forbearance causes acts of love, this difference is not captured in a neat distinction between what is due and what comes as gift. While the tolerant do indeed render to others the patient endurance they are due by right, they do so only as they share a society of some sort with those they endure. It's their participation in this society that generates this due, that makes this act required, and the right relations of this society is a good held in common among those who give and receive this act. Their shared love for this good helps generate this tolerance; it makes possible this commerce. Here the point is that the object of this love and the source of this due—this shared society—is quite often inherited, not created, its benefits given, not merited. In most instances, it is received from persons who have come before and from powers and circumstances that transcend its members. Even those societies that are voluntary in origin, that are constituted by the deliberate choices of those who participate, can have antecedents and circumstances that make these choices possible and that are themselves given not chosen. If this is right, then tolerance has its beginning in love's response to something gratuitous. This beginning does not turn every social relationship into a species of friendship or every just act of toleration into an instance of love's well-wishing, if only because it is one thing to love the common goods of a society, quite another to act in every instance as a friend to each of its members. But it does compel us to concede that an act of tolerance can be both due and desired precisely because it follows and assumes love's response to gift, to an antecedent grace.

Acts of love within a friendship reproduce the pattern. Friendship's love is not due anyone in particular, not at the beginning. At the start, it always comes as grace and gift. And yet once given and then returned, it creates a society, a friendship, with its own orders and norms that justice honors and safeguards. Some acts of love will continue to be gratuitous, but others will be constrained by those norms. They will be requirements of the relationship that love has created. Again, if this is right, then, as with tolerance, we must refer to both what is given and what is due in an account of forbearance. Some of its acts come as gifts, as love's blessings that outstrip what is owed. Others can be due a friend, due by right given the relationship they share, and the love that forbears can be constrained by norm.

A more promising way to distinguish these siblings begins with their shared material object, with the act of patient endurance that each offers in response to some objectionable difference, and then considers the distinct rules that give form to these acts. Since these are *human* actions, they will be formed *secundum regulam rationis humanae*, in accord with a rule of human reason (*ST* I-II.63.4). Since both are *virtues*, both will generate this act in accord with the norms of *right* human reason, and yet in each case the norms applied are distinct. For tolerance, they are the norms of justice, for forbearance, the norms of friendship's love. The tolerant endure some objectionable difference because this act is the good that is due some person in accord with those norms. Full stop. Nothing more. By contrast, the forbearing endure another's difference because they are friends, because friends wish each other well and share a life together, and because this act in this instance delivers a good to the beloved. This good might be due the beloved in accord with norms of the friendship, or it might be offered as gratuitous gift. But in either case, it comes as an act of love, of friendship's well-wishing and desire for union.

This formal distinction between tolerance and forbearance comes into focus when we consider the different ends their acts are ordered to achieve. As we have just seen, habits can differ in species according to their objects or "proper matter," the "matter about which" their acts regard, and the object of a *virtue* is the good with respect to its proper matter as determined by some formal rule (*ST* I-II.63.4; 55.4; 60.2). But habits also differ as a result of "the things to which they are ordained," and a virtue is well directed to those things (*ST* I-II.63.4). Here Thomas has in mind the *proximate* ends of a virtue's act, for "moral matters do not receive their species from the last end, but from their proximate ends" (*ST* I-II.60.1.3).[9] And here the point is that these two different ways of distinguishing virtues—by object or act and by ends—bear on each other precisely because a virtue's acts are conducive

---

9   If actions were specified by their distant ends, then we would have to say that the person who steals in order to give alms performs the same act as the person who does an honest day's work for the sake of that same remote end. In fact, as should be obvious, these are materially distinct acts with their own proximate ends that may or may not be further ordained to the remote end of alms giving. Stealing is different from working. In Thomas's language, each has a different object, a different matter about which each regards (*ST* I-II.18.2 and ad 2). No doubt, these two different actions might be ordained to the same proximate end, to the acquisition of money. Would this shared proximate end make them identical acts? Yes and no. Actions and virtues have a twofold specification: materially from their objects and formally from their ends. This means that stealing and working are materially distinct even as they might be formally identical according to their common proximate ends. Both can be instances of moneymaking. Both can be informed by this one intention. And the same logic of specification applies when these acts and their common proximate ends are further ordained to almsgiving. The intention of that remote end further *informs* the act. It does not erase the prior specification or transform the stealing, working, and moneymaking into nothing but almsgiving. Rather it gives these antecedently distinct acts an intentional form that they would not otherwise have apart from their ordination to this remote end (*ST* I-II.18.6; cf. *DV* 10.9–10).

to its ends. Attend to its ends, and the distinct character of its acts should come into view.[10]

The tolerant, I have argued, endure the objectionable differences of another in order to maintain the relationship they share and autonomy with respect to those differences. Along with the good of acting tolerantly, of working to deliver what is due and expressing regard for the value of that relationship, these are the ends they seek, nothing more. As we noted in chapter 3, they do not hope that the differences that divide them from those they endure might dissolve, that hearts and minds will be united and parties reconciled. At the very least, their tolerance does not depend on this hope; it is not essential to it. In fact, in some circumstances they know that intending this end and proceeding with this hope would be unreasonable, even unjust. Of course, they do hope that their actions succeed in sustaining the relationship, in keeping it whole, but they assume that this whole will include the differences that now divide and that require their ongoing act.

The forbearing, by contrast, endure what is objectionable for the sake of a somewhat different collection of ends and proceed with a distinct hope. Like the tolerant, they intend to maintain the relationship shared with those they endure and the autonomy enjoyed with respect to their differences, and they want their act to express the regard they have for that relationship. But in addition to these ends, they also intend to be reconciled with those from whom they are divided, or at the very least, this is their hope, and they endure what they despise for the sake of this additional end. Unlike the tolerant, they are not content with a relatively modest union of judgment and love, one that admits of distance and difference. Rather, they assume a more substantive union at the start, one constituted by the mutual love and well-wishing, the shared life and common projects, that distinguish friendships, and they hope their endurance will eventually yield an ever more perfect union, one that eliminates the need for their act. Until it does, they will be filled with yearning for that increased union, hope for reconciliation, and sorrow over the differences that still divide. And note, their sorrow is different in kind from that which accompanies tolerance. Both passions regard something lost, the estrangement from others that difference creates, and yet the mood and object of each are distinct. The tolerant experience sorrow over the inability to recognize some of their own loves and commitments embodied in the society they share with those they endure. So for example, the person who considers abortion unjust killing but who nevertheless concedes toleration's just necessity in certain political circumstances and with respect to certain pregnancies will surely experience sorrow of precisely this sort. She

10 We witnessed this relationship between form and finality, between ends identified and acts ascribed, in chapter 4's discussion of tolerance and contestation. See especially note 13.

wants her society to refuse this injustice and embody her deepest commitments, but right now it doesn't, and there's no reason to hope that it will any time soon, or so she concludes. If things were different, if the harmful effects of an outright ban were not gravely disproportionate, then she would happily forsake this painful act of patient endurance and recoup this loss. Returning again to Aquinas's useful idiom, her will's velleity toward that act is negative. She would forsake it if she could, but right now, given the circumstances that she finds herself in, she can't. So she endures this objectionable difference—this injustice that she despises—with patience and regards this loss with sorrow.

The sorrow of the forbearing is different. It regards a different loss, not the inability to recognize oneself in the society one inhabits, but the divide that has opened up within a friendship across lines of objectionable difference. The object of friendship's love is the friend herself and the friendship shared, and while love's act creates and sustains a certain union of friend with friend it also *assumes* a certain antecedent correspondence of judgment, love, and activity. If friends discover that they differ in significant ways about the most important judgments and loves, if one party commits to an activity that either confounds or horrifies the other, or if wrongs go unrecognized and kindnesses unnoticed, then contest and correction are likely to follow. If the differences are deep and hard to dislodge, if a compromise cannot be struck, or if one party remains blind to whatever wrongs have been inflicted and endured, then love's forbearance will have to be exchanged for the friendship to be sustained. Since love endures difference for the sake of friendship's unity, sorrow will surely come, as will negative velleity toward the act and its circumstances. Friendship's love still abides, indeed the forbearance is an expression of it, but the union its act sustains is less substantial precisely because it assumes less of the antecedent union that it once had, or at least assumed. As an act of friendship, this forbearance proceeds in the hope that this frayed union will be restored in some way; that differences might be resolved, that judgments and loves might once again converge, that friends once divided by hurts and wrongs might be reconciled. Its endurance creates the time and space for its hope to be fulfilled, and yet until then, this sorrow over lost union will accompany its love.[11]

These facts about forbearance—that its act is ordered to the ends of friendship, that it hopes for union, for a resolution of the differences that divide, and that it regards the friend herself—confirm Aquinas's insistence that it is an act of love. Its endurance is an instance of love's well-wishing, and the goods offered to the beloved come in two parts, one given in the act, the

11   The sorrow of the tolerant regards the fact that they cannot see their own loves and commitments in the social union they share with the tolerated. The sorrow of the forbearing regards this same fact, but also the frustrated hope for a deeper social union with those endured.

other deferred in hope. The act itself sustains the friendship in the face of differences that would otherwise undo it, and one portion of the good that the forbearing wish for the other is nothing but this friendship sustained by this act.[12] The other portion is deferred and is the object of hope: that the friendship now sustained might increase in substance as the differences that now divide it might pass away and the union of friend with friend, of lover and beloved, might become ever more perfect. The truly forbearing do not offer this hope lightly or blithely. The objectionable differences that divide friend from friend can be serious and difficult to resolve: deeply held convictions, habitual modes of action, or vehemently felt passions. Some might involve substantial injustice and its attendant harms, and these will typically demand contestation and correction, whether fraternal or political, not simply forbearance. Reconciliation across differences of this kind will require growth in moral insight and self-knowledge on both sides of the divide followed by confession and repentance, recognition and forgiveness. None of these transformations are easy or likely and thus the reasons that sustain hope for reconciliation will often be hard to find. In circumstances like these, the reconciliation deferred in hope by the forbearing resides on a distant horizon. Still, regardless of circumstances or reasons, forbearance comes packaged with this hope precisely because its patient endurance is an act of friendship. It assumes an ongoing union of life and loves, a commitment to mutual well-wishing and understanding, and a desire that each might increase. When faced with serious objectionable differences, it cannot retain this assumption or sustain this desire without this hope.

It is not the hope that might accompany the pursuit of some arduous good by our own powers. It is not, in other words, the irascible passion perfected by magnanimity, the part of courage that regards great deeds and high honors.[13] It is, rather, an action caused by a virtue that resides in the will and that in general regards two things: the good intended and the help by which it is obtained. The good one intends must be difficult to achieve; the help must come from another. Once again, I am borrowing from Aquinas, in this instance, from his discussion of the faith and hope that come packaged with charity (*ST* II-II.17.2, 6–8). The love that abides in friendships, and so too the virtues that perfect and sustain its act, must also come packaged with faith and hope, not gracious and infused, but natural and acquired. Apart from this packaging, friendship's love will be imperfect, its expression inconstant.

---

12   Referring to the friendship elicited by God's love, Aquinas writes, "Charity is itself the fellowship of the spiritual life, whereby we arrive at happiness: hence it is loved as the good which we desire for all whom we love out of charity" (*ST* II-II.25.2.2).

13   For hope as an irascible passion, see *ST* I-II.40.1–3; for great deeds and honors as an object of this hope, and of this hope moderated by magnanimity, see *ST* II-II.129, passim, but esp. 129.1.2.

It's not an assumption that Thomas makes, and yet, as I said, he develops his account of charity—of the friendship with God and neighbor that comes by grace—in part by considering analogies with ordinary friendships (*ST* II-II.23.1), and this does seem to endorse the thought that love abides within these friendships only as its finds expression in virtues (such as forbearance) that are accompanied by something like natural faith and hope.[14]

In the case of forbearance, the good that one intends to have and yet finds difficult to achieve is the resolution of differences and the reconciliation of friends, and the help that one hopes to have comes from the friend endured.[15] This good cannot be had without his help, without his moral and spiritual work, but not only his. The lines of assistance cut in both directions. If it's serious injustice that divides the friends, and if confession and repentance are required along the way to reconciliation, then the one who forbears must be willing to bear witness to these reconciling acts, and if necessary, to offer forgiveness in reply. Indeed, forgiveness *must* be offered if the injustice endured has wronged the one who forbears. At the same time, they must express gratitude for their friend's willingness to repent of this injustice and for the reconciliation that comes to their friendship as a result. Not only that, they must proceed with humility, recognizing that their judgment about the differences that divide could miss the mark in various ways and that some of their own words and deeds are likely to require their friend's forbearance. Like love, its source, the forbearance of friends must be mutual, its hope must rest in each other. And like friendship's love, forbearance tends to generate this mutuality through its own act. It tends to secure the object of its hope through its sacrifice. If I help bear the burden of my friend's objectionable difference, neither ignoring its reality, nor discounting its significance, and if I make this sacrifice out of love for him, out of desire for continued union and in hope that these burdens might pass and this union deepen, then I put my love on display, and love tends to elicit love in return. Love offered and recognized, sacrifices made and acknowledged: these tend to create, restore, and perfect friendship's union. Will these tendencies have these effects in every instance? Past evidence will always be mixed at best, and thus the forbearing cannot know with clear sight what will follow from their acts. They cannot know whether their hope for reconciliation will be fulfilled or whether the forbearance they offer will be returned in kind. As Moshe Halbertal reminds us, most sacrificial offerings proceed under this cloud of uncertainty. There is always the possibility that a heartbreaking gap might open up between the offering, on the one hand,

---

14   For a fully developed account of natural hope, modeled on Aquinas's treatment of its supernatural sibling, see Lamb, "Aquinas and the Virtues of Hope."

15   As Aquinas says, "we hope chiefly in our friends," and thus charity precedes hope (*ST* II-II.17.8).

and the receiving and the returning, on the other—a gap that creates a potential for rejection and trauma.[16] Nevertheless, the forbearing believe in this reception and return, this object of their hope, and their assent to this belief follows from the reality of their friendship. It is a faith founded on the fact that love already abides between the friends and on the endurance that each already provides to each. At the very least, their mutual forbearance creates the time and space they need for reconciliation to come. Whatever else must be said about the causes and substance of reconciliation, forbearance is certainly its medium, just as faith regards its possibility and hope its reality, for "faith is the substance of things hoped for" (Heb. 11:1)[17].

So far so good. As virtues, tolerance and forbearance generate materially identical acts that are ordered to some of the same proximate ends. At the same time, the formal principles that specify their acts are distinct (the norms of justice versus the norms of friendship), and this specific difference in act can be seen in the proximate ends they do not share, in their different sorrows and hopes, and in the different social relationships in which they reside.

Now, two caveats. First, the fact that forbearance resides in friendships, in a relationship of mutual well-wishing and care, implies a willingness to endure what the tolerant will not. The forbearing endure some things the tolerant simply cannot bear. Some of these things need not be endured according to the norms of justice, others *ought* not be, and in each case it's the character of the relationship sustained by the virtue and expressed in its act that accounts for the difference. Friends endure in each other what colleagues or acquaintances might not precisely because they are friends, and the object of this endurance can be either trivial or not. Suppose my wife, somewhat ragged after a long day at work and somewhat anxious over looming deadlines, comes through the door with sharp words and sour looks, and suppose there is a habit of mutual forbearance between us. In that event, I'll endure those words and looks and persist in her company for the sake of the friendship we share—out of the love that I have for her and for our friendship, in the faith that this too can pass, and in the hope that, with her help, it will. And note, it's the friendship we already share that is a portion of the good I wish *for* her in my endurance *of* her. But now imagine I receive those same sharp words and sour looks on a regular basis from a colleague

---

16   Halbertal, *On Sacrifice.*

17   In faith, Thomas tells us, the intellect assents to that which is believed, not because it is moved to this assent through knowledge of its object, but rather "through an act of choice, whereby it turns voluntarily to one side rather than to the other," and not in fear or doubt but in confidence (*ST* II-II.1.4). Hope accompanies this assent precisely because faith "contains virtually all things hoped for." With the assistance of another, we hope to secure the good that we confess, that is the object of our belief. (*ST* II-II.4.1).

at work. There's no friendship between us to generate an act of forbearance, and it's unlikely that I'll respond tolerantly. Indeed, it's unlikely that justice demands it. Or suppose that I have committed some grave injustice. The wrong done is serious, the goods lost are substantial, and the act itself is public in two senses—everyone knows what I have done and our shared life is harmed in the doing. Betrayed a trust, drove under the influence, fudged the numbers, trampled the weak, ignored the needy, and so on: something along these lines. My friends will certainly correct me, but they are also likely to help me bear the burdens of my injustice, neither forsaking my company nor denying me their love. Others may not be so generous. Acquaintances may tolerate my presence in whatever common life we share, even as I am corrected and restrained by public justice, or so one hopes. But it's unlikely that they will be able to marshal a more robust endurance of my company, and it's not clear that they must. Without a friendship that already unites us, why should they?

In both of these examples, it's the antecedent friendship that generates the obligation to endure what the merely tolerant would not, and it's friendship's forbearance that fulfills love's obligations when differences like these divide. But we also know of cases where no such friendship exits, no such obligation, and where love's endurance comes nevertheless, where it arrives as grace. No friendship unites Priam and Achilles; indeed they are enemies. Achilles has killed Hector, Priam's son, but only after Hector has killed Patroclus, Achilles's friend. And yet when they grieve together in the final chapter of the *Iliad*, surely it's forbearance that enables them to put aside their anger, endure each other's company, share each other's sorrow, and hope for some measure of reconciliation—not a measure that puts an end to all enmity but one that allows a grief-stricken father to bury his son and a friend to purge rage from his mourning. And surely Priam approaches Achilles's camp with something like faith in this possibility, with hope for its reality.[18]

We can also imagine cases where, taken together, the character of the antecedent friendship and the nature of the objectionable difference generate no obligation to offer love's forbearance. The friendship exists, but neither party is obliged to endure *this* from the other. Sharp words and sour looks are one thing, curses and abuse another, and it's not at all clear that the latter

---

18   *Iliad* 24.592–647. Hecuba, Priam's wife, has no faith in this unseen possibility: "No, no—where have your senses gone?—that made you famous once . . . How can you think of going down to the ships, alone, and face the glance of the man who killed your sons, so many fine brave boys? . . . If he gets you in his clutches, sets his eyes on you—that savage, treacherous man—he'll show no mercy, no respect for your rights!" (*Iliad* 24.238–246). She finds nothing loveable in her enemy. She cannot sympathize with his loss. Her rage gets in the way and so preempts her forbearance. "Oh would to god that I could sink my teeth in his liver, eat him raw! *That* would avenge what he has done to Hector." *Iliad* 24.252–253.

should be endured, even for the sake a friendship that abides between be-loveds. Correct and depart and see what can be salvaged later on: none of love's obligations are broken in this response, or so it seems to me. The trouble, of course, is that love's endurance might come nevertheless in a case of precisely this sort. The act is not required by the antecedent relationship, it outstrips the demands of *both* tolerance and forbearance, and yet still it comes. The wrong done might be identified, but it is also endured. The wrong doer might be corrected, but their company is also retained.

Cases like these are hard to assess. Love's endurance offered to those who have committed grave wrongs and inflicted serious harms is odd, if not mysterious, and it is doubly so when the offering comes from their victims. The interpreter who believes in the possibility of *virtuous* endurance in cases like these will have to temper this faith with caution. The forbearing will say that he endured out of love for the friend, for the relationship they share and in hope for reconciliation, and of course, this might be true. The act might express a perfection of forbearance that is difficult to recognize precisely because it exceeds the norms and demands of more familiar virtue. It might bear witness to a mysterious and unfamiliar quality of perfect friendship. But then again, it might express some combination of disordered love, cruel self-hatred, and self-deceived longing. It might emerge from a relationship that on the surface appears as friendship but underneath exists as pathology or domination. Given these opposing possibilities, an endurance that surpasses the norms and demands of familiar virtue should obviously be approached with suspicion. The charitable interpreter will look for real excellence, for genuine forbearance, but will not be surprised to find a semblance.

So goes the first caveat; it adds needed complexity. Some of love's acts are required by the norms of an antecedent friendship, some come as gratuitous favor, and in each instance the endurance delivered can surpass what tolerance provides in both range and object.[19] The second offers a necessary denial: the distinction that divides tolerance from forbearance does not depend upon whatever it is that divides public and private relationships. Rather, the tolerance-forbearance distinction cuts across the latter and depends instead upon the distinction that divides relationships that have friendship-like qualities from those that do not. The point is that many private relationships are clearly not friendships just as some public relationships exhibit bonds

---

19   The difference that divides love from justice and that regards their objects comes into focus just here. Their material objects are the same; both regard operations that mediate relations with other persons. And yet love's acts fall under a different formal aspect (*sub alia tamen ratione*). When they are required, they fall under "the aspect of a friendly or moral duty," not a legal due, and when they come as gift they fall under the aspect of "a gratuitous favor" and exceed whatever friendship requires (*ST* II-II.23.3.1).

of solidarity and mutual well-wishing that bear witness to something like friendship's love. The former are perfected by tolerance, the latter by something like forbearance, and (as before) the effects of this difference are visible most plainly in the quality of hope that accompanies these acts. In private relationships that are not friendships, we are willing to allow tolerable differences to remain; indeed, we have seen that tolerance can require a willingness to endure without hope for reconciliation across *some* differences. By contrast, hope for union of some kind is an ordinary feature of the forbearance that sustains our civic friendships and political solidarities. The reality of that union, the essence of that hope, might be modest: not a final resolution of all disagreement, but a peaceful coordination of differences that no longer require patient endurance, that now command mutual admiration and respect. The substance of those relationships might be thin: not the deepest loves of closest friends, but the shared life and mutual well-wishing of fellow citizens. Insofar as those citizens have some measure of this modest hope with respect to at least some collection of disagreements and differences, it will be forbearance that generates the patient endurance that sustains them. Indeed, to take one obvious example, the stories we tell of democratic life and progress in the United States typically direct our attention to a forbearance that hopes for a more perfect union across at least some painful differences and scars of wrong.[20]

CHARITY'S FORBEARANCE AND ITS NATURAL SIBLINGS

Now that we have distinguished naturally acquired varieties of tolerance and forbearance, we need to distinguish each of these from the forbearance that Christians will say belongs to charity, to the love for God and neighbor that God's grace alone makes possible.[21] The distinction between natural

---

20   For examples, see Stout, *Blessed Are the Organized*, 235–259; and Chappell, *Stone of Hope*, 67–104.

21   Aquinas contends that God's grace re-creates the soul and infuses habitual love for God and neighbor (*ST* II-II.23.2–3). Many Protestants—from Luther to Barth—have doubted this contention. Grace, they say, elicits God's love in us but without making us anew and without infusing a habit. Many interpreters—from de Lubac to Milbank—doubt that Thomas draws a sharp distinction between the loves of created human nature and those of human nature graciously re-created. While I have no theological objections to the idea of grace re-creating the soul and no exegetical worries about Thomas's analogical pairing of creation and re-creation, the issues are too many and too complex to explore here. For my purposes, it is enough to identify a consensus, more or less, among Augustinian Christians: (1) the distinction between things natural and gracious does not require belief in free-standing nature, nature that is in-

forbearance and its gracious sibling is, in principle, relatively easy to draw, even if similarities in act make them difficult to distinguish on the ground. Imagine two people, one acts with the patient endurance of natural forbearance, the other endures with a forbearance that grace makes possible, that participates in God's love. Both offer this act as an instance of love's well-wishing, as an expression of love's regard for the friend. Both intend to maintain the friendship shared with those they endure and mutual autonomy with respect to their differences. And both endure what they despise, at least in part, for the sake of reconciliation with their beloved. Both hope that the differences that now divide will one day be resolved. At the same time, Christians will say that the person whose loves have been transformed by the Holy Spirit will endure another's difference out of love for God, out of the recognition that God loved them first. They will say that God's forbearance and correction express this love, and that God's love heals and elevates their own and so gathers them up into the shared life and mutual well-wishing that abides among members of the household of God. Loving God entails loving all who belong to God, and the good that one wishes for them is a share in this divine friendship, this fellowship of mutual love, of friend with friend in God. Given the reality of sin—its ubiquity and power—this activity must include forbearance, which sustains the temporal possibility and future perfection of this fellowship despite the normative divides that sin creates and that now threaten its peace. Christians will say that the forbearing love their neighbor as God in Christ has loved humanity, bearing the burden of their sin for the sake of friendship's union with them. Just as God has become present in time through love's sacrifice, so too the forbearing remain present to the neighbor as they endure her sin and help her bear its burdens. And just as Christ's sacrifice enables the Gentiles to be united with God, in part as temporal reality, in part as future promise, so too the endurance of a neighbor's difference creates a portion of that union and authorizes hope for its perfection. In fact, Christians will contend that the person who bears the burdens of another's sin out of love for God is already united with God through that love (ST II-II.17.6). For them this union is a present, if imperfect, reality. Their hope is that the example of their love, the sacrificial reality of their endurance, will be made vivid by the Holy Spirit

---

dependent of God's work as creator and sustainer or untouched by God's ongoing love and care; (2) the God of Israel and the church cannot be known and loved without the gracious self-disclosure of this God and without the transformation of our loves; and (3) the grace that makes love for God possible transforms the soul (somehow) and makes this love habitual. So, I will speak of God's love transforming the soul, not re-creating it, and I will refer to charity—the friendship of humanity for God—as its effect.

and thus encourage those they endure to will as they do, to put aside their sin, to share in this union, and to love God as they are loved (*ST* II-II.25.6.4).

These features of gracious forbearance regard its ends. Others regard its act or object. In fact, Christians will say that gracious forbearance is distinguished from both the forbearance that abides in ordinary friendships and the tolerance we have considered all along by the *distinct formality* of its object. Thomas writes: "Now the object of every virtue is a good considered as in that virtue's proper matter" (*consideratum in materia propria*) (*ST* I-II.63.4). Taking our lead from this remark, we have said that both naturally acquired tolerance and forbearance have the same object considered *materially*; both regard the same act in its natural species, the patient endurance of some objectionable difference. As virtues appropriate to our human nature, we have also said that they fix the good in this act according to a shared rule, the "rule of human reason" (*regulam rationis humanae*) (ibid.). This rule gives this material object a certain form, and this form is provided, in the case of tolerance, by wise judgment about the demands of justice, and, in the case of forbearance, by wise judgment about the gifts and requirements of friendship. If we say, as we should, that gracious forbearance has this same object considered materially, that it also regards an act of patient endurance in response to objectionable difference, we must also admit that the formal aspect of its object and thus its *materia circa quam*—the matter about which it is concerned—comes, not from the rule of human reason, but *secundum regulam divinam*, "according to the Divine rule" (ibid.). The good in its act is fixed by divine judgment, not by right human reason, or so Christians will insist. As a result, it differs in species from the other two, not only because of its end—union with God and neighbor—but also because of "the specific and formal aspects" of its proper object (*ST* I-II.63.4 and ad 1).[22] All three offer a good act in response to an objectionable difference, an act that mediates our relations with others, but in the case of gracious forbearance, the character of that goodness is determined by fundamentally different reasons, reasons that come from divine, not human, judgment (*ST* I-II.63.4.2). It is united to

---

22   The distinction that Aquinas draws here does not imply that he thinks human judgment is somehow different from God's. As we noted in chapter 2, for Aquinas, the natural law is nothing but our rational participation in the eternal law, in God's judgment about our good. It follows that judgment in accord with the rule of human reason is always, in some measure, a consequence of this participation in divine judgment, this rational knowledge of the human good that God has bestowed upon us. It is precisely this participation, this rational knowledge of the human good, that enables us to act and judge as human beings do, and it is *right* judgment about this good that enables us to identify and perform virtuous actions appropriate to our created nature. When grace transforms the soul, it deepens our participation in the eternal law, it directs the will to aspects of the human good that cannot be grasped by our ordinary rational capacities, and the actions that follow in turn are counted among the virtuous, not by the rule of created reason, but *secundum regulam divinam*.

these others through the shared material content of their objects, through the fact that all regard the same action in its natural species. And yet, the *materia propria* of gracious forbearance is distinct on account of the different rule that specifies the formal character and goodness of its act. To summarize: gracious forbearance is distinguished in one way from both of its natural siblings by the fact that it is ordained to union with God and neighbor and by the Christological repetition of its sacrifice, and it is distinguished from both in yet another way by its proper object, by the divine rule that specifies the good in the act itself.

These differences emerge most vividly in comparison with natural tolerance. Consider, first, the distinct *range* of operation exhibited by charity's forbearance. On Thomas's rendering, it requires a *sanum rationis iudicium*, a "sound judgment of reason" in accord with our gracious participation in God's eternal law (*ST* II-II.33.3.2; cf. 45.2), and of course ordinary tolerance demands something quite similar. By habit, the tolerant intend to deliver the good that is due to the person from whom they are divided by some objectionable difference, some unsettling disagreement. And they cannot choose aright among those acts that might deliver this due, those things that we listed at the start of chapter 4—endurance, acceptance, respect, indifference, contest, correction, coercion, expulsion, or exit—unless they "counsel, judge, and command aright, which is the function of prudence and the virtues annexed to it" (*ST* I-II.58.4). Still, the ordinarily tolerant and the graciously forbearing will reach different conclusions about the persons and differences their respective acts regard. Those who forbear out of love for God proceed with the gift of wisdom, or so Christian confess. This gift enables them to judge human actions in accord with divine things (*quod per divina*) and direct human actions in accord with divine standards (*per divinas regulas*).[23] They do not ask whether this sin or that objectionable difference is so vile, so intolerable, that the relationship must be abandoned. For them, exit and expulsion are never real options, and thus they need not determine which sinners must be endured or which sins they must help bear. The tolerant will make these distinctions; justice demands it.[24] But those who have been

---

23 *ST* II-II.45.3. According to Thomas, the gifts are habits that make us amendable to the inner promptings of the Spirit. Their purpose is to address the deficit that remains in us, in our reason and will, once we have been transformed by grace and in-formed by the theological virtues. These virtues perfect us imperfectly, since through them we know and love God, but not so as to avoid "all folly, ignorance, dullness of mind and hardness of heart" (*ST* I-II. 68.2.3). Thus the need for the gifts, above all wisdom, which enables the faithful to be moved by the Spirit and so "to judge aright of Divine things, or of other things according to Divine rules" (*ST* II-II.45.4).

24 Naturally acquired forbearance draws similar distinctions; love demands it. The forbearing judge these matters according to the norms of friendship and for the sake love's ends, not, as with tolerance, according to the norms and ends of justice. But the point is the same. Some

moved by the Holy Spirit to love God and neighbor, and who judge the objectionable differences of another in accord with divine wisdom and in the spirit of this love, will not. For them, all sins, all objectionable differences, must be endured with patience. No sinner generates burdens that are, in principle, unbearable, that the forbearing are unwilling to endure. They may, of course, fall short of this ideal, but it remains an ideal nevertheless. The tolerant have their list of actions and things they find so objectionable that the relationship must be abandoned, but those who endure with the forbearance of Christ proceed with no equivalent list. They must distinguish those sins that harm persons or threaten the common good from those that do not. The latter, we have noted, require charity's forbearance and whatever fraternal correction seems warranted, while the former require, in addition, the just correction that protects persons and safeguards the common good as it restrains the sinner and deters those tempted to emulate his sin. But no matter how this distinction is drawn, sins of all kinds are patiently endured, for "love bears all things" (1 Cor 13:7) and "the good bear with the wicked . . . in accord with what is proper" (*mali tolerantur a bonis . . . secundum quod oportet*), which is to say that the forbearing endure with the sinner and help him bear his burdens even when his sins are grave, even when the wrongs done are substantial and the harms inflicted real (*ST* II-II.108.1.2). What the tolerant would find literally unbearable, the forbearing endure nevertheless.

The point can be put in terms of membership. In chapter 5, we noted that some differences and disagreements are so intolerable that they define membership in the community in question. Those who persist in these differences lose standing. The rights and privileges that belong to members are no longer theirs, their company is no longer desired, their tolerable differences no longer endured. Not so with the burdens endured immediately for God's sake or with the community shared with all sinners through Christ's sacrifice. In principle at least, no sin, no injustice can separate a sinner from the fellowship with God and the blessed that the forbearing assume, for that fellowship is based on God's love, on God's willingness to bear the

---

differences are so great, so difficult to confront, so horrific—think of the worst injustices, the greatest violations—that endurance cannot be offered, regardless of what remains of the friendship. It cannot be ordered to this love's ends. Its act cannot express the well wishing of friends. Even reconciliation deferred becomes impossible to intend, an obscene, perverse object of hope. When this act and hope appear nevertheless, even the most generous interpreter will struggle to account for them. Christians may suspect that another Spirit is somehow at work, another love somehow in play, even if its causes and contents go unrecognized. There are dangers here on both sides. Reference to the Holy Spirit can be received as patronizing by those who do not share Christian commitment, and it can be a source of self-deception, masochistic desire, and false hope for those who do. For this reason, Christians pray for grace upon grace and for friends who can critique and correct their judgments, desires, and hopes.

burdens of every sin, and on the ability of this love to transform every sinner. In this life, hope for that transformation always abides. If the sin generates substantial and public harm, then the instruments of just coercion must be brought to bear against the sinner, but resort to these means does not remove the need for forbearance or diminish its hope. Sinners must be endured no matter how cruel or hurtful the sin, and the forbearing must hope for repentance and reconciliation no matter how unlikely these may seem. "If we hope for what we do not see," for the gracious transformation of the sinner, "we wait for it with patience" (Rom 8:25). The forbearing live in this hope and by this patience even with respect to those actions, things, and persons that the tolerant cannot endure.

And note, to hope that the sinner might join the one who forbears in friendship with God is to hope that he might begin to forsake his sin. Those transformed by grace are not only redeemed from their alienation from God, but also from a portion of the disorder in their souls that inclines them to cowardice and injustice.[25] Thus the forbearing wait upon the amendment of the sinner, and their patient endurance gives him the time he needs to receive God's grace and reform his ways. Again, not so with the tolerant, whose patient endurance, we have noted, has no equivalent hope. It does not necessarily come packaged with desire for the differences endured to pass. In some circumstances and relationships and with respect to some differences, the tolerant will find this hope unreasonable. If they are to retain the company of those they endure and sustain whatever society they share, then their tolerance must bend to the recognition that these differences will remain. This humility is a portion of their virtue's response.

Are the graciously forbearing humble? Yes, but their humility does not follow from an equivalent recognition. At the very least, it does not follow from this recognition alone. Rather, Christians will insist that humility comes with this variety of forbearance by means of its Christological form. "There is no distinction," the Apostle writes. "All have sinned and fall short of the glory of God," both Jew and Gentile alike. All deserved punishment, not access to the fellowship of everlasting happiness, and yet that access is given nevertheless "by His grace as a gift," for "in His divine forbearance he had passed over many sins" (Rom 3:22–25). For Paul, this gift comes to Israel as an expression of divine mercy, of God's willingness to save God's people (Rom 9:14–18). While all have sinned according to the Law, "all Israel will be saved" according to the promises made to the patriarchs (Rom 11:25–32). And this gift comes to the Gentiles from this same source, from God's mercy and promise, but this time "through the redemption which is in Christ Jesus,

---

25 *ST* I-II.109.2. Of course, in this life the soul's gracious transformation is always incomplete, never perfect. Charity can always increase (*ST* II-II.23.4), and thus those who forbear will always require forbearance in return.

whom God put forward as an expiation by His blood, to be received by faith"
(Rom 3:24–25). According to the Apostle, those who receive this gift in faith
"walk not according to the flesh but according to the Spirit" (Rom 8:4).
It is this same Spirit that raised Jesus from the dead, or so Christians confess,
and when it dwells in the faithful, they regard themselves as they are, as
children of God, "and if children, then heirs, heirs of God and fellows heirs
with Christ" (Rom 8:17). As faithful participants in this household, those
who have been transformed by this Spirit are both obliged and empowered
to bear witness to God's grace by reproducing God's act, by offering mercy
and forbearance to those who sin and fall short of the law. So too, they must
recognize that they participate in this household only as God shows mercy
to them and forbears their sin, which in turn makes their own forbearance
humble. They will find themselves confessing something like the following:
"[T]he sin I forbear in another might also be found in me, or, if not this
sin, then surely some other. Thus I forbear, not because my virtue gives me
power over another, but because the endurance I provide I need in return
and because it is this gift and return of love, this mutual bearing of burdens,
that abides among members within the household of God."[26]

So does suffering, at least in this life, and here another difference emerges
between naturally acquired tolerance and graciously given forbearance. Of
course, the tolerant suffer as well. They suffer the differences they despise
and must live among, and, as we noted in chapter 3, this is why they must exhibit patience and perseverance. But the suffering of the graciously forbearing is different. Their patient endurance comes to a friend whose life they
share, its joys and sorrows, and so they suffer under the burden of the sin
they help their friend bear. This claim can be spun in various Christological
directions, and there are multiple (if not competing) accounts of the atoning effects of suffering the sins of others in the New Testament witness. Paul
seems to indicate that Christ bears our sins as he accepts the punishment
we deserve (Gal 3:10–14). But substitution theories of atonement overlook
the suffering involved in forbearance. It is not the punishment due another
that is borne by those who forbear, but rather the sins that might deserve
punishment. How then do the forbearing bear the burden of another's sin?
How does their endurance carry the iniquity that belongs to another?

Well, consider again those cases that most plainly call for the patient
endurance of the forbearing. The sin is serious, and it wrongs the person
who must forbear. For the Christian, the harm done extends to God as well,
and it might also extend to a neighbor's good, but let's concentrate on the

---

26 Who exactly belongs to the household of God, who has been elected to this divine fellowship and who, if anyone, has not, is a question that has divided Christians across the centuries. I will not address it here. I will simply point out that the question of forbearance, like
the question of tolerance, requires an answer to the question of membership.

immediate relationship. Instead of abandoning the sinner or resisting her sin, the graciously forbearing endure this evil, this threat to their own good. Instead of forsaking the sinner's company, they remain close at hand and wait for her redemption. The Christological substance in this progression—enduring the sin of another, suffering its harm, and expecting the redemption of the sinner—cannot be denied. We see it most plainly in the Gospel of Mark, where enduring sin, suffering as a result of that endurance, and redeeming sinners as a result of that suffering are placed front and center. From the beginning, the reader understands the secret that escapes the disciples: Jesus is the Son of God, the Messiah foretold by the Prophets (Mark 1:1–3).[27] After eight chapters of signs and wonders designed to display this identity, Jesus poses the question directly: "[W]ho do men say that I am?" Peter seems to know. "You are the Christ," he says, but his understanding tests negative. As soon as Jesus reveals that the "Son of Man must suffer many things, and be rejected by the elders and the chief priests and the scribes, and be killed, and after three days rise again," Peter objects and is promptly rebuked: "Get behind me, Satan." With a chastened and confused Peter before him, Jesus spells out the meaning of his divine Sonship: "If any man would come after me, let him deny himself and take up his cross and follow me. For whoever would save his life would lose it; and whoever loses his life for my sake and the gospel's will save it" (Mark 8:27–35). This is the climax of Mark's narrative of hidden identity and hereafter the story slides unavoidably toward Jerusalem and the Cross. Along the way, Peter shows that he cannot follow this path of suffering servanthood: he can't stay awake in Gethsemane and he cannot admit his connection to Jesus after the arrest. As predicted, he denies his friend (Mark 14:37–42, 66–72). Soon after, Jesus is beaten, mocked, stripped, and crucified. Then, at last, a breakthrough: someone finally understands, but not a disciple who has seen signs and wonders, but a man who has helped torture and kill. "And when the centurion, who stood facing him, saw that he thus breathed his last, he said, 'Truly this man was the Son of God'" (Mark 15:39).

How did the centurion come to this conclusion? Once a sinner who tortures, now a friend who confesses Christ crucified: how did this happen? Well, consider the fact that his sin is brought into sharp relief by the blood he has spilled, in this instance, the innocent blood of the one who endures the evil he does. Perhaps in this blood he sees himself for the first time, his violence and disorder, and he is able to repent of this evil only as Jesus is willing to endure this wrong and allow his own blood to be shed. In this divine forbearance, in this grace—an act that far outstrips the demands of ordinary tolerance—the centurion is redeemed, not so much from the punishment he is due, but from the violence he does and his alienation from the person

---

27   My reading of Mark's gospel has benefited from Hays, *Moral Vision of the New Testament.*

it afflicts. So too, as Jesus sacrifices his own good in this act of forbearance, he atones for the sin he suffers. In his patient endurance of this sin, in his willingness to suffer its harmful effects, he does not forsake the sinner, but retains hope for union with him, a hope that is fulfilled as the centurion sees in the blood he has spilled both the sin he has done and the grace he has received. Thus Christ's forbearance and his sacrifice are one. He can't abide with the centurion and endure this sin without putting his own life at risk, and it's precisely his willingness to suffer this sin and endure its deadly effects that enables him to wait on the redemption of this sinner.[28] In the end, it is Christ's forbearance that helps the centurion carry his sin and eventually shake off its burden.[29] This is the gift that Jesus offers, or so Christians confess. Once relieved of this burden, the centurion can now participate in a relationship that his sin had severed. At one with Christ, he can now count himself, as Paul would put it, among the sons of God (Rom 8:15–17).[30]

---

28   The point must be put carefully lest we misread the passion story and encourage masochism among the vulnerable or sadism among the hardy. Christ does not want to die. He does not intend to sacrifice himself. He does not choose his own death as a means to some other end. He does not want to suffer, and he does not count his suffering good in itself or singularly redemptive. To think otherwise not only reduces his death to self-slaughter and discounts his genuine sorrow, his real fear, but it also implies that suffering redeems and that redemptive suffering can be rightly desired. But it doesn't, and it can't. What redeems is love, love that is willing to suffer for the sake of a beloved, a beloved held captive by his capacity for injustice and alienated from the one who loves. Jesus loves human beings. He wants to redeem them from their sin and to be reconciled with them, and to do this he must retain their company. He must be willing to endure their injustice and suffer their violence, not because he wants to, but rather because these other aims cannot be achieved without staying put, seeking union, and bearing burdens. In the language I have borrowed from Aquinas more than once, we can say that his velleity toward this patient endurance is negative. He would avoid it if he could. Even so, he knows these aims cannot be achieved apart from this act and without suffering what comes, and he knows that this suffering and endurance are very likely to bring about his own death. When Christians say that he offered himself as a willing sacrifice, they mean (or ought to mean) that he willed these ends in light of this knowledge and with this particular negative velleity.

29   This account of redemptive suffering is indebted to the one developed by Marilyn Adams. See her "Redemptive Suffering" and *Horrendous Evils and the Goodness of God*. It should be noted that her account is a theodicy, mine is not.

30   My interpretation of Mark's account of Christ's sacrifice, its atoning effects and the sacred lineage it creates, owes much to Jay, *Throughout Your Generations Forever*. The same applies to my interpretation of the Apostle Paul's understanding of Jesus and the Gentiles. At the same time, the cosmopolitan community that Paul thinks Christ's sacrifice creates, a community in which there is "neither Greek nor Jew, slave nor free, male nor female," where all are "heirs according to the promise" (Gal 3:28–29) and all can justly cry our "Father" (Rom 8:15) defies her claim that, in every instance, sacrifice severs the natural ties of mother to child and replaces it with a sacred lineage of men. Paul may be on to something. Jesus had a mother, after all, and it was not his connection to Mary that was sacrificed on the Cross. Rather, his sacrifice regards

Or rather, according to this sacrificial logic, we can now expect him to participate in that fellowship of friends as it proceeds on its temporal sojourn. Notice the condition Paul places on participation: "provided we suffer with him in order that we may also be glorified with him" (Rom 8:17b). It confirms the call to discipleship in Mark 8:34–9:1. The centurion must now share in Christ's priestly self-sacrifice. He must be willing to endure the sins of others and risk the loss of his own good for the sake of the society he hopes to share with them. So too he must hope that this imitation will reproduce (however imperfectly) the redeeming and atoning effects of Christ's decisive sacrifice, of his perfect forbearance. He must hope, in other words, that his forbearance will be a medium of God's grace, that it will be recognized and received as a gift and thus initiate the redemption of the sinner endured.

The dangers here are obvious and should not be denied. These theological symbolics can encourage the sadism of some and the masochism of others. Inequalities of power and the lust to dominate only encourage this misuse. Those who have been victims of these symbolics, who have suffered under their misuse, will be inclined do without them.[31] It is an understandable response; I have no desire to discount it. But virtue's ideal offers another. We have seen that forbearance always comes with voice, with criticism and correction that accompanies its willingness to endure. The Gospels bear witness to this as well, to Christ's prophetic words. We have also noted that while the truly forbearing are willing to suffer loss for love's sake, they do not desire that loss. Their velleity toward it remains negative. These cautions give some comfort. They address some of the questions that critics should ask and identify some of the traps that we should avoid, but they are no substitute for genuine forbearance. As in all things, dangers and difficulties can be addressed only as real virtue is had and expressed, real grace received and returned.

MIXING THINGS UP

At this point, some readers will object. "The world is more complicated than *this*. Yes, some acts of patient endurance clearly belong to the tolerance

---

the sins human beings commit and the evils they suffer, and it gathers all into the household that Mary already shares with God, not severed from their mothers but ever in their company. Nature is not overcome, but assumed, its lineages enhanced and so perfected, or so Christians confess. That said, there's no denying the evidence Jay piles up: many sacrifices work just as she says. They replace a natural lineage founded on maternity with a "spiritual" connection to patriarchal power.

31   See, for example, Williams, *Sisters in the Wilderness*.

annexed to justice, others to the forbearance that abides in natural friendships. And yes, Christians will speak of a forbearance that comes by God's
grace and participates in God's love. But surely some acts of patient endurance belong to more than one virtue, to both justice and love. Consider, for
example, the tale of fathers and sons that you told in chapter 3. The virtue
that enables you to endure your son's objectionable music is tolerance, you
say, a virtue that belongs to justice. Love's ends and norms have no part in
the relationship you describe. But how can *this* be when surely you love
your son, wish him well, and long for your relationship with him to ever
deepen. Moreover, if you confess what Christians do about God and grace,
then surely you hope that this love will be elevated and perfected by this
grace, that an image of God's love will be expressed in your own. If this is
right, then how can it be tolerance that perfects your response to the difference posed by his annoying music? Doesn't love complicate the matter?"

Yes it does. If, in my better moments, something like love's care, well-
wishing, and desire for union order and animate my words and deeds as I
respond to my son, then my endurance of his objectionable differences will
obviously show signs of love's effects. That said, I don't want to retreat from
the claims made in chapter 3. The endurance described there was, in object,
an act of tolerance. It was due my son regardless of the love that I have for
him. Moreover, it was ordered to the just ends that the tolerant intend, and
it was offered without hope for the difference endured to pass. If, as we have
said, actions and virtues are specified by their formal objects and proximate
ends, then this act of patient endurance belongs to tolerance, the virtue annexed to justice. It is not an act of forbearance, the virtue that perfects and
sustains ordinary friendships. Full stop. And yet insofar as a tolerant act can be
elevated by love beyond its ends and ordained to love's own, then that same
act can also belong to that love. Will it then become an act of forbearance?
No, not necessarily. It remains an act of tolerance according to its twofold
specification (*ST* I-II.63.4). In proper object, it is an act of patient endurance
with respect to some objectionable difference that has been chosen in accord with the norms of justice. Differences of this kind are the matter about
which this act regards (*ST* I-II.18.2 and ad 2). In intention, it is ordered to
the ends of tolerance: to a society shared, to the peace that abides among
members, to the regard this relationship deserves, and to the autonomy enjoyed with respect to the differences in dispute. And the virtue that perfects
this act belongs to justice as one of its parts precisely because this act comes
as something due and because the obligation to deliver that due emerges
from the fact that I am his father and he is my son, not from the love that,
in this instance, animates our relation. The point is that I would owe him
this endurance for the sake of these ends even if, in some other instance, our
love relationship was badly frayed or broken. This could happen after all,
and if it did, he would remain my son, and fathers, it seems to me, owe their

teenage sons endurance of this particular difference regardless of the love—its quality and intensity—that binds them. In fact, we can easily imagine circumstances in which my obligations toward my son are determined neither by my parental status, nor by the love that binds us. Other roles and relationships will make that determination. Suppose I coach my son's baseball team, and suppose the boys are doing what they know they should not—tossing water bottles at each other in the dugout. The hour is late. The day is hot. The game is already lost. So I endure this behavior with patience. And note, I tolerate my son's participation in it, not because he is my son and deserves this endurance from me, his father, and not because he is my beloved and this is what love offers or its norms require. Rather, if I am truly tolerant, if I treat him justly, then I will endure him as I do the others: because I am the coach, because they are my players, and because on this day, in this moment, their rambunctiousness deserves this patient endurance from me.

But let's suppose that love does bind us, as it surely does, and let's say this love is virtuous. What then? In that event, the act of tolerance that I owe him because he is my son and I am his father or because he is my player and I am his coach would be the object of my action, its matter, we might say, and the end specified by love would give that matter its form. Materially, it would be an act of tolerance; formally it would be an act of love. I would treat him tolerantly because this is what justice requires in this instance and because I hope to secure the proximate ends of the tolerant, and I would ordain this act to love's ends in accord with love's graces and demands. I would treat him justly for love's sake, and I would need *both* virtues up and running to do so with the ease and consistency of habit.[32] For of course, if I have love for my son but no tolerance that accords with our respective roles within the relationships we share, then I might wish him well and long for union in some abstract way, but I will very likely act unjustly when confronted with his objectionable differences. And if I treat him unjustly, then it's not clear what remains of my love beyond a semblance. It goes without saying that parents who coach teams that include their own children are particularly susceptible to these corruptions of justice and love.[33]

32   Once again I follow Aquinas's usage. "The object is not the matter of which a thing is made (*materia ex qua*), but the matter about which something is done (*materia circa quam*); and stands in relation to the act as its form, as it were, through giving it its species" (*ST* I-II. 18.2.2). This same act, this same matter, is further specified as it is ordered to an end, an end that functions as an additional form. Thus, "the species of a human act is considered formally with regard to the end, but materially with regard to the object of the action" (*ST* I-II.18.6).

33   Thomas speaks of charity's effect upon the other virtues in precisely these terms, and these terms apply just as well to ordinary love's effects upon justice and its parts. "To perform a right action, we must be well disposed not just as regards the end, but also as regards what contributes to the end.... Therefore, it is clear that even though charity disposes people so

A tolerant act ordained to love's ends is transformed in various ways. Informed by those ends, it is has a different spirit and character. First and foremost, it is no longer *simply* an act of just endurance. It is, rather, justice infused with love, put to the service of love, and expressive of the love that binds this particular father with this particular son. Ordered to love's ends, its act is quickened by love's desire, and thus it comes more eagerly and promptly than an act moved by tolerance alone. And it serves a new social relationship without abandoning the old, a relationship with more depth and intimacy than the one specified by the abstract roles of father and son or coach and player. Borrowing the language Thomas uses to speak of the effects of God's love on human agency, we might say that virtuous love perfects justice and its parts (*ST* I-II.61.5; II-II.23.7–8). In this instance, tolerance is not erased by that love, any more than the relationship in which it resides is abandoned. Rather, tolerance is transformed and thus perfected by love; perfected as it is ordered to an end that transcends its own and brought into a relationship that it does not assume. Its integrity and goodness are preserved, even as it is so transformed.

No doubt, the transformations that love might effect can be more or less radical, and it may be that love so thoroughly governs my response to my son and his music that whatever fatherly tolerance I am able to muster is transfigured into forbearance. It may be that I come to endure what I despise, not so much because this is what fathers are obliged to provide, and not for the proximate ends of the tolerant, but rather because we love each other, because I want to retain the relationship shaped by that love, and because I long for the differences that divide us to pass. And yet, insofar as this forbearance has tolerance as its seed and root, and insofar as love transforms but does not eliminate what it perfects, traces of tolerance remain even as it is transfigured into forbearance. Put another way, we remain father and son even as the power and importance of that relationship have faded, even as love has transformed it into something like a friendship. As everyone knows, friendships between parents and children are complicated, mixed-up affairs, largely because the roles, requirements, and perfections of the parent-child relationship are constantly returning and intruding. In this instance, these remainders can be seen in the fact that the union I hope for with respect to *this* difference is deferred to a distant future.[34] If my love forbears as transfigured tolerance, then I do not expect my hope for reconciliation across this difference to be fulfilled anytime soon. Indeed, if I proceed with that hope, if my love yearns for the

---

that they are correctly related to their ultimate end, they must have other virtues to dispose them correctly toward what contributes to that end" (*DC* 5).

34 This love-transformed relationship is *something* like a friendship, not perfectly so. Genuine friendship requires equality, which, in many respects, fathers and teenage sons lack. See Aristotle's discussion of friendship between parents and children, *NE* 1161b16–1162a9.

immediate overcoming of our differences, then as I said in chapter 3, it treats my son unjustly, and surely love that does injustice cannot be love.[35]

If Christians take their cue from Aquinas, they can say that the effects of charity on tolerance reproduce this pattern. Charity comes by grace, and grace works on whatever it finds. If it finds some measure of acquired tolerance in the soul, then it heals, reorders, and further perfects this virtue and its acts (*ST* I-II.109.2).[36] Already ordered to the shared life and common goods of some temporal society, tolerance is now elevated by grace, by the charity it provides, into ends and purposes that transcend its own. It is gathered up into a new social relationship, into "the fellowship of eternal happiness" that God's gracious love creates between God and neighbor (*ST* II-II.23.5). This grace disrupts—as grace always does—but in this instance its disruptions regard the sins and imperfections it redeems us from, not the virtues it happens upon. Naturally acquired human excellences are retained even as they are now perfected in act, elevated to new ends, and situated in a new relationship created by God's love. Tolerance remains, as does the social relationship that it orders and perfect, but each is now gathered into a friendship created by God's love and ordained to the ends of this new relationship. The tolerant intend to achieve the proximate ends that distinguish their virtue's act, and they regard these ends as good in themselves, even as their achievement of them is further ordained to a final end specified by charity. This redirection with respect to final end does not convert this act

35   So long as traces of this relationship and these roles remain, I can't imagine my son objecting to the fact that my endurance of his difference comes as love alone, that it is ordered directly to love's ends and not through the proximate ends of tolerance. But there are other relationships that we might share, and in some of these I can imagine him regarding the transfiguring effects of love upon justice as a corruption of each. Consider, again, the baseball team. As one player among others, he wants no special treatment from me, his coach, simply because I love him. He doesn't expect me to forsake our love relationship, but nor does he want that love to determine how I treat him, at least not immediately. On the field, he is a player and I am a coach, and it's the roles and requirements of this relationship that should determine how we regard each other. If I ignore those roles and requirements, if I regard him as my beloved son alone, then he is likely to doubt the quality of that love and long for the just treatment that it has eclipsed.

36   Some of Thomas's interpreters have found remarks that appear to show grace meeting acquired moral virtue, not with elevation and perfection, but with elimination. After all, he does say that a full complement of infused *moral* virtues accompany charity's reformation of the soul (*ST* I-II.63.3), and it's not at all clear how infused and acquired versions of the same moral virtue could coexist in the same life. (See Mattison, "Can Christians Possess the Acquired Cardinal Virtues?" and Knobel, "Can Aquinas's Infused and Acquired Virtues Coexist in the Christian Life?") For an account of how they might, see Bowlin, "Elevating and Healing." It's an account that suggests a possibility I do not explore here, namely, that the infused moral virtues mediate grace to the acquired. If this is right, then acquired tolerance and forbearance will be elevated and perfected by God's love through the mediation of infused versions of these same virtues.

of justice into an act of charity precisely because it retains its proper object and proximate end.[37] It remains an act of tolerance, of patient endurance due another, and it is ordered to the preservation of a shared life, to a collection of goods held in common, and to autonomy across some important difference.[38] Yet this act of tolerance is done and these ends are sought out of love for God and neighbor. The tolerated are now endured at least in part because they are loved, because they participate in charity's friendship, and the justice done by the tolerant is now a temporal expression of this love's eternal life.

As an act of *tolerance*, this patient endurance of objectionable difference need not be chosen for the sake of reconciliation with the tolerated; reconciliation is not a necessary object of its proximate hope. As an act ordained to *charity's* final end, this patient endurance is indeed ordered to reconciliation, and it proceeds in the hope that God's grace will be its partner and cause. Yet in this instance, reconciliation is deferred, perhaps to some temporal future, perhaps to eternity. The divide between proximate and final ends makes this deferral possible. The circumstances of the act make it necessary. The point is *not* that charity's *love* is deferred to an eschatological horizon, that it is an impossible ideal, a portion of eternity that cannot touch time. Rather the point is that some neighbors are best loved only as they are treated justly, in accord with the norms and ends of a temporal relationship, a relationship whose goodness love cannot deny. In cases like these, God's love becomes incarnate in time not directly through acts of forbearance, but indirectly, through acts tolerance. Indeed, in some circumstances, with respect to some persons and differences, it would not only be unjust to endure patiently in the hope of immediate reconciliation, but also uncharitable. Offense, scandal, or insult would be the likely fallout, not reconciliation, not the relationship preserved and its common goods sustained. In cases like these, justice must embody love in time. Tolerance must be love's immediate response to difference, not forbearance.

We can imagine the tolerant person who has been transformed by grace and who is relatively reflective about her actions thinking something like the following when confronted with such a case: "This person deserves my tolerance. Its patient endurance is what they are due by right from me, and besides, there are goods worth having that this act will help secure, above

---

37   Since proximate ends specify virtues and their acts (*ST* I-II.1.3.2; 60.1.3), actions ordered by charity to God as to their final end are not, as Augustine at times suggests, reduced to so many acts of love. They are, rather, acts of specifically distinct virtues ordained to God out of love for God. This ordination gives these other virtues charity's form even as they remain specifically distinct (*DC* 3.5).

38   Charity commands the acts of other virtues, directs them to its end (*DC* 3), and its end becomes their form (*DV* 10.10). Materially, they remain acts of these other virtues; formally they are converted into acts of love (*ST* II-II.23.8).

all the particular relationship I have with this person and the autonomy we share. What's more, I do not hope for reconciliation, for the resolution of our differences, for this, it seems, would be a foolish and unjust hope. Rather, I recognize that while breath remains, so will these differences, or so it would seem. At the same time, I have been commanded by God to love as God does, to direct all that I do to God in love, and to extend that love to my neighbor, even to strangers, sinners, and enemies. If this neighbor is loved best in this instance only as he is treated justly, then I will also tolerate these differences for God's sake and for the union I hope one day to share with this neighbor in God's company and among blessed. I will hope for that final reconciliation and for the grace that will cause it, but in order to do justice now I will defer the object of my hope and settle for something less. Strangely enough, in this instance, this what love demands."[39]

These shared effects of divine and human love on acquired tolerance do nothing to diminish their substantial differences. A just act of patient endurance that has been transformed by love but not offered for God's sake is formally distinct from that same act offered in charity. The love expressed by the act might be required given the norms of the temporal relationship it assumes, but it does not fall under divine command and it does not presuppose the covenant of grace that authorizes and specifies the love that God requires. The best evidence of this difference comes in the *reach* that Christians confess charity actually has. Our natural, human love has limits with respect to persons. It extends to some, but not all. Our list of civic friends and dearly beloveds will always come to an end, and our tolerance, will always respect that limit. Of those we are obliged to tolerate, we will love only some, and only these will be tolerated for love's sake. With these alone will we hope for reconciliation across the differences that now divide us. All others might be tolerated but not for love's sake or with hope for some future reconciliation. By contrast, those who have been transformed by the Holy Spirit and who, as a result, have a share in God's love will proceed with no equivalent restraints, or so Christians confess. All that they do will be reordered by this love, which means that friendship with God and neighbor will be the final end of their every act of tolerance and the deferred substance of their hope. As with natural, ordinary loves, the transformations that charity effects might be so thorough, so complete, in the lives of some that their tolerance is transfigured into forbearance. In that event, every act of patient endurance that accords with the norms and requirements of a temporal relationship will be offered directly for the sake of charity's ends. And as with ordinary love, charity that forbears as transfigured tolerance will retain traces of the virtue it

39   Since tolerance is a moral virtue, and since the moral virtues are connected through prudence, then it is indeed likely that the tolerant will be reflective about the moral content of their acts.

transforms and aspects of the relationship it transcends in its willingness to defer a portion of the end it intends to a future horizon. In *this* love's endurance, the neighbor is regarded as a participant in the fellowship of the Holy Spirit, and a portion of its intended end is achieved in the temporal fellowship this eternal love creates. But insofar as difference still divides, perfect union is yet to come, and a charity that forbears as transfigured tolerance is willing to allow those differences to stand within the original relationship even as it anticipates a final reconciliation.

The effects of divine charity on naturally acquired forbearance, the kind that abides in ordinary friendships, reproduce this pattern. In some cases, the social relationship in question begins as something other than a friendship. The parties to it might be colleagues, fellow citizens, or neighbors on the block, but the point is that mutual well-wishing is not one of the acts normally required by the relationship and desire for union is not ordinarily one of its ends.[40] But then, as we know, a friendship can be added to these other relationships and whatever measure of tolerance abides in them can be ordered by friendship's love to love's final ends. And, as we noted, in some instances, the friendship might deepen, grow, and so overshadow these other social bonds that tolerance is transfigured by friendship's love into natural forbearance. In other cases, the friendship itself is the primary relationship. It builds its own foundation; it rests on no other. And the patient endurance of objectionable difference that abides within it will be, right from the start, an act of well-wishing ordered directly to love's ends. In each case, God's love can be added to love's virtue, charity to natural forbearance, infused habit to acquired, and when it is, the person transformed by that love will forbear the objectionable differences of their friend, not simply in accord with the graces and requirements of their natural friendship, but now, in addition, for the sake of the fellowship she has with God and hopes to share with her friend. As before, God's love does not erase the virtues it transforms but rather heals their deficits and elevates their acts to union with God and neighbor (*ST* I-II.109.2). Concretely this means that natural forbearance transformed by grace and quickened by God's love will be elicited by that love with greater ease and constancy. More, this act will be required, not simply by the demands of the natural friendship, but also by the requirements that emerge within the relationship that now obtains between the person who forbears, the God whom she loves, and the friend she endures for God's sake.

Thomas puts the point in terms of love's reasons. Natural forbearance that has been infused with charity will proceed with more reasons to love than

---

40   The caveats are designed to bear witness to an earlier concession: a relationship that is not a friendship may nevertheless have friendship-like aspects.

natural forbearance alone. Its beloved will be regarded in more than one way, as participating in more than one social relationship, and its act will be required by more than one collection of normative demands. Thomas writes: when grace transforms the soul, "the good on which every other friendship is based, is directed, as to its end, to the good on which charity is based." When this happens, "charity commands each act of another friendship, even as the art which is about the end commands the art which is about the means." But this means that "the very act of loving someone because he is akin or connected with us, or because he is a fellow-countryman or for any like reason that is referable to the end of charity, can be commanded by charity, so that, out of charity both eliciting and commanding, we love in more ways those who are more nearly connected with us" (*ST* II-II.26.7). When natural forbearance animates natural friendships, we can assume that charity will multiply its reasons for acting in much the same way. The objectionable differences of the beloved will be endured, not simply for the sake of the natural friendship already shared, but also for the sake of fellowship with God that, by grace, might be shared with the beloved. And presumably the range of that forbearance transformed by grace will increase, such that things once unbearable according to the norms of the natural friendship are now endured for the sake of that same divine fellowship.

Returning one last time to fathers and sons, suppose I tolerate the thumping racket coming out of my son's bedroom in part because this is what fathers owe sons in circumstance like these, in response to music like this. And suppose further, as is surely the case, I love my son and order this act of patient endurance not merely to the ends of just tolerance but also to the union that I share with him and that I hope will be sustained and (someday) deepened. Finally, suppose that my soul has been transformed by the sanctifying work of the Holy Spirit and that my loves and relationships bear witness (however dimly) to its healing and elevating effects. In that event, I will have to regard my son in three ways: as a member of my household who is owed certain actions and things in accord with that membership; as a beloved with whom I share a life and a society of mutual well-wishing; and as a fellow member of the household of God, as one who is beloved of God as I am and loved by me for God's sake. In some circumstances, the father/son relationship will fade into the background, its norms put aside, and the natural friendship perfected by grace will determine my actions. In other circumstances, those roles and norms will retain their purchase and so too my natural loves and their precepts. I will tolerate his objectionable differences because he is owed this endurance from his father, because I love him and hope to retain and deepen our union, and because (by grace) I love God and all those who belong to God, my son included, and I hope that my patient endurance of his difference will be received by him (with God's assistance) as a recapitulation of that love.

Such is the potential complexity, the combination of things natural and divine, of things gracious and owed, that Christians might identify in any particular instance of enduring the objectionable differences of another. When this potential complexity is actual, the conceptual depth of that endurance is greater and the reasons to love more substantial than the depth and substance of that same act when it is produced *either* by natural forbearance alone, *or* by the singular grace of divine forbearance. The former emerges from but one kind of temporal relationship, one kind of love, one collection of gifts and requirements. The latter transcends, as much as is possible, the norms and gifts that emerge from the roles and relationships of temporal life and replaces them with the graces and requirements that come with membership in the household of God. The latter is ordered immediately to union with God and unburdened by the frailties and inconsistencies of naturally acquired virtue, or so Christians confess, and yet like the former, it also proceeds with a short list of reasons to love. It would be love's endurance that comes by grace alone. Perfect and powerful, it would, as much as humanly possible, imitate the divine mind and regard the beloved as simultaneously temporal stranger and eternal friend (*ST* I-II.61.5). At the same time, it would not be nested in an ordinary set of social relations and as such it would not be quickened and intensified by reasons that come with natural love and its forbearance. Thus Thomas writes: "Out of charity, we love more those who are more nearly connected with us, since we love them in more ways. For, towards those who are not connected with us we have no other friendship than charity, whereas those who are connected with us, we have certain other friendships" (*ST* II-II.26.7).

We began with contemporary discontent with tolerance. Some doubt that it is a moral excellence. Others concede that it is but find its posture in the world either too demanding or too unstable. The acts of toleration we need must be secured by policy, procedure, or self-interest, not by tolerance, not by a people commited to this virtue's ideals. Both discount the contribution that tolerance might make to our moral and political lives. Others use these discontents to confirm what they already suspect about naturally acquired virtue: that it's a swindle and a fraud, that we must look to divine blessing and Christian love for a proper response to the differences that divide us, to gracious forbearance but never to tolerance.

This book has explored what these critics deny: the place of tolerance among the moral virtues, its relation to love's endurance, and the light that secular and theological discourses might shed on each other. If its arguments are sound, then the moral resources for responding to the differences that divide us are much richer and more compelling than these critics imagine. In social relationships of all kinds—friendships, households, citizens organizations, and political communities—acts of patient endurance are offered and returned across various lines of normative difference. Some are offered in the hope that these relationships will be set right, these differences not denied; some in the hope that a friendship will be retained, its divisions eventually resolved. This is the world as we find it. What's needed is more reflectiveness about this world, more self-knowledge about our place within it, and a deeper appreciation for the virtues that perfect resort to this act, tolerance and forbearance among others.

EPILOGUE
NATURE, GRACE, AND COCKFIGHTS

But how does this work? Where might we see tolerance and forbearance, contest and correction, sacrifice and endurance in action, and can the vocabulary developed in this book shed light on what we see? Well, we found these virtues at work and this vocabulary deployed in various examples along the way, but, as promised, consider another, a story from the spring of 2000, a story about a visit to the Collinsville Game Club.

At the time, cockfighting was an ordinary feature of rural life in Oklahoma. Few regarded it with indifference. In small towns and distant counties, many with Hispanic or Native American roots, cockfighting was considered a noble activity, an ancient inheritance, and a mark of resistance against a wider culture that has little regard for rural lives and local traditions. In the suburbs and cities it tended to elicit disgust and, most prominently, embarrassment. One might think that mutual toleration could address these differences and to mutual benefit. It would secure protection for a cherished tradition and recognition for lives entangled with dirt and death. And it would allow high-tech suburbanites and cosmopolitan city dwellers to retain their disgust while encouraging both to abandon their embarrassment. But the matter resolved itself as George Fletcher might have predicted. Citing the unacceptable harm cockfighting does to the roosters who fight and the subtle moral threats it poses to the citizens who watch, the state of Oklahoma banned cockfighting by referendum in 2002.

But old loves die hard, and cockfighting persists in the Ozark hollows of the southeastern corner of the state.[1] As recently as February 2005, a state

1 It persists even as participants are threatened with stiff fines and jail time. Seven men were arrested in late January 2005 for staging several fights one evening in a barn north of Muldrow. The seventy-eight spectators in attendance cut and run. "Charges Prepared in Cockfighting Case," *Tulsa World*, February 2, 2005.

senator from Henryetta, a town on the western edge of those hollows, proposed a bill that would reverse the ban and return this elicit love to his constituents. His argument began with an appeal to equity and ended with a proposal that flirted with the burlesque. If the laws allow human beings to fight, to box and wrestle, then why not roosters? If civil statute regulates the conditions under which human beings may punch and jab, can't we do the same for fowl? In fact, why not protect fighting cocks as we do boxing bruisers; why not fit them with tiny gloves and chest protectors, and why not call it quits on a five-count when one cock has a clear advantage? The *New York Times*, whose stories about Oklahoma tend to have self-satisfied appeal, parsed Senator Shurden's moral calculus this way: "Who's going to object to chickens fighting as humans do?"[2]

But my story regards the time before the ban. In those days, cockfight clubs dotted the countryside, gamecock weekends attracted visitors to the county seat towns of the southeast, and legislators had been known to float bills that would enshrine in the state constitution the right of roosters to fight and of Oklahomans to bet and cheer.[3] During the heyday of the Cold War, a different state senator, an old salt from Sallisaw, was reported to have said that cockfighting would be the first thing to go when America caved in and the communists took over. Freedom is just another word for cockfighting, or so it seems. Yet, as I said, the threat to freedom eventually came from precincts closer to home, in the petition drives of the animal rights activists, mostly from Tulsa and Oklahoma City. Their aim was to put before the voters a proposal that would ban cockfighting by amendment to the state constitution. As the signature count mounted late in the spring of 2000, the divide between rural and urban became sharp and nasty. The activists were described by their opponents in predictable terms—as liberal elites, outsiders from the coasts, patronizing do-gooders who are ignorant of rural traditions, who have never had red dirt on their boots, and so on—or, rather, they were described in these terms until it appeared that the petition drive would succeed. Then the tone turned conciliatory and eventually the Collinsville Game Club invited all registered voters to attend a weekend bout.

Peace-loving by conviction, and, by twisted habit, a pushover for anticosmopolitan sentiments, I was of divided mind about the matter. I needed to know more. So, mustering my courage—I said to my wife, if Clifford Geertz can stomach this, so can I!—and with three colleagues in tow, I drove thirty

---

2   "Cockfighting for the Squeamish," *New York Times*, January 28, 2005.

3   The Oklahoma State Senate had legislation pending that would call for a vote of the people on a proposal that would give constitutional protection to hunting, trapping, rodeo, raising livestock, and cockfighting, activities that Speaker of the House Larry Adair calls "the traditions and long-standing customs of people in certain areas of our state." "Speaker Defends Cockfight Protection," *Tulsa World*, April 22, 2001.

miles north of Tulsa to Collinsville.[4] What I found there, among other things, was a sturdy intermediate association, doing the kinds of things political scientists tell us intermediate associations are supposed to do in societies like ours. Here was a seedbed of citizenship if ever there was one, and the means of cultivation were surprisingly familiar. Weekend rituals and midweek gatherings, youth groups, potlucks, educational opportunities (in gamecock lore), a governing board, a newsletter, membership that crossed generations, and collective memory that went back to before statehood. Here was a thriving social world situated between *oikos* and *polis*. Here was an independent community accustom to self-rule and primed for the rigors of democratic life. Perhaps Robert Putnam is right about the decline of civil society and the rise of toxic individualism, but at least in Collinsville neither trend was apparent. No one was cockfighting alone.[5]

The fights themselves are mostly horrifying. Rising bleachers surround a small ring on a dirt floor. Angry and eager, the cocks are made lethal by their handlers, who fit each leg with razor-sharp spurs. Placed center ring, the birds explode at each other, leaping and slashing. The excitement is brief. Gamecocks tire easily. If neither receives a lethal blow in the first few minutes, the fight quickly degenerates into pecking and rolling. After about ten minutes, both birds are bloodied, blinded, and breathless. Handlers remove the combatants to a smaller ring behind the far bleachers where a crowd gathers—friends offering support, gamblers chasing a bet, gawkers seeking a conclusion. The bout ends only as one bird refuses to fight, or dies.

After the first fight, I couldn't watch any more, so I concentrated on the audience. There were many children in the crowd, children of all ages, scampering over and under the bleachers, some watching the proceedings, some chatting with friends, others shouting encouragement to their favorite bird, still others gazing passively on the contest before them. My eyes followed a small boy of about seven or eight who was being chased by three or four other children of about the same age. He slipped between the seats and dropped beneath the bleachers, trying to escape, but his pursuers were faster and cornered him just below us. "Get him! Get his eyes!" one of them shouted, and they began to peck and pinch his head and face with thumbs and fingers. The boy fought back with kicks and jabs, broke out of the circle, and then, crying, fled the building into the yard with the others close at his heals.

We had seen enough and followed the children out the door. We too were pursued. "Whad'ya think? Pretty exciting, eh?" We turned, and there was a man in his seventies, flanked by three others, fiftyish and scowling. Apparently the seed caps I had distributed in the car did nothing to conceal our geeky, out-of-place identities. The older man was eager to talk, and so we did.

4   Geertz, "Deep Play."

5   Putnam, *Bowling Alone*.

We gave our impressions, our mixed feelings about what we had seen, and he gave us what was plainly the party line, that old Stoic theology. Gamecocks love to fight. It is in their blood. By pitting them together, we allow nature to take its course, nothing more. Yes, the consequences are violent and bloody, but the fight itself is fitting and beautiful. Nature is like that.[6] Indeed, death by noble struggle is a fate far better than the one met by most of their kind, better than the pluck and chop at the local Tyson plant. His voice trailed off, and then, almost apologetically, he encouraged us to vote against the proposed constitutional amendment.

The other men said nothing, but we could tell that they didn't care for us. In their eyes, we were the enemy. Active hostilities had ceased, but for tactical reasons, and it was plain that they neither welcomed nor accepted our company. We were tolerated—our persons and views—if only just barely. As we thanked them for their hospitality and turned to go, we noticed the children repeating their imitation of the cock fight ritual with a new victim among the cars in the parking lot. The boy we had watched was now an aggressor, pecking and kicking with ferocity unmatched by the others. The sun was high and the day was hot. We got into our car and drove back to Tulsa.[7]

Looking back on that afternoon much remains opaque, but a couple of things have come into focus. First, my colleagues and I had been swept up into a debate about the tolerable and the intolerable, about the items on these lists, and about the prospect of moving certain items from one list to another. Urbanites wanted cockfighting moved from the list of actions and things one must tolerate to the list of actions and things one need not, and perhaps must not. Rural participants wanted to keep these lists unrevised. The means of debate were ordinary and the venues local: town meetings, editorial pages, conversations in coffee shops and VFW posts, petition drives, site visits, and, in due course, a proposal put before the voters. In the end, as I said, the friends of cockfighting lost. The practice was banned by a vote of the people. The request for tolerance was denied, which brings me to the second thing that matters here.

It was the friends of cockfighting who asked for tolerance and who appeared willing to offer it in return, not the urban hipsters or suburban soccer moms. They wanted cockfighting endured by their fellow citizens who

---

6 Augustine describes a cockfight in roughly the same terms, as *concinnum et pulchrum* and thus a sign of transcendent order. Its beauty draws him in and makes him attend. In "every movement of these animals devoid of reason, there was nothing improper, precisely because another reason from above governs all things." *Ord.* I.8.25, my translation.

7 Had we just witnessed a reversal of Girardian themes? Sacrifice had not dissipated mimesis and its rivalries, as René Girard suggests it should. Rather, sacrificial violence had been imitated. It had fueled fraternal rivalry.

found it objectionable, and they counted this endurance among the goods they were due as citizens, as members of a political community sustained by mutual tolerance. And they asked for this due without assuming that the difference in dispute would be resolved. They had little hope for reconciliation with their urban and suburban critics; but no matter, mutual tolerance would be enough to sustain their life together within this political community and across this difference.

This should be obvious but it bears repeating if only because it contradicts the assumptions of culture war critics on both the left and the right. Conservatives would have us believe that tolerance is incompatible with the traditional morality that is thought to thrive in places like Collinsville, while critics on the left tend to regard the rural inhabitants of middle America as incapable of exercising the virtue, respecting difference, or appreciating the importance of each.[8] But the facts on the ground in Collinsville defy both assumptions. They expose the prejudices and fantasies that have captivated critics on both sides of this debate. In its own odd way, the Collinsville Game Club was a seedbed of tolerance. No doubt, its members asked for tolerance from those *outside* the club, from the inhabitants of the political community they shared with the rest of us in the state, but I suspect they made the request because they were familiar with the activity (if not the virtue) in their own precincts. They asked for tolerance because they were already in the habit of regarding its patient endurance as a useful response to the differences that divided their own little society.

Complaints of the critics aside, these facts on the ground shouldn't surprise us, and not simply because tolerance is natural to us and tends to appear in some form almost everywhere and always, even in rural Oklahoma. The Collinsville Game Club was obviously a thriving civil society and it generated the benefits that intermediate associations are said to produce. Within their walls, "the taste and habit of self-rule" are cultivated.[9] Shared interests are pursued and collective efforts made, and along the way, social capital accumulates. Informal networks form, trust grows, and tolerance emerges, all in a context of cooperation for the sake of mutual protection and common welfare. The consequences are political and altogether positive, or so the story goes. A people schooled in these tastes and habits will most likely become active, robust citizens. "Engaged men and women tend to be multiply engaged."[10] Already involved with one kind of society, already

---

8   That the rural inhabitants of Middle America might have slightly different lists of things tolerable and intolerable, different from urbanites on the coasts, goes without saying, but this is a different matter. It does not regard the status of tolerance as a virtue or the capacity of rural people to recognize its merit.

9   Taylor, "Invoking Civil Society," 222.

10   Walzer, *What It Means to Be an American*, 11.

tending to its affairs, they will be primed to care for the common goods of political society. Already skilled in cooperative ventures at the parochial level, they will not be threatened by the conflicts and compromises of public life. With little effort they will come to understand that give-and-take among equals is the soul of democratic politics, and, with varying degrees of self-consciousness, they will realize that this soul flourishes only as certain moral virtues are cultivated and exercised—humility, courage, justice, and tolerance.

And it certainly was tolerance that our hosts in Collinsville requested. They didn't expect city slickers and suburban swells to regard cockfighting favorably, to find it unobjectionable. They understood how someone who spends little time on farms and ranches or among livestock and fowl might consider the practice objectionable, and they didn't expect those of us who object to forsake our response. Whether reflectively or not, they accepted this epistemic divide between us, acknowledged reasons on both sides, and concluded (again, whether reflectively or not) that tolerance salted with humility offered the best course. So too, they didn't want our tolerance of their cock-fighting to come with the expectation that those who love it will, over time, abandon their rural ways. That would be condescending. No, they wanted us to regard cockfighting as a permanent feature of Oklahoma life, to recognize that some of our fellow citizens might find beauty and sport in it, not simply violence and blood, and to admit that this justified difference in perception warrants our endurance of their difference. By their lights, the tolerance that they hoped to secure would not be an interim virtue that awaits the redemption of the objectionable but rather a permanent feature of our shared life.

But, as I said, this request was denied, and this outcome turned the moral tables. Those who had requested toleration's patient endurance now had to offer it. This is how things tend to go. Contestation and debate proceed about some particular attitude or activity, about its moral status as tolerable or not, and those who had hoped for tolerance may have to tolerate in turn. So it was in Collinsville. Democratic debate had concluded, an election was lost, and the political society was now drawn in a direction the friends of cockfighting had opposed, in accord with loves and commitments they do not share. If this loss cannot be recouped by democratic means—further contestation, a counter petition drive, a second ballot initiative, and so on—and if insurrection and exit are refused, then this transformation of their po-litical society and this difference that divides them from their fellow citizens will have to be endured. The question, of course, is whether the patient en-durance required in this instance—like the endurance requested before the vote—might in fact be an instance of true tolerance. There are some differ-ences that one despises and yet endures with patience, some losses that one laments and yet suffers nevertheless. As we have seen, the difficulty comes in determining which differences are in fact objectionable and which persons are owed toleration's patient endurance given the norms and requirements of the relationship in question. It comes in determining when this response is right and due, in finding the will to act in accord with this determination, and in delivering this act across a proper variety of circumstances and for the sake of the right collection of ends. Over time, the difficulty comes in generating this act with the constancy of habit and in cultivating a variety of the habit that is fitted for democratic life. Cockfighting may be intolerable—I certainly find it so—and yet some in Collinsville experienced the ban as loss. I will leave it to others, to their friends and neighbors, to judge whether the acts of toleration that have been offered in reply amount to true tolerance or something else.

Did cockfighting disappear in rural Oklahoma? No, it simply went underground. Weekend bouts are now held in isolated pole barns and backwater Quonset huts, clandestine but not exactly anonymous. In small towns people talk, word gets out, and soon enough most will know who's involved in this now illegal activity. This muddies the moral waters even more.[11] Most rural Oklahomans are Protestants of one sort or another. Many are church members, and traditional piety is the norm. I'm speculating now, but imagine what relations are like in those local congregations. Most of the faithful take the Apostle Paul's injunction to subject themselves to governing authorities with unbending seriousness (Rom 13:1–6). Authority to rule comes from God, or so they believe, and those who resist the authorities resist what God has appointed. From the perspective of their ecclesial membership, the inhabitants of these small towns will regard the injustice of cockfighting as a sin precisely because a just governing authority prohibits it. From the perspective of their temporal citizenship, the activities of the person who attended the previous night's cockfight and who now sits in the pew on Sunday morning cannot be tolerated. These activities have been discredited by democratic means and prohibited by legal statute. They injure the principal common good of the political community: its relationships set right in accord with legal precept. Insofar as citizens are obliged to care for this good and deliver it to all, these actions not only damage that good but wrong the members of this community. The local sheriff will have to be notified. Correction must be offered and persuasion tried. If favorable attitudes toward cockfighting remain even after participation in the activity comes to an end, then these will have to be endured with patience—at least at the close of the day. This is an endurance that citizens owe each other, or so they are likely to conclude.

Now imagine that a certain quality of friendship abides among members in these congregations and a certain love and desire for union animates their

---

11   In the spring of 2014, Delaware County deputies discovered a cockfight while making a drug arrest. They found twenty game birds kept and trained for fighting. "Cockfight Found in Progress during Drug and Weapons Bust," *Tulsa World*, April 10, 2014.

life together. They will say that, by grace, these relationships bear witness to the friendship that Jesus shared with his disciples, that this love is a participation of God's life (John 15:12–15). They might say that grace enables them to ordain these acts of legal coercion, fraternal correction, and patient endurance beyond the proximate ends of citizenship to a final end, to friendship with God and neighbor. They may even hope for a change in judgment and love and for the prospect of an ever-deeper union with those from whom they are now divided. If they regard the object of this hope as long coming, then they will admit that tolerance will have to suffice in the meantime. But they might also long for that object even now, for that change in judgment and love and that ever-deeper union. They might say that it will come as grace does, as assistance from another. In that event, we might say that their tolerance has become forbearance, their endurance a work of love.

Now imagine two additional possibilities. In these small towns, fellow citizens might also be public friends. A certain mutual well-wishing, desire for union, and hope for the resolution of differences might animate their civic relations. In that event, the coercion, correction, and endurance traded among citizens, regardless of religious commitment or affiliation, might be ordained to these ends and offered with these hopes. And if these ends and hopes come to dominate their response to the differences that divide them, then we might say that forbearance has displaced tolerance, that their endurance has become a portion of love's political work. In that event, those citizens who also happen to confess what Christians do about God and grace will not only forbear for the sake of a shared temporal citizenship. Acting in the faith that human love can express and bear witness to divine love, they might say that their political loves have been ordained to a distant hope: that these neighbors corrected and endured might one day know that they are beloved of God and so put aside their sin.

So it is with churches, cockfight clubs, and small towns in Oklahoma. Each can be a seminary of virtue, where tolerance and forbearance might be cultivated and exercised, where differences are contested and corrections exchanged, and where some will say that nature and grace intermingle and yet remain distinct.

ACKNOWLEDGMENTS

This book was started in Tulsa and finished in Princeton. In both towns, I accumulated debts and received gifts. I was on the faculty of the University of Tulsa with a remarkable collection of moral philosophers, political theorists, and historians of political thought. Our conversations were frequent, lively, and, for me, enormously beneficial. Thanks to Jane Ackerman, Nicholas Capaldi, Eldon Eisenach, Lars Engle, Stephen Gardner, Russell Hittinger, Thomas Horne, Jacob Howland, Michael Mosher, and Paul Rahe. Now at Princeton Theological Seminary, I work among systematic theologians, Christian ethicists, and historians of doctrine, as well as moral philosophers, political theorists, and religious ethicists. This mix includes colleagues, friends, and students. This community has been a blessing. I am especially grateful for conversations and exchanges with Alda Balthrop-Lewis, Anthony Bateza, Ellen Charry, Joseph Clair, David Decosimo, Emily Dumler-Winckler, Adam Eitel, Gordon Graham, Clifton Granby, Eric Gregory, Lindsey Hankins, Davey Henreckson, George Hunsinger, Stacy Johnson, Cambria Kaltwasser, Brian Lee, Daniel May, Gustavo Maya, Bruce McCormack, Jeffrey Skaff, Sarah Stewart-Kroeker, Mark Taylor, Melanie Webb, and Derek Woodard-Lehman.

Scott Davis, C. J. Dickson, Molly Farneth, Gabrielle Girgis, Melissa Lane, and Jeffrey Stout read and commented on an earlier version of the entire manuscript. I owe special thanks to Scott Davis for suggesting the title and to Melissa Lane and Jeffrey Stout for indispensable advice about content and organization. Others read individual chapters: Leora Batnitzky, Ernesto Cortes Jr., Eddie Glaude, Jacob Howland, Michael Lamb, Cornel West, and James Wetzel. To all of these colleagues and friends, I am happily indebted. For their wisdom and encouragement, I am enormously grateful. Thanks as well to the institutions that gave me a chance to test-drive ideas: Boston University, University of Bucharest, Emory University, Florida State University, Gonzaga University, IAF/Southwest, Princeton Theological Seminary, Princeton University, University of Tulsa, Villanova University, and University of Virginia.

A grant from the Louisville Institute funded a sabbatical leave during the 2004–2005 academic year, which I used to work through some of the vast literature on toleration. This launched the project. I am grateful for the grant and indebted to James Lewis for his support. I owe a special word of thanks to Fred Appel, religion editor at Princeton University Press. Early on, Fred expressed interest in the project, and over the years his faith and encouragement never failed. Thanks as well to editors Joseph Dahm, Juliana Fidler, and Jenny Wolkowicki for their wise counsel and steady patience.

Portions of chapter 1 and the epilogue include reworked material that first appeared in "Nature, Grace, and Toleration: Civil Society and the Twinned Church," *The Annual of the Society of Christian Ethics* 21 (2001): 85–104. Chapter 2 includes revised portions of "Nature's Grace: Aquinas and Wittgenstein on Natural Law and Moral Knowledge," in *Grammar and Grace: Reformulations of Aquinas and Wittgenstein*, edited by Jeffrey Stout and Robert MacSwain (London: SCM Press, 2004), 154–174. Fragments of the introduction and chapter 6 appear in "Democracy, Tolerance, Aquinas," *Journal of Religious Ethics* 44, no. 2 (2016): 278–299. I am grateful to these publishers and editors for their permission to reproduce this material. Thanks as well to John Wiley & Sons Ltd and to the Master and Fellows of Trinity College, Cambridge for permission to reproduce selections from Ludwig Wittgenstein, *On Certainty*, ed. G.E.M. Anscombe and G. H. von Wright, trans. Denis Paul and G.E.M. Anscombe. Copyright © 1969 by Basil Blackwell.

I owe the greatest debt of gratitude to Mimi, Isaac, and Nicholas. It exceeds all measure or accounting. Every day, I am sustained by their love, by their capacity for joy, by the inspiration of their lives.

BIBLIOGRAPHY

Abrams, M. H. *Natural Supernaturalism: Tradition and Revolution in Romantic Literature*. New York: Norton, 1973.

Adams, Marilyn M. *Horrendous Evils and the Goodness of God*. Ithaca, NY: Cornell University Press, 2000.

———. "Redemptive Suffering: A Christian Solution to the Problem of Evil." In *The Problem of Evil: Selected Readings*, edited by Michael L. Peterson, 169–187. Notre Dame, IN: University of Notre Dame Press, 1992.

Adams, Robert Merrihew. *Finite and Infinite Goods: A Framework for Ethics*. Oxford: Oxford University Press, 2002.

Anscombe, G.E.M. *Intention*. 2nd ed. Cambridge, MA: Harvard University Press, 2000.

Aquinas, Thomas. *Corpus Thomisticum: Opera Omni*. Edited and maintained by Enrique Alarcón. http://www.corpusthomisticum.org/iopera.html.

———. *Disputed Questions on Truth*. 3 vols. Translated by Robert W. Mulligan, James V. McGlynn, and Robert W. Schmidt. Chicago: Henry Regnery, 1952–1954.

———. *Disputed Questions on Virtue*. Translated by Jeffrey Hause and Claudia Eisen Murphy. Indianapolis: Hackett, 2010.

———. *Opera Omnia cum hypertexibus in CD-ROM*. 2nd ed. Edited by Robert Busa. Milan: Editoria Elettronica Editel, 1992.

———. *Quaestiones Disputatae*. 2 vols., 9th ed. Edited by P. Bazzi, M. Calcaterra, T. S. Centi, E. Odetto, P. M. Pession, R. Spiazzi,. Turin: Marietti, 1953.

———. *Summa Contra Gentiles*. 4 vols. Translated by A. C. Pegis, J. F. Anderson, V. J. Bourke, and C. J. O'Neill. Notre Dame, IN: University of Notre Dame Press, 1975.

———. *Summa theologiae. Opera Omnia iussu Leonis XIII p.m. edita*, Vol. *4–12*, Cura et studio Fratrum Praedicatorium. Rome: Typographia Polyglotta, 1888–1906.

———. *Summa Theologica*. 3 vols. Translated by the Fathers of the English Dominican Province. New York: Benzinger Brothers, 1947–1948. Reprint, 5 vols., Westminster, MD: Christian Classics, 1981.

Aristotle. *Metaphysics*. 2 vols. Edited and translated by W. D. Ross. Oxford: Oxford University Press, 1924.

———. *Nicomachean Ethics*. 2nd ed. Translated by Terence Irwin. Indianapolis: Hackett, 1999.

Assheton, William. *Toleration disapprove'd and condemn'd*. 2nd ed. Oxford: William Hall, 1670.

Augustine. *The City of God against the Pagans*. Edited and translated by R. W. Dyson. Cambridge: Cambridge University Press, 1998.

———. *Confessions*. Translated by Henry Chadwick. Oxford: Oxford University Press, 1991.

———. *Earlier Writings*. Edited and translated by J.H.S. Burleigh. London: SCM Press, 1953.

———. *The Happy Life; Answer to the Skeptics; Divine Providence and the Problem of Evil; Soliloquies.* Translated by Ludwig Schoop. *Fathers of the Early Church: A New Translation (Patristic series)*, vol. 5. Washington, DC: Catholic University of America Press, 1948.

———. *Letters, Volume 2 (83–130).* Translated by Wilfred Parsons, S.N.D. *Fathers of the Early Church: A New Translation (Patristic series)*, vol. 18. Washington, DC: Catholic University of America Press, 1953.

———. *Letters, Volume 3 (131–164).* Translated by Wilfred Parsons, S.N.D. *Fathers of the Early Church: A New Translation (Patristic series)*, vol. 20. Washington, DC: Catholic University of America Press, 1953.

———. *The Trinity.* Translated by Edmund Hill, O.P. Hyde Park, NY: New City Press, 1991.

Barth, Karl. *Church Dogmatics.* 4 vols. Translated and edited by G. M. Bromiley and T. F. Torrance. Edinburgh: T & T Clark, 1956–1975.

Bawer, Bruce. "Tolerance or Death!" Reason.com, November 30, 2005. http://reason.com/archives/2005/11/30/tolerance-or-death. Accessed July 7, 2015.

Bejan, Teresa. "'The Bond of Civility': Roger Williams on Toleration and Its Limits." *History of European Ideas* 37, no. 4 (2011): 409–420.

Bejczy, Istvan. "Tolerentia: A Medieval Concept." *Journal of the History of Ideas* 58, no. 3 (July 1997): 365–384.

Bennett, Jonathan. *Locke, Berkeley, Hume: Central Themes.* Oxford: Oxford University Press, 1971.

Bilgrami, Akeel. "Secularism: Its Content and Context." In *Secularism, Identity, and Enchantment,* 3–57. Cambridge, MA: Harvard University Press, 2014.

Boguslawski, Steven. *Thomas Aquinas on the Jews: Insights into His Commentary on Romans 9–11.* Mahwah, NJ: Paulist Press, 2008.

Borges, Jorge Luis. *The Book of Sand.* Translated by Norman Thomas di Giovanni. New York: Dutton, 1977.

Bowlin, John R. "Augustine Counting Virtues." *Augustinian Studies* 41, no. 1 (2010): 277–300.

———. "Augustine on Justifying Coercion." *The Annual of the Society of Christian Ethics* 17 (1997): 49–70.

———. *Contingency and Fortune in Aquinas's Ethics.* Cambridge: Cambridge University Press, 1999.

———. "Democracy, Tolerance, Aquinas." *Journal of Religious Ethics* 44, no. 2 (2016): 278–299.

———. "Elevating and Healing: Reflections on *Summa Theologiae* 109.2." *Journal of Moral Theology* 3, no. 1 (2014): 39–53.

———. "Psychology and Theodicy in Aquinas." *Medieval Philosophy and Theology* 7, no. 2 (1998): 125–152.

———. "Tolerance among the Fathers." *Journal of the Society of Christian Ethics* 26, no. 1 (2006): 3–36.

Brandom, Robert. *Articulating Reasons: An Introduction to Inferentialism.* Cambridge, MA: Harvard University Press, 2000.

———. "Freedom and Constraint by Norms." *American Philosophical Quarterly* 16, no. 3 (July 1979): 187–196.

———. *Making It Explicit: Reasoning, Representing, and Discursive Commitment.* Cambridge, MA: Harvard University Press, 1994.

———. *Tales of the Mighty Dead: Historical Essays in the Metaphysics of Intentionality.* Cambridge, MA: Harvard University Press, 2002.

Bretherton, Luke. *Hospitality as Holiness: Christian Witness Amid Moral Diversity.* Surrey: Ashgate, 2006.

Brett, Annabel. *Changes of State: Nature and the Limits of the City in Early Modern Natural Law.* Princeton: Princeton University Press, 2011.

Brock, Stephen L. *Action and Conduct: Thomas Aquinas and the Theory of Action.* Edinburgh: T & T Clark, 1998.

———. "The Legal Character of Natural Law According to St. Thomas Aquinas." PhD diss., University of Toronto, 1988.

———. *The Philosophy of Saint Thomas Aquinas: A Sketch*. Eugene, OR: Cascade Books, 2015.

Bromwich, David. "How Moral Is Taste?" In *Skeptical Music: Essays on Modern Poetry*, 232–251. Chicago: University of Chicago Press, 2001.

Brown, Wendy. *Regulating Aversion: Tolerance in the Age of Identity and Empire*. Princeton: Princeton University Press, 2008.

Budziszewski, Jay. *True Tolerance: Liberalism and the Necessity of Judgment*. New Brunswick, NJ: Transaction, 1992.

Burke, Edmund. *A Philosophical Enquiry into the Origin of Our Ideas of the Sublime and Beautiful*. New York: Oxford University Press, 1998.

Caesar, Julius. *The Gallic War*. Translated by H. J. Edwards. Loeb Classical Library. Cambridge, MA: Harvard University Press, 1917.

Carey, George. "Tolerating Religion." In Mendus, *Politics of Toleration in Modern Life*, 45–64.

Cavell, Stanley. *The Claim of Reason: Wittgenstein, Skepticism, Morality, and Tragedy*. Oxford: Oxford University Press, 1979.

———. *Little Did I Know: Excerpts from Memory*. Stanford: Stanford University Press, 2010.

Chappell, David. *A Stone of Hope: Prophetic Religion and the Death of Jim Crow*. Chapel Hill: University of North Carolina Press, 2004.

Cicero, Marcus Tullius. *On Duties*. Translated by Walter Miller. Loeb Classical Library. Cambridge, MA: Harvard University Press, 1913.

———. *On Invention. The Best Kind of Orator. Topics*. Translated by H. M. Hubbell. Loeb Classical Library. Cambridge, MA: Harvard University Press, 1949.

———. *On the Orator: Book 3. On Fate. Stoic Paradoxes. Divisions of Oratory*. Translated by H. Rackham. Loeb Classical Library. Cambridge, MA: Harvard University Press, 1942.

———. *On the Republic. On the Laws*. Translated by Clinton W. Keyes. Loeb Classical Library. Cambridge, MA: Harvard University Press, 1928.

Compte-Sponville, André. *A Small Treatise on the Great Virtues: The Uses of Philosophy in Everyday Life*. Translated by C. Temerson. New York: Henry Holt, 2001.

Conyers, A. J. *The Long Truce: How Toleration Made the World Safe for Power and Profit*. Dallas: Spence, 2001.

Creppell, Ingrid. *Toleration and Identity: Foundations in Early Modern Thought*. New York: Routledge, 2003.

Davidson, Donald. "On the Very Idea of a Conceptual Scheme." *Proceedings and Addresses of the American Philosophical Association* 47 (1973–1974): 5–20.

Davis, G. Scott. *Warcraft and the Fragility of Virtue: An Essay in Aristotelian Ethics*. Boise: University of Idaho Press, 1992.

Decosimo, David. *Ethics as a Work of Charity: Thomas Aquinas and Pagan Virtue*. Stanford: Stanford University Press, 2014.

D'Entrèves, Alexander Passerin. *Natural Law: An Introduction to Legal Philosophy*. New Brunswick: Transaction, 2004.

Digeser, Elizabeth DePalma. *The Making of a Christian Empire: Lactantius and Rome*. Ithaca, NY: Cornell University Press, 2000.

Dobson, Ryan. *Be Intolerant: Because Some Things Are Just Stupid*. Colorado Springs: Multnomah Books, 2003.

Dodaro, Robert. *Christ and the Just Society in the Thought of Augustine*. Cambridge: Cambridge University Press, 2004.

Douglas, Mary. *Natural Symbols: Explorations in Cosmology*. New York: Vintage, 1973.

Drake, H. A. *Constantine and the Bishops: The Politics of Intolerance*. Baltimore: Johns Hopkins University Press, 2000.

Eitel, Adam. "*De Beata Vita:* Love and Friendship in Thomas Aquinas." PhD diss., Princeton Theological Seminary, 2015.

Elbow, Steven. "Reince Preibus Doesn't Like the Word 'Tolerance.'" *Capital Times,* July 23, 2013. http://host.madison.com/news/local/writers/steven_elbow/reince-priebus-doesn-t-like-the -word-tolerance/article_eb94c906-aa2e-5e55-b442-b9268b1c39d6.html (accessed June 11, 2015).

Elster, Jon. *Ulysses and the Sirens: Studies in Rationality and Irrationality.* Cambridge: Cambridge University Press, 1979.

Fergusson, David. *Church, State, and Civil Society.* Cambridge: Cambridge University Press, 2004.

Fiala, Andrew. *Tolerance and the Ethical Life.* London: Continuum, 2005.

Finnis, John. *Natural Law and Natural Rights.* Oxford: Clarendon, 1980.

Fish, Stanley. "Boutique Multiculturalism." In *The Trouble with Principle,* 56–72. Cambridge, MA: Harvard University Press, 1999.

Fletcher, George. "The Instability of Tolerance." In Heyd, *Toleration,* 158–172.

Forst, Rainer. "Toleration as a Virtue of Justice." *Philosophical Explorations* 4, no. 3 (2001): 193–206.

———. *Toleration in Conflict: Past and Present.* Translated by Ciaran Cronin. Cambridge: Cambridge University Press, 2013.

Frankfurt, Harry G. *The Reasons of Love.* Princeton: Princeton University Press, 2004.

Fredriksen, Paula. *Augustine and the Jews: A Christian Defense of Jews and Judaism.* New York: Doubleday, 2008.

Galston, William A. *Liberal Purposes: Goods, Virtues, and Diversity in the Liberal State.* Cambridge: Cambridge University Press, 1991.

Garnsey, Peter. "Religious Toleration in Classical Antiquity." In Sheils, *Persecution and Toleration,* 1–27.

Geertz, Clifford. "Anti-Anti-Relativism." In Geertz, *Available Light,* 42–67.

———. *Available Light: Anthropological Reflections on Philosophical Topics.* Princeton: Princeton University Press, 2000.

———. "Deep Play: Notes on the Balinese Cockfight." In *Interpretation of Cultures,* 412–454. New York: Basic Books, 1973.

———. "The Uses of Diversity." In Geertz, *Available Light,* 68–88.

Gibbon, Edward. *The History of the Decline and Fall of the Roman Empire.* 8 vols. London: J. Murray, 1887.

Gray, John. *Two Faces of Liberalism.* New York: New Press, 2000.

Greenberg, Steven. *Wrestling with God and Men: Homosexuality in the Jewish Tradition.* Madison: University of Wisconsin Press, 2004.

Grisez, Germain. "The First Principle of Practical Reason: A Commentary on the Summa Theologiae, 1–2, Question 94, Article 2." *Natural Law Forum* 10 (1965): 168–201.

Halbertal, Moshe. *On Sacrifice.* Princeton: Princeton University Press, 2012.

Hall, Pamela M. *Narrative and the Natural Law: An Interpretation of Thomistic Ethics.* Notre Dame, IN: University of Notre Dame Press, 1994.

Harel, Alon. "The Boundaries of Justifiable Tolerance: A Liberal Perspective." In Heyd, *Toleration,* 114–126.

Harned, David Baily. *Patience: How We Wait upon the World.* Cambridge, MA: Cowley, 1997.

Hauerwas, Stanley. *After Christendom? How the Church Is to Behave if Freedom, Justice, and a Christian Nation Are Bad Ideas.* Nashville: Abington, 1991.

———. "Hauerwas on 'Hauerwas and the Law': Trying to Have Something to Say." *Law and Contemporary Problems* 75, no. 4 (2012): 233–251.

———. *Performing the Faith: Bonhoeffer and the Practice of Nonviolence.* Grand Rapids, MI: Brazos, 2004.

Hauerwas, Stanley, and Charles Pinches. *Christians among the Virtues: Theological Conversations with Ancient and Modern Ethics.* Notre Dame, IN: Notre Dame University Press, 1997.

Hays, Richard. *The Moral Vision of the New Testament: Community, Cross, and New Creation. A Contemporary Introduction to New Testament Ethics*. San Francisco: Harper, 1996.

Herdt, Jennifer. *Putting on Virtue: The Legacy of the Splendid Vices*. Chicago: University of Chicago Press, 2008.

———. *Religion and Faction in Hume's Moral Philosophy*. Cambridge: Cambridge University Press, 1997.

Herman, Barbara. "Pluralism and the Community of Moral Judgment." In Heyd, *Toleration*, 60–80.

Heyd, David. "Is Toleration a Political Virtue?" In Williams and Waldron, *Toleration and Its Limits*, 171–194.

———, ed. *Toleration: An Elusive Virtue*. Princeton: Princeton University Press, 1996.

Hill, Christopher. "Toleration in Seventeenth-Century England: Theory and Practice." In Mendus, *Politics of Toleration in Modern Life*, 27–43.

Hirschman, Albert O. *Exit, Voice, and Loyalty: Responses to Decline in Firms, Organizations, and States*. Cambridge, MA: Harvard University Press, 1970.

Hittinger, Russell. *First Grace: Rediscovering the Natural Law in a Post-Christian World*. Wilmington, DE: ICI Books, 2003.

———. "Two Modernisms, Two Thomisms: Reflections on the Centenary of Pius X's Letter Against the Modernists." *Nova et Vetera* 5, no. 4 (Fall 2007): 843–880.

Homer. *The Iliad*. Translated by Robert Fagles. Introduction and notes by Bernard Knox. Harmondsworth: Penguin, 1990.

Horton, John. "Toleration as a Virtue." In Heyd, *Toleration*, 28–43.

Hume, David. *Dialogues Concerning Natural Religion*. London: Penguin Classics, 1990.

Ignatieff, Michael. "Nationalism and Toleration." In Mendus, *Politics of Toleration in Modern Life*, 77–106.

Incandela, Joseph. "The Appropriation of Wittgenstein's Work by Philosophers of Religion: Towards a Re-evaluation and an End." *Religious Studies* 21, no. 4 (1985): 457–474.

Jay, Nancy. *Throughout Your Generations Forever: Sacrifice, Religion, and Paternity*. Chicago: University of Chicago Press, 1992.

Kahlos, Maijastina. *Forbearance and Compulsion: The Rhetoric of Religious Tolerance and Intolerance in Late Antiquity*. London: Duckworth, 2009.

Kantorowicz, Ernst H. *The King's Two Bodies: A Study in Medieval Political Theology*. Princeton: Princeton University Press, 1957.

King, Martin Luther, Jr. "The Ethical Demands for Integration." In Washington, *Testament of Hope*, 117–125.

———. "Experiment in Love." In Washington, *Testament of Hope*, 16–20.

———. *Why We Can't Wait*. San Francisco: Harper & Row, 1963.

Knasas, John F. X. *Thomism and Tolerance*. Scranton, PA: University of Scranton Press, 2011.

Knobel, Angela McKay. "Can Aquinas's Infused and Acquired Virtues Coexist in the Christian Life?" *Studies in Christian Ethics* 23, no. 4 (2010): 381–396.

Lactantius. *Divine Institutes*. Translated by Anthony Bowen and Peter Garnsey. Liverpool: Liverpool University Press, 2003.

———. *Institutions divines/Lactance*. Vols. 1–2, 4–6. Translated by Pierre Monat. Paris: Editions du Cerf, 1973–2007.

Lamb, Michael. "Aquinas and the Virtues of Hope: Theological and Democratic." *Journal of Religious Ethics* 44, no. 2 (2016): 300–322.

———. "A Commonwealth of Hope: Virtue, Rhetoric, and Religion in Augustine's Political Thought." PhD diss., Princeton University, 2014.

Laursen, John Christian, and Cary J. Nederman, eds. *Beyond the Persecuting Society: Religious Toleration Before the Enlightenment*. Philadelphia: University of Pennsylvania Press, 1998.

Lessing, Gotthold Ephraim. "Nathan the Wise." In *Nathan the Wise, Minna Von Barnhelm, and Other Plays and Writings*, edited by P. Demetz and translated by B. Q. Morgan, 173–276. New York: Continuum, 1991.

Lisska, Anthony. *Aquinas's Theory of Natural Law: An Analytic Reconstruction*. Oxford: Clarendon, 1996.

Locke, John. *A Letter Concerning Toleration*. Edited by James Tully. Indianapolis: Hackett, 1983.

Lovibond, Sabina. *Realism and Imagination in Ethics*. Minneapolis: University of Minnesota Press, 1983.

Macedo, Steven. *Liberal Virtues: Citizenship, Virtue, and Community in Liberal Constitutionalism*. Oxford: Oxford University Press, 1990.

MacIntyre, Alasdair. "Toleration and the Goods of Conflict." In Mendus, *Politics of Toleration in Modern Life*, 133–155.

MacKinnon, Catharine. *Toward a Feminist Theory of the State*. Cambridge, MA: Harvard University Press, 1989.

Manning, Christel. *God Gave Us the Right: Conservative Catholic, Evangelical Protestant, and Orthodox Jewish Women Grapple with Feminism*. New Brunswick, NJ: Rutgers University Press, 1999.

Marshall, John. *John Locke: Resistance, Religion, and Responsibility*. Cambridge: Cambridge University Press, 1994.

Mattison III, William C. "Can Christians Possess the Acquired Cardinal Virtues?" *Theological Studies* 72 (2011): 558–585.

McDowell, Josh, and Bob Hostetler. *The New Tolerance: How a Cultural Movement Threatens to Destroy You, Your Faith, and Your Children*. Wheaton, IL: Tyndale House, 1998.

McInerny, Ralph. *Aquinas on Human Action: A Theory of Practice*. Washington, DC: Catholic University of America Press, 1992.

Mendus, Susan, ed. *Justifying Toleration: Conceptual and Historical Perspectives*. Cambridge: Cambridge University Press, 1988.

———, ed. *The Politics of Toleration in Modern Life*. Durham, NC: Duke University Press, 2000.

———. *Toleration and the Limits of Liberalism*. Atlantic Highlands, NJ: Humanities Press International, 1989.

Milbank, John. *Theology and Social Theory: Beyond Secular Reason*. Oxford: Blackwell, 1990.

Mill, John Stuart. "On Liberty." In *On Liberty and Other Essays*, edited by John Gray, 5–130. Oxford: Oxford University Press, 1998.

Nederman, Cary J. "Discourses and Contexts of Tolerance in Medieval Europe." In Laursen and Nederman, *Beyond the Persecuting Society*, 13–24.

———. *Worlds of Difference: European Discourses of Toleration, c. 1100–1550*. University Park: Pennsylvania University Press, 2000.

Nederman, Cary J., and John Christian Laursen, eds. *Difference and Dissent: Theories of Tolerance in Medieval and Early Modern Europe*. Lanham, MD: Rowman & Littlefield, 1996.

Nelson, Daniel. *The Priority of Prudence: Virtue and Natural Law in Thomas Aquinas and the Implications for Modern Ethics*. University Park: Pennsylvania State University Press, 1992.

Newey, Glen. "Tolerance as a Virtue." In *Toleration, Identity, and Difference*, edited by John Horton and Susan Mendus, 38–64. London: Macmillan, 1999.

———. *Toleration in Political Conflict*. Cambridge: Cambridge University Press, 2013.

Niebuhr, Gustav. *Beyond Tolerance: Searching for Interfaith Understanding in America*. New York: Viking/Penguin, 2008.

Nietzsche, Friedrich. *On the Genealogy of Morals and Ecce Homo*. Translated by Walter Kaufmann and R. J. Hollingdale. New York: Vintage, 1989.

Nussbaum, Martha. *Political Emotions: Why Love Matters for Justice*. Cambridge, MA: Harvard University Press, 2013.

Oberdiek, Hans. *Tolerance: Between Forbearance and Acceptance*. Lanham, MD: Rowman & Littlefield, 2001.

O'Meara, William. "Beyond Toleration." In Razavi and Ambuel, *Philosophy, Religion, and the Question of Intolerance*, 94–108.

O'Neill, Onora. "The Public Use of Reason." In *Constructions of Reason: Explorations of Kant's Practical Philosophy*, 28–50. Cambridge: Cambridge University Press, 1989.

Perry, John. *The Pretenses of Loyalty: Locke, Liberal Theory, and American Political Theology*. Oxford: Oxford University Press, 2011.

Pettegree, Andrew. "The Politics of Toleration in the Free Netherlands, 1572–1620." In *Tolerance and Intolerance in the European Reformation*, edited by Ole Peter Grell and Bob Scribner, 182–198. Cambridge: Cambridge University Press, 1996.

Porter, Jean. *Nature as Reason: A Thomistic Theory of the Natural Law*. Grand Rapids, MI: Eerdmans, 2005.

Proast, Jonas. *The Argument of the Letter Concerning Toleration Briefly Considered and Answered*. London: Theater for George West and Henry Clements, 1690.

Putnam, Robert D. *Bowling Alone: The Collapse and Revival of American Community*. New York: Simon & Schuster, 2000.

Raphael, D. D. "The Intolerable." In Mendus, *Justifying Toleration*, 137–154.

Rapoport, Chaim. *Judaism and Homosexuality: An Authentic Orthodox View*. Portland, OR: Vallentine Mitchell, 2004.

Ratzinger, Joseph Cardinal. "Homily *Pro Eligendo Romano Pontifice*: Addressed to the College of Cardinals, April 18, 2005, in the Vatican Basilica." *Common Knowledge* 13, nos. 2–3 (Spring–Fall 2007): 451–455.

———. *Truth and Tolerance: Christian Belief and World Religions*. Translated by Henry Taylor. San Francisco: Ignatius Press, 2004.

Rawls, John. *A Theory of Justice*. Cambridge, MA: Harvard University Press, 1971.

Raz, Joseph. "Autonomy, Toleration, and the Harm Principle." In Mendus, *Justifying Toleration*, 155–175.

———. *The Morality of Freedom*. Oxford: Oxford University Press, 1986.

Razavi, Mehdi Amin, and David Ambuel, eds. *Philosophy, Religion, and the Question of Intolerance*. Albany: State University of New York Press, 1997.

Redhead, Mark. "Debate: Nietzsche and Liberal Democracy: A Relationship of Antagonistic Indebtedness?" *Journal of Political Philosophy* 5, no. 2 (1997): 183–193.

Rhonheimer, Martin. *Natural Law and Practical Reason: A Thomistic View of Moral Autonomy*. Translated by Gerald Malsbary. New York: Fordham University Press, 2000.

Rogers, Eugene F., Jr. *Aquinas and the Supreme Court: Biblical Narratives of Jews, Gentiles, and Gender*. Oxford: Blackwell, 2013.

Rommen, Heinrich A. *The Natural Law: A Study in Legal and Social History and Philosophy*. Translated by Thomas R. Hanley. Indianapolis: Liberty Fund, 1998.

Rorty, Richard. "The Historiography of Philosophy: Four Genres." In *Philosophy in History: Essays in the Historiography of Philosophy*, edited by Richard Rorty, J. B. Schneewind, and Quentin Skinner, 49–75. Cambridge: Cambridge University Press, 1984.

———. "On Ethnocentrism: A Reply to Clifford Geertz." In *Objectivity, Relativism, and Truth: Philosophical Papers*, vol. 1, 203–210. Cambridge: Cambridge University Press, 1991.

Rose, Gillian. *Love's Work: A Reckoning with Life*. New York: Schocken, 1997.

Sabl, Andrew. "The Last Artificial Virtue: Hume on Toleration and Its Lessons." *Political Theory* 37, no. 4 (August 2009): 511–538.

———. "'Virtuous to Himself': Pluralist Democracy and the Toleration of Tolerations." In Williams and Waldron, *Toleration and Its Limits*, 220–240.

Scanlon, T. M. "The Difficulty of Tolerance." In Heyd, *Toleration*, 226–239.

Schneewind, J. B. "Bayle, Locke, and the Concept of Toleration." In Razavi and Ambuel, *Philosophy, Religion, and the Question of Intolerance*, 3–15.

———. *The Invention of Autonomy: A History of Modern Moral Philosophy*. Cambridge: Cambridge University Press, 1998.

Scott, James C. *Domination and the Arts of Resistance*. New Haven: Yale University Press, 1990.

Sheils, William J., ed. *Persecution and Toleration*. Oxford: Blackwell, 1984.

Shklar, Judith. "Liberalism of Fear." In *Liberalism and the Moral Life*, edited by Nancy Rosenblum, 21–38. Cambridge, MA: Harvard University Press, 1989.

———. *Ordinary Vices*. Cambridge, MA: Harvard University Press, 1985.

Steyn, Mark. "It's the Demography, Stupid." *New Criterion* 24, no. 5 (January 2006): 10–19.

Stout, Jeffrey. *Blessed Are the Organized: Grassroots Democracy in America*. Princeton: Princeton University Press, 2010.

———. *Democracy and Tradition*. Princeton: Princeton University Press, 2004.

———. "A House Founded on the Sea: Is Democracy a Dictatorship of Relativism?" *Common Knowledge* 13, nos. 2–3 (Spring–Fall 2007): 385–403.

———. "The Spirit of Democracy and the Rhetoric of Excess." *Journal of Religious Ethics* 35, no. 1 (March 2007): 3–21.

Strawson, P. F. *The Bounds of Sense: An Essay on Kant's Critique of Pure Reason*. London: Methuen, 1966.

Strong, Tracy B. *Friedrich Nietzsche and the Politics of Transfiguration*. Rev. ed. Urbana: University of Illinois Press, 2000.

Sutherland, N. M. "Persecution and Toleration in Reformation Europe." In Sheils, *Persecution and Toleration*, 153–161.

Taylor, Charles. "The Diversity of Goods." In *Utilitarianism and Beyond*, edited by Amartya Sen and Bernard Williams, 129–144. Cambridge: Cambridge University Press, 1982.

———. "Invoking Civil Society." In *Philosophical Arguments*, 204–224. Cambridge, MA: Harvard University Press, 1995.

Tinder, Glenn. *Tolerance and Community*. Columbia: University of Missouri Press, 1995.

———. *Tolerance: Toward a New Civility*. Amherst: University of Massachusetts Press, 1975.

———. "What Can We Reasonably Hope For? A Millennium Symposium." *First Things* 99 (2000): 33–34.

Tucker, Robert, ed. *The Marx-Engels Reader*. 2nd rev. ed. New York: Norton, 1978.

Vainio, Olli-Pekka. "Virtues and Vices of Tolerance." In *Religion in the Public Square: Proceedings of the 2010 Conference of the European Society for Philosophy of Religion*, edited by Niek Brunsveld and Roger Trigg. *Ars Disputandi Supplement Series* 5 (2011): 273–284.

Walzer, Michael. *On Toleration*. New Haven: Yale University Press, 1997.

———. *What It Means to Be an American: Essays on the American Experience*. New York: Marsilio, 1992.

Washington, James M., ed. *A Testament of Hope: The Essential Writings and Speeches of Martin Luther King, Jr.*. San Francisco: Harper & Row, 1986.

Webb, Melanie. "Rape and its Aftermath in Augustine's *City of God*." PhD diss., Princeton Theological Seminary, 2016.

Wetzel, James. "Splendid Vices and Secular Virtues: Variations on Milbank's Augustine." *Journal of Religious Ethics* 32, no. 2 (2004): 271–300.

———. "A Tangle of Two Cities." *Augustinian Studies* 43, nos. 1/2 (2012): 5–23.

Williams, Bernard. "Tolerating the intolerable." In Mendus, *Politics of Toleration in Modern Life*, 65–76.

———. "Toleration: An Impossible Virtue?" In Heyd, *Toleration*, 18–27.

Williams, Delores S. *Sisters in the Wilderness: The Challenge of Womanist God-Talk*. Maryknoll, NY: Orbis, 1993.

Williams, Melissa S., and Jeremy Waldron, eds. *Toleration and Its Limits*. New York: New York University Press, 2008.

Wittgenstein, Ludwig. *On Certainty*. Edited by G.E.M. Anscombe and G. H. von Wright and translated by Denis Paul and G.E.M. Anscombe. Oxford: Blackwell, 1969.

———. *Philosophical Investigations: The German Text with a Revised English Translation*. 3rd ed. Translated by G.E.M. Anscombe. Oxford: Blackwell, 2001.

Wolfe, Alan. *One Nation, After All: What Americans Really Think about God, Country, Family, Racism, Welfare, Immigration, Homosexuality, Work, the Right, the Left and Each Other*. New York: Penguin, 1999.

Wolff, Robert Paul, Barrington Moore, Jr., and Herbert Marcuse. *A Critique of Pure Tolerance*. Boston: Beacon, 1969.

Wolterstorff, Nicholas. *Justice: Rights and Wrongs*. Princeton: Princeton University Press, 2008.

Wood, Alan W. "The Marxian Critique of Justice." *Philosophy and Public Affairs* 1, no. 3 (1972): 244–282.

Yearley, Lee. *Mencius and Aquinas: Theories of Virtue and Conceptions of Courage*. Albany: State University of New York Press, 1990.

Zagorin, Perez. *How the Idea of Religious Toleration Came to the West*. Princeton: Princeton University Press, 2003.

Žižek, Slavoj. "Tolerance as an Ideological Category." *Critical Inquiry* 34, no. 4 (Summer 2008): 660–682.

———. *Violence: Six Sideways Reflections*. New York: Picador, 2008.

INDEX

tolerance — patient endurance of another's objectionable
          difference